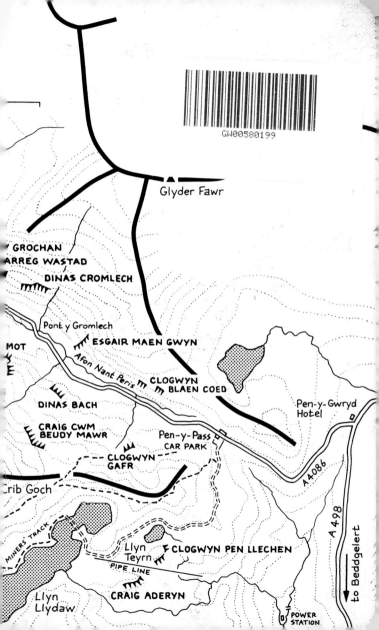

GW00580199

GROCHAN
ARREG WASTAD
DINAS CROMLECH

Glyder Fawr

Pont y Gromlech
MOT
ESGAIR MAEN GWYN
Afon Nant Peris
CLOGWYN
BLAEN COED
DINAS BACH
Pen-y-Gwryd
Hotel
CRAIG CWM
BEUDY MAWR
Pen-y-Pass
CAR PARK
CLOGWYN
GAFR
Crib Goch
A 4086
MINERS TRACK
Llyn
Teyrn
CLOGWYN PEN LLECHEN
PIPE LINE
Llyn
Llydaw
CRAIG ADERYN
POWER
STATION
A 498
to Beddgelert

Climbers Guide to Snowdon
by H R C Carr   1924

Three Cliffs in Llanberis
by J E Q Barford   1944

Llanberis Pass – First Edition
by P R J Harding   1950

Llanberis North – First Edition
by D T Roscoe   1961

Llanberis South – First Edition
by P Crew   1966

Cwm Glas – Second Edition
by P Crew and I Roper   1970

The Three Cliffs – Second Edition
by M P Hatton   1974

Llanberis Pass – Second Edition
by G Milburn   1978

Llanberis Pass – Third Edition
by G Milburn   1981

Llanberis – First Edition
by P Williams   1987

Llanberis Pass – Fourth Edition
by P Williams   1993

Front Cover: Nigel Smart on *Slape Direct* (E1), Clogwyn y Grochan. Photo: David Wilkinson

Rear Cover: Steve Mayers on his own route, *Overlord* (E7), Dinas Cromlech. Photo: Ray Wood

Williams, Paul

Llanberis Pass

(Climbers' Club Guides)

British Library Cataloguing in Publication Data

A catalogue record for this book is available from the British Library

796.522

ISBN 0-901-601-53-5

Output by Pickards, Sheffield
Printed by Hi-Tec Print, Dinnington, South Yorkshire
Distributed by Cordee, 3a De Montfort Street, Leicester, LE1 7HD

Contents

The South Side of The Pass

List of diagrams and photodiagrams

The Climbers' Club

The publisher of this guidebook is the Climbers' Club, which was founded in 1898 from origins in Snowdonia. The Club is now one of the foremost mountaineering clubs in Great Britain. Its objects are to encourage mountaineering and rock-climbing, and to promote the general interest of mountaineers and the mountain environment.

It is a truly national club with widespread membership and currently owns huts in Cornwall, Pembrokeshire, Derbyshire and Snowdonia. Besides managing six huts, the Climbers' Club produces an annual Journal, runs a full programme of climbing meets, dinners and social events. Club members may also use the huts of other clubs through reciprocal arrangements. The club publishes climbing guidebooks (currently 15 in number) to cover the South East, the South West, Pembrokeshire, and Mid Wales and North Wales regions. The club is a founder member of, and is affiliated to, the British Mountaineering Council; it makes annual contributions to the BMC's Access Fund.

Membership fluctuates around 900 and at present there are no limits on growth. Members of two years standing may propose a competent candidate for membership and, providing adequate support is obtained from other members, the Committee may elect them to full membership; there is no probationary period.

Guidebook Disclaimer

This guidebook attempts to provide a definitive record of all existing climbs and is compiled from information from a variety of sources. The inclusion of any route does not imply that it remains in the condition described. Climbs can change unpredictably; rock can deteriorate and the existence and condition of *in situ* protection can alter. All climbers must rely on their own ability and experience to gauge the difficulty and seriousness of any climb. Climbing is an inherently dangerous activity.

Neither the Climbers' Club nor the authors and editor of this guidebook accept any liability whatsoever for any injury or damage caused to climbers, third parties, or property, arising from any use of it. Whilst the content of the guide is believed to be accurate, no responsibility is accepted for any error, omission, or mis-statement. Users must rely on their own judgement and are recommended to insure against injury to person and property and third party risks.

The inclusion in this guidebook of a crag or routes upon it does not mean that any member of the public has a right of access to the crag or the right to climb.

Before climbing on any crag in this guide please read any appropriate access and conservation notes.

Climbing Style

The following policy statement on climbing style was agreed in principle at The Climbers' Club Annual General Meeting on 25th February 1990:

The Climbers' Club supports the tradition of using natural protection and is opposed to actions which are against the best interests of climbers and users of crags. This applies particularly to irreversible acts which could affect the crags and their environs.

Such acts include: the placing of bolts on mountain and natural crags; retrospective placing of bolts; chiselling, hammering, or altering the rock appearance or structure; excessive removal of vegetation and interference with trees, flowers and fauna.

The Climbers' Club policy is that guidebooks are written to reflect the best style matched to the ethos and traditions of British Climbing.

Acknowledgments

The writing of the 1987 Llanberis guide proved to be a task of epic proportions. The slate boom of the early '80s with new routes going up daily, plus the abundance of freshly available archive material meant that the number of new climbs for inclusion more than doubled, and that the guide was four years in the making.

When asked, about three years later, to do an update which would omit the slate section, I readily agreed. It seemed a relatively straightforward task to insert a few new climbs into a comprehensive text, but of course, nothing in life is simple or straightforward. The more detailed documentation of lesser crags and shorter routes had brought whole new areas under scrutiny, including Scimitar Ridge, but most notably the fecund crags of the Cwm Glas Bach Area (previously referred to as Bumhole Buttress) opposite Clogwyn y Grochan, where routes initially mushroomed with an amazing rapidity.

With time pressing against me, and the Climbers' Club Publications Sub-Committee anxiously awaiting a manuscript, the complex walls and outcrops of Cwm Glas Bach were always going to be something of a nightmare to document quickly and accurately, even after several visits. Fortunately for me (and the CC) help was at hand when this area's most prolific pioneer, Iwan Jones, agreed to write the Cwm Glas Bach Area script.

Once again, in the words of Peter Harding, 'No guidebook can be compiled by one climber without the help and co-operation of many others'. This stands as true today as in 1950 when those words were written. Besides having some excellent guides to use as a foundation for this new tome: Carr 1926, Barford 1944, Harding 1950, Roscoe 1961, 1964, Crew 1967, Crew and Roper 1970, Hatton 1974, Milburn 1978, 1981, and of course Llanberis 1987, there have been many people who have given invaluable criticism and help for both this latest edition and the one previous to it, including: John Allen, Martin Atkinson, John Banks, Sue Bird, Bob Bradley, Joe Brown, Martin Boysen, Stuart Cathcart, Martin Crook, C Davies, Claude Davies, Johnny Dawes, Nick Dixon, Harold Drasdo, Bob Drury, Ron Fawcett, Gary Gibson, B Grantham, Ray and Ruth Greenall, Andy Grondowski, Fred Hall, Sue Harland, Stevie Haston, Perry Hawkins, Trevor Hodgson, Graham Hoey, Mike Howard, Steve Howe, Wil and Grace Hurford, J James, Paul Jenkinson, Phil Jewell, Dave Jones, David B A Jones, Owen Jones, S Kent, Dai Lampard, Dave Lawson, Pat Littlejohn, Simon Lee, Steve Long, Stan Lowe, Richie Lyon, P G Martin, Steve Mayers, Geoff Milburn, Jim Moran, Andy Newton, Andy Pollitt, Jim Perrin, Mick Pointon, Andy Popp, Paul Pritchard, Dave Pycroft, John Redhead, Ian Riddington, Dave Roberts, P Roberts, Lynn Rogers, Chas Sewell, Colin Shone, Jon Silvester, Craig Smith, George Smith, Jon Sonczak, D Summers, Phil Targett, Terry Taylor, Mike Thomas, Willy Todd, Dave Towse, Paul Trower, Mike Turner, Adam Wainwright, Hugh Walton, Phil Waters, Bob Wightman, W Wright, Chester Climbing Club, The Cromlech Climbing Club, Manchester Rucksack Club, Malc Campbell and Jon de Montjoye, both ex-Plas y Brenin, and the Bangor University Mountaineering Society.

My apologies to anyone whose name I have omitted from the above list, including the gentleman who sent me some information on Beorn, and whose letter, despite my most diligent efforts to locate it, remains lost.

However fraught, guidebook writing is ultimately like climbing a difficult route; the planning, the anticipation, the execution, the occasional self-doubt, and the exhilaration of the finish. But with a guide, no matter how hard one strives for perfection, there are inevitably going to be inaccuracies as holds break off, pegs corrode... and then there is the subjective matter of grading. So why update the guide? The inspiration came as I recalled that day a few weeks after Llanberis was published...a letter dropped through the door of my cottage signed, 'From the author of the First Bumper Fun Book, to the author of The Second...'

P W 1993

Introduction

This latest edition of *Llanberis Pass* is a definitive (I hope) record of all the climbs discovered on both the North and South sides of The Pass. Slate climbing, a popular part of *Llanberis 1987* has been omitted, slate information is available in either *Slate – A Climbers' Guide* by IA Jones, A Newton and L McGinley, or *Rock Climbing in Snowdonia* by P Williams.

The trend over the past few years has been for the focus of first ascensionists to centre mainly around hard problems on the smaller outcrops, many of which would not have merited a second glance 20 years ago. In the caring '90s, when size doesn't matter, and 'small is beautiful', this new approach has come as a breath of fresh air, blowing away some of the cobwebs that have wafted around in The Pass since that legendary spider spun them across Cobweb Crack, thus stimulating a healthy new interest in the area. Traditional and contemporary routes now coexist comfortably alongside one another, but more importantly, several interesting and diverse locations having been opened up, thus enabling teams to escape the more crowded cliffs during busy weekends. Scimitar Ridge, however, goes against the current trends, as it is a large serious cliff sporting many of the most committing routes in the area. With many bold new routes, well-protected new routes, and quality new routes from VS upwards to go at within the pages of this guide, there is something fresh for most parties. Technical standards have been raised on a par with those found on mountain crags anywhere in Britain and The Pass is buzzing once again.

The comprehensive 1950 guide by Peter Harding was affectionately known as 'the bumper fun book' by an older generation of climbers, but was too thick to act as the format for subsequent guides. It was eventually split into three guides. After several Llanberis North and South guides, stricter editing enabled the CC to revert back to one complete Llanberis Pass guide in 1978, 1981 and 1987. This is also the style for the current edition.

The two sides of the Llanberis Pass though rather different in character, are a fine complement to each other. On the north side the five main cliffs are situated low down on the hillside below the Esgair Felen ridge and southern slopes of Glyder Fawr. They are steep, impressive, fast drying (apart from Craig Ddu) and mostly have solid well-gardened rock, picked clean by the passage of countless climbers, save on Scimitar

Ridge where there are no easy climbs. Most of the lines on the other four cliffs are trade routes in what has become one of our most popular mountain outcrop areas. Here a climber at work is watched keenly from the road by critical fellow climbers (some using binoculars) amongst a horde of idle car-bound tourists.

The south side of The Pass is a totally different proposition. Here the crags are generally bigger, more serious and are slower to dry out. The extensive cwms reach up 3,000 feet to the Crib Goch ridge and the summit of Crib y Ddysgl, which together form the northern half of the famous Snowdon Horseshoe. And then there are the new additions to the outcrops of Cwm Glas Bach, surely destined to become popular as much for their ease of access as well as the merit of their climbing.

All the main crags on the north side and many of those on the south side can be reached from the road in less than half an hour. For the climber who desires peace and tranquillity there are the subtle delights of Clogwyn y Ddysgl, the mind-boggling exposure of the routes on Cyrn Las (although these are very popular on sunny summer weekends), or how about a visit to Llechog?

Every effort has been made to ensure that the routes in this guide are fairly and accurately graded, though this is very difficult when some of the newer routes are unrepeated. The standard adjectival grading system has been used and it assumes that climbers are carrying a modern rack of gear and wearing 'sticky' soled rock boots. The grades are as follows:

Easy	Severe
Moderate	Very Severe
Difficult	Hard Very Severe
Very Difficult	Extremely Severe

The Extremely Severe grade is now an open-ended system represented by the symbols E1, E2, E3, E4, E5, E6, E7, E8... etc, the E grades give an overall impression of the difficulty of a climb, be it a desperate well-protected physical effort or a thin and poorly protected 'mind game'.

Numerical pitch grades have been included in the text; starting at 4a running through to 7b for the current hardest route in the area, although this may well be downgraded, as several of the old desperates have been, once they get a repeat.

In 1987, some of the older routes were upgraded in response to overwhelming opinion amongst middle grade climbers e.g. Cemetery Gates E1 5b, Karwendel Wall 5b, and the one desperate move on Surplomb 6a, after all, most climbers had known that for years. On the easier side, Flying Buttress, was upgraded to V Diff. Fortunately there seem to be few grading anomalies amongst the established routes, the main bones of contention being; Cenotaph Corner down to 5b/c; Left Wall up to E2/3; Right Wall down to E4 from E5. Well, as Right Wall is three grades harder than Left Wall, and that in its turn has felt easier than Cenotaph Corner on occasion... and as someone has written of Left Wall, on my manuscript, 'E2 – low to middle of the grade' it seems that some people are going to be rather upset. Grading is a contentious and subjective issue at the best of times, but now The Pass has a host of short hard desperate outcrop style climbs to contend with; how do you compare the short, technically precocious Vlad the Arête with the long, bold and run-out Nightmayer? You can't, these are two distinctly different types of route which have to be judged on different criteria.

Bolts, a five letter word to make any ancient climber choke on his pint... we don't want them! We don't need them in The Pass! Bolts in traditional areas such as mountain crags and outcrops are regarded as decidedly unethical; it's just not cricket, and any climber caught placing one should be restrained from doing so if possible. If this proves impossible, point him out in The Heights one Saturday night so that local climbers can forcefully state their case. For those who need their fix of bolt climbing, North Wales Limestone is a bolt climber's Mecca.

Wherever aid of any form has been used, the minimum number of points of aid for each climb is given in brackets after the grade of the route, e.g. Very Severe (1 pt. aid). The nature of the aid will be made clear in the route description. Many of the old routes now go free owing to extensive gardening, a wide selection of nuts, Friends, chalk, climbing-wall fitness and most important of all a healthier attitude towards climbing ethics. The word peg is used in three contexts; 'peg runner', 'aid peg' and 'peg belay'. It is hoped that all pegs mentioned in the text will be left in place (if they haven't corroded). If any pegs are found to be missing, please record the fact in Pete's Eats new route book. All routes are described in their freest form.

The familiar 'star' system is used to indicate the quality of routes irrespective of grades. A route must be excellent in all respects to qualify for ★★★ and even a ★ must be out of the ordinary. The absence of stars does not mean that a climb is unsatisfactory, as poor climbs are specifically described as such.

Hedonist or traditionalist, there is bound to be something in the guide to suit your taste, but remember, all the crags in this guide can be seen from the road in good weather and if any crag can't be seen then:

a) it is probably out of condition.
b) it is the middle of the night
c) you are probably drunk as a skunk lying face down under a table in The Heights.

And now... from almost indecipherable scribblings on around 200 pieces of paper... at long last... the guide.

Editor's Acknowledgments

Introduced during the production of the Ogwen Carneddau guidebook the newly created North Wales Climbers' Club guidebook team has once again been in action to produce this new guidebook to the Llanberis Pass. Paul Williams has done his usual excellent job as the principal author; Iwan Jones used his extensive knowledge of recent events to produce the section to the highly developed crags of the Cwm Glas Bach area, and has researched diligently to discover whether the names we climbers have given to the numerous crags of The Pass are correct; Simon Cardy has once again undertaken the difficult job of putting the route lines onto the diagrams and photodiagrams, and amongst others Andy Newton, Neil Foster, Nick Dixon and Andy Popp have helped with proof reading and advice. Bob Moulton has, as usual, been an excellent Business Manager, as well as an helpful adviser, and Dave Farrant has given vital help on computing matters. Barabara Jones generously provided the increasingly important Conservation Notes. A variety of photographers have offered their work for consideration and inclusion, particularly Ray Wood and John Cleare, my thanks to all of them.

Ian Smith

Please note: At a very late stage in the production of this guidebook the diagram for Clogwyn Gafr (Craig Fach), was unfortunately lost in the postal system. It seemed that even if it was found it would be too late to include it, however it was found in time and does appear, sadly not in its proper place but as an Appendix on pages 316 and 317.

Conservation Notes

Before the construction of a road through Llanberis Pass in around 1830, the usual way to reach Llanberis was by a 'dreadful horse-path' or by boat up Llyn Padarn. This topographically imposed isolation maintained a near natural 'wilderness' in the valley and, until around 1700, eagles still soared above the hills of Snowdonia. With the construction of the road, access improved dramatically and by the end of the century climbers were exploring many of the cliffs and crags once considered to be the abode of demons. With over 100 years of climbing in the Llanberis Pass, now one of the most popular climbing areas in Britain, it is tempting to ask whether there is anything left to conserve?

Indeed there is and a little awareness will reward you with views of darting peregrine and diving chough, or, meadow rue, starry saxifrage and insectivorous butterwort, with banks of bluebells and primroses on some ledges and descent gullies in spring. Climbing activities may have had an impact, but the occasional sight of a tiny oak or rowan tree starting to grow alongside a popular route gives hope that all is not lost.

Both sides of Llanberis Pass are part of the Snowdonia Mountains Site of Special Scientific Interest, an internationally important upland site designated for its varied, and sometimes rare, upland plant and animal life and its geological features, reflecting the effects of glaciation on the complex of rock types in Snowdonia. Sheep grazing has produced a dominant cover of acidic grassland with abundant clubmosses, but the heather is still locally abundant. The complex geology has resulted in areas of base rich rocks where the vegetation becomes herb-rich with luxuriant cover of roseroot, ladies mantle, moss campion and mountain sorrel amongst many others, where grazing sheep cannot reach.

The main climbing cliffs on either side of The Pass however are composed of solid tuffs of the Upper Rhyolitic Series which are more acidic and tend to form dense, hard rocks, less conducive to vegetation growth and more conducive to climbing. The animal life of Snowdonia is similarly varied ranging from a relict artic-alpine invertebrate fauna including the rare Snowdon Rainbow Beetle through to nesting peregrines and chough, both of which have regular breeding sites in the Pass. Feral goats can often be seen browsing on the vally sides.

We can climb on most of the cliffs described in this guide without causing any further damage or disturbance to the fauna and flora, if a sense of awareness is coupled with a minimum impact philosophy in the form of no gardening and care in descent, especially avoiding wet gullies which are often the refuge for a luxuriant diversity of plant life. Avoiding too much trampling on any still vegetated ledges and using trees as little as possible will also prevent further deterioration of the vegetation cover. Avoiding climbs close to nesting sites during the breeding season will protect the tenuous hold birds such as chough and peregrines have on these mountains. Despite all these measures however, there are some areas covered by this guide which are still relatively uncrowded and little used, where an increase in exploration and activity could be disastrous for the wildlife. Most notable in this respect is Cwm Glas which, due to the nature of the rocks in the cwm, supports a luxuriance of artic-alpine and lower ground plants, including some very rare species. These plants are restricted essentially to the cliffs and steep rocky ground due to sheep grazing and, needless to say, gardening and cleaning in any new route activity on these cliffs would severly deplete these uncommon plant communities and render the mountains a much poorer place as a result.

The mountains, plants and animals of Snowdonia yearly attract hundreds of botanists, naturalists, photographers and walkers who delight in the presence and diversity of wildlife found here; they have as much right to experience and enjoy it as we do, and they would be rightly concerned and angry at any wilful destruction. For these reasons, tread lightly, and, as the production of this guide is likely to stimulate new activity, if you intend to develop a new cliff or crag, please contact the Countryside Council for Wales before you start so advice can be given on the likelihood or known existence of any rare plants, sensitive vegetation communities or birds being damaged or disturbed by climbing activities.

Remember these plants and birds are protected by law and offences are prosecuted under the 1981 Wildlife and Countryside Act; gardening could result in prosecution so make yourself aware and if in doubt ask first.

Nearing the end of the first century of climbing activity in Llanberis Pass, why not take a new, radical and positive approach to the cliff environment and appreciate it all for what it is, including the so called 'nasty, scruffy, vegetated ' parts?

For information on the conservation interest of areas within the guide, the CCW warden Marc Jones can be contacted through the CCW regional office on 0248 372333.

Barbara Jones

Historical

Climbing in Snowdonia started in earnest in the 1860s and 1870s when members of the then recently formed Alpine Club came to stay at the Pen y Gwryd Hotel, owned by Henry Owen. This venue became the social centre of Welsh climbing at that time, one of the most prominent regulars being C E Mathews who founded the Society of Welsh Rabbits, an informal club which explored Snowdonia in winter. With the better snow conditions at that time it was an ideal centre for Alpine training. The rock remained for the future.

The earliest ascents in about 1879 are credited to R Pendlebury and in 1884 the *Clogwyn y Person Arête* was ascended after the *Western Gully* start. E R Kidson, an enthusiastic pioneer, climbed the Crib Goch gullies during this period.

The beginning of Welsh rock-climbing was marked by the formation of the Climbers' Club in August 1898 with a nucleus of P y G regulars headed by Matthews. The activities of the climbers were recorded in the journals, and traditions were soon established. Kidson led a party of CC members up *The Parson's Nose*, which was rumoured to have been climbed as long ago as the 1840s by the 'climbing parson'.

By this time J M Archer Thomson was firmly established as one of the leading Welsh climbers. His *Black Cleft* on Dinas Mot was, for some time, the hardest route in Wales. For the next 13 years he dominated Welsh climbing and when not on Lliwedd he ascended many of the gullies in this area with the Williams brothers, R F Blackwell, E R Turner and M K Smith. The formidable *Great Gully* of Cyrn Las finally fell to Thomson in 1904 after two years of serious attempts. It was in this period that a large party of schoolmasters attacked the gullies of Cyrn Las and named the last in honour of their profession. Towards the end of the gully epoch, *Crib Goch Buttress* was climbed first by the Abrahams then by G W Reade who put up his excellent buttress route. Thomson added several routes on Clogwyn y Ddysgl, including the fine *Gambit Climb*, prior to his sudden death in 1912.

Geoffrey Winthrop Young was active in the area before The Great War and opened up Craig Cwm Beudy Mawr. George Mallory climbed during the war and added *The Black Gates*; but sadly the war took its toll of many who loved the hills.

Herbert Carr and Maurice Guinness were active in the post-war years leading up to the Climbers' Club Guide to Snowdon in 1926. In it there was no reference to the steep crags on the north side of Llanberis Pass. These were left for the next generation, which took advantage of developments in equipment and in particular, rubber footwear.

Ivan Waller added the infamous *Fallen Block Crack* in 1927 and then in 1930 the Bathursts became the first team to use artificial aids when they climbed *The Cracks*. Colin Kirkus made a significant advance in 1930 with his classic *Direct Route* on Dinas Mot and followed it the next year with another masterpiece, *West Rib*.

In 1931, J Menlove Edwards made his debut with *Western Slabs* on Dinas Mot before moving across to the north side of The Pass, where he opened up his great period of exploration with *Holly Buttress* on Dinas Cromlech. During the next 10 years he dominated both sides of The Pass putting up a host of excellent new routes including the classics, *Flying Buttress* and *Crackstone Rib*, as well as harder routes such as *Pharaoh's Wall* and *Shadow Wall*. His lines invariably involved fights with vegetation, overhangs and loose rock, much of which has now disappeared. The names of some of Edwards's routes show the extent of his lively imagination. His early ones are all derived from a biblical knowledge. *Nebuchadnezzar's Crawl* gets its name from the seven years which Nebuchadnezzar spent on his belly with the beasts in the field and his head buried in the long grass, as a climber might have once done on the route. The overhangs at the foot of another climb looked like an Egyptian hat, hence *Pharaoh's Passage*. *Dives* was so named because the pioneers hoped for better things above. *Sexton's Route* was named because of the sombre attire of the third man who wore a black tail coat to protect him from the elements. Edwards did not have it all his own way, however, for in 1935 E Pentir Williams succeeded in climbing one of the three great Cromlech corners to give *Sabre Cut*. The same year, Jake Cooke and P L Roberts found the superb and impressive *Main Wall* on Cyrn Las, as well as other minor lines on the south side of The Pass.

By far the greatest step forward in The Pass was Arthur Birtwistle's remarkable ascent of *Diagonal* in 1938. The route was not repeated for 10 years and even now demands a great deal of respect. Edwards was very active during the war and added the fine routes of *Brant* and *Slape*. Both Edwards and John Barford had been responsible for many pre-war developments and the interim guide by Barford, reprinted from the CC journal, marked the end of the Edwards era. It is sad that Barford was killed in the Alps before completing his guide to Dinas Mot, but Arnold Carsten took over the work, and even climbed routes solo when short of a companion. His manuscript was eventually included in Harding's Pass guide.

The Second World War robbed us of many fine climbers, but in the post-war period another generation of 'tigers' was developing rapidly on the northern gritstone outcrops. In this group were the aforementioned Peter Harding and Tony Moulam, who, aided by an improved crack technique and modern protection, began to push the standards even higher. *Spectre* fell in 1947 and at the time was thought to be a standard harder than previous routes. Despite this, Harding soloed it in 1948. Another fine Harding route from 1947 was the imposing corner of *Ivy Sepulchre* which was inspected and gardened from abseil on the day prior to its ascent, a practice more in keeping with the '70s rather than the '40s. In 1948 Harding opened up the rather forbidding-looking Craig Ddu, then farther up The Pass sorted out *The Wastad Girdle* and *Kaisergebirge Wall*. On the first ascent of the latter, seven pegs were used and the climb was thought to be a good deal harder than the other routes on the cliff with perhaps the exception of *Spectre*. Today no pegs are needed but there is a curious piece of metal (now a blob of rust), reputed to be part of a bicycle crank, driven into one of the cracks below the crux by Colin Goodey; it has saved many falling leaders in the past. A year later *Unicorn* and *Lion* were discovered just in time to get into Harding's magnificent Llanberis Pass Guide, published in 1950, which soon became known as 'The Bumper Fun Book'.

Soon after the guide came out, a young wiry climber appeared on the scene with the apparent intention of making it obsolete; a man with the ability to make first ascents in shocking weather conditions and who reigned for nearly a quarter of a century despite many up and coming young climbers; the legendary Joe Brown. The first feature to attract Brown's attention was the commanding line of *Cenotaph Corner* which had so far repelled all attempts; jamming and bridging up to the niche about 20 feet from the top, Brown hammered up a peg, in the process of which he dropped his hammer onto the head of Wilf White who was belaying. Fortunately, White was all right; unfortunately, Brown had no pegs left, so *Cenotaph Corner* won this first encounter with 'The Baron'; but not for long.

In 1951 Brown ascended *Hangover* and in the same year teamed up with Don Whillans for their first Pass route, the intimidating *Cemetery Gates*. Classic lines began to fall thick and fast. Inevitably *Cenotaph Corner* yielded to Brown in 1952 and then the following year, with Whillans he added the strenuous *Surplomb*, whose single aid point was removed in 1959 by young sandstone ace Phil Gordon. In early 1953, Brown and Whillans turned their attention to the south side of The Pass alternating leads on *Subsidiary Groove* six months prior to the ascent of Brown's super-classic *The Grooves*, which is still no pushover for its grade. Whillans powered his way up *Erosion Groove Direct* in 1955 a characteristically bold and serious lead which still 'collects the occasional scalp'. *Grond* and *The Thing*, both short vicious problems, also belong to this era, but the major route at the time was undoubtedly *The Cromlech Girdle*. Tales from this era are legion: *Surplomb* for many years was rumoured to have been done wearing nailed boots during a snowstorm; *Cobweb Crack* is said to have been named after a spider which spun its web above Brown's stance ensuring that on that particular day there would be no flies on Brown.

After the initial onslaught by Brown and Whillans, other leaders such as Ron Moseley and later Hugh Banner took up the challenge and produced a variety of hard climbs. In particular Moseley's ascent of the intimidating *Left Wall*, using bootlace slings and Meccano nuts to overcome the crux, stands out, as does Banner's exposed masterpiece, *Overhanging Arête* on Cyrn Las.

As a result of long hard work, Don Roscoe produced his much needed guide to Llanberis North in 1961 and this has formed the basis for all subsequent guides. At the time of publication it cleared up many rumours about the 'impossible' Brown and Whillans routes. Things quietened down somewhat in The Pass until Brown emerged once more to explore the wings of Dinas Mot. His ascent of *The Mole* initiated a wave of exploration and extensive gardening on the steep overhanging cliffs which had remained in the shadows for so long.

May 1962 saw the first Pass route by that accomplished team of Pete Crew and Baz Ingle, when they produced *Trauma Grooves* on Cyrn Las. The early 1960s saw a host of high grade routes by this forceful team when they were not up on Cloggy. Perhaps *Plexus* on Dinas Mot and *The Great Buttress* on Cyrn Las are the best of their routes. Also in this period *Epitaph*, the fierce left arête of Cenotaph Corner was top-roped and assaulted in earnest by several teams until a successful lead by Ron James using some aid. The route was eventually climbed free by John Ewbank in 1965. Good winter conditions are very rare in this country but in January 1964 *Waterfall Climb* on Craig y Rhaeadr was thoroughly frozen allowing Ingle and Martin Boysen to make a well-timed ascent.

The Llanberis South guide by Pete Crew came out in 1966 and was the last of the three guides to replace Harding's classic work. This in turn led to even more pioneering on the south side of The Pass. Boysen made his mark with several fine routes on Dinas Mot in the early 1960s and two of his finest efforts were *Black Spring* and *The Plexus Girdle* in 1965.

The Skull, which he put up in 1966 still retains its reputation as one of the harder routes in The Pass, especially as it now goes completely free. The left arête of *Ivy Sepulchre* held out for a long time despite many assaults till *The Crucifix* fell to Lew Brown in 1966.

The Pass was quiet for a while with only a few filling-in routes being produced, but in 1969, Boysen and Dave Alcock created the excellent *Black Shadow* while Joe Brown and Crew teamed up together to add another hard route, *'T'ouse Wall*, the description of which has been incorrect in every guide over the last 25 years, up until now.

In 1970 the practice of soloing routes was at its height, leading exponents in The Pass being Alan McHardy and Cliff Phillips. Phillips in fact fell over 200 feet while soloing on Dinas Mot and lived to tell the tale. Alan Rouse, trying to solo a new Extreme on sight, got up what is now the first hard pitch of *Ten Degrees North*; unfortunately it rained and he had to finish up *Plexus*. Another notable effort from this time was a solo ascent of *The Thing* by Welshman Eric Jones, but even this was capped by a tremendous on sight solo ascent of *The Overhanging Arête* on Cyrn Las by McHardy. The terminal consequence of a fall from such a route is only too obvious.

Although in the 1960s peg moves had been eliminated on some routes, in the 1970s there was a welcome and more thorough reappraisal of the aid situation. The trend was set by Ado Garlick in autumn 1970 with his superb free ascent of *Left Wall*. In 1974 Alec Sharp added several new lines on Dinas Mot. Of these *Ten Degrees North* is probably the best and most popular. In the same year Pete Livesey brought a new approach to the Welsh scene and having inspected his line over several days he eventually led the *Right Wall* of Cenotaph Corner. It was a bold and committing lead, undoubtedly the hardest in Wales at that time; still meriting an E5 grade, it was astonishingly soloed by Phil Davidson twice, in 1982 and 1983. Another major free ascent of this era was that of *The Skull* by Ray Evans and Hank Pasquill. Evans also created routes of his own such as the technical *Roll On* and the delectable *Superdirect*.

1975 saw the appearance of Gabriel Regan, a talented young climber from the Peak District who free-climbed *Spectrum* as well as *Hangover Direct*. In the same year, Rowland Edwards climbed *Resurrection*, a strenuous and technical line up the left wall of the Corner. It has rapidly become a classic route like its famous neighbours.

In addition to making a long awaited second ascent of *Right Wall* in 1976, Ron Fawcett straightened out *Roll On* to give the sustained *Stroll On*. Livesey's contributions that year were *Memory Lane*, the immaculate

Foil and a hard start to *The Crucifix*. During the hot dry summer of 1976 a strong Lakeland team consisting of Ed Cleasby, John Eastham and Rob Matheson came south and picked off a spectacular route, *Lubyanka* on Cyrn Las – done entirely on sight. Gordon Tinnings went one better when he made an amazing solo ascent (in extremis on the exposed top pitch) in 1980.

A 'Free The Pass' campaign was started by Geoff Milburn in 1977 to push modern free-climbing standards in North Wales and it soon brought a blitz on the aid routes when several young leaders set to work. In the forefront was Jim Moran who freed *The Toad* and *Jawbone* as well as adding several short but technical new routes of his own, such as *Quasar*. His finest achievement was, with Dave Hollows, to free *Black Mamba* of all its aid to give *Times Past*. Hollows himself excelled by freeing the roof pitch of *Sexus*. In July, Chris Hamper and Dave Roberts made the third and fourth ascents of *Right Wall*. Roberts then freed the frightening *Nexus Direct* – on sight, and also beat Moran to free *Mole Direct*, but the latter added an independent start and finish two days later to give *The Molehill*. Competition for lines during the summer was keen and several teams were operating in the area. Alec Sharp stormed up over the *Shadow Wall* overhang to give the powerful, frightening, *Zangorilla*; Moran went for the fine arête of *Curfew*, while Roberts climbed the now classic *SS Special*. Later in the year four new routes appeared on the already overcrowded Wastad, including *Elidor* which had in fact been done but not recorded many years before. Moran now picked off the much tried groove of *Leftover* and before the winter set in added another hard route, *Runnymede*, up the obscure Groper buttress. His final contribution for the 1978 guide, *Peeping Tom*, was only completed during a spell of very bad weather after a potentially serious fall on the lethally loose first pitch.

It was now felt by some climbers that as The Pass was sufficiently close to being worked out, a new guide might not be needed again. However in May 1978 the new guide brought climbers flooding back to the valley not only to climb the old favourites and repeat the most recent routes but also to look at the spaces between the existing routes. Dave Roberts and Paul Williams took a perverse delight in adding *First Amendment* solely to put the new guide out of date. This was followed by Moran's free ascent of *Crossbones*, which knocked out three points of aid in one fell swoop. Later in June, Fawcett solved the long-standing problem of *The Pump* to give a short but very hard test-piece. July brought Gary Gibson, a Peak District devotee, to the Llanberis new route scene; of his climbs in The Pass from this period, *Black and White* proved to be the best. Moran added a very hard route, *The Heretic*, to Craig Ddu in August and in the same month Pete Whillance wiped out the two points of aid on *Groper*. During the autumn local activist Paul Williams, started a campaign to plug some of the unclimbed gaps on the Cromlech. To this end he kept beavering away on the cliff in all but the foulest of weather.

The savage winter of 1978/79 will long be remembered as its icy grip brought most of the cliffs in The Pass into condition. There were even epic ascents of the Grochan gullies but the main action centred on Craig y Rhaeadr which was iced up from top to bottom. Mick Fowler temporarily deserted his beloved loose rock to bring modern winter techniques to The Pass and added several Grade V ice routes. The best two, *Cascade* and *Central Icefall Direct* (which has a sensational hanging icicle 200 feet up it) have formed a few times in recent years and have had many ascents, epic ascents, and just epics. The Air Sea Rescue Squadron from R A F Valley has been called out to the cliff so many times rumour has it that the pilots can fly there blindfolded.

During 1979 more minor lines succumbed, but in addition several big routes were to appear. Williams first took Roberts up *Brute 33*, a vicious overhang, and then teamed up with Leigh McGinley for *Golgotha*, a rather serious climb to the left of *Ivy Sepulchre*. In the summer of 1979 two routes stood out from the rest, especially as they were well-known problems. Ed Cleasby once again came south, this time for *Hindenburg* on Cyrn Las which was eventually completed in two pushes after a mammoth cleaning session. The big news of the year however was the long awaited ascent of *Lord of the Flies* by Ron Fawcett and Chris Gibb. Described as being considerably harder than its neighbour *Right Wall* (which incidentally received almost as many ascents as Cenotaph Corner in 1985) this creation set a new standard for The Pass although this too was considered to be a hard man's trade route by 1986. In addition, this route was not only the scene of a television spectacular, but was also the cause of the trundling of a huge block which used to reside above *Right Wall* – this was levered off at 'dead at night'.

Early in 1980 Fawcett completed the often tried problem of *Quantum Jump*, then packed in yet another super-route, *Precious*, on the right wall of the Cromlech after persuading a bystander to belay him. Over a period of some six weeks Fawcett was to bring new standards of difficulty to the Welsh crags. During this time, after teaming up with Williams, he well and truly blitzed the Cromlech doing all the major unclimbed lines. *Hall of Warriors* was a particularly bold route up a friable wall involving the use of a tiny sapling but *Atomic Hot Rod*, a short brutal crack, was to provide what was then thought to be a 7a testpiece. Even with marked improvement in fitness and general rise in climbing standards it is still rated 6b. Fawcett's other Cromlech routes, *J R* and *True Grip* were high quality eliminates but *Ivory Madonna*, a new girdle was a brilliant major addition to the central walls. At about this time general feeling seemed to indicate that it would be a good idea to make the grading system open ended, not only to cater for the hardest new routes, but also to allow an upgrading of some of the easier Extremes to avoid overcrowding in any one grade.

Not surprisingly, after the exceptionally dry spring, Pat Littlejohn added *Ghosts* and *Silent Spring* to Craig y Rhaeadr, a cliff which usually seeps, and which has rarely been dry enough to merit much attention. This self-same spell of good weather enabled Steve Haston and Leigh McGinley, both climbing extremely well, to amaze the pundits with *The Red Ring*, their completely free ascent of the massive *Grinder* roof. Another ferocious piece of climbing around this time was the much looked at right arête of *Brant Direct* which gave John Redhead some exciting moments. *Cockblock* was a powerful effort, hard move after hard move with little respite, it was soloed by a hyper-fit Phil Davidson in 1984.

On the Cromlech in 1981, Dave Jones ascended his controversial excursion up and around Left Wall and Epitaph to the heckling of a team of locals who could not believe their eyes. *Tess of the D'Urbevilles*, as the 'route' was called, came in for much criticism. The style of ascent was so dubious with an overriding element of conceptualisation that a description was omitted from the 1983 Pollitt New Climbs supplement, however, Paul Jenkinson ascended the line some seven years later, much to the relief of many local activists. The best new route discovered in The Pass during 1982 was probably *A New Austerlitz*, on the East Wing of Dinas Mot by Gary Gibson and Neil Harvey.

At the beginning of June 1983 Mark Lynden and John Silvester climbed *Rootorooni*, a counter-diagonal route to *The Thing*. Another activist on the scene at this time was Stuart Cathcart who, after putting up *Silent Thunder*, *Gorty's Triangle* and *Stalling Out*, a fine trilogy of routes on the right side of Dinas Mot, shifted his attention to the smooth walls on the right of Cyrn Las. Before his ascents, Cathcart controversially placed three bolts, (the first since the MacInnes saga on the Cromlech back in the '50s) an act which had the 'Old Guard' on the verge of a coronary, and the 'young hot shots' casting aspersions on both his ethical style and lineage. Fortunately, within a couple of months the bolts were chopped and replaced with pegs by Nick Dixon and Andy Popp who both led a combination of the provocatively named *New Era* and *Steel Appeal*, starting up the former and finishing via the latter to produce *Mild Steel* E6 – a particularly sterling effort from Popp who was leading E4 at that time. In the same area, Andy Sharp and John Harwood climbed *Hooded Crow* on little frequented Clogwyn y Ddysgl.

Clogwyn Gafr (Craig Fach), a small outcrop containing several aid routes, came under the scrutiny of various climbers. Dave Pycroft started the ball rolling with free ascents of *The Slash* and *Diapason* then Phil Davidson was co-opted to free *Pulsar*, a fine crack. The 'holdless' groove just to the left gave Martin Crook and Pete Norton a good workout some months later when they freed *Pi*, now *Sacred Idol*.

Standards became so high that virtually anything seemed possible. Jerry Moffatt soloed half a dozen routes on the Cromlech including *Right Wall* and *Foil,* pronouncing it, "an easy and outdated crag", while Andy Pollitt, the Dyserth Dynamo, led *Quantum Jump, Cockblock, Venturi Effect, Mural, S S Special, C Minor* and *Stroll On* – all in the same day. On a sadder note, the 1940s classic, *Nea,* suffered a major rockfall from its top pitch; as a result the route was upgraded to VS.

In early 1985, Willy Todd added several short hard routes in the vicinity of Craig Ddu. This trend was repeated on Dinas Bach where Bob Drury put up *Body Rock*, with its one mighty move, and on Little Buttress where the best of a crop of new additions was *Ryley Bosvil*, a technically precocious crack from Redhead. Another interesting find was on the very traditional Carreg Gwalch, which yielded *Shadow of Youth*, a slanting crack, to Ray Wood and Lew Hardy. All new finds in the Pass were dwarfed however, by the discovery of *Long Kesh* on Cyrn Las, a route of mind-blowing exposure between *The Skull* and *Lubyanka*, the first major find for about five years and a great effort from Steve Boydon and Simon Cardy.

The hard winter of early 1986 gave brilliant snow and ice conditions; February was outstanding – bright sunny days with clear blue skies split by hard frosty nights; numerous new ice routes were ascended. Right Wall and Central Icefall Direct received ascents (by different teams) on the same day – what a double that would make. There were several interesting discoveries unearthed later on in the year; with few really major lines left unclimbed, these were mainly on the smaller, more esoteric crags though nonetheless worthwhile... *Marlene on the Wall,* the prominent roof on Clogwyn Blaen Coed, went on sight to Trevor Hodgson; *The Nectarine Run* by Jon de Montjoye, on little known Clogwyn Gafr was one of the year's best finds, while no less worthy, on the then obscure Cwm Glas Facet was *Pretty Girls Make Graves* – a fierce finger crack from Craig Smith. Smith was again active on the left arête of *Grond* with his sensational, *Rumblefish*, a lonely lead. Not to be left out, Nick Dixon ascended *Grand*, the right arête, and then climbed the blank scoop right again, *Awesome*. A few weeks later, Dixon put up *Melancholony* on Cwm Glas Facet, and Martin Crook found

Killerkranky on Scimitar Ridge, both routes being pointers towards the future.

The publication of a new Llanberis guide in 1987 triggered off a wave of frenetic development with over 70 new routes recorded that year. Amongst the best of these were *The Bog of the Eternal Stench* on Craig Ddu, *King Wad* and *Surgical Lust* on Scimitar Ridge, three sensational finds for Lancastrian exile Paul Pritchard. Also on Scimitar Ridge *The Kicker Conspiracy, Romany Soup* and *The Bells, The Bells, The Bells* from Crispin Waddy, plus *Mutiny on the Mouse Organ* and *The Tufty Club Rebellion* by Andy Popp, were all excellent, hard, sustained routes in the modern idiom. Another addition, *The 39 Slaps* gave Johnny Dawes a strenuous, technical and dynamic redpoint which was superbly on sighted by Popp. Dawes also added *Satsumo Wrestler,* alongside *The Nectarine Run* on Clogwyn Gafr as well as developing some desperate bouldering on the Barrel Boulder below The Nose of Dinas Mot. The Barrel's F8b girdle was added later by Moffatt. On the walls and boulders of Cwm Glas Bach, many good routes were unearthed including the taxing off-width, *Fear of Infection*, from George Smith, *Rimsky Korsakov* and *Wagner's Ring* from Dawes, *Lasagne Verdi* from Pritchard, *Melon Transplant* and *Nick's Sexual Problem* with its mighty move, from Dixon, and the brilliant *Weasels Rip My Flesh* from Steve Howe, to name but a few.

The development of Cwm Glas Bach continued throughout 1988, though at a much slower pace than the previous year, Popp's first ascent solo of *King of Rumpy* being particularly noteworthy. Pat Littlejohn, a new arrival to the area quickly made his mark, climbing the prominent thin crack/seam on the Equator Walls to produce the aptly named *Alchemy* – it's magic! Other notable routes were *Outspan* by Al and Phil George, and *Red Giant* from Howe and Phil Baxter, both on Clogwyn Gafr, and *Vlad the Arête*, an excruciatingly hard micro-route from Dixon.

In 1989, Dai Lampard added five big routes to the south side of the Pass; on Plexus Buttress: *The Smodge*, which runs up to the right of *The Windmill* took one visit to the crag to complete, whereas *Perplexus*, a bold route through the overhangs near *The Red Ring* took four; *Tales of the Riverbank*, on which leads were shared with Al George, was an eliminate, climbed on sight, which breached some impressive ground on the East Wing of Dinas Mot; on Cyrn Las, the inverted V-groove between *The Grooves* and *The Prune* gave the main chapter and verse of *Sunday School Outing*, but the plum find was *The Edge of Time* (on which Nige Bonnett led the second pitch) a spectacular and airy expedition up the right arête of the crag, rumoured to be so exposed that oxygen was used on the top two pitches, and surely destined to become popular.

Elsewhere, on Clogwyn Tyllau, above Carreg Wastad, Owain Jones climbed his eponymous arête and Dave Holmes found *Unleashing the Wild Physique*, both powerful modern test-pieces. At the top of the Cromlech, the frightning and previously brutalized wall left of *Grond* yielded a short but serious pitch, *The Bastard Practice*, to Adam Wainwright, whilst over the hill towards Capel Curig, on the roadside crag of Dyffryn Mymbyr, Dixon joined the dots together on the finger-shredding *Jiggit*.

There was little new activity in 1990 and 1991; Iwan Jones continued to find gaps that provided amenably graded routes on Cwm Glas Bach; Ed Stone tackled *The Roc-Nest Monster* on Scimitar Ridge, and an almost unbelievable solo of *Lord of the Flies* by cellar-dweller Dave Thomas on a sunny weekend afternoon nearly gave half the spectators a coronary. In 1992, with rumours of another guide imminent, frenetic activity resulted in four very hard routes. Firstly, on Scimitar Ridge, *The Trumpet Blowers*, a steep, uncompromising and oft-eyed line, fell to Wainwright; Cwm Glas Bach yielded the desperate rounded arête of *Melondrama* to Dixon; but those timeless walls of Dinas Cromlech still held the biggest prize of all. After solving the intricacies of the overhanging, square cut arête above *Cenotaph Corner* to give *Overlord*, Steve Mayers, originator of many hard climbs on North Wales limestone turned his attention to the last(?) great problem, the space left of *Lord of the Flies*. The Line had been tried by Pritchard some years previously, but after reaching the Girdle ledge an escape was made up the upper part of *Lord of the Flies*. After thorough top rope and abseil inspection, Mayers psyched himself up and succeeded in leading the most challenging pitch in The Pass to date... aptly named *Nightmayer*, the strenuous and run-out nature of the final headwall means that it will be many years yet before the route receives a true on sight ascent. But then again, those words been written before... who knows what the next generation will have to say on this matter?

As the guidebook was in its final production stages Nick Dixon created another desperately difficult micro-route with his *Beginners' Mind* on the Dinas Mot boulders above the Cromlech bends. In contrast, Iwan Jones made the long walk up to Craig yr Haul, a previously undeveloped crag well above the road between Pen y Gwyrd and Plas y Brenin, and climbed a dozen or so routes at E1 and below.

The North Side of the Pass

Dinas

OS Ref. 614 585

This isolated little outcrop sits forlornly on the lower slopes of Y Garn, above a wooded spur, almost due east of Nant Peris. The main feature is its central corner with an overhanging left wall. The corner has been climbed, as have the walls around to the left and right, some being originally pegged in the '50s. The two best, and probably hardest problems are; the crack in the prow which forms the left arête of the central groove, and an exposed hand-traverse of the left wall.

Craig Ffynnon Peris

(Crag of St Peris's Spring)

OS Ref. 611 584

This tiny crag is almost buried in the trees about 200 metres down to the left of Dinas, on the left side of the flat wooded spur which dominates the village of Nant Peris. It is easily recognised by a small clean square-cut arête jutting out from the foliage, above an isolated white cottage sitting at about 10 o'clock, as one reaches the 30mph signs at the bottom end of Nant Peris. After passing the Vaynol Arms on the right, take the first left turn and follow a track which gradually peters out as it rises. Many of the problems and variations that exist have been left for the itinerant boulderer to rediscover for himself, only the main routes are described. To the left of the prominent central arête (Nick's Arête) past an off-width crack, a rounded arête where the crag peters out gives:

★**Nappy Brown and the Red Hot Pokers** 30 feet E1 5b (1988)
Pull onto the front of the arête from the left (or start direct – much harder E2 6a) and continue direct on sound rock to finish – a mini classic.

Autumn Acorns   30 feet   E3 6a   (1992)
From the foot of the off-width, take a tenuous left-trending line up the
wall, finishing direct (and right of Nappy Brown etc).

Fists of Fury   30 feet   E2 5c   (1988)
The painful off-width is painfully obvious.

Nick's Arête, the well-brushed square-cut arête has been ascended on
a top rope... well, each individual move has been done – but the
sequence has yet to be linked together... it may yet yield to an inspired
'slapper' – at an estimated British 7b.

★**Big Brother is Belaying Me!**   35 feet   E5 6b   (1988)
A heart-stopping little pitch. Starting just right of the arête, climb the
flake and thin crack to a tied-off peg. Lunge right past this for good
holds. Finish direct passing two ancient pegs.

Four Horsemen of the Apocalypse   35 feet   E3 6a   (1990)
Though short, this route requires a stable approach, being good value
for its grade. Either, start in the obvious right-hand corner and climb it
for 10 feet before moving out left, hands just above the overlap, to
make a hard move up for an obvious flake – high peg runner, or
climb direct to the same point. Traverse left to a large foothold then
pull up rightwards to finish at slings.

Times Laughin' Stocks   30 feet   E2 6a   (1988)
Squeezed in between the direct start to the previous route and the
corner, this serious micro-pitch is no laughin' matter. Using obvious
holds (next to pockets) or just the pockets without the holds – harder,
climb the wall trending right to join the corner route, which is 4b if
done direct, at the top.

Rediscovered   30 feet   E1 5b   (1988)
A slight pitch up the right edge and corner.

Craig Ddu   (The Black Crag)

OS Ref. 618 574

The most westerly of the cliffs on the north side of Llanberis Pass. Its black
glint suggests a wet, unpleasant cliff but some of the rock is intrinsically
jet black and rather smooth. Drainage from the steep hillside makes the

cliff unusually slow to dry out. Boiler-plate formation gives the crag a slabby appearance, but it is uniformly steep and in the central part, up which Canol forces a way, slightly overhanging. Many of the routes are better than their appearance would suggest and there is a greater element of seriousness than on other cliffs on the north side of The Pass.

The cliff is halved by Garlic Groove, a wet vegetated gully left of which lies the major section, bounded at its left end by Short Tree Chimney, topped by a tree. Just right of this, a boulder on the right edge of a watercourse at the foot of the cliff marks the start of Crown of Thorns. Left of Garlic Groove is a massive pinnacle. Between this and Crown of Thorns are Zig-Zig and Canol. The pinnacle marks the starts of Black Wall and Scrog. The main feature right of Garlic Groove is another flat topped pedestal, the left side of which forms the obvious slab and vertical corner of Rift Wall. To the right, the cliff, still very steep, gives The Heretic, The Bog of the Eternal Stench, Yellow Groove, Yellow Wall, Petite Fleur and several other short but entertaining routes. Descent is down the easy hillside well to the left of the crag or on the right down a gully just right of Grooved Rib.

At the left-hand side of Craig Ddu just beyond the point where the descent path turns back along the foot of the crag, there is a clean isolated wall, clearly visible from the road, and split by a thin sloping crack, Mabinogion.

Telegram Sam 40 feet E2 5c   (1985)
The wall left of the thin sloping crack is just little harder than the crack itself.

★**Mabinogion** 45 feet E2 5c   (1985)
A little gem. Climb the crack to a good pocket (crux). Step left and continue up on pockets to a ledge. Finish up the thin crack in the short, overhanging headwall (good wire – difficult to place).

Stumpy the Dragonslayer 40 feet E2 5c   (1985)
Climb the wall right of Mabinogion.

Health and Efficiency 40 feet E2 6a   (1987)
The groove right of Stumpy... is an oft-tried devious problem. Climb the groove to good pockets on the right wall. Finish direct.

Sound as a Trout 40 feet E2 5c   (1992)
Start at the obvious flake right of the groove of Health and Efficiency. Climb the centre of the flake to a small horizontal slot. Move left to the arête and ascend to a good flaky spike. Move right on good holds, place a runner in the top crack, and scuttle round right to belay.

Craig Ddu

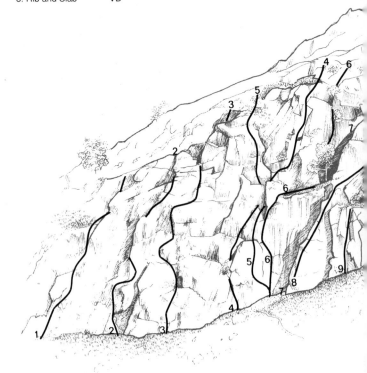

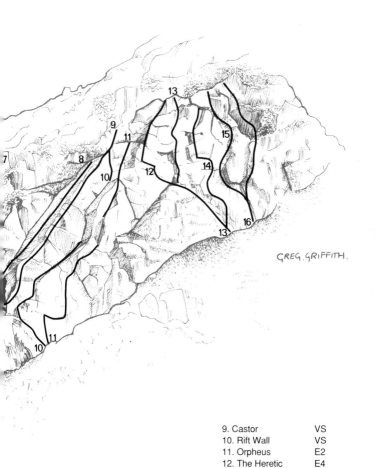

GREG. GRIFFITH.

9. Castor	VS
10. Rift Wall	VS
11. Orpheus	E2
12. The Heretic	E4
13. Yellow Groove	VS
14. Yellow Wall	E2
15. Fever	HVS
16. Petite Fleur	HS

Buoux in a Tin (Without a Tin-opener)   40 feet   E5 6b   (1987)
Thirty yards around to the right of Mabinogion sits a huge flake
whose front face presents a severely undercut wall. From a large
flake, exacting climbing up a faint left to right diagonal weakness
leads hopefully to a safe finish via a big groove thus avoiding the
alternative finish – via a yellow helicopter... the direct start is
Saussuave, 6c.

Short Tree Chimney   165 feet   Difficult   (1949)
At the left-hand of the main cliff proper, 10 feet left of a watercourse,
is an obvious right-facing chimney capped by a tall tree. Start left of
this.
1 55 feet. Climb the chimney or its drier left wall to a ledge. The
chimney is bridged by a large chockstone. Climb up and swing to the
left, make a difficult mantelshelf and go back into the corner. Climb
this to a large ledge and tree.
2 40 feet. Move left and climb the short wall past a tree to a belay.
3 70 feet. Scramble to the top, traversing first right, then left.

Variation.
2a The wall directly behind the first stance may be climbed – about
Severe/Hard Severe. Lethal if wet.

★**Sea Panther**   120 feet   Hard Very Severe 5a   (1980)
Fine climbing up the centre of the wall of Short Tree Chimney. Only
really feasible during periods of drought. Start three feet right of Short
Tree Chimney. Climb steeply up the wall moving slightly left after a
few feet. Go up on small flakes past an awkward move at 25 feet to
gain good holds and easier climbing, runner on the left. Traverse
right at 60 feet to reach an obvious ledge below the steep upper
wall. Ascend this on good holds via a hidden central crack until
forced to move left. Cross a ramp and continue up to a good tree
belay on the left. Scramble off left to finish.

★**Crown of Thorns**   135 feet   Severe   (1949)
Pleasant if dry, but still serious for its grade. Start 12 yards right of
Short Tree Chimney where a boulder protrudes three feet out of the
ground at the right-hand edge of the watercourse.
1 60 feet. Ascend direct to the right end of a grassy ledge at 25 feet.
Climb the groove on the right, then move back left to the top of the
pedestal.
2 40 feet. Climb the wall on good holds to a sloping ledge, then take
a grassy groove until an entry can be made into a large scoop.
Belays in the corner.
3 35 feet. Climb the flaky wall on the right. Step up and across the
groove on the left, a difficult move then brings the top within reach, or

climb directly up the corner above the wall and back through the 'thorny crown' onto the grass. Belay well back.

Variation.
1a Start 15 feet left of the boulder at the bottom of the watercourse and climb diagonally right to the grassy ledge 25 feet up the normal start.

Blackguard   200 feet   Hard Very Severe   (1975)
Start immediately right of Crown of Thorns at the foot of an indefinite crack.
1 60 feet. 4a. Follow the crack to join Crown of Thorns half-way up the groove on its first pitch. Continue as for Crown of Thorns to the pedestal stance.
2 50 feet. 4c. Traverse right for 20 feet. Climb a steep wall past a small quartzy area on good holds to reach ledges. Step up left to belay.
3 90 feet. 4c. Traverse right beneath an overhanging wall to a projecting block. Climb onto this from the right and surmount the bulge above to a slab. Climb this then finish up a short corner crack.

Flying Trapeze   205 feet   E1   (1975)
Start 25 feet right of the Crown of Thorns starting boulder, and just left of a clump of grass 20 feet up the crag.
1 70 feet. 4b. Climb the wall to a ledge at 25 feet. Step left then go up trending right, making for the foot of the right-slanting groove on Zig-Zag. Follow this for 10 feet to a small ledge. Nut and ancient peg belays.
2 55 feet. 4c. Continue up rightwards then move left to a shallow groove. Climb this to a large hanging block at the top. Traverse right below this to a sloping ledge and peg belays.
3 90 feet. 5a. Move back left and climb the crack in the left side of the block, scary. Go up the wall to just below the bulge. Traverse right for 15 feet to a sloping ledge, the last few feet on undercuts. Layback up on the left round the bulge to a precarious finish.

★★Zig-Zag   210 feet   Very Severe   (1952)
A very fine climb, not hard technically, but rather serious because of spaced protection. Small wires are useful. Start under a prominent overhang 20 feet up, and about 50 feet right of the Crown of Thorns starting boulder.
1 120 feet. 4b. Climb up leftwards to a grassy ledge at 30 feet. Go diagonally up right, steep, to another grassy ledge. Step left into a short shallow groove and climb leftwards across an easy ramp line to the foot of a right-slanting groove 10 feet higher. Climb this groove to a grassy stance. Care needed with belays.

2 90 feet. 4b. Continue diagonally right to a ledge and finish up the black groove 20 feet right of the stance.

China Girl 210 feet E2   (1983)
A direct line up the centre of the main face which crosses some loose rock. Start immediately right of Zig-Zag below the bulge at 20 feet.
1 80 feet. 5c. Start up the quartz vein leading to a small overhang. Go over this at the small hanging groove. Continue directly up the crack above to easier but shattered rock. Belay on the ledge. Care needed to find belays.
2 130 feet. 5b. Climb the overhanging groove above the stance, then easier rocks to the top. A poorly protected pitch.

★★Canol 230 feet E1   (1952)
A good route, steep and technically interesting. Start 40 feet left of the slanting crack on the left side of the massive pinnacle, below a holly tree on a grassy ledge.
1 80 feet. 4c. Climb steeply up to the holly tree. Bushwhack through the grass and ascend diagonally leftwards to a sloping shelf which leads left to a blocky belay.
2 80 feet. 5b. Climb the short steep wall on the left behind the belay using an indefinite crack to reach a rightward sloping ramp. From the top of this, turn the overhang on its left side, peg runner, and continue to a ledge. Traverse easily right for 30 feet to an enormous block belay.
3 70 feet. 4b. Climb the obvious groove just left of the block turning the shattered overhang on the left to finish.

Variations

Direct Start
1a 60 feet. Very Severe 4c. From a point 25 feet left of the normal start i.e. 10 feet right of Zig-Zag, climb the ledgy wall to the block belay at the top of Canol pitch 1 stepping right at 30 feet.
3a 80 feet. E1 5b. As for Canol to the peg runner below the overhang then traverse right using a fang of rock to a good hold. Climb diagonally down right past a quartz hold and round a corner to a detached block. A shallow groove leads to flat holds, which are traversed right until it is possible to climb up to trees.

★Jupiter 220 feet E3   (1982)
A bold and intimidating outing. Start as for the normal start to Canol, below the holly tree growing 30 feet up the crag.
1 60 feet. 5a. Climb the wall and groove up to the holly. Go up the shattered groove above, a bit grassy, to a peg belay. This is level with, but 25 feet right of, the blocky belay at the top of Canol pitch 1.

2 70 feet. 5b. Step left and climb the overhanging wall via a dubious flake to the overhang. Move left round this and follow the steep quartzy crack diagonally left to a second roof. Boldly climb this moving right, then left, to the traverse ledge of Canol. Move right to belay on the large block, as for Canol. An exposed pitch.
3 90 feet. 5a. Traverse back left for about five feet, past Canol's final groove to a shallow scoop. Go up this using two good pockets to a ledge and finish direct.

The Despicable Act   220 feet   E2   (1982)
A bold slabby lower section contrasts with the highly technical finale up an overhanging groove. Start at a small shattered spike eight feet right of the Canol start.
1 120 feet. 5b. Step left off the spike and climb steeply up the black streak to reach a large sloping niche at 30 feet. Pull rightwards around the overlap and ascend boldly on good sharp holds, first right then left to a grassy ledge. Climb up over ledges to the foot of an overhanging groove. Go up this exiting leftwards to the large block belay on Canol.
2 100 feet. 5c. Move up leftwards from the top of the block. Traverse back right to beneath an overhanging groove. Make very hard moves past a peg runner to enter the groove, up which the climb finishes. Scrambling remains.

Grey Wall   210 feet   E1   (1957)
An interesting line. Start below a slanting crack with a tree at its foot on the left side of the massive pinnacle.
1 50 feet. 5a. The overhanging crack on the left side of the pinnacle leads to a tree on the black slab. Continue up to a grassy ledge below an overhanging groove.
2 80 feet. 5c. Climb the groove to the small stance of Black Wall pitch 2. Follow Black Wall pitch 3 to the peg runner, then traverse 20 feet right to a stance below an overhanging crack.
3 80 feet. 4c. Climb the crack to below the overhang, then traverse right to good holds and the finish.

Variation
1a 50 feet. 5a. Step up onto a ledge just left of the tree. Pull boldly round the arête and go up to the tree at the top of the diagonal crack.

★★**Black Wall**   210 feet   E1   (1954)
A good route but it is usually greasy and intimidating. Start below the wide crack on the right side of the obvious pinnacle.
1 45 feet. 4b. Traverse left and climb the arête to the top.
2 50 feet. 4a. Climb the steep wall on the left into a scoop. Traverse

diagonally left to a small stance and good belays.
3 80 feet. 5c. Climb the crack to the overhang then swing out left.
Climb direct for 15 feet until it is possible to step right to a thin crack.
Climb this for 10 feet, peg runner. A shallow groove on the left leads
to the overhang. Traverse diagonally left across greasy slabs. Good
stance and belays.
4 35 feet. Climb direct to the top.

Scrog 320 feet E1   (1955)
An interesting route with some good moves. Start as for Black Wall.
1 60 feet. 4b. Climb the wide crack on the right-hand side of the
pinnacle.
2 90 feet. 5b Step across and ascend the short overhanging crack on
the right. Go up the arête above for 15 feet, then traverse right to a
good tree belay in a large bay.
3 60 feet. 5a. Ascend the steep crack behind the tree, then follow the
groove over an overhang and continue to a prickly holly stance.
4 80 feet. 5a. Move left for six feet to a groove leading back right to
the foot of an overhanging crack. Climb this and continue bearing
right to a large block.
5 30 feet. Climb the pleasant finishing wall.

Variations
3a 90 feet. 5c. Climb the crack behind the tree, then step left to the
foot of an overhanging layback crack. Climb this with difficulty and
belay on the holly above. Continue up the groove of pitch 4.
4a 70 feet. 5b. Instead of moving back right, continue direct.

Sheep in Situ 315 feet E1   (1975)
A rambling expedition with a deceptively steep second pitch. Start at
a quartzy ramp about 10 feet right of the wide crack of Scrog.
1 40 feet. 4a. Climb the ramp to a sloping ledge on the right and a
peg belay.
2 30 feet. 5b. Step down and move steeply right to a peg runner.
Climb the groove above on the right to an awkward finish on a
grassy ledge.
3 50 feet. 4c. Step up left and follow the ledge until it is possible to
climb up to a large ledge with blocks (on the girdle).
4 50 feet. 4c. Climb the groove behind the blocks until a traverse left
leads to below the left end of a ledge with trees.
5 35 feet. 5a. Climb the vegetated groove behind the tree past a peg
runner to a rightward traverse which finishes over a large block to a
holly tree belay – painful for the 'shorts and T-shirt brigade'.
6 80 feet. 5a. Traverse right to pitch 4 of Scrog, follow this.
7 30 feet. 4a. Finish up the wall as for Scrog.

Garlic Groove   210 feet   Severe   (1949)
Quite a pleasant climb above the initial slimy chimney. Start in the
black gully a few yards right of the massive pinnacle.
1 80 feet. The wet chimney leads to a grassy corner. Continue up this
with interest to the tall tree.
2 60 feet. The groove continues in a curving line. Climb the corner
for a few feet then step into a subsidiary groove on the right. Ascend
this until a step to the edge. Go up to a large block then climb the
steep rib on the right to a holly tree.
3 70 feet. Scramble up the continuation of the gully. A short chimney
below a tree proves awkward. Finish in the same line.

Dill   220 feet   Hard Severe   (1982)
Start between Garlic Groove and Rib and Slab.
1 90 feet. Climb the tapering slab, continue up the broken rib, then
traverse left to the tree on Garlic Groove.
2 60 feet. 4b. Above is an arête which is gained direct, or from the
right. Climb this to join Garlic Groove. Follow this to belay at a holly
tree.
3 70 feet. Scramble up via a square-cut chimney to reach the final
wall. Finish directly up this.

★**Rib and Slab**   250 feet   Very Difficult   (1948)
A popular beginners' climb. Start at the foot of the rib right of Garlic
Groove.
1 100 feet. Climb the tricky rib past a steepening near the top to a
broad terrace. Tree root belay.
2 150 feet. Climb the delightful slab to finish (the line is just left of
centre). Care is needed with the final belay.

My Mum's Slabby Arête   100 feet   E4 6a   (1987)
On the left, at the top of the central gully (the initial part of Garlic
Groove), and left of the top pitch of Rib and Slab, is a pocketed arête
with a tree to its right. The arête is hard to start, gradually easing to a
pleasant afternoon outing.

The Tickle   100 feet   Severe   (1962)
This avoids the slab of Rib and Slab by taking the wall on the left.
Start below the slab of Rib and Slab. In the gully is a slight bay with a
roof about six feet up the gully, on the left.
1 60 feet. Climb the crack in the back of the bay, move left under the
roof, round the corner into a niche. Go up to a block, then climb a rib
or vegetation on its left to belay at a holly tree.
2 40 feet. Climb the steep rocks behind, keeping left – harder than it
looks – the finish of Dill.

Castor   180 feet   Very Severe   (1967)
A rather disjointed and disappointing climb. Start from a
quartz-topped boulder by the path, just left of the prominent rib,
midway between Rib and Slab and the fence.
1 50 feet. 4b. Mantelshelf onto a large block and continue up the
wide crack to a large bay and tree belay.
2 50 feet. 4c. Traverse right through trees, over an arête, then go up
a crack and the overhang above. Move left to belay.
3 80 feet. Finish up the right-hand side of the slabs.

Black Mike   70 feet   Hard Very Severe 5a   (1987)
Really only a variation start to Castor, but having some good moves,
and making the original route much more continuous. Start to the right
of Castor pitch 1. Climb the flaky groove and small overhang to a
junction with Castor pitch 2.

★**Carlos**   90 feet   E1   (1969)
A fierce little pitch taking the right-hand of three steep grooves. Start
about 12 feet left of the fence.
1 55 feet. 5b. Climb the overhanging groove until an awkward move
enables the right wall to be gained. From a precarious position, bold
climbing leads to a rest below the small roof on the right. Traverse left
along the obvious line to a small stance, junction with Castor. Peg
belay on the left.
2 35 feet. 5a. Swing into the groove on the left. Continue up the
crack to finish. Belay on the slabs above.

Samson Too   50 feet   E3 6a   (1991)
A slight, but deceptively steep and awkward little pitch. Start
immediately right of the overhanging groove of Carlos. Climb the
right-hand side of the arête to a large jug. Move diagonally right to a
good hold, crux, then boldly take the right wall of the corner to a tree
belay – the top six feet needs care to be taken with the rock. Abseil
off.

Black Letter Day   70 feet   E1 5b   (1987)
Start behind the fence between Carlos and the Black Pig. Gain a
leftwards leaning ramp. Follow this awkwardly, then take the groove
and crack above to a tree belay (on Samson Too). Abseil off.

★**The Black Pig**   135 feet   E3   (1981)
A deceptively steep and absorbing line between Carlos and Rift
Wall. Start at a boss of rock five feet right of the fence.
1 50 feet. 5c. Climb the black shattered wall keeping right of the
groove. Make a hard pull over the bulge and step right to climb a
four-foot groove. Continue to a large ledge, then ascend a short wall
to another ledge. Peg and nut belay on the right.

2 50 feet. 5b. Gain the top of the large flake above the stance. Ascend a few feet then move left to the arête. Traverse back right and climb the bulging wall using an inverted spike. Pull strenuously into the scoop. Climb this to a stance below a thin crack on the right.
3 35 feet. 6a. Climb the crack, which overhangs alarmingly, to a good hold. Exit left with difficulty.

★★**Rift Wall** 200 feet Very Severe (1949)
A varied route up the large slabs and overhanging corner which form the left flank of the flat-topped pedestal. Start in a bay at a rock step 25 feet right of the fence.
1 70 feet. 4b. Go diagonally left on easy rock to a ledge. Climb up a few feet then traverse right on steep rock to gain the bottom of the slab. Climb this to a belay below the overhanging corner crack.
2 90 feet. 5a. Struggle up the overhanging corner, then breeze up the easy slab to the top of a pedestal. Belay.
3 40 feet. 4a. Move up left to the foot of a steep corner. Swing sensationally onto the left arête on large flakes. Finish easily.

★**Orpheus** 180 feet E2 (1967)
A juggy wall climb with well-spaced protection. Start 20 feet right of Rift Wall at two quartz bands.
1 80 feet. 5b. Go diagonally left up a shallow depression to a good flake runner. Traverse 20 feet right across a slab to a small platform on the arête. Move boldly up on pockets then go slightly left to a small niche. Traverse a few feet right and take the overhang at its weakest point to a slab and spike belay.
2 50 feet. 4c. Climb diagonally right up a short wall, then go easily up to a small bay on Pedestal Route. From the right-hand end of the bay, move right round a bulge and climb the arête to the top of the pedestal.
3 50 feet. 4c. Traverse right to a crack. Climb this and the overhang above to enter a groove. Finish up this.

★**Pedestal Route** 210 feet Very Difficult (1948)
This reaches the top of the pedestal by a rising traverse from the short right-hand side, then descends to escape along a weakness in the slabs of Rift Wall. Start by 30 feet of scrambling up into the grassy bay right of the pedestal.
1 60 feet. Traverse left and round the corner to a small bay. Climb the far corner to the slab top, or, the corner crack of the grassy bay leads directly to the same point.
2 150 feet. Descend the slab by the corner to a small sapling, then traverse out onto the far edge. The awkward slabs near the edge lead up to grass (this is the slab of Rib and Slab).

Slab and Groove 120 feet Hard Very Severe (1986)
Start below the steep slab, above the start of Pedestal Route.
1 50 feet. 4a. Climb the middle of the slab.
2 70 feet. 5a. Follow the steep groove above via some bold
laybacking – the rusty peg half-way up, is useless.

★★**The Bog of the Eternal Stench** 100 feet E6 6b (1987)
A mighty pitch which forges directly up the leaning black wall crossed
by The Heretic. Scramble up the first pitch of Yellow Groove to the
large block at the top of the rock pyramid, then descend the ramp on
the other side for 15 feet to the start. Climb straight up, then slightly
left to reach The Heretic's groove which is followed to the break. A
powerful move up and right to a peg at the overlap lands one below
the crux. The headwall above gives a frantic finale; sprint straight up
now, reachy and dramatic moves plus scant protection combine well
to keep the adrenalin flowing... only for the bold!

The Heretic 100 feet E4 6a (1978)
A deceptively powerful pitch across the sombre black wall left of
Yellow Groove with a problematical finish. Start just left of the large
block (Yellow Groove pitch 2 start). Traverse left, then climb the
groove in the centre of the impending wall to a slanting crack. Sidle
awkwardly left to a precarious finish. Scramble up for 30 feet to
belay.

★★**Yellow Groove** 140 feet Very Severe (1955)
A steep and exposed line with good holds which gives superb
climbing up the left-hand side of the yellow wall. Start on the
right-hand side of the rock pyramid 40 feet right of Pedestal Route.
1 50 feet. Scramble easily up the rock pyramid which is crowned by
a large block.
2 90 feet. 4b. From the block climb a groove to an overhang then
move right to a ledge below a clean-cut groove. Ascend this, step left
and continue up the wall; a previously underrated pitch.

★**Blackhead** 100 feet E3 6a (1981)
This independent line between Yellow Groove and Yellow Wall gives
a superb and varied pitch. Start 10 feet right, and slightly lower than
the start of Yellow Groove pitch 2, at a leftward slanting weakness.
Follow the leftward slanting line up the wall, strenuous, to the foot of
the groove of Yellow Groove. Move right and climb the short
left-facing groove, crux, to a sloping ledge. Surmount the large
overhang on the left and finish up the crack past two hollies. Brute
force and technique are an advantage.

★★**Yellow Wall** 160 feet E2 (1962)
A fine sustained climb of interest and character. Start on the

right-hand side of the rock pyramid at the foot of the steep wall, directly below the hanging groove of Fever.

1 90 feet. 5b. Climb the steep wall for 20 feet to a resting place. Trend up leftwards to the base of a shallow groove. Climb this and continue to a large foothold. Turn the overhang on the right and go up to a ledge and belay.

2 70 feet. 5b. Traverse left past a perched block, under an overhang to a sloping ledge (junction with Blackhead). A strenuous pull round the overhang leads to precarious climbing up a groove; face left to finish.

Fever 135 feet Hard Very Severe (1966)

An interesting climb with an excellent groove. Start a few feet right of Yellow Wall below a hanging boss of rock, and an overhanging chimney.

1 75 feet. 5a. Climb the steep crack and wall. Traverse left under the overhang to the foot of a groove. Superb moves up the groove past a peg runner at the top lead to a step right along a flake. Climb the slab to a ledge behind a holly.

2 60 feet. 4c. Make a rising traverse left to a perched block. Climb a crack and traverse left from a holly to the top.

★**Petite Fleur** 110 feet Hard Severe 4b (1961)

Pleasant but short, start as for Fever. Climb the steep crack and wall to the overhang. Move up right into the overhanging chimney. Climb this and the slabby continuation groove to a grassy bay. One hundred feet of scrambling remains.

Grooved Rib 110 feet Very Severe 4c (1962)

A worthwhile pitch at the top end of its grade. Start 10 feet right of Petite Fleur at the foot of a steep rib. Climb the rib direct avoiding rightward possibilities to a steepening at 60 feet. A difficult stretch and a high step enable a ledge to be reached. Step left and climb a shiny slab into a groove. Finish at the Petite Fleur belays.

Rolling Stone 100 feet E1 5b (1981)

Better than it looks, although a little mossy. Start 10 feet right of Grooved Rib at an obvious crack. Climb the crack and pull directly over the bulge onto the slab above. Go straight up to the roof and climb it into the narrow V-groove, crux. Follow this for 15 feet to a grassy terrace. Traverse 20 feet right on easy ground to a broken holly tree. Ascend direct for 20 feet to a tree belay.

Wounded Knee 100 feet Hard Very Severe 5b (1981)

Start 10 feet right of Rolling Stone. Climb the arête and short slab to the bulge. Take this direct, crux, and traverse left to the slab and roof of Rolling Stone. Follow the short groove right of the roof to a grassy terrace. Traverse right to belay as for Rolling Stone.

★★★**The Black Belt** 645 feet Hard Severe   (1949)
A traverse of the cliff from left to right with fine situations but little technical difficulty. Absorbing and interesting, it is the best expedition of its standard on the north side of The Pass. Start at the left-hand end of the cliff, around the corner from Short Tree Chimney.
1 70 feet. Climb the groove to a tree at 25 feet. Move right and climb Short Tree Chimney past the chockstone to a tree belay.
2 60 feet. Descend five feet and traverse horizontally right on good holds to reach a ramp. Peg and nut belay on top of the pedestal (as for Crown of Thorns).
3 90 feet. Descend a few feet and traverse horizontally right for 40 feet to the base of a rightward-slanting groove. Climb this (as for Zig-Zag) to a stance on a small grassy ledge with poor belays.
4 50 feet. Climb Zig-Zag for 15 feet to a narrow ledge. Traverse right along obvious ledges descending slightly to the grassy ledge and block belay on Canol.
5 100 feet. From the right-hand end of the ledge, climb down six feet and go across a groove. Follow the ledge right and step down into the corner, peg runner. Move right to a good thread. Pull round onto a large ledge then cross a field to the tree belay at the top of Garlic Groove pitch 1.
6 35 feet. Walk right to belay at the foot of the large white slab of Rib and Slab
7 70 feet. Climb easily up the right-hand edge of the slab to a small grassy ledge with a ramp descending rightwards. Good nut belay 10 feet up on the left.
8 40 feet. Descend the steep ramp and climb the slab to the top of the pedestal (Pedestal Route in reverse).
9 50 feet. Descend the steep corner crack and scramble up to the large block belay on Yellow Groove. Care should be taken to protect the second on this pitch.
10 80 feet. 4c. From 20 feet down the ramp at a grassy quartz niche, climb up, then make a descending rightward traverse across the wall on the obvious line to finish just right of Grooved Rib – an excellent pitch which although Very Severe is avoidable.

★**What a Jump** 300 feet Very Severe   (1983)
An interesting low-level girdle of the left-hand part of the crag. Start below the right-hand side of the massive pinnacle, as for Black Wall.
1 50 feet. 4b. Traverse left and climb the arête to the top.
2 80 feet. 4b. Traverse left along the prominent weakness to the blocky belay on Canol.

3 70 feet. 4b. Traverse left across to Zig-Zag. Continue left past some pieces of quartz at the foot of a rightward-slanting groove (Zig-Zag). Keep traversing more easily to the large ledge on Crown of Thorns. Peg and nut belay.

4 100 feet. 4a. Step down slightly and traverse across above the mantelshelf on Short Tree Chimney. Climb this to the tree (possible belay). Finish up the second pitch of Short Tree Chimney.

Hit the Basement   525 feet   Hard Very Severe   (1983)
An intricate series of pitches split by some strolling. If the 15-foot crack on pitch 6 is bypassed the route becomes Very Severe. Start from the stile on the patch half-way up to the Crag.

1 140 feet. 4b. From the top of the stile climb up to a grassy ledge at 50 feet. Make a steep move up the rib on the right, step left and ascend the broken wall to block belays 10 feet back.

2 75 feet. 4a. Scramble rightwards for 40 feet to a 'pock-marked' wall. Move right into a crack and ascend pleasantly to block belays. Walk back 50 feet to the foot of the open rib which comes down from 20 feet right of Orpheus.

3 70 feet. 4c. Climb the rib and step left at the top onto a ledge. From the left-hand end of this move steeply up to a sloping ledge and nut belays. Good spike 10 feet higher.

4 80 feet. 4a. Move round and descend the slab (below the crux corner of Rift Wall). Step across the gap and follow the sloping ledge round the corner to belay at the foot of Rib and Slab. Walk 30 feet left to belay on the tree at the top of Garlic Groove.

5 65 feet. 4c. Step up and climb to the top of the leaning corner crack just left of Garlic Groove. Pull straight over onto a grassy ledge below a short overhanging crack.

6 25 feet. 5a. The crack yields quickly to bold laybacking. Flake and nut belays 10 feet back.

7 70 feet. 4b. Climb the shallow groove on the right, then finish up the smart little wall above

Little Buttress   OS Ref. 619 573

Between Craig Ddu and Clogwyn y Grochan, and about 100 yards from the latter, is a small buttress capped by a steep yellow wall with hollies on its right-hand side. With new rock getting scarcer, it now boasts several desperate micro-routes. The climbs are described from right to left.

The Three Cliffs 120 feet E1 (1985)
Start 15 feet right of and above the foot of a Y-shaped crack, below a dog-leg shaped groove.
1 50 feet. 5b. Climb the wall via layaways to a steep finish. Block belay.
2 40 feet. 5a. Take the thin crack behind the belay to easier ground below the final wall.
3 30 feet. Finish up the last pitch of Little Buttress Climb.

Little Buttress Climb 125 feet Severe (1949)
Start left of the holly trees at the foot of a steep Y-shaped crack.
1 55 feet. Strenuously ascend the wide crack taking its right fork.
2 40 feet. Climb up over shattered blocks to the foot of the final wall. Large block belay.
3 30 feet. From the top of the block move out onto the steep yellow wall, by a large shallow niche. The crack above is taken on good holds.

★**Ryley Bosvil** 50 feet E5 6c (1985)
The obvious much tried peg-scarred crack left of Little Buttress Climb. A classic product of the '80s, extremely technical. Climb the crack past the peg; sustained, precarious and a very sensational effort.

Little Groover 60 feet E1 5b (1984)
The slanting groove left of Ryley Bosvil has a hard move at 15 feet to reach a ledge. Continue in the same line then finish easily up the slab.

Too Late to Hesitate 50 feet E4 6b (1990)
From just left of Little Groover climb the obvious flake system to a set of good holds. Tiny wires on the left and right. Move up and right to a good hold on the arête, crux, then finish up Little Groover.

Down on the left side of the crag, twin cracks rise up to merge at 30 feet.

Toms Plums 30 feet E3 6b (1985)
Climb the right-hand crack with extreme difficulty, crux low down. Scramble up the slab to finish.

Bell Fruit 30 feet E4 6b (1985)
The left-hand crack proves a desperate struggle with a finger-severing jam at half height.

The crack just to the left has also been climbed.

Drws y Gwynt

(Door of the Wind)

OS Ref. 621 574

This steep little crag, standing out from the hillside above and to the left of Clogwyn y Grochan is well worth a visit as the rock is on the whole very clean, sound and rough. The cliff, rising in two tiers, is like a miniature Dinas Cromlech, consisting of large blocks and corners. The most conspicuous feature towards the left-hand side is the steep right-angled corner of Little Sepulchre. On its right-retaining wall lies a thin finger crack, then a wide crack which rises from the top of a pillar. To the right again a large holly marks the groove of Holly Gate, beyond which a number of side walls, gradually diminishing in height, give several short problems of varying difficulty.

★**A Touch of Class**   80 feet   E2 5b   (1991)
Excellent holds, perfect rock and good protection where it matters all combine to give a worthy outing. Unfortunately, at present, the route is a little dirty but should improve and get slightly easier as it cleans up. Start left of the arête left of Little Sepulchre, under an obvious V-groove. Pull into the V-groove and climb it to a step up and right onto an uncomfortable ledge. Ascend the wall direct at first, then move right to better holds. Go up left to a fairly wide crack and follow it to the top.

Demi Sec Dame   80 feet   E3 6a   (1984)
The arête left of Little Sepulchre. Move left across the arête on underclings (fangs) to gain a shallow groove. Go up and climb the crack which initially trends left then right to a prominent ledge on the arête. Take the final wall via a crack just left of the arête on superb finger-locks.

★**Little Sepulchre**   80 feet   Very Severe 4b   (1948)
A superb little climb reminiscent of Curving Crack on Cloggy. Start below the clean-cut corner. Scramble up to tall spikes then traverse into the corner. Climb the excellent corner crack with surprising ease.

★**Too Hard For Jim Perrin**   80 feet   E1 5c   (1978)
A classic test of finger jamming. The name is a misnomer as Jim has romped it. Start as for Little Sepulchre. Climb the thin crack between Little Sepulchre and Cracked Wall, hardest at the start.

★Cracked Wall 100 feet Very Difficult   (1948)
A fine route on perfect rock. Go up to the spikes as for Little
Sepulchre. Climb the wall to the overhanging crack (this point can
also be reached by cracks on the right). The crack is tricky to enter
but holds are large where it is steepest. Finish up a short wall.

Holly Gate 145 feet Very Difficult   (1948)
A good, interesting line though artificial in its lower part. Start below
and to the left of the large holly tree.
1 80 feet. Climb the slabs delicately and go into the corner below the
tree. Ascend a strenuous flake crack on the right to a stance.
2 65 feet. Go up a little on the right, then traverse back into the
groove behind the tree. Climb the groove then ascend a crack in the
wall to finish.

Reluctant 190 feet Hard Severe   (1958)
This takes the outside edge of the buttress, right of Holly Gate but
escapes left for belays. Start just right of Holly Gate.
1 50 feet. Go up from the lowest corner of the buttress, keeping as
much as possible to its crest. At 40 feet traverse left along a grassy
ledge to belay on Holly Gate.
2 40 feet. Return to six feet left of the ridge and climb awkwardly
past a protruding chockstone at 30 feet to gain a large ledge (belay
top left).
3 50 feet. Traverse down along the ledge and continue the original
line to a large grassy ledge sloping down to the left (where the other
climbs end). Belay at the foot of a crack.
4 30 feet. Climb the crack on good holds, strenuous, to another
grassy terrace.
5 20 feet. Ascend the left-hand crack to finish; the chimney on the
right is poor.

Leesled 105 feet Severe   (1951)
Rather dirty and unpleasantly vegetated. Beyond the wall which meets
the cliff high on the right is a rowan tree; start beneath this.
1 20 feet. Go up the broken wall to a large ledge and belays.
2 85 feet. Climb the mossy slab to gain a ledge on the right with
difficulty. Awkward steps up left lead to twin cracks. Ascend to the
large holly and exit left, or in the right-hand corner.

The following routes are on the upper tier of the crag; above and behind
Little Sepulchre. The main part consists of a wall seamed with cracks and
divided by a huge blocky chimney, about 25 yards down and left of the
chimney is a wedge-shaped grey wall which gives...

Play Safe, Be First 60 feet E4 6a   (1987)
Hard starting moves precede bold but easier climbing to a juggy break and first protection at 30 feet. The easier cracks above are something of an anticlimax.

Left of the blocky chimney are two thin cracks.

Featherlight 50 feet E1 5b   (1984)
Climb the left-hand crack, similar to, but easier than Foil on the Cromlech.

Barnstormer 50 feet E1 5b   (1984)
The right-hand crack is undercut by a niche and escaping from this provides the crux.

Chopping Block 50 feet E2 5c   (1987)
The benign-looking right arête of the Barnstormer wall does not yield easily. Climb the arête using holds and runners on either side until it is possible to a swing left into a fist crack. Fight this to reach the break and the lurking chopping block – this should be treated circumspectly. Having negotiated this, amble up the easy crack to finish.

Three large cracks break the wall to the right of the huge blocky chimney.

Left-hand Crack 35 feet Hard Very Severe 5a   (1984)
An awkward V-chimney leads to an off-width struggle.

New Form 35 feet E1 5c   (1984)
Start just right of the last route. Climb the wall using thin shallow cracks.

Right-hand Crack 30 feet Very Severe   (1984)
The off-width right of New Form gives a 5a struggle.

Unison 30 feet Hard Severe   (1984)
On the right-hand edge of the crag and just right of the last route is a short jamming crack – climb this with pleasure.

Some 200 feet left of the top of Little Sepulchre is a crag characterised by a gravestone-shaped wall facing up The Pass and forming the left wall of a corner... this is Tombstone Wall. The right-hand side of the crag is rounded and concave; beneath it is a good bivouac site formed by a leaning flake. The wide corner crack is Very Difficult.

★**Tombstone Wall** 40 feet E4 5c   (1985)
Go directly up the wall just left of centre on pockets and creaky flakes – a bold undertaking devoid of protection.

Round the corner to the left are two overhanging pillars, the left one being a detached pinnacle split by a crack giving:

Masochist's Mambo   60 feet   E3 6a   (1985)
No pain, no gain! A real bruiser! Climb the fiercely overhanging finger-to-hand crack to a small ledge. Boulder the summit block then step across the gap to belay.

Fred   60 feet   E3 6a   (1987)
The prominent scoop 50 feet right of Tombstone Wall is tenuous, strenuous, and quite bold. A sustained section protected by small wires leads up to the base of the overhanging bulge. Pull up on a poor pocket (Fred will be the *last* four letter F-word that comes to mind at this point) and make hard precarious moves to gain the slab above. Belay 10 feet up and left.

Above the right-hand section of Craig Ddu are three prominent boulders; a square one trapped between two thin ones – like a sandwich. Just below these is a small buttress with a clean pillar that has a narrow overhanging face split by a crack.

Overhanging Deckchair   50 feet   E2 5c   (1985)
Certainly no picnic on the beach. Reach the crack using loose flakes. Barbarous jamming up this leads to a welcome finishing bucket. Painful.

About half-way along the path from the right-hand end of Craig Ddu to Drws y Gwynt, and 40 feet above it is a crag with a deep V-groove/corner in its right arête – Very Severe, 4c. Below the left arête of the groove/corner is a curving overlap with a scooped wall to its right above a quartz marker.

Sheepslayer   90 feet   E3 5c   (1982)
A deceptively steep pitch. Follow the curving groove to the right. Pull over the roof and move onto the arête. Climb this past a large rock scar to the top.

Clogwyn y Grochan   (Cliff of the Cauldron)

OS Ref. 622 573

This popular crag lies a short way up the valley from Craig Ddu, just over 100 yards from the road. It has three buttresses, all extremely steep in the lower half and divided by two fierce gullies. The rock is sound and gives good protection, but unfortunately the upper sections are more broken and vegetated, although the angle eases. Several prominent features make route finding easy. The left-hand buttress, Goats' Buttress, is split by the curving line of Nea. Right of this is the dome-shaped block of Spectre whilst to the left are the walls and ribs of Phantom Rib, Hazel Groove and Delphos. Right of Goats' Gully is a steep wall with a curving line of overhangs; S S Special accepts the challenge of the steep wall direct, whilst Sickle traverses under the overhangs after starting from an immense flake down on the right. Abutting this flake is the clean-cut V-groove of Brant Direct with the improbable line of Cockblock on its right arête. A little farther along is the severely overhanging groove of Surplomb, about 20 feet before one comes to the broad groove of Hangover. The steep wall between the grooves is taken by Stroll On. The next smooth wall is Kaisergebirge Wall with its hard crack climbs, topped by a broad grassy ledge, Lords. Then comes the impressive Central Gully with a tall tree on the right marking Long Tree Gate. The right wall of Central Gully gives Fear and Loathing, N'Gombo and Ochre Groove. A damp wall and corner on the right are taken by Slime Wall and Broad Walk. Right again above The Gardens (a 'vegetable plot' about 40 feet up) is an imposing overhanging wall with Perygl and Jawbone. The last obvious feature is the short chimney of Fa. Descent is via the steep and tricky gully left of Delphos. A finger-stone marks the initial chimney at the top of the gully.

At the foot of the descent gully, on the right, and above a couple of rock steps sits a clean, smooth, short oval wall reached by an easy scramble. It gives three routes.

Bogtrotting   30 feet   E4 6a   (1989)
The wall and crack left of centre is too hard for most bogtrotters.

The Yuppification of Deiniolen   30 feet   E4 6b   (1989)
The central wall and crack line is a technical little teaser... Filofaxes are 'neither use nor ornament' here; but a stiff gin and tonic may help calm the nerves, after an ascent.

Grochenspiel   30 feet   E1 5b   (1989)
The easiest line on the right side of the wall is available for those who
wish to play.

At the foot of the main crag proper is...

Delphos   280 feet   Very Severe   (1949)
A sustained and varied route. The wide crack on the first pitch,
(harder now that several old and misused trees have gone) gives an
amusing problem. Start on the left-hand side of Goats' Buttress below
an obvious corner, well down and right of the three previous routes.
1 125 feet. 4c. Climb the corner to a damp scoop. Traverse left from
a small tree to a good ledge. Climb the difficult thin crack to the
overhang, then move diagonally right into the corner. Struggle up the
wide and awkward crack to a stance and belay. This pitch can be
split.
2 95 feet. 4a. Cross the wall on the right to a shattered ledge. Climb
up, then step left into a clean-cut groove. Continue up via a large
flake to a broad ledge. Scramble up to below an overhanging red
wall. Belay.
3 60 feet. 4a. The pleasant wall is steep but has good holds.
Scramble up to finish.

Hazel Groove   310 feet   Hard Severe   (1935)
Quite a good route for its grade but it deteriorates towards the top.
Start 20 feet left of the lowest point of Goats' Buttress.
1 40 feet. Scramble up the gully to a large grassy corner.
2 55 feet. Climb the corner on good holds. At 20 feet, where it
divides, traverse left along a narrow ledge then swing down to a
small sloping platform below the overhang. Step across to a tree then
climb 10 feet to a ledge (junction with Phantom Rib).
3 65 feet. Climb the groove until it splits. Follow the left-hand crack
until a step out left onto the nose, then go straight up, or take the
harder right-hand branch. Large yew tree above.
4 50 feet. A vegetated gully leads to a ledge on the left rib.
5 50 feet. Climb the wall then traverse past an oak to a holly.
6 50 feet. Finish up the steep wall on good holds.

Variation
Direct Start   60 feet   Very Severe   4b   (1949)
This takes the clean-cut V-groove which runs up to enter Hazel Groove
from the left. Start just left of the normal start. Go up into the corner.
Step right and swing up to a sloping platform. Continue up the
groove and awkward crack to the stance at the top of pitch 2.

Last of the Summer, Whine   255 feet   Hard Very Severe   (1979)
A slight eliminate but with some nice moves.
1 60 feet. 4b. As for Hazel Groove Direct start.
2 55 feet. 5a. Step left and climb a small groove. Move left onto the rib and go round to a crack. Climb this and continue direct to the yew tree. Belay.
3 80 feet. 5a. Climb the fine crack in the wall on the right of the vegetated gully of Hazel Groove, to a difficult exit. Belay on a higher ledge.
4 60 feet. 5a. Go up to the oak tree. Climb the wall behind the tree trending slightly left, then go up using a slot to a move right and the top.

★★**Phantom Rib**   245 feet   Very Severe   (1949)
An excellent and exposed route. The crux consists of an exhilarating rib with small holds. Tiny wires on this section help to reduce the stress of a quite committing lead. Start at the foot of the small gully leading up to the large grassy corner of Nea/Hazel Groove.
1 40 feet. 4b. Climb parallel cracks in the left wall of the gully, awkward. Step right and climb past a tree to belay at the top of Hazel Groove, pitch 2.
2 40 feet. 4c. Ascend the groove for a few feet, then traverse steeply right and pull up onto a ledge on the rib. An exciting section up the rib on small holds (crux) gains a stance just above in a corner.
3 60 feet. 4b. Climb the corner behind the tree, runner, then move up and follow small ledges rightwards below two hanging grooves to a short groove in the arête. Climb this and step right into another groove. A couple of moves up lead to the foot of a large sloping ledge, belay, good nuts in the wall behind.
4 45 feet. 4a. Move right along the ledge then climb the corner. Traverse 10 feet back left along a narrower ledge. Ascend for 10 feet to a spike and nut stance directly above the previous stance.
5 60 feet. Climb easily to an oak tree, then go diagonally right to a corner which leads to the top.

Wang   70 feet   E3 6a   (1980)
An excellent little technical test-piece. It takes the groove just left of the cornet-shaped groove on the dome of rock forming the headwall of Hazel Groove (Phantom Rib traverses below this wall at the start of its third pitch). Start in the aspen coppice just above the second stance of Phantom Rib, below and left of the wall. Climb the awkward smooth groove to a bulge capped by a jug. From the jug, gain the groove above with difficulty and reach the arête on the right to finish.

★★**Nea**   245 feet   Very Severe   (1941)
The central curving line up Goats' Buttress. A very fine climb which

Drws y Gwynt

1. Little Sepulchre
2. Too Hard For Jim Perrin
3. Cracked Wall

	10. Goats' Gully	VS
	11. S S Special	E2
4. Delphos	VS	12. Sickle	HVS
5. Hazel Groove Direct	VS	13. Brant Direct	HVS
6. Phantom Rib	VS	14. Cockblock	E5
7. Nea	VS	15. The Pump	E4
8. Spectre	HVS	16. Slape Direct	E1
9. Spectrum	E2	17. Brant	VS

Clogwyn y Grochan

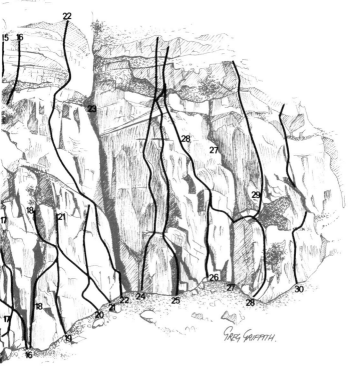

GREG GRIFFITH.

18. Surplomb	E2	26. Central Gully	HS
19. Slape	HVS	27. N'Gombo	HVS
20. Hangover	E1	28. Ochre Groove	E1
21. Leftover	E3	29. Slime Wall	VS
22. Quasar	E3	30. Broad Walk	VS
23. Mural	E3	31. Pergyl	E4
24. Kaisergebirge Wall	HVS	32. Scrambler's Gate	S
25. Babel	VS	33. Jawbone	E3

only just merits its Very Severe status. Once graded Severe, a rock fall in 1984 obliterated its third pitch making Spectre pitch 5 the only viable finish. Start as for Hazel Groove.

1 65 feet. 4b. From the grassy corner climb the groove until it divides. Take the left-hand branch for 15 feet then delicately step right round the rib to reach a crack which quickly leads to a constricted stance and belay.

2 75 feet. 4a. Follow the slabby corner crack until a small chimney leads to a large ledge. Care needed here with unstable blocks on the stance.

3 65 feet. 4b. Swing out onto a ledge on the steep left wall then move up a short corner. Make an exposed step left to gain the start of a shallow bottomless groove. Climb this on improving holds to a large ledge.

4 40 feet. Finish up the steep wall behind. Belay well back.

At the top of pitch 2 it is possible to traverse right across Goats' Gully and abseil 150 feet down the wall left of Sickle from the obvious tree – great care needed.

God Told Me To Do It   60 feet   E5 6a   (1993)
This route takes the vertical seam on the right-hand side of the overhanging wall left of the second pitch of Nea. Start from a belay above pitch 1 of Nea and climb the seam, which is both technical and sustained, to reach a rounded finish. Finish easily up and left to belay on a tree.

★★**Spectre**   295 feet   Hard Very Severe   (1947)
A fierce and well-protected classic. The crack on pitch 4 gives 'food for thought' on first acquaintance. Start at the lowest point of Goats' Buttress.

1 65 feet. 4c. Climb the thin crack or a slab to a good ledge on the right. Continue up easier rock on the right to a holly tree belay below a steep groove.

2 65 feet. 5a. Climb the steep groove with difficulty to a ledge below a butterfly-shaped overhang. A delicate move round the arête to the left leads to a short but tricky slab. Cross this high or low, then climb a groove to a belay. The slab can be avoided by a rather savage pull up the wall just right of the butterfly-shaped overhang.

3 30 feet. Climb easily across the slab to the foot of a steep wide crack.

4 30 feet. 5a. The crack is best started by laybacking. Steep jamming soon leads to the stance at the top of Nea pitch 2.

5 65 feet. 4b. Swing out and climb the left wall by a shallow groove. Step left into a bottomless groove which leads up to a good stance and belay.

6 Finish up the wall behind the stance.

The Revenge 120 feet E2 5c (1987)

A reasonable eliminate which just about merits a mention in this already overcrowded part of the crag. Start either by scrambling up from the left to belay below the chimney of Nea, or, up the first crack of The Vendetta – more appropriate. Climb the chimney then continue directly up the wall to an obvious flake. Pull up and stand on the ledge by the holly (No. 1 Friend). Traverse rightwards and ascend to a flake. Step up onto this and use a pocket to reach a good hold. Stand on this hold to gain two small flakes, step right, then trend leftwards up the slab to belay at a flake on Nea.

The Vendetta 280 feet E1 (1979)

A variation on Spectre, the best of several hereabouts. Start just left of Spectre.

1 40 feet. 5c. Climb the crack (nearest the arête) in the wall left of Spectre pitch 1.

2 105 feet. 5b. From the back of the ledge ascend the chimney just right of Nea and exit on good holds. Move slightly right and pull over the overhang into a crack which leads awkwardly to easier ground. Climb the short slab to gain the slab below the last crack of Spectre.

3 30 feet. 5a. The crack of Spectre.

4 & **5** 105 feet. 4b. Finish up Spectre pitches 5 & 6.

F B Madonna 220 feet E5 (1981)

A ferocious finger-wrecking eliminate which now sadly sports a chipped hold at the start. Start below the hanging rib right of Spectre.

1 40 feet. 6b. Climb the boulder problem wall and overhang right of Spectre pitch 1. Hard!

2 80 feet. 6a. From the Nea starting ledge, climb a thin crack just right of Phantom Rib to reach another crack above a grassy ledge on the right. Follow a curving flake and the continuation crack above.

3 100 feet. 6b. Move up to climb the cornet-shaped groove in the domed headwall above the traverse on Phantom Rib. Exit left over the bulge and follow a crack to a loose finish.

★ Spectrum 280 feet E2 (1965)

An exposed and strenuous route on good rock. Start 40 feet left of Goats' Gully below some shattered overhangs.

1 45 feet. 5b. Boldly climb the innocuous looking overhangs from the left. Pull directly into a shallow groove with good handholds which quickly lead to a ledge and belay.

2 100 feet. 5c. Move right onto the wall and climb thin cracks to the overhang. Pull round this to better holds and follow the crack

diagonally right to a ledge. Move back left and pull over the left side of the overhang. Climb a groove to a ledge. Move right to a crack at the end of the ledge and climb it to belay on Spectre.
3, 4 & 5 135 feet. Finish up Spectre pitches 4, 5 & 6.

Spectrological Arête 100 feet E2 5c   (1982)
A slight pitch up the arête right of Spectrum. Climb directly up the arête to the overhang. Move left and pull over the overhang to a ledge. Take the crack on the right to the belay on Spectre. Abseil off, or finish up Spectre.

'C' Minor 75 feet E2 5c   (1977)
Start just left of Strapiombo at a crack in the steep gully wall. Climb the crack to reach slabs and a runner on the Strapiombo flake. Move back left on undercuts to the arête. Swing round the arête on long layaways and go up on good holds to a belay (on Spectrum). Abseil off or finish up Spectre.

Pus 70 feet E4 6b   (1979)
An exceptionally perplexing groove problem. Start below the 'C' Minor. Follow 'C' Minor to the flake runner on the right. Move back left and ascend the 'holdless' groove above to the Spectrum stance. A route which sees many failures.

Strapiombo Direct 275 feet E1   (1978)
A better and tidier version of the parent route.
1 75 feet. 5b. Climb the crack as for 'C' Minor. After 25 feet step right and go up behind the flake. Continue to hollies.
2 55 feet. 5b. Climb up as for Strapiombo pitch 2.
3 40 feet. 5a. Ascend the crack of Spectre.
4 & 5 105 feet. 4b. Finish up Spectre pitches 5 & 6.

Strapiombo 120 feet Hard Very Severe   (1957)
A short difficult climb of character. Worth doing despite its repulsive start.
1 40 feet. 4b. Climb Goats' Gully pitch 1.
2 55 feet. 5b. Step left to below the large overhang and climb this with difficulty. Climb the crack to the Spectre belay.
3 25 feet. 5a. Traverse right into Goats' Gully. Scramble up carefully to abseil off the small prominent tree just right of the gully (150 feet to the foot of the crag).

Goats' Gully 250 feet Very Severe   (1949)
A vile route if wet – and it usually is! The grade is debatable depending on one's attitude to slimy rock. Start below the gully.
1 40 feet. 4b. Back up the initial deep chimney until a pull round the overhang. Belay on the tree above.

2 60 feet. 4a. Climb easily to another tree at the foot of an open chimney which slants up left to the perched block stance of Nea.
3 150 feet. Loose and dirty scrambling to finish.

The Scapegoat   175 feet   E1   (1982)
1 70 feet. 5b. Climb the crack left of S S Special to a ledge. Traverse left then continue diagonally left towards the roof. Step across into a groove, then climb it into a cave, often wet. Go left onto the arête and make a hard move onto the triangular slab above. Climb this to its apex and belay in the gully.
2 50 feet. 5a. Step down and climb the groove in the left wall of the gully. Exit left onto the large ledge and move up to follow the crackline diagonally back right to a sloping ledge. Climb the wall stepping left onto the arête and continue up this to the Nea stance.
3 55 feet. 4b. Step left onto the wall and finish up Spectre.

Cunning Stunts   80 feet   E3 5c   (1983)
Start as for The Scapegoat. Climb the crack left of S S Special to a ledge. Move up left to the obvious groove and exit direct to join the final moves of Sickle.

★★**S S Special**   150 feet   E2 5b   (1977)
A steep and popular eliminate running directly up the Sickle Wall. Start on the left of Sickle. Climb the right-hand crack of the wall to a wide ledge. Go up the steep thin right-hand crack to join Sickle at the roof. Make exposed moves round the roof using a flake to reach easier climbing above. Belay in a short corner above slabs.

★**Sickle**   190 feet   Hard Very Severe   (1953)
A worthwhile and technical route which crosses the slabby wall beneath the overhangs. Hard for its grade. Start at a huge flake about 10 yards right of Goats' Gully.
1 70 feet. 5a. Climb the flake by the crack on its right or left-hand side. From its top step left onto the wall and climb the thin crack to a ledge. Continue to a niche, then traverse right past some blocks to a sloping stance.
2 60 feet. 5b. Step down and make a hard starting move to cross the steep wall on the left with difficulty to a groove. Climb this to the overhang. Pass this delicately on the left then climb the slab to a stance and belay in a small corner on the right.
3 60 feet. 4c. Climb across slabs on the left and follow a short steep crack in the left wall of Goats' Gully to the perched block stance of Nea or climb up left to the prominent tree and make a 150-foot abseil to the ground.

Variation
2a 5a. From the stance, climb up and traverse under the roof on undercuts and sidepulls to join the normal route at the top of the groove.

★★**Venturi Effect**   120 feet   E5 6a   (1980)
A thrilling pitch with some heart-stopping moves up the groove above the schizophrenic threat of the Sickle flake – a sort of 'hard man's' S S Special. Start as for Sickle. Climb the left-hand side of the Sickle flake. Painfully wide bridging up the groove above the flake leads to the overlap. Step right and climb the short, hard overhanging groove (in the left arête of the Brant groove). Continue direct in a fine position to finish up a thin flake.

★★★**Brant Direct**   75 feet   Hard Very Severe 5a   (1949)
A popular and well-protected exercise in bridging and jamming. Climb the obvious, slightly overhanging, clean cut chimney/groove past a couple of awkward sections to a long ledge and belay on the right.

★★★**Cockblock**   75 feet   E5 6b   (1980)
A fierce, much attempted and much fallen off pitch. Start below the right arête of Brant Direct. Boulder up to a ledge at 10 feet. Continue with difficulty past a small pillar and a good nut. Make a long reach up and right, then pull up, all very tiring and technical, to an easing at 50 feet. Belay thankfully on the long ledge above.

Dried Voices   75 feet   E5 6b   (1985)
Yet another ferocious test-piece which takes the obvious eliminate line right of Cockblock. Start under the hanging groove between Cockblock and The Pump. Climb the wall with considerable difficulty directly up into the hanging groove. Finish up Cockblock. The first protection, an RP2 and an RP1 can be placed by a traverse right from Cockblock.

★**The Pump**   70 feet   E4 6b   (1978)
A well-named climb up the obvious hanging groove and crackline to the right of Brant Direct. Climb the wall on the right and stride left into the top of the groove. Continue up the crack on good holds stepping right at the top. Easier climbing soon leads to the Brant ledge and belays.

Variations
The initial groove has been climbed direct to the foot of the crack – hard 6b. It is also possible to exit from the crack direct. This used to be done in ignorance of the normal finish i.e. stepping right at the top of the crack. It is harder and very prickly. The wall between The Pump and Slape

Direct has been climbed at 6b, but the pitch is contrived with little new climbing.

★★ Slape Direct 70 feet E1 5c (1954)

A classic little problem. The crux moves give food for thought. Start a few feet right of The Pump, and about 15 feet down and left of the Brant sentry box, at a leftward-slanting crack. Reach the crack from the right and ascend to a small quartz ledge on the right. Some technical moves and an enigmatic pull round the bulge gain a crack and better holds. Continue easily to a holly belay.

★ First Amendment 150 feet E2 (1978)

A problem wall and groove (pleasant E1) lead to an intimidating second pitch which is serious for its first few moves. Start 10 feet right of Slape Direct.

1 70 feet. 5c. Climb the thin crack to the Brant traverse. Continue up the corner to the tree.

2 80 feet. 5b. Behind the tree is a large flake. From the top of this climb boldly up the smooth wall then continue up the superb, well-protected hanging groove above.

Variation

Between First Amendment and the first pitch of Corruption is a testing, eliminate pitch, **Horizontal Departure** E4 5c. A peg runner used on the first ascent has now gone, although runners in Corruption can be used instead. The route moves left onto, and then continues up the arête overlooking First Amendment.

★★ Brant 370 feet Very Severe (1940)

A fine traditional, devious, route with steep wall and slab climbing. Start about 20 yards right of the Brant Direct groove, on top of a rock step and below a sentry box niche.

1 70 feet. 4c. Move up into the niche. A delicate traverse left leads to a good jug. Pull up on this and continue left along a ledge. From its left-hand end, climb up to hollies. Go up a little corner on the left then swing left round a pinnacle to a ledge and belays.

2 50 feet. 4c. Continue the traverse stepping down a few feet to enter a short V-chimney. Climb this awkwardly to a ledge on the right.

3 140 feet. 4a. From the right-hand end of the ledge an ascending traverse left up the wall leads to a slab (possible belay). Climb the overlap and slabs to an obvious corner. Follow this for a few feet then move right to ledges. Go up these and easy slabs to a large yew tree (the crux pitch if wet – leaders often get gripped).

4 110 feet. 4a. Follow the main nose of the buttress behind the yew.

Corruption   150 feet   E3   (1966)
A technical and exhausting route. Harder since the demise of the tree
which once sprouted out of the crack above the sentry box. Start as
for Brant below the sentry box.
1 50 feet. 6a. Bridge up the Brant sentry box and climb the crack to
an overlap, where a hard move gains quartz holds on the right.
Climb the short wall to a grassy bay and tree belay (on Slape).
2 100 feet. 5c. Finger jam the corner crack to a small ledge. Bridge
up the corner to a large block on the left. Pass this and continue up
the dirty corner to another ledge. Either finish up Slape or step round
the arête on the right to abseil off the tree at the top of Hangover.

★★**Surplomb**   130 feet   E2   (1963)
This strenuous and impressive route has a bold first pitch. Start as for
Brant.
1 80 feet. 6a. Climb into the sentry box at 10 feet. Make hard moves
right to a finger-jug (crux). Go boldly up on well-spaced holds,
trending right to the Slape traverse ledge. Climb the short
overhanging V-chimney (good protection) to a belay.
2 50 feet. 5b. Bridge up the chimney until a swing onto the left arête
can be made. Continue up a shattered crack to a stance.

Pus in Boots   130 feet   E3 6a   (1980)
A superdirect version of Surplomb at the very top end of its grade.
Start a few feet right of Surplomb above some cruel blocks. Ascend
direct to the finger-jug on the Surplomb traverse. Follow Surplomb to
the Slape traverse ledge. Climb the difficult groove on the left
stepping right at the top onto the belay ledge of Surplomb. Finish
directly up the chimney.

Variation
★**Right-Hand Finish**   50 feet   E4   (1982)
An intimidating pitch. From the belay ledge on Surplomb move right
round the arête. Climb the wall just to its right; bold and 6a.

★**Slape**   365 feet   Hard Very Severe   (1940)
A devious but worthy companion to Brant. Start at a large groove 30
feet right of Brant.
1 80 feet. 4c. Climb the corner for a few feet then step right onto a
ledge. Spike runner. Swing back round the corner on the left and
make an awkward traverse under a bulge on good holds to a ledge.
Continue left past a large tree to a junction with Brant at the pulpit.
2 25 feet. 5a. Step left off the top of the flake onto a steep wall, crux.
Climb a crack and overhanging blocks to Brant pitch 2 belay.
3 70 feet. An easy chimney on the right leads to a large triangular
grassy ledge. Belay in the far corner.

4 80 feet. 4b. The crack in the centre of the wall leads to a tiny ledge. Traverse right a few feet and climb the yellow overhang on dubious holds. Climb mossy quartz slabs to the ancient yew tree.
5 110 feet. Climb up behind the yew keeping right of the edge to a shattered ledge. Trend right past a large yew to finish.

★**Roll On** 150 feet E3 (1971)
A fine steep route based on the crack-line between Surplomb and Hangover; little climbed since the creation of Stroll On.
1 85 feet. 5c. Start up Slape and the pinnacle at the base of the first groove of Hangover. Climb the crack in the wall to the overhang. Traverse left under the overhang to Surplomb pitch 1 belay.
2 65 feet. 5c. Step right round the arête to a steep wall. Traverse right to the continuation of the pitch 1 crack-line and follow it with difficulty.

★★★**Stroll On** 130 feet E3 6a (1976)
The logical line for Roll On is one of the most popular hard crack pitches in The Pass giving superbly sustained climbing with one very difficult move. Climb the crack of Roll On direct; the crux is pulling round the roof, but above there is little respite.

★**Hangover** 340 feet E1 (1951)
An exposed route of considerable character. The second pitch has seen many epics. Start as for Slape.
1 70 feet. 5a. Climb the groove for a few feet and step right to a ledge at the foot of another groove. Climb this, then step left and go up a crack to a small ledge. Care is needed with belays here.
2 80 feet. 5b. Step right round the arête to a shallow groove in the wall. Awkward moves gain a traverse line which leads easily to the main groove, which is steep and hard to start. Bridge up to holly trees. Abseil off or:
3 30 feet. Climb the wall by its left edge.
4 40 feet. Traverse left then go up on good holds to a large ledge and yew trees (Ledge Way).
5 & 6 120 feet. Finish as for Ledge Way or Sunset Boulevard.

Leftover 160 feet E3 (1965/1977)
A fine technical exercise. Start 25 feet right of Hangover.
1 80 feet. 5c. (Hangover Direct). Climb the crack for 20 feet into a scoop and move out left over the roof into another crack. Climb this for 15 feet to a resting place. Move left and go up to belay as for Hangover pitch 1.
2 80 feet. 6a. The steep stubborn corner behind the belay is even by today's standards, mean and fingery. Finish via the main upper groove of Hangover pitch 2.

★★★**Quasar**   120 feet   E3 6a   (1977)
A fine steep eliminate at the upper limit of its grade with an obdurate crux that has slowed many teams. Start just right of Leftover/Hangover Direct. Ascend the strenuous groove to the overhang. Pull out right to a good flake and resting ledge. Follow the thin crack above the flake to reach a ledge on the left. Climb the wall to the Kaisergebirge ledge. Finish up the groove as for Kaisergebirge Wall.

Quantum Jump   120 feet   E5 6b   (1977)
An exceptionally fierce and technical pitch – the nemesis of many a 'climbing wall hero'. It takes the short but fierce crack to the right of Quasar. Start as for Karwendel Wall. Climb up, traverse leftwards as soon as possible, and move up to the steep crack; or gain the crack direct – 6b! This leads strenuously yet precariously to the end of the Kaisergebirge ledge. Finish up the wall to the right of Kaisergebirge Wall.

Mural   110 feet   E3 6a   (1977)
A tricky wall leads to a 'pumpy' crack. Start as for Karwendel Wall. Take a diagonal line left up open rock to the overhang and move right, to cross Kaisergebirge Wall; or more easily start up Karwendel Wall to climb the strenuous crack past one very technical pod to reach a ledge above all difficulties. Finish easily up to Lords, a large terrace, or, traverse right about eight feet, then climb the problematical crack (Scavenger's Daughter Finish) – a 'must' for those who found the lower section easy.

★**Karwendel Wall**   110 feet   Hard Very Severe 5b   (1958)
A short but interesting wall. Start at a small spike left of Kaisergebirge Wall. Climb the shallow groove right of the spike to join the Kaisergebirge Wall traverse. From the sloping platform climb up bearing slightly left until a difficult move right to a sharp hidden hold enables the obvious traverse line to be followed up right to easy ground. Ascend to Lords.

Al Fresco   90 feet   E4 6a   (1991)
A steep and strenuous eliminate which is escapable. Start just left of the start of Wind. Climb the pocketed and disjointed cracked wall to a finger-pumping finale up the thin crack of Scavenger's Daughter Finish (to Mural).

★★**Kaisergebirge Wall**   120 feet   Hard Very Severe   (1948)
A lead that gradually increases both in difficulty and exposure. Protection is good where it matters. Much fallen off. Start 30 feet left of Central Gully.
1 100 feet. 5b. Follow the rising traverse line steeply leftwards to a

Baz Ingle and Pete Crew on *Hangover* (E1) Clogwyn y Grochan.
Photo: John Cleare

Andy Sharp attempting to make the second ascent of *Brute 33* (E3) Carreg Wastad. Photo: Paul Williams

good ledge. Move left again to the foot of a steep shallow groove. Climb this, crux, to a good ledge and belays.

2 20 feet. The short wall on the right leads to Lords where one can abseil off, or continue up Ledge Way, or abseil off the tree (at the top of Hangover) after the first pitch.

★**Divertimento** 220 feet E2 (1980)

A girdle of the steeper lower walls of the cliff below Sunset Boulevard. Start as for Kaisergebirge Wall.

1 100 feet. 5c. Follow Kaiser for 30 feet, then drop down and traverse under steep walls into Quasar at the flake. Swing across into Leftover and follow it to the Hangover stance.

2 30 feet. 5c. Traverse into Roll On and continue to the Surplomb stance.

3 20 feet. 4c. Traverse around into Corruption.

4 70 feet. 5c. Finish up Corruption; originally the route finished across the wall on the left at 6b, but this was thought to be out of character with the rest of the route.

★**Sunset Boulevard** 365 feet Hard Very Severe (1954)

A worthwhile girdle which links sections of some of the best routes on the cliff. Start as for Kaisergebirge Wall.

1 120 feet. 5a. Follow Kaisergebirge Wall to the foot of its crux groove. Continue traversing and stride across the final groove of Hangover. Traverse round into a V-chimney and go up to a good belay. Care should be taken to avoid rope drag on this pitch.

2 40 feet. Go round the block on the left and ascend to grass, then cross to the block belay above Slape pitch 3.

3 70 feet. Go down the grassy ledge to a short chimney. Descend this to a good ledge and belays (Slape pitch 3 in reverse).

4 25 feet. 5a. Descend the short difficult wall of Slape pitch 2.

5 70 feet. 5a. Cross to the foot of Brant's V-chimney, step down left and continue the traverse under the overhangs on awkward undercut holds. Ascend to a niche and flake belays on Sickle.

6 40 feet. Go diagonally left up the slab to a flake on the edge of Goats' Gully. Most parties finish here, but one can descend slightly and go left to reach the crack of Spectre pitch 4. After the crack, a finish can be made by crossing Phantom Rib and Hazel Groove.

★★**Wind** 90 feet Hard Very Severe 5b (1977)

A stiff little test-piece for its grade. Start as for Kaisergebirge Wall. Ascend the steep thin crack to the final part of Babel pitch 1. Finish on Lords.

Advert 90 feet E3 5c (1978)

A very serious pitch which starts just right of Wind. Ascend the wall past some flakes to the flared crack. Climb this with difficulty. Slabs then lead to Lords.

Babel   300 feet   Very Severe   (1949)
An interesting route with a serious third pitch. Start 10 feet left of Central Gully.
1 90 feet. 4c. Climb steeply up on good holds just right of a ledge to reach a line of holds at 15 feet. From their right-hand end, make an awkward move onto a ledge (this can be avoided by scrambling up the gully on the right). Move up onto a second ledge, then traverse easily left to climb a shallow flaky groove eight feet right of the corner (for purists) or more easily climb the corner itself, to Lords. Belay just behind the tree.
2 50 feet. 5a. Walk 20 feet left. A problem start up the middle of three small grooves leads to an easier finish up the left one. Block belays.
3 60 feet. 5a. Ascend the wall behind the block belay. This is hard and poorly protected initially but gradually eases to a small oak tree. Thread and nut belays 20 feet higher.
4 100 feet. 4c. Move diagonally right over a rock scar and climb a short open corner at the back of a broad ledge finishing on juggy holds in superb bubbly rock. Cross the ledge and climb directly up the wall behind the corner trending right to finish.

Variation   40 feet   Hard Very Severe 5a   (1969)
3a Step right and climb the obvious steep, dirty crack.

Second Wind   100 feet   E4 6a   (1991)
Bold and a little loose. Start from the abseil at the top of Wind. Climb up for 25 feet with poor protection, crux, traverse right for 15 feet. Continue direct with slightly less difficulty. Abseil off.

Ledge Way   345 feet   Very Difficult   (1935)
A rambling route with its share of water and walking. Start at the foot of Central Gully.
1 110 feet. Climb the right-hand corner of the gully. Chimney up through the waterfall to the cave, then traverse out across the left wall to Lords. Walk across Lords.
2 70 feet. Beyond the little tower where the ledge narrows a steep short wall leads back right to a pile of large blocks. Step off the blocks and traverse left to a slab. Continue to a yew tree.
3 45 feet. Climb up over awkward ledges behind the second yew tree to a large grassy ledge.
4 60 feet. Continue up the ledge to the right, then go back left.
5 60 feet. Climb the steep wall avoiding shrubs by keeping right.

Central Gully 210 feet Hard Severe (1949)

A somewhat wet and greasy outing that masochists refer to as 'a traditional climb'... perhaps best done as a superb ice climb.

1 70 feet. Climb the bed of the gully to where Ledge Way traverses out onto Lords.

2 90 feet. Descend and cross over right to the Long Tree. Climb a groove slanting steeply up between two perched blocks, then a series of steps leading back into the gully bed above the overhang, crux.

3 50 feet. Climb up and out over the roof to easier ground. The upper part of the gully is easy.

Variation

★ **Superdirect Variation** 80 feet Hard Very Severe 5b (1975)

2a When completely dry, a direct line through the overhang gives a spectacular and unusual pitch on good holds. Well-protected.

Left-Hand Variation 260 feet Very Severe (1951)

Start from Lords, above the first pitch of the normal route.

1 30 feet. From a point overlooking the gully, climb a steep crack (hard to start) to good holds and a traverse across into the gully. Climb this a few feet to a stance.

2 80 feet. Go up the gully, then steeply back across it into the left-hand crack. Climb this to where it comes back out into the gully, with a bit of a swing over the top. Belay.

3 50 feet. Ascend the left wall to a large yew tree. Belays above.

4 100 feet. Climb the steep pock-marked left wall of the gully, just right of the yew tree, then move right a few feet and climb steeply on better holds. Continue among some loose blocks by a holly and a long open crack to the top.

★ **N'Gombo** 180 feet Hard Very Severe (1955)

An exposed and worrying diagonal line up the steep right wall of Central Gully. The highlight is to climb over a huge precarious flake which has stood the test of time – so far. Start just right of the foot of Central Gully.

1 50 feet. 4c. Climb the short steep crack below The Long Tree, often greasy. Continue in the same line until a traverse right over some large blocks leads to the foot of a vertical corner.

2 130 feet. 5a. Climb the corner with difficulty to a step round onto the left wall. A series of ledges leads diagonally left to the foot of a huge flake. Wedge the crack on its right-hand side to a ledge. Swing out left over the void and pull up (hard) to a small cave. Step right and finish on good holds. Belay in a corner 25 feet back.

Long Tree Gate 215 feet Very Severe (1935)

A good route although somewhat contrived. Start at the foot of the

buttress right of N'Gombo, below and right of The Long Tree.
1 50 feet. 4c. Gain the ledge on the arête using widely spaced holds. Make a tricky move up left on a hidden hold and continue up to The Long Tree.
2 25 feet. Climb a short corner to the N'Gombo/Ochre Groove ledge.
3 40 feet. Traverse round the arête to the right on poor rock. Exposed. Climb to a small stance and thread belay.
4 60 feet. 4a. Ascend the interesting crack to a tree belay.
5 40 feet. Climb steeply up to grassy ledges.

Variation
1a 50 feet. 4a. Start more easily by climbing a sloping rake left of the toe of the buttress, until the traverse back left to The Long Tree.

Fear and Loathing   205 feet   E1   (1982)
A route to get the pulse racing. It takes the shattered N'Gombo Wall and is well-named. Start just around the corner from Long Tree Gate.
1 75 feet. 5a. Climb the strenuous wall to the ledge on the arête of Long Tree Gate. Follow this to a large block belay left of the N'Gombo corner.
2 130 feet. 5a. Move up and left to the foot of a shattered wall. Climb this on juggy but suspect holds to a poor thread (or Friend). Swing out right and layback up to join N'Gombo at a peg. Climb the corner above pulling out onto Ochre Groove. Move back left to the foot of a lichenous groove. Ascend this delicately, exiting right at the top.

Toots Direction   70 feet   E3 6a   (1989)
Short and steep. Takes the wall and groove left of Ochre Groove Direct. Start below the centre of the wall. Climb flakes and continue to a spike. Step right and go directly up to the roof. Pull over this moving rightwards and finish straight up to belay as for Ochre Groove.

★Ochre Groove   215 feet   E1   (1954)
A fine route which merits its grade thanks to an ankle-snapping crux in the lower part of its initial groove – the peg having long gone. Start 20 feet right of Long Tree Gate at an obvious V-groove capped by an overhang.
1 80 feet. 5c. Climb the technical V-groove – take care placing protection here. Move out right at the overhang to a ledge. Go back left between the overhangs to a grassy ledge and block belays. Junction with N'Gombo.
2 95 feet. 4c. Climb the corner as for N'Gombo and continue up the corner crack. Exit right to a tree belay on Long Tree Gate.
3 40 feet. Ascend steep rock to grassy ledges.

Gizzard Puke 90 feet E1 5b   (1982)
The name is very apt. Climb the wall between Ochre Groove and
Slime Wall to a convenient abseil tree.

Slime Wall 200 feet Very Severe   (1961)
A serious route of its grade, for which it needs to be dry – it seldom
is. Start at a large flake about 25 feet right of Ochre Groove.
1 90 feet. 4c. Climb the crack to the top of the pinnacle. Step
awkwardly left onto the wall. Traverse diagonally left to the foot of a
steep crack. Climb this to a good ledge.
2 60 feet. 4a. From the right-hand end of the ledge, trend right for
15 feet, then climb the slab direct.
3 50 feet. Easy ledges lead up left, then from a corner, break back
right and traverse under the overhangs. Finish up a little wall.

Broad Walk 285 feet Very Severe   (1954)
Another route that is often wet, but is pleasant when dry. Start 25 feet
right of Slime Wall in a corner.
1 95 feet. 4c. Climb the prominent damp black corner to a sloping
ledge on the right. Continue up the corner or traverse right, then climb
a groove to a stance and belay.
2 55 feet. 4c. Climb the tree to reach holds. Follow the corner then
traverse left and take the left wall to a stance and belay.
3 60 feet. 4a. Climb the corner for 25 feet then step right and
ascend a grassy rake.
4 40 feet. Traverse left and go up a groove to a grassy ledge.
5 35 feet. The groove above has large but doubtful holds.

Perygl 305 feet E4   (1965/1982)
A serious climb through the shattered overhangs right of Broad Walk
with a technical and strenuous crux. Much of the loose rock which
once gave this climb a fearsome reputation has disappeared but the
route still demands respect. Protection is reasonable.
1 95 feet. 4c. As for Broad Walk pitch 1.
2 30 feet. Walk right along a ledge to The Gardens.
3 120 feet. 6a. Climb the wall to a small overhang and into an
overhanging groove. Fight up the difficult groove; some care is
needed in handling suspect holds on its right wall. Move right from
the top of the groove into a good crack leading to a large ledge.
4 60 feet. Move round the corner on the left and go up easy rock.

Scrambler's Gate 215 feet Severe   (1935)
Jungle bashing leads to better climbing up some steep rock. Start on
the right of Broad Walk at a chimney.
1 40 feet. Climb the short easy chimney to a holly tree rake.
2 30 feet. Ascend a short wall on good holds, then go through

heather to a ledge and the sturdy trees of The Gardens.

3 35 feet. Traverse the ledge to the left, round a corner to an oak tree and continue to a holly.

4 80 feet. Descend 10 feet and traverse across Broad Walk to the foot of a little crack. Climb this to a stance. Step left onto a rake and go up this for 15 feet. Move right onto a reddish slab. Traverse left on a narrow ledge below a steep wall to an oak tree.

5 30 feet. A weakness in the wall behind the tree leads to a little corner on the right. Climb this awkwardly to a heathery ledge. Scramble up to a good stance.

Bluebell Traverse   725 feet   Severe   (1935)

An outdated girdle traverse of the cliff with plenty of walking and endless variations. Follow Scrambler's Gate, but on pitch 4 keep traversing across Broad Walk to the pitch 1 belay of Ochre Groove, on the big ledge. Cross in to Central Gully and go up to Lords, then descend to a large triangular grassy ledge 40 feet away. Continue along a rocky gangway leading out left. After 10 feet climb a slab to a small tree then meander across slabs, crossing Goats' Gully to the perched block stance on Nea. Descend slightly to cross Hazel Groove high or low.

Jawbone   160 feet   E3   (1968/1977)

The easiest line through the large overhangs is rather loose, rarely repeated and not recommended. Start below the big tree.

1 60 feet. 4b. An obvious crack rises up to the big tree.

2 100 feet. 5c. Go up right on suspect rock to the overhang, aiming for the prominent undercut groove which can be seen above it. Pull round the overhang and ascend the tricky groove. Exit right and climb to a ledge and tree belay. Abseil off to avoid the horrific jungle which awaits a victim.

Fa   200 feet   Severe   (1949)

An unsafe route on unstable rock. Start 50 feet left of the gully which bounds the crag on its right. Follow the obvious chimney. Frequent belays.

Fatha   260 feet   Very Severe   (1949)

A steep climb on vegetation, good and bad rock, up the buttress between the chimney of Fa and the bounding gully. Start up the obvious break in the overhang 20 feet left of the gully.

1 40 feet. Go diagonally up the steep wall by a rib and groove to a small stance and low belay.

2 80 feet. Step down and traverse right to a small slab. Climb this, then go round the corner where a line of flakes leads to the rib above. This breaks at 50 feet, and vegetation followed by a 15-foot

traverse left leads to a platform with poor belays.
3 80 feet. The vegetable groove is quitted by a black mantelshelf, and the wall climbed to some rotten flakes. Belay 20 feet right below the overhangs
4 60 feet Traverse back to the flakes. Gain the groove above and climb its left wall to a good belay. Eighty feet of scrambling leads to the finish.

Carreg Wastad Fach   OS Ref. 624 572

This is the broken yellowish crag left of the gully bounding Carreg Wastad on the west. Its right-hand side has a short orange and quartz scooped wall below grey bulges.

Question Mark   160 feet   Very Severe   (1955)
Start at a grassy ledge at the lowest part of the buttress.
1 30 feet. The rib has good holds to a large stance and belays.
2 50 feet. Traverse horizontally right under the overhangs on small sloping ledges to a stance and spike belay.
3 35 feet. 4b. The crux. Step right onto the slab and go up on small holds round the overhangs to large detached blocks.
4 45 feet. Continue for 10 feet, then step left and climb a slab with a small overhang. Finish up a heathery rib.

Boston Spa Climb   145 feet   Severe   (1958)
Start at the left-hand end of the slab.
1 60 feet. Move up, then step right and continue up again to a small stance and peg belay below an overhang.
2 50 feet. Traverse leftwards to the corner and go up a groove in this to steep grass below a rib.
3 35 feet. Climb the pleasant rib.

Friday Night Beaver   120 feet   E2   (1987)
Start below a crack running up to the overhang.
1 40 feet. 5c. Battle up the vicious crack to better holds and continue to belay below the prominent large overhang. Friend belays.
2 80 feet. 5b. Step right and climb direct to a tricky mantelshelf. Climb the groove above before stepping out left onto the final straightforward arête. Descend by scrambling down diagonally rightwards.

Carreg Wastad

(The Flat Crag)

OS Ref. 625 571

This crag with its fine yew trees lies a few hundred yards up the valley from Clogwyn y Grochan and is opposite Ynys Ettws, the Climbers' Club hut. It stands well out from the hillside and consists mainly of solid rock, which can, however, be very unstable in places where the rock has an organ-pipe structure. At the left-hand end of the crag are the fluted slabs of Skylon and Wrinkle. Right of these are the overhanging corner of Gryphon and the groove of Unicorn with the roof of Brute 33 in between. Overhanging Chimney and The Crevice both stand out well. The latter is just left of Crackstone Rib. In the centre of the cliff is a large corner, Erosion Groove, which runs the full height of the crag. On the right is a steep face topped by the large slanting overhang of Shadow Wall; the rib of Trilon leads up to the right-hand end of this. The upper part of a scoop containing a line of yews is part of Dead Entrance, and Yew Link connects the first two yews.

Right of the scoop lies the tower of Old Holborn and the obvious upper groove of Bole Way. Main Scoop Route takes the line of the huge scoop in the right-hand side of the cliff. At the right-hand end is a fine prow of rock supported on Red Rock, a triangular buttress of reddish rock whose summit is an earthy ledge. Each side of the cliff has an easy descent gully.

Skylon 200 feet Hard Severe (1952)
A popular and well-protected route, quite hard for its grade. Start at the left-hand end of the cliff below a small bulge at 70 feet (as for Wrinkle).
1 120 feet. Climb easily up to a ledge below a small overhang. Move up right and climb a crack until it is possible to make a difficult step left onto the overhang, then move up to a ledge. Climb diagonally right to a terrace. Belay behind the large flake at its upper left edge.
2 80 feet. The wall above the flake leads via a bulge at 30 feet to a stance. Scramble to the top.

★★★Wrinkle 235 feet Very Difficult (1947)
A very popular climb which finishes up the fluted slabby walls right of Skylon. The rock in some sections has been polished to a high gloss. Start left of the overhang as for Skylon.

1 80 feet. Move right up slabby steps then work back left to below the Skylon overhang. Make an exposed traverse right to a ramp, and then to nut belays in a corner.
2 65 feet. Climb the corner then awkwardly gain a ledge on the right. Climb a shallow groove slanting back left then a wrinkled slab to a good ledge.
3 90 feet. Take a short crack on the right to the top of a small pedestal. Ascend the slabby grooves above with care to a ledge. Finish up the broken corner on the right. Protection is well-spaced – belay well back.

Sun Valley 200 feet Very Severe (1977)
A contrived line with some interesting climbing. Start just right of Wrinkle to the left of a shallow cave.
1 70 feet. 4c. Climb easily to a large sloping ledge. Traverse right just above the lip of the cave to a small niche. Climb direct to the end of Wrinkle pitch 1.
2 70 feet. 4b. Go up behind the stance to a good ledge. From its left end make some difficult moves up the wall then follow an easy crack until a move right to a small grassy bay.
3 60 feet. 4b. Climb the thin crack to a quartz ledge. Ascend the overhang on good holds and finish up a slab.

★First Test 200 feet Very Severe (1977)
A direct line up to the large corner above the traverse on Wrinkle. Start 10 yards right of Wrinkle at a short corner.
1 70 feet. 4c. Climb the corner and continue straight up the steep broken white wall (hard) to a good ledge.
2 130 feet. 4c. A rightward sloping groove leads to easy ground. Get into the big corner on the left with difficulty and continue to the overhang above. Move 10 feet right and up a second corner for six feet. Make an exposed step out left onto the arête. Finish up slabs.

Gryphon 210 feet Hard Very Severe (1954)
A rather tedious line, but the crux corner is interesting. Start at a pedestal, 20 feet left of Unicorn, where a prominent overhanging corner runs up to the left end of an overhang.
1 35 feet. 4c. Follow a gangway up left until a direct ascent can be made to a step right onto the sloping floor of the corner.
2 60 feet. 5b. Climb the crack in the corner to the top of the flake on the right. Move left to the top of the corner by very trying moves. Continue to the holly tree in the corner above.
3 115 feet. 4c. Go diagonally right to a spike runner on the rib adjacent to Unicorn (possible stance). Continue up the rib zigzagging to avoid difficulties.

1. Skylon	HS
2. Wrinkle	VD
3. Gryphon	HVS
4. Brute 33	E3
5. Unicorn Direct	HVS
6. Unicorn	HVS
7. Elidor	E1
8. Lion	VS
9. Overlapping Wall	E1
10. Jayway	E3
11. The Crevice	VS
12. Rackstone Crib	VS

13. Crackstone Rib	S
14. Ribstone Crack	VS
15. Erosion Groove	HVS
16. Erosion Groove Direct	E2

Carreg Wastad

GREG. GRIFFITH.

17. Shadow Wall	VS	22. Bole Way	VS
18. Yellow Crack	HVS	23. Bole Way Direct	HVS
19. Zangorilla	E4	24. Dead Entrance	VD
20. Trilon	VS	25. Main Scoop Route	HS
21. Old Holborn	HVS	26. Peeping Tom	E3
		27. Cornix	HVS
		28. The Castle	VS
		29. Halan	HS

★**Brute 33** 180 feet E3 (1979)
An exhausting and thrilling line through the big overhangs just left of
Unicorn Direct – worthy of the attention of any aspirant jug-thug. Start
at the foot of a white groove below the roof.
1 40 feet. 5b. Climb the groove and trend right to belay as for
Unicorn – delicate and poorly protected.
2 40 feet. 6a. Attack the roof by the obvious crack to belay on some
flakes 20 feet higher. Strenuous but well-protected.
3 100 feet. 4c. Finish direct up the Gryphon arête.

★**Unicorn Direct** 195 feet Hard Very Severe (1949)
A more sustained line than the original route.
1 50 feet. 4a. As for Unicorn
2 65 feet. 5a. From the left-hand end of the ledge, climb the
overhanging crack with difficulty. Go through trees as for Unicorn.
3 80 feet. 5a. Climb the groove, awkward at 30 feet. Ascend to the
final chimney splitting the overhang. Doubtful rock.

★**Unicorn** 200 feet Hard Very Severe (1949)
Quite a good route with a fierce little groove on its second pitch. Start
below the obvious groove, just right of the Brute 33 overhang 50 feet
up.
1 50 feet. 4a. Zigzag up the wall to avoid difficulties, then go over
cracked blocks to a good ledge.
2 50 feet. 5b. Climb the V-groove behind the stance and make a
difficult move up and left, crux, to enter the main groove. Carry on
through trees to belay below an overhang.
3 100 feet. 4b. Take the groove on the right a few feet then traverse
delicately right to a small ledge on the far rib. Climb the delightful rib
in a fine airy position.

★**Elidor** 200 feet E1 (1977)
Some steep moves up the blank-looking groove above the Lion
traverse lead to an easier finish up the top arête of Unicorn.
1 60 feet. 4a. Climb the wall as for Unicorn to the block stance.
2 140 feet. 5b. Step right onto the black slab. Climb diagonally right
then straight up to the foot of the blank little groove. Bridge up this
and exit left at the top. Continue up to a rightward traverse. Follow
this and finish up the arête. A good pitch.

★**Lion** 290 feet Very Severe (1949)
An old classic which is both technical and interesting despite having
a contrived finish.
1 60 feet. 4a. Zigzag up the wall to the block stance as for Unicorn
pitch 1.
2 80 feet. 4c. From the foot of the V-groove on Unicorn step right

onto a black slab. Cross this diagonally rightwards to the overlap and traverse right to the foot of Overhanging Chimney. Climb this, then cross the right wall to a stance and belay. A fine pitch.

3 90 feet. Ascend the slab on the right, step across the short chimney and swing up onto Crackstone Rib. Follow this to belay at a sloping stance.

4 60 feet. 4a. Traverse into the upper part of Ribstone Crack. Ascend to a tree from which a huge flake leads to the top

★★**Overlapping Wall** 250 feet E1   (1948)

A fine open climb with a fairly bold crux that is much harder than the rest of the route. Protection below the crux is quite good; above, it is well-spaced, and the climbing is balancy. Start directly below Overhanging Chimney just left of a large overhang.

1 90 feet. 4c. Go up for 20 feet, then traverse right on good holds to a ledge. Climb the steep wall moving left then right to a large quartz ledge. From its left-hand end, a shallow groove leads to a stance below the large chockstone of Overhanging Chimney.

2 70 feet. 5b. Climb the groove then gain its left rib. Move left and climb the overlap at its weakest point, crux. From a good nut, traverse left a few feet, then go up and follow a groove back right to a ledge. Move right to belay in the corner. Serious.

3 90 feet. 4c. Make a rising traverse across the right wall and go up onto the rib. Finish up this in an exhilarating position.

Variation

This makes the whole route an excellent Very Severe in standard.

2a 50 feet. Very Severe 4c. Ascend Overhanging Chimney (as for Lion) direct.

Jayway 235 feet E3   (1975)

The vicious little wall on the second pitch should not be underestimated. Start as for Overlapping Wall.

1 90 feet. 4c. As for Overlapping Wall to the pitch 1 stance.

2 45 feet. 5c. Climb the incredibly awkward, thin jagged crack in the right wall of Overhanging Chimney to belay as for Lion pitch 2.

3 100 feet. 4b. Move right and finish direct.

The Crevice 255 feet Very Severe   (1947)

A pleasant route for the slim but a fiendish problem for the corpulent and those of above average girth. It is the right-hand of the two chimneys. Start directly below Crackstone Rib.

1 100 feet. Ascend the leftward-slanting rake to a tree. Traverse delicately right onto a slab, then go up to a stance at the foot of the chimney.

2 50 feet. 4c. Climb the strenuous chimney (folk often get stuck here for hours) to a slab. Ascend this to a good crevasse stance.
3 40 feet. 4a. Climb up and swing round onto Crackstone Rib. Follow this to the sloping belay at the top of pitch 2.
4 65 feet. 4a. Finish as for Crackstone Rib.

Rackstone Crib   190 feet   Very Severe   (1958)
An inferior but more direct variation on Crackstone Rib. Start 20 feet right of The Crevice.
1 70 feet. 4b. Ascend a short wall and step left to the foot of a cracked corner. Follow this to a ledge then climb a shallow groove until forced onto the rib on the right to reach a stance and belay (junction with Crackstone Rib).
2 70 feet. 4b. Climb the easy groove on the right of the rib of Crackstone Rib then ascend a short wall on the right and continue to belay at the top of Crackstone Rib pitch 2.
3 50 feet. 4a. Finish up the corner crack.

★★★**Crackstone Rib**   175 feet   Severe   (1935)
One of the great Welsh classics. It has a very fine exposed rib pitch which is especially photogenic. Start at the foot of Erosion Groove.
1 30 feet. Climb a short crack to a ledge. Belay on the left.
2 80 feet. Follow the well-worn traverse leftwards to the arête passing a depression, good runners. Step round boldly and follow the arête in an exposed position to reach a ledge. A short wall leads to a better ledge.
3 65 feet. Climb the easy groove on the right to a corner. Continue up to a traverse line on the left wall. Follow this to finish up a short steep crack.

Variation
Direct Start   50 feet   Hard Very Severe 5a   (1982)
Start left of Ribstone Crack. Climb directly up the rib to join Crackstone Rib – tricky.

Slipstone Slab   220 feet   Very Severe   (1989)
A wandering route which covers little new ground. Protection is sparse. Start midway between Crackstone Rib and Ribstone Crack below a patch of grass at 20 feet.
1 60 feet. 4c. Take a thin wet crack to the grass. Step left into a shallow niche then continue up a faint rib to the traverse line. Move left to belay in the depression.
2 100 feet. 4c. From the right end of the ledge, climb an awkward shallow groove and continue to a holly. Climb steeply up a thin crack behind the holly to reach another ledge. Make an exposed traverse right below the overlap into the groove of Ribstone Crack. Follow this

to belay on the right.
3 60 feet. 4a. The wide crack behind the belay.

★**Ribstone Crack** 170 feet Very Severe   (1951)
A steep, exposed and well-protected crackline just left of Erosion
Groove. Hard for its grade. Start at the foot of Erosion Groove.
1 110 feet. 4c. Climb the obvious crack direct to belay on
Crackstone Rib. Sustained with a difficult move near the top.
2 60 feet. 4a. Traverse back right for a few feet and go up to a tree
on the left. Finish via a huge flake.

Erosion Groove 175 feet Hard Very Severe   (1953)
A popular but rather disappointing route with some suspect rock. It is
the obvious groove cleaving the cliff from top to bottom. Start at the
foot of the groove below two holly trees.
1 50 feet. Scramble up past the first holly and step left into a crack
which leads to a stance and belay on a huge flake.
2 65 feet. 5a. The main corner groove on the left is hard to start and
leads to a small overhang at 45 feet. Pass this on the left (crux) and
follow the overhanging groove above to a stance and belay.
3 60 feet. 4a. Climb the corner with a wide upper crack.

★★**Erosion Groove Direct** 65 feet E2 5c   (1955)
A strenuous and technical problem; in the past it had a notorious
reputation as a 'chop route' but although it has been somewhat
tamed by modern protection, it is still no pushover. From the belay on
Erosion Groove at the top of pitch 2, step right and enter the groove
with difficulty. Finish more easily up the wide overhanging crack.

★**Twisted Sister** 165 feet E2   (1983)
An excellent eliminate between Erosion Groove and Shadow Wall.
Start from the first holly on Shadow Wall.
1 90 feet. 5c. Move left and climb up to the obvious crack. Follow
this and move left to a belay under Erosion Groove Direct.
2 75 feet. 5c. Follow Erosion Groove Direct past its crux. Move right
across the wall to finish up the superb airy crack.

★★**Shadow Wall** 155 feet Very Severe   (1935)
A scrappy start leads to an exciting crux traverse under the large
overhang. Start by scrambling up to the foot of a corner which leads
up to the left end of the large diagonal overhang.
1 90 feet. 4a. Climb the groove to a holly tree (possible stance) and
continue up to a stance and belay under the huge roof.
2 40 feet. 4c. A series of three ledges leads up rightwards under the
roof. From the top ledge, a hard move right gains a short groove.

Climb this to a tree belay.
3 25 feet. Climb easily to a good ledge.

Variation
★**Yellow Crack**   70 feet   Hard Very Severe 5b   (1958)
   1a Start from the holly tree on Shadow Wall pitch 1. Climb the
   stubborn, steep, wide crack in the wall to the traverse of Shadow
   Wall below the big overhang, strenuous. Finish up Shadow Wall.

★★★**Zangorilla**   160 feet   E4   (1977)
An intimidating and impressive route which blasts directly through the
large capping overhang above the Shadow Wall traverse. Bolder
and more strenuous since the rattling block came off the top pitch.
Start 10 feet right of Shadow Wall beside a huge flake.
1 110 feet. 6a. Gain the steep groove above and climb it, then the
wall above to the ledge on Trilon. Step across left into the steep,
smooth, leaning groove about eight feet right of Yellow Crack. If you
can start it, climb the fingery and technical groove to reach good
holds. Move up left to belay on the ledges of Shadow Wall.
2 50 feet. 6a. Spacewalk boldly and strenuously out left on
undercuts, across the roof, with an awkward move to get established
on the airy wall above. Ascend direct in a sensational position, with
only imaginary protection, to finish.

Trilon   205 feet   Very Severe   (1949)
A poor start leads to an airy rib. Start on the right and below the
overhang of Shadow Wall at the lowest point of the buttress.
1 70 feet. 4a. Climb the wall on good holds to a large perched
block. Traverse right to a pleasant yew tree ledge.
2 110 feet. 5a. Climb the crack to a large spike then go diagonally
left on good flakes to the overhang. Step left onto a sloping ledge
and make a fierce move up into a niche. After a few steep moves up
the groove ascend the delightful rib to a holly tree belay.
3 25 feet. Finish easily as for Shadow Wall.

Goldcrest   120 feet   E1 5b   (1983)
This takes the obvious groove between Trilon and Quasimodo. Start
from the yew tree ledge of Trilon. Climb the slab to the overhang. Pull
over this via a thin crack. Follow the crack and groove above to a
tree belay above Trilon. A good sustained pitch.

Quasimodo   120 feet   Hard Very Severe 5b   (1964)
A strenuous and obscure pitch through the overhangs right of
Goldcrest. Start from the yew tree ledge of Trilon. Climb the crack a
few feet right of that of Trilon to the niche in the large overhangs.

Ascend these with difficulty to a small ledge. Step right and jam the corner crack.

Yew Link 45 feet Hard Very Severe 5b   (1953)
A short awkward pitch between the yew trees of Trilon and the upper yews of Dead Entrance. Start from the yew tree ledge of Trilon. Climb the wall behind the yews to a small holly in a groove. Swing out right and climb a mossy wall to a peg in a niche. From a peg runner above, pull up to the yew trees of Dead Entrance.

★**Old Holborn** 240 feet Hard Very Severe   (1963)
A brilliant finish up the steep tower between Trilon and Bole Way more than compensates for an indifferent start.
1 90 feet. 4c. As for Bole Way pitch 1.
2 30 feet. 4a. Climb the steep slanting groove up left to the large ledge and tree belay (First Bole) below the tower.
3 60 feet. 5b. Ascend a steep groove in the front face of the tower to the large roof, peg runner. Reach a good handhold under the roof and make a bold swing out left to a hidden ledge. Go back onto the steep arête and climb to small ledges. Poor belays.
4 60 feet. 4c. Climb the steep slabby face trending right to finish. A fine exposed pitch.

Bole Way 320 feet Very Severe   (1951)
This devious line up the cliff has some suspect rock. Start at a small rib with a gully groove on either side about 100 feet right of Trilon and 30 feet left of Main Scoop Route.
1 90 feet. 4c. Climb the groove on the right side of the rib until a swing onto the rib, possible holly stance. Step across awkwardly right to gain a slanting rake and ascend to a cosy stance at holly trees.
2 120 feet. 4c. Climb the wall behind the hollies (or step off the tree) both hard, and go up the groove. Step right onto a rib which leads up to an obvious line (Dead Entrance) running back left. A stance can be taken here on top of the rib using a large ivy root and nut belays, or a stance can be taken at an ash tree down on the left (First Bole). It is better to continue; move down left under the overhang to a groove. The steep and interesting groove leads to a holly stance (Second Bole). Care should be taken to avoid rope drag if this pitch is not split.
3 65 feet. 4b. From the holly above traverse right below the overhang. Follow a long rake easily to a break in the steep headwall. Belay at a tree in a bay.
4 45 feet. 4b. Climb the break above trending slightly left to a steep finish.

Variations

Left-Hand Finish   70 feet   Hard Very Severe   (1984)
Start from the second tree in the main groove.
3a 30 feet. 5a. Traverse left across the steep wall to a stance on Old Holborn.
4a 40 feet. 5b. Climb the groove left of Old Holborn finish.

Direct Finish   50 feet   Hard Very Severe 4c   (1958)
3b Traverse right below the overhang to a traverse back left to gain the crack above. Finish up the exposed crack on good holds and jams.

Dead Entrance   350 feet   Very Difficult   (1935)
A jungle-bashing saga which contains some pieces of rock. On the right side of the cliff is Red Rock, a semi-detached buttress defined on the left by a grassy fault. Start below this.
1 105 feet. Ascend the obvious gangway then continue up an interesting chimney. Scramble to a ledge on the summit of Red Rock.
2 100 feet. Follow the grass left and descend an awkward grassy scoop until a traverse can be made to two large loose spikes. Either ascend to a derelict block, then go down by an ash tree and a greasy groove to the tree of Green Park, or descend from the spikes and cross a little rock bay to the edge beyond where a jump or descent can be made to Green Park.
3 145 feet. Traverse left to a yew tree. Climb a little slab on the right then follow trees to the top via numerous belays.

Main Scoop Route   255 feet   Hard Severe   (1935)
A pleasant route, less vegetated than Dead Entrance. The groove on pitch 3 can be rather stubborn if damp.
1 105 feet. As for Dead Entrance to the summit of Red Rock.
2 40 feet. Climb diagonally left up an easy gangway to a stance.
3 40 feet. Descend 10 feet left to a ledge in The Great Scoop. Go over a small square block and climb the groove (crux) to hollies.
4 30 feet. Climb two short chimneys to a good ledge.
5 40 feet. Ascend the final wall to a strenuous pull over the last bulge. This pitch is aptly called the Hard Court.

Variation
Koala Finish   120 feet   Hard Very Severe 5b   (1969)
An entertaining pitch. The hard section is quite short and reasonably well protected.
3a Move up the wall on the right to the small overhang. Step right and then down into a groove; move right again to a difficult mantelshelf onto a sloping ledge. Climb to a good thread runner then

step left and continue until forced left again. Climb direct to a large pinnacle belay. Protection is well-spaced above the crux.

Peeping Tom 240 feet E3 (1977)
The loose left arête of Red Rock leads to a fierce crack pitch. Start at the foot of Red Rock just left of Cornix.
1 80 feet. 5b. Go steeply up the wall via obvious flakes then traverse left to a ramp sloping right. Follow this until a traverse left to the exposed arête. Climb this to the summit of Red Rock. A very serious pitch.
2 90 feet. 5c. Go easily up to the big overhang. Climb this and the steep groove/crack above, passing an old peg, hard, to the hollies of Halan.
3 70 feet. Follow Halan to the second tree and finish steeply.

Cornix 235 feet Hard Very Severe (1953)
A chossy initial pitch leads to superb groove climbing above. Start under Red Rock below an obvious groove.
1 75 feet. 4b. Climb a groove for a few feet then go diagonally left until a traverse right up a prominent rake to below an obvious groove. Ascend the left wall of the groove and exit on the left. Stance and belay on the summit of Red Rock.
2 100 feet. 4c. Traverse right to a shallow open corner. Bridge up this with a tricky exit at the top to the holly tree belay of Halan pitch 2. An excellent pitch.
3 60 feet. 4a. Climb up to a tree as for Halan. Traverse right onto the steep wall and ascend to the top.

The Red Rock has been girdled following the obvious diagonal fault from left to right. (**Fester** Severe/Very Severe, 1969) the grade depending on one's attitude to handling loose rock.

The Castle 205 feet Very Severe (1963)
A poor route with some loose rock which meanders up the arête of the tower-like buttress on the extreme right of the crag. Start at the foot of the grassy slope bounding Red Rock on the right.
1 50 feet. 4b. Climb up on the right of the damp break to a spike below the bulge; step right and climb the steep crack to a small stance. Holly tree belay.
2 45 feet. 4c. Descend a little and go left to the foot of an open groove on the front of the tower. Climb the groove to the top of a pedestal. Stance on the right.
3 110 feet. 4b. The wall above is undercut, so swing right into a shallow groove. Step up, then move left onto the arête where good holds lead to a ledge (junction with Halan). Move up right to an

obvious traverse line leading round the arête to a possible belay. The short crack and wall above lead to a detached flake; pull up to the right on huge holds, in a fine position, to the final slab. Trend left to finish on the arête.

Halan   150 feet   Hard Severe   (1949)

A devious route which spirals up the tower-like buttress on the right of the cliff. Fairly vegetated, but contains some interesting rock. Start up grass on the right of the crag to a quartz ledge about half-way up the buttress.

1 50 feet. Climb over a block on the left and go up into a groove. Here an obvious line traverses the buttress. Pull up with difficulty onto the sloping ledge above and on the left. Follow this to a niche below the overhang. Belay.

2 30 feet. Continue traversing under the overhang to a holly.

3 70 feet. Climb to a tree, then pull onto the wall above to another tree. From this regain the wall. Go right to a sloping ledge then traverse for a few feet until a steep and exposed mantelshelf leads to the top.

The New Girdle   665 feet   Very Severe   (1953)

A good expedition, continually interesting, which takes a high line across the cliff face. Much better than The Old Girdle. Start at the left end of the cliff.

1 80 feet. As for Wrinkle to the first stance.

2 90 feet. Go right to the far arête and climb it on good holds.

3 45 feet. Descend a groove to the lower of two hollies, then abseil 30 feet to a good ledge (Unicorn pitch 2 in reverse).

4 & 5 160 feet. As for Lion pitches 2 and 3.

6 70 feet. Traverse right using trees and walk 20 feet to more trees (junction with Dead Entrance). From the far end of the ledge work out right round the corner, then go under an overhang to Bole Way, arriving below the steep groove half-way up its second pitch (45 feet below The Second Bole).

7 70 feet. Descend slightly right, go over the derelict block' of Dead Entrance and cross a fluted slab below an overhang. Climb up and ascend the scoop of Main Scoop Route to the evergreen ledge.

8 70 feet Climb two short chimneys to a ledge, then continue up the wall and final bulge as for Main Scoop Route.

The Old Girdle   800 feet   Very Severe   (1948)

Mainly Severe in standard, with a much harder crux. Follow The New Girdle and make the abseil. Stroll under Lion and The Crevice to the arête. A steep wall leads to the foot of Ribstone Crack. Traverse across Erosion Groove to the holly tree on Shadow Wall. Climb the steep crack with a bulge (crux), then traverse right below the rib of

Trilon and descend to the yew trees. Follow Bole Way until the Dead Entrance traverse can be reversed to the summit of Red Rock. One can finish here or get another mediocre pitch.

Clogwyn Tyllau

(a.k.a. Arêteland)

(Cliff of Holes)

OS Ref. 626 572

Just above Carreg Wastad is a small compact buttress with the obvious rightward-slanting crack of Ampyx at its centre and the impressive square-cut overhanging Owain's Arête at its left end.

Follow the path up and left of Owain's Arête to an obvious white wall with incipient cracks, this gives a finger-wrecking problem:

Indoor Bowling Here I Come 40 feet E5 6c (1989)
A striking micro-route. A boulder problem start, protected by a sideways RP 3 in an obvious crack, leads to a mantel and easier climbing above. Move slightly left at the top. Belay well back.

Back to Trivia 40 feet E3 6b (1989)
Aptly named. Takes a crozzly crack in the left side of Owain's Arête; start 10 feet left of that route. The crack on the left side of the pillar front will feel anything but trivial during an ascent. A difficult exit left at 25 feet precedes a mediocre rambling finish.

At the left end of the main crag lies the much-tried (by Owain that is)...

★★**Owain's Arête** 80 feet E6 6b (1989)
This exacting, high quality pitch accepts the all too obvious challenge of the overhanging arête, giving some alarming moves in dramatic situations. If the small wire is not *in situ* the route is probably E7... a long reach may prove useful. Start below an obvious pillar and some stacked pegs at about 15 feet. Climb the pillar to the pegs. Pass these via a long stretch for a pocket, crux, and rock over onto a ledge. Reach through via a crozzle on the arête to gain a niche, *in situ* wire. Stand in the niche, small nut in a horizontal crack at head height, exit precariously left and stretch for a large break, thread, good nuts and a rest. Move right and go up via a downwards-pointing bubbly niche and obvious protruding spike. Take the groove above on sidepulls,

finishing at a huge jug. An easy arête leads up to the final spike belay.

★**Unleashing the Wild Physique**   80 feet   E5 6b   (1987)
A powerful route up the overhanging corner groove right of Owain's Arête requiring a well-ripped physique to unleash. Start right of the arête above a wide crack. Aggressively layback the overhanging groove past two pegs to reach an equally steep headwall... power up this to prime the pump.

Ampyx   105 feet   Very Severe 4a   (1963)
A pleasant little climb, though lacking the charisma and quality of its harder neighbours. Start below the central slanting crack.
1 35 feet. 4a. Climb the wall then the crack proper to a good ledge, thread belay.
2 35 feet. 4c. Move right along the ledge until small flakes lead up the steep wall. An awkward move leads to a wide crack beside a huge perched block.
3 35 feet. 4b. Go through the tree and climb the overhanging crack.

Queer   70 feet   E4   (1988)
Down on the right end of the crag a perfect white groove provides a frustrating little problem.
1 30 feet. 6b. The contortionate white groove has good RP protection which is hard to place – the trick is not to pull on it. Step left to belay in the gully.
2 40 feet. Step up and climb the thin crack above the cave moving left to a block belay – a mundane pitch.

About 30 yards right of Queer, the crag is bounded on the right by three prominent pinnacles... beware the awkward slippery approach.

No More Queensway Sales   35 feet   Hard Very Severe 5a
        (1991)
The left-hand arête of the first pinnacle is unremarkable.

Penal Colony   35 feet   E2 5b   (1991)
The right-hand arête of the first pinnacle has its moments.

Stand Prow'd   30 feet   E3 6a   (1991)
The best of this bunch of routes. The obvious sharp arête on the second pinnacle is started from the right, with a crux to gain the obvious flat ledge. Finish more easily.

Bang Utot   40 feet   Hard Very Severe 5a   (1988)
The corner crack on the east wall of the third uppermost pinnacle. Climb the crack for 30 feet stepping left onto the headwall to finish.

Carreg Wastad Uchaf

OS Ref. 628 571

This lies above and to the east of Carreg Wastad and right of Bryant's Gully. The crag consists of a smooth, shallow, scooped cwm with a steep right wall above heather terraces and broken rock. From Bryant's Gully, a subsidiary gully runs up rightwards to scree (opposite the east end of Carreg Wastad). A steep path breaks out left across rock and heather leading into a small cwm. On the left wall of the cwm stands a large holly tree below twin cracks, the right one containing numerous beards of grass and heather.

The Bearded Crack   100 feet   Hard Severe   (1963)
Start 10 feet right of the holly i.e. 40 feet right of a shattered yellow wall with three pinnacles in front of it.
1 25 feet. Awkwardly climb the crack to a stance on top of the flake.
2 75 feet. Move left and climb the wall between the cracks on good holds, moving into the left-hand crack near the top. Pleasant.

Pholidomya   90 feet   Very Difficult   (1963)
The rib right of The Bearded Crack. Start as for the latter. Climb the rib, steeply at first, then go slightly right on good holds to a grassy ledge. Ascend the crack to the overhang then traverse left and finish up the nose.

For Carreg Wastad Uchaf proper, follow the path left under the three pinnacles. It now turns right and runs up into the cwm. The routes are described from right to left and are not immediately obvious from below.

Little Whizzer   150 feet   Hard Severe   (1956)
Start below a large rowan tree growing from a crack about 10 feet up.
1 30 feet. Climb up bearing right to a spike belay.
2 60 feet. Step up to a small quartz ledge; traverse this for about 18 feet, then move back at a higher level and go up the overhanging wall on small holds. Stance and belay on the left.
3 60 feet. Traverse left to a conspicuous V-groove, then go up on finger holds just to the right. Step round the corner and finish on a slab.

Solen   160 feet   Very Severe   (1963)
The wall between Ensis and Little Whizzer. Start just left of the latter, below an obvious groove slanting left.

1 75 feet. 4c Climb a short wall into a groove; go up this and exit left to a heather clump. Climb the slab to a mossy line leading right. This is followed to a short crack below and right of the first stance of Ensis. Ascend the crack and the difficult steep wall to a quartz shelf. Peg belay.

2 45 feet. Traverse the shelf until it peters out and continue steeply across a corner to the grassy bay on Ensis.

3 40 feet. Climb the corner on the left of the chimney.

★**Punk Puffins on Rock**   120 feet   E3 5c   (1990)
A surprisingly good pitch approached via a surprisingly steep scramble, taking a direct line up the centre of the scooped wall, through Solen. Start in the centre of the wall and boldly climb the beautiful slab to gain the ramp of Solen. Continue up moving first right, then back left to an interesting finish.

Ensis   170 feet   Hard Severe   (1963)
The obvious undercut, mossy cracks on the left of the wall. Start at the foot of a gully 40 feet left of Little Whizzer.

1 45 feet. Traverse right with difficulty above the overhang and pull into the groove above. Continue on good holds until an awkward step to a grassy ledge on the right. Belays on the right.

2 75 feet. Step left across the groove and go up on good holds to a ledge on the arête. Traverse left and go up a V-groove, pulling out left onto a quartz-streaked slab which leads to a grassy bay.

3 50 feet. Climb the steep chimney on the right, moving left up a pleasant slab at the top.

Craig Nant Peris

(The Crag of St Peris's Brook)   OS Ref. 626 575

This is the fine-looking but very broken crag which forms the gable end of the Esgair Felen ridge. It is well worth a visit, for the scenery and position are superb, 2,000 feet above the valley floor. The tall organ pipe sills of felstone are a unique sight, but much of the rock is unfortunately very rotten although it is climbable if handled with care. The usual approach is by Bryant's Gully, one of the longest and finest climbs of its type in Wales. The crag is about 200 feet high and consists of three buttresses. The West Buttress is defined on the left by very light greenish coloured rock. On its right are the twin gullies of Tweedledum

and Tweedledee divided by a gaunt subsidiary buttress, The Rattle. The
Central Buttress has a gendarme on its right edge overlooking the upper
part of Bryant's Gully. The East Buttress is very broken but gives good
scrambling.

West Buttress Arête 200 feet Difficult   (1935)
Start at the foot of the twin gullies at an obvious traverse line beneath
bulging rock.
1 60 feet. Traverse round into a groove and go up to a stance on the
left – no secure belays.
2 40 feet. Climb the chimney to another stance.
3 60 feet. Either traverse 20 feet left, then go up a groove to a large
quartz platform, or continue direct on poorer rock to the platform.
4 40 feet. Steeply up the edge then scramble to the top.

Tweedledum 180 feet Difficult   (1935)
The left of the twin gullies. There is one small chimney pitch below the
chockstone at 120 feet. The final section is interesting if climbed
direct.

The Rattle 200 feet Very Difficult   (1935)
Start at the foot of the buttress dividing the two gullies.
1 110 feet. Scramble up the centre to a ledge below an overhang.
Cross into the groove on the left at 70 feet or continue up the rib on
the right. Take the groove or the left-hand rib to the ledge below the
large overhang.
2 90 feet. Traverse diagonally to the right corner and climb up on the
edge. Move back to the left after a few feet and ascend direct to
finish.

Tweedledee 200 feet Difficult   (1935)
The right-hand gully is moderately grassy. Jammed blocks form a cave
at the top.

Central Buttress Arête 310 feet Very Difficult   (1935)
Care is needed with the rock. Start by scrambling up for 150 feet on
the left of the broad shallow gully, then take a rib on its right to a
large flake at the foot of the buttress proper – a ledge runs round to
the right.
1 40 feet. Climb the groove on the right to a ledge below the
gendarme.
2 70 feet. Go up to the gendarme. Step delicately across left and up
behind the gendarme to easier rock. Fifty feet of scrambling remains.

Dinas Cromlech

(Fortress of the Cromlech)

OS Ref. 629 569

This imposing cliff, the showpiece of The Pass, stands starkly on the hillside 600 feet above Pont y Gromlech looking out over the upper reaches of the valley like some grim medieval castle. Its massive rhyolite walls and pillars, steep and exposed, are furnished with sound and often abundant holds giving probably the finest and most exposed top-grade climbing on either side of The Pass, plus several first-class easier routes which are enhanced because of their dramatic surroundings. Modern protection has made all but the hardest climbs relatively enjoyable and safe. The rock, although seemingly brittle, is generally reliable but caution should be exercised when climbing on the East Wing (to the right of Cemetery Gates) as the cliff tends to be more unstable in this area.

The dominant feature of the Cromlech is its magnificent open-book corner whose apex is taken by Cenotaph Corner, perhaps the most famous Welsh rock-climb. To the left lies the West Wing the first feature of which is the corner of Sabre Cut. This rises from The Forest, a once vegetated, but now barren sloping ledge lying 80 feet up the face. Moving left past the cracks of Dives and Holly Buttress the cliff rapidly diminishes in height and is cut by three right-facing corners; these are Pharaoh's Wall, Pharaoh's Passage, Parchment Passage and finally the overhanging groove of The Thing before broken rocks appear. To the right of Cenotaph Corner, past the prominent crack in its right wall, Cemetery Gates, lies another corner, Ivy Sepulchre, at the start of the East Wing. Farther over, beyond the shattered crack of Jericho Wall, the cliff becomes less steep deteriorating into vegetated rock with a large heathery ledge, The Heath, at about one-third of its height. Next comes the castellated Flying Buttress which leans drunkenly against the base of the cliff and marks the end of the East Wing. Just to the right of this is Castle Gully with three short routes high up on its right wall, then the descent gully, isolated pinnacles, and scree. Above Cenotaph Corner sits The Valley, a series of large grassy ledges traversing the face of the cliff, the starting point for all routes on the smaller upper cliff.

Descents: For West Wing routes (those finishing left of Sabre Cut) scramble up and around the top of the cliff to find the steep but easy descent gully which curves round its right-hand side. The gullies on the left-hand side of the cliff are hard to find and follow at dusk and are best avoided. For climbs finishing on The Valley it is usual to abseil down the wall a few feet right of Cenotaph Corner; great care should be taken to avoid knocking stones down during this operation. For those who don't fancy the abseil or one of the shorter routes above an escape is possible via Tributary Crack, the easy diagonal flake which splits the short wall above and left of Cenotaph Corner.

The West Wing

Millwood's Wall   100 feet   Severe   (1953)
Left of the overhung chimney/niche of The Thing is a large heather terrace from which rise three corners, the right-hand one being the top part of Vanishing Point. Start between the left and central corners. Climb the centre of the wall past a small grassy ledge at half-height trending right.

Vanishing Point   110 feet   E1 5b   (1977)
A scrappy start leads to a few good moves up the final groove. Start as for The Thing at the foot of a corner (often wet). Ascend the corner to a heathery ledge. Finish up the slim groove in the wall above.

★★**The Thing**   125 feet   E2   (1956)
A fierce and technical climb which still sees its share of epics! Start at the left-hand end of the crag beyond Parchment Passage where an overhanging crack slants up merging into an overhanging groove/niche.
1 80 feet. 5c. Follow the rightward-slanting crack past a couple of very thin moves and strenuous pulls into a niche. Jam up to inverted flakes and use these to gain a foothold on the left. Continue up trending right past a sapling and after 20 feet move right round the arête to belay at the tree of Parchment Passage.
2 45 feet. 4c. Move back left to rejoin the crack which leads more easily to the top.

Variation
1a 125 feet. 5c. It is possible to climb directly over a bulge into the finishing crack thus avoiding the rightward excursion onto Parchment Passage. Slightly harder but better.

★**Rootorooni**   155 feet   E3   (1983)
A steep and surprising route. Start to the right of The Thing by some jagged boulders.
1 80 feet. 5c. Climb the shallow groove to the roof and move left to pull over it. Continue up to the curling roof. Move right then hand-traverse back left to reach a small ledge. Go up to belay on The Thing.
2 75 feet. 5c. Follow The Thing for 15 feet to a small chockstone.

Traverse left across the wall to a large spike and pocket. Trend slightly rightwards along a line of pockets then finish up a groove in the middle of the wall.

Parchment Passage   125 feet   Very Difficult   (1933)
An interesting route up the leftmost corner of the crag. The top section is very polished. Start below the corner.
1 90 feet. Scramble up to a tree. Ascend leftwards until an exposed high step on polished holds gains a gangway running back up into an awkward corner stance.
2 35 feet. Ascend to the left-hand of two short cracks. Step right when it becomes difficult to a steep finish.

★**Cobweb Crack**   110 feet   Very Severe   (1951)
A very good climb which is stiff for its grade. Start below and a few feet left of the start of Parchment Passage at the foot of a short crack.
1 40 feet. 4a. Climb the crack on good holds and traverse left to a stance and belay.
2 70 feet. 5a. Above is a pocketed T-shaped crack undercut at the start. Climb this strenuously past a tricky section at 20 feet; continue up on improving jams and move left to a junction with Parchment Passage. Finish up this.

Scarab   140 feet   Hard Very Severe   (1982)
A surprisingly worthwhile eliminate whose second pitch is a more direct version of the variation finish to Pharaoh's Passage. Start just right of the foot of Parchment Passage below a tree.
1 50 feet. 5b. Climb past the tree and follow the slim groove above, stepping right to a belay on Pharaoh's Passage.
2 90 feet. 5a. Go up and move right to good pockets, then up and slightly left to the top of a flake. Continue directly up the centre of the wall to finish.

Pharaoh's Passage   130 feet   Very Severe   (1933)
A wandering climb which takes the central right-facing corner and wall to its right. Start at the foot of the corner.
1 50 feet. 4c. Surmount the overhang with difficulty until a strenuous pull out leftwards leads to a holly tree ledge.
2 80 feet. 4c. Ascend the wall behind the first holly then from its top traverse right to the skyline and finish up the rib.

Variation
The Original Finish
2a 70 feet. Ascend the Moderate chimney.

Scroll 40 feet Hard Severe   (Traditional)
Useful as an extra pitch to Pharaoh's Passage or Wall; start from the
terrace on which these routes finish. Climb the obvious corner for 15
feet, finishing up the crack above past a couple of loose chockstones.

Speedfreak 140 feet E2 5b   (1972)
A serious arête. Start 15 feet right of Pharaoh's Passage above a
sharp flake. The first 25 feet are strenuous and a little loose. Finish
more easily up the arête above.

★**Pharaoh's Wall** 110 feet Very Severe   (1933)
Steep and enjoyable. Start below the right-hand corner at the foot of
a short wall.
1 25 feet. Easily up the edge of the wall to a sloping platform and
thread belays below the corner.
2 85 feet. 4c. Trend diagonally up the wall just right of the corner
crack to a series of potholes. Continue directly up the wall by steep
but straightforward climbing. A good pitch.

Variation
2a 85 feet. 4c. Go diagonally up the wall, traverse back left into the
corner at the level of a large pothole. Finish up the corner crack
which has now widened into a chimney.

★★**Noah's Warning** 220 feet Very Severe   (1951)
A fine sustained route of some character high in its grade which
follows the obvious pock-marked crack right of Pharaoh's Wall. Start
below the crack.
1 130 feet. 4c. Ascend the crack on good holds to the large pothole
on Pharaoh's Wall. Continue up the wall past several bulges to an
overhang. Turn this on the left to a ledge. Belay.
2 90 feet. 5a. Climb the chimney/crack splitting the steep wall above
to reach an overhanging flake. Move round this to the right then go
straight up and move left to a thin crack. At the top of this exit left
with difficulty – a memorable rounded finish.

Rameses Wall 200 feet E1   (1957)
An artificial line with some interesting moves, and a sting in its tail.
Start as for Noah's Warning.
1 100 feet. 5a. A high step onto the right wall gains a rising traverse
which leads to the arête. Climb the wall round the corner left of the
Holly Buttress crack and scramble up over broken ground to belay by
a holly tree.
2 60 feet. 4c. Step down onto the right wall and climb the obvious
steep groove trending to the arête. Step left and go straight up to
belay on Spiral Stairs.

Dinas Cromlech

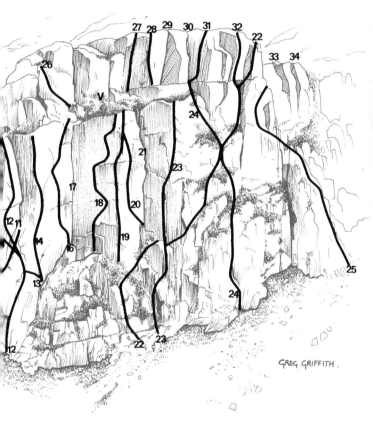

GREG GRIFFITH.

3 40 feet. 5b. Climb the short wall just left of the arête on the right a testing little problem. Finish easily.

The Nubian 180 feet E1   (1978)
A pleasant eliminate taking the arête left of Holly Buttress. Start five feet left of the arête.
1 100 feet. 5b. Climb diagonally right to join the arête at the overlap. Pull round left strenuously to good holds (crux). Follow the arête, and its little continuation, to belay half-way up Holly Buttress at the tree.
2 80 feet. 4c. Step left and follow the arête direct.

Holly Buttress 170 feet Very Severe   (1931)
A steep and direct climb. Start at the foot of the steep polished crack leading up to hollies around the corner to the right of Rameses Wall and just to the left of Dives.
1 100 feet. 4c. Struggle up the crack (this is much harder since the demise of the holly tree) to a possible stance. It is better to continue easily in the same line to a holly tree. Belay.
2 70 feet. 4b. Climb the steep corner crack.

Variation
2a 85 feet. 4b. From the foot of the crack traverse right across the steep wall to reach a slab. Follow this back up left to the top.

Zimbabwe 200 feet E1   (1979)
A rambling route up the arête right of Holly Buttress. Start just right of Holly Buttress.
1 70 feet. 4b. Climb the narrow wall with a steep finish to a prickly stance by some holly bushes below a short steep wall.
2 100 feet. 5c. Scramble up about 10 feet then ascend the wall to a prominent pocket. A hard traverse right to the arête (crux) is followed by exposed moves rapidly easing and a stroll up to the final belay of Spiral Stairs.
3 30 feet. 4c. Finish up the short finger crack above the stance.

★★**Dives/Better Things** 200 feet Hard Severe   (1933/1949)
A great classic climb whose highlight is the excellent airy V-groove of the aptly named Better Things finish. Start a few feet right of Holly Buttress where a steep corner crack rises up to the black diagonal overhang which leads to The Forest.
1 80 feet. Go up the strenuous crack on good holds. Continue diagonally right (often wet) below the overhang on curious pumice-like rock. Belay on The Forest at the foot of the slab.
2 40 feet. Climb the short crack as for Spiral Stairs and belay above

Jethro Kieran on one of the most popular routes in The Pass — *Crackstone Rib* (Severe) Carreg Wastad. Photo: Ray Wood

Pete Crew on *Erosion Groove Direct* (E2) Carreg Wastad.
Photo: John Cleare

David Smart on the second pitch of *Zangorilla* (E4) Carreg Wastad.
Photo: David Wilkinson

Nigel Baker on *The Thing* (E2) Dinas Cromlech. Photo: Chris Craggs

it below the steep V-corner crack.
3 80 feet. Finish up the crack in a fine position.

Variation
The right-hand arête has also been climbed. This gives a very contrived pitch of HVS 5a.

★★**Sabre Cut** 180 feet Very Severe (1935)
An excellent route with a very fine top pitch – the first of the big corners on the Cromlech to be conquered. Start at a vertical corner 10 feet right of Dives.
1 105 feet. 4c. Climb the corner until it divides. Step out right and ascend the wall to The Forest. Climb easily to a good belay on its upper right edge.
2 75 feet. 4b. Traverse left and ascend the enjoyable corner crack to the top.

★**Curfew** 220 feet E1 (1957/1977)
A popular eliminate with an exposed finish. Protection is adequate where it matters. Start 15 feet right of Sabre Cut at a rib to the right of the black overhang
1 100 feet. 5a. (Sabre Cut Direct) Climb the rib to a gangway leading rightwards. From the end of this step right into a steep corner which leads to Spiral Stairs, and thus to The Forest.
2 120 feet. 5b. Climb the steep wall just right of the tree on Spiral Stairs (poorly protected). Ascend the left arête past a ledge to a horizontal break. Traverse this rightwards until the wall above bulges. A few hard moves around the bulge lead to superb juggy climbing up the top arête.

★★★**Foil** 80 feet E3 6a (1976)
A sparkling and superbly sustained pitch up the finger crack in the wall right of Sabre Cut. Exceptionally well-protected. Start as for pitch 2 of Epitaph. Start up Epitaph then follow the thin crack which becomes mean at 50 feet – possible escape left into Sabre Cut here. Continue to a semi-rest at a pocket. Strenuous moves above lead to a precarious exit. Traverse off leftwards to belay at the top of Sabre Cut – and a view of one's second.

Cenotaph Corner Area

The Cromlech Walls, the focal point of Welsh climbing, are probably unmatched in Britain for their unique concentration of hard, high quality and atmospheric mountain routes. Well over a dozen fine Extremes ascend or cross these hallowed walls each offering steep crack or pocket climbing mainly on impeccable rock... an irresistible magnet which draws climbers back time and time again.

★**Epitaph**   220 feet   E3   (1962)
The original way up the left arête of Cenotaph Corner. Though now superseded by Memory Lane and Foil, it is still a very worthwhile route. Some suspect rock and spaced protection make this a bold lead. Start as for Curfew.
1 120 feet. 5a. Begin as for Curfew but continue up through The Forest to belay on its upper right edge.
2 100 feet. 5c. Move left and climb a thin crack until a reachy move right gains a ledge on the arête. Climb the arête trending slightly left on two friable flakes. Step up, then a long reach and pull on a small flake leads to easier climbing, and thankfully the top. The crack behind the stance is Hard Severe.

★**Corridors of Power**   100 feet   E4 6a   (1989)
A harder and more direct way of doing Memory Lane adding a few new feet of climbing to the Cromlech's considerable repertoire. From The Forest, climb the crack and groove right of Foil to the overhang, pull boldly onto the arête and follow pockets up to the large ledge – junction with Memory Lane, finish up the arête above, as for Memory Lane.

★★**Memory Lane**   150 feet   E3 5c   (1976)
A fine open and exhilarating route. Serious and sustained. Start below the left arête of Cenotaph Corner at the first belay on Spiral Stairs. A crack runs up to The Forest. Climb the crack to a ledge on the arête. Move right onto the left wall of The Corner. Ascend direct to the ledge on Epitaph (runners in Left Wall will be found necessary by most leaders). Finish up the arête as for Epitaph – a testing pitch.

★★**Spiral Stairs**   280 feet   Very Difficult   (1931)
An exposed and highly polished trade route. Not recommended for complete novices as the traverse on pitch 2 is quite serious to second. Start on the screes below Cemetery Gates.
1 100 feet. Scramble leftwards up polished ledges. Continue along the narrow path to nut belays just up on the left by a short crack.
2 70 feet. Pull up the crack onto the obvious leftward traverse line. Follow this, descending slightly for 50 feet, until a rib leads up to The Forest. An exposed pitch which is apt to terrify nervous seconds.
3 70 feet. Move across left into the prominent short crack. Climb this to a ledge on the left. Trend up leftwards on good holds via an easy slab to a poor stance and spike belays.
4 40 feet. Climb a chimney/groove to easy slabs.

★**Tess of the d'Urbevilles**   150 feet   E6 6b   (1989)
A scintillating pitch; once the black sheep of the Cromlech, this
controversial climb has now been welcomed into the fold. Extremely
bold, start between Memory Lane and Left Wall. Climb directly up the
wall and do the crux of Memory Lane. Break right and follow a rising
crack via a hard move to reach Left Wall. Runners, step back left and
go up to small ledges and several reasonable RPs. From the centre of
the ledge, boldly run it out straight up the wall to the top with minimal
RP protection going nowhere near Left Wall, or the buckets to its left.

★★★**Left Wall**   130 feet   E2 5c   (1956)
A brilliant route at the top end of its grade. Still a contender for the
most popular, most fallen off, and finest Extreme pitch in North
Wales. It takes the crack which splits the left wall of Cenotaph
Corner. Start on the large sloping ledge below Cenotaph Corner.
Climb diagonally left to stand on a flaky ledge below the crack
proper. Follow this on good holds past an awkward section where it
slants up rightwards to a good resting place below the fork. The thin
left-hand branch gives 20 feet of sustained climbing before a series of
large dubious holds leads left to the arête. Finish easily.

★★**True Grip**   130 feet   E4 6a   (1980)
Essentially a superb direct version of Left Wall. If the pegs on
Resurrection are clipped the grade is reduced. Start as for Left Wall.
Climb up for about 15 feet then pull out rightwards. Go directly up
the wall to join Resurrection at a faded thread runner. Step left, and
after a long reach for a pocket, gain The Girdle ledge. The leftward
curving flake above is climbed with one's feet on it. Where the flake
disappears make a reachy move for a pocket and so to Left Wall.
Continue up Left Wall to finish direct.

★★★**Resurrection**   145 feet   E4 6a   (1975)
A magnificent pitch of undeniable quality, sustained and strenuous,
with a fingery crux at the top. Start just left of Cenotaph Corner.
Climb leftwards for 15 feet then go directly up past a faded thread
runner to The Girdle ledge. Move right to a flat rib of rock. Ascend
the left side of this past a couple of peg runners with a hard move to
reach better holds. Move across to join Left Wall where the crack
splits. Follow the right-hand fork with difficulty, very sustained for 30
feet, to a good spike and runner. The crack now closes. Make a long
reach left to sharp finger holds and finish up a shallow groove.

Variations

The Right-Hand Finish
Harder but better protected and more popular than the original. From

Dinas Cromlech
Cenotaph Corner Area

1 Dives/Better Things	HS
2. Sabre Cut	VS
3. Curfew	E1
4. Foil	E3
5. Spiral Stairs	VD
6. Memory Lane	E3
7. Left Wall	E2
8. Resurrection	E4
9. J R	E5
10. Cenotaph Corner	E1
11. Lord of the Flies	E6
12. Nightmayer	E8
13. Right Wall	E5
14. Precious	E5
15. Cemetery Gates	E1
16. The Crucifix	E2
17. Ivy Sepulchre	E1
18. Hall of Warriors	E5
19. Misty Wall	E2
20. Cenotaph Corner Finish	S
21. Overlord	E7
22. Gruel	HVS
23. Ivy Sepulchre Crack	VD
24. Rumblefish	E7
25. Grond	E2

where the crack closes continue in the same line on small face holds. Make a massive reach for a flat hold (6b for the short) and finish direct.

Redhead's Finish
From the spike go straight up the wall between the left and right-hand finishes – solid 6b.

★ **J R**   140 feet   E5 6b   (1980)

A fierce eliminate up the wall to the right of Resurrection which has seen some l-o-n-g falls. Unfortunately it is possible to step into Cenotaph Corner for a rest at 80 feet. Only the purist will resist this temptation. Start as for Resurrection. Follow Resurrection for 10 feet then climb direct to The Girdle ledge. Climb the flake above (as for Resurrection) to the pegs then step right. A difficult pull on a rounded hold gains sharp finger jugs. Climb up to a flake runner then move right and upwards until a layback on a small edge and a pinch grip move lead to the ledge below the crux of Resurrection. Follow the Resurrection Right-Hand finish.

★★★ **Cenotaph Corner**   120 feet   E1 5c   (1952)

Perhaps the most famous of British rock-climbs and the focal point of the Llanberis Pass. Although the passage of countless feet has polished its holds to a high sheen, to lead this route for the first time is both a thrilling and satisfying experience. Immaculate climbing with good protection. Start at the foot of the huge right-angled corner. Ascend to a difficult but well-protected move at 25 feet. Continue more easily using a crack on the left to a widening of the corner crack. Struggle up this with an awkward move into a shallow niche at 100 feet just past a chockstone (The Pudding Stone). Bridge delicately up to thin jams and exit via a good hold to a tree belay over on the right.

★ **Nightmayer**   130 feet   E8 6c   (1992)

A formidable test of nerve and stamina which makes the most of the baffling blank section of the wall between Cenotaph Corner and Lord. An abseil inspection will be found necessary by most parties. Follow Lord of the Flies to the finger-traverse ledge. Pull straight up and continue direct on pockets, moving right to gain the large pocket on Lord, thread runner. Crank up and left on a two finger pocket then continue direct to The Girdle ledge. Move right for a rest. Move back, and ascend past a good wire just above The Girdle ledge. A reasonable small wire protects the sharp dynamic crux about half-way up. More tenuous climbing on small pockets leads to a point six feet from the top. Move left and finish up the last piece of the wall, exiting onto rock... a heart-stopping lead.

★★★**Lord of the Flies**   130 feet   E6 6a   (1979)

A stunning route of great difficulty and quality between Cenotaph Corner and Right Wall which should be on the hit list of every 'wall creature'. Since the disappearance of, first, the peg, and more recently the crucial nut placement that once protected the crux, the route is now a much more serious proposition. Start 12 feet right of The Corner below thin vertical cracks. Climb the cracks until they run out, then go directly up to a thin ledge. Finger-traverse right along this with a hard move up at its end to gain a large pocket. Continue up on reasonable holds for a few feet, until a short but fierce and fingery section leads up left to another pocket, runner in the pocket and also good nut out to the right. Step right and ascend to better holds, and so reach The Girdle ledge. A few moves up the wall gain a finger ledge leading right to the base of a shallow groove and improving holds. Finish up the groove past a large nut runner.

★**The House of God**   130 feet   E6 6a   (1989)

Rather contrived! A more serious and sustained way of doing Lord of the Flies – though not as classic as the original. Start up Lord then follow Nightmayer to The Girdle ledge. Move right and finish up Lord.

★★★**Right Wall**   150 feet   E5 6a   (1974)

Although it has lost its awesome reputation through many ascents this brilliant climb is still a big lead and should not be underestimated. The original way up the wall, it is a route-finding masterpiece, the holds only coming to light at close quarters. Start at the right-hand end of a grassy ledge at a short wall and short corner below some old bolts. Ascend the short wall to a ledge. Climb the corner breaking out left up the diagonal crack. Move back right and continue up the wall on pockets to a narrow ledge, and so to a good rest on the right. Step up onto a prominent foothold and climb leftwards to a large broken pocket; or move left a few feet and ascend direct. From the top of the pocket step left and climb up on small pockets to a line of holds rising rightwards to The Girdle ledge. Traverse right until directly below a shallow pocket, The Porthole, 20 feet above. Start up the crux wall just to its right then step into it and so reach a series of good holds which run rightwards past a good spike. Traverse along these to finish up a thin crack.

Precious   130 feet   E5 6b   (1980)

A scary start and thrilling finish make this route a memorable outing. Unfortunately the line is very escapable. Start 15 feet right of Right Wall below an inverted V-slot. Go straight up through the V-slot. Continue via a shallow scoop then slightly up left to a resting ledge (on Right Wall). Climb to good runners 10 feet higher. Ascend rightwards to a large pocket and so to another pocket. Move left a few feet and pull up onto The Girdle ledge (often dirty). Follow Right Wall past The Porthole to the traverse line. Instead of moving right finish direct to a small tree by superb pockety climbing.

Variations
The Original Start 6a. Gain the shallow scoop above the inverted V-slot by a horizontal traverse from the diagonal crack on Right Wall. From The Girdle ledge climb up between Right Wall and Cemetery Gates to the rightward traverse of the former route at a similar standard.

★★★**Ivory Madonna**   260 feet   E5   (1980)
A majestic, rising, right-to-left girdle of the Cenotaph Corner walls in two demanding pitches, with a particularly intense crux. Start as for Cemetery Gates.
1 140 feet. 6b. Climb Cemetery Gates to the first good resting ledge. Traverse easily left to join Lord of the Flies. An adrenalin pumping 20-foot sequence of 'brick edge' climbing (yes, this is the crux) enables 'non-fliers' to gain the sanctuary of Cenotaph Corner. Ascend 15 feet to belay.
2 120 feet. 6a. A hard move left just below an overlap on the left wall gains two good pockets. Continue left to a flake runner, step down five feet and move across to join Left Wall where the crack forks. Climb boldly left along a line of rising pockets to join Epitaph at a perched block 15 feet from the top. Finish easily.

★★★**Cemetery Gates**   170 feet   E1   (1951)
The exhilarating and exposed crack-line at the right arête of Cenotaph Corner is much more accomodating than it appears from below. Except for a few feet, the route is furnished with large holds but the climbing is still quite strenuous; leaders trying to push up their standard frequently have epics on it. A hard move up into the crack proper at 40 feet is fairly serious but above protection is excellent. Start from the top of a huge flake right of Cenotaph Corner. Carefully descend this to a tree belay below the right arête.
1 110 feet. 5b. Climb up first right and then left to the foot of the chimney/crack. Enter this boldly and follow it past an awkward section to a good ledge at 60 feet. Continue up the crack to belay on The Girdle ledge, the last few moves being the crux.
2 60 feet. 4c. From the right-hand end of the ledge climb the wide crack for 15 feet. Step round the arête to the right and go up to reach a series of 'Thank God' holds which lead airily to the top.

The Grim Jim   170 feet   E2   (1981)
An obvious line up the arête and wall between Cemetery Gates and The Crucifix. Start as for Cemetery Gates.

1 130 feet. 5b. Follow Cemetery Gates to the long ledge at 60 feet. Move right round the arête, go up on dubious holds, then step back left to a ledge on the arête. Ascend a few feet then go strenuously over the bulge using a layaway hold in a pocket. Trend left up to the ledge and belay on Cemetery Gates.
2 40 feet. 5b. Follow the crack behind the stance to the top; a superbly exposed pitch.

Variation
The Direct Start   60 feet   E4 5c   (1981)
Climb the Gates to the chimney. Move boldly up the bulge on disposable holds to rejoin the Gates at the first ledge.

The East Wing

The Crucifix   210 feet   E2   (1966)
A bold outing at the upper limit of its grade which runs up a groove in the centre of the wall left of Ivy Sepulchre. The climbing is not too hard but friable rock and well-spaced protection combine to give a high 'grip' factor. Start as for Ivy Sepulchre.
1 80 feet. As for Ivy Sepulchre pitch 1.
2 130 feet. 5b. Traverse out leftwards and ascend steeply to a flake runner. Continue for 10 feet to a small ledge, then trend up left to a shallow groove. Climb this boldly to a shallow niche (junction with The Girdle). Surmount the bulge move left and climb the wall to 'Thank God' holds to finish.

Crucifix Direct   150 feet   E4 5c   (1976)
A menacing version of the parent route – with even more suspect rock. Start from a ledge and tree belay below the centre of the wall. Boldly climb straight up to join Crucifix at the flake runner after 60 feet of climbing.

Golgotha   130 feet   E4 5c   (1979)
This route takes a surprisingly independent line between Ivy Sepulchre and Crucifix and is very serious, as the peg runner can only be clipped after the crux; the name means 'Place of the Skull'. Start at the foot of the Ivy Sepulchre corner. Climb the crack just left of the corner. Trend left under the overlap and step down to a resting ledge. Pull rightwards over the bulge using a pocket to reach a hidden fyake on the white wall. Stand on this with difficulty to reach the peg runner then finish boldly up the wall just to its right.

★★**Ivy Sepulchre**   190 feet   E1   (1947)
An interesting and varied climb up the large corner right of Cenotaph. Start below this on a grassy ledge.

1 80 feet. Climb vegetated rock and continue up left via a crack leading to trees. Traverse right along a ledge and go up over two rock steps to belay at the foot of the corner.

2 110 feet. 5b. Climb the corner, awkward at first, but soon easing up, to a large overhung niche. Climb out of this with difficulty to better holds. Finish up the corner without further problems to an oak tree belay just below the top.

★**Hall of Warriors**   130 feet   E5 6a   (1980)
A rivetting route which has its harrowing moments and one very hard move. Start a few feet right of Ivy Sepulchre. Climb the wall with an awkward move left to a ledge at 25 feet. Continue up until it is possible to pull out onto the centre of a large ledge (on The Girdle) – all very serious so far. Step up left to a pocket. Go straight up with a telescopic reach for a jug, crux, and so to a sapling and grass ledge. Move six feet right (a bit of a shock horror) then go up to finish via a crack.

Jericho Wall   250 feet   E2   (1952)
A steep and nerve-racking route on friable rock with only moderate protection. It follows the shattered chimney/crack up the edge of the wall right of Ivy Sepulchre. Start below the wall at a 15-foot triangular buttress.

1 80 feet. 5a. Climb the left-hand side of the buttress and go up to a small wet overhang. Move right and climb a smooth white corner/groove on small holds to below another overhang. Go left to the Ivy Sepulchre ledge.

2 65 feet. 5a. Traverse down right across the ledge to a damp scoop. Climb this, and the wall above, then step left to an overhung niche. Step up and trend right with difficulty to a large ledge. Stance and belay.

3 105 feet. 4c. Traverse 15 feet left and ascend to a holly tree. Traverse back right and go up to a scoop; continue up until it is possible to traverse left to a small pinnacle. Finish direct to The Valley.

Wardance   90 feet   E1 5b   (1982)
A poor route on doubtful rock up the arête just right of Jericho Wall starting from the ledge below its second pitch. Follow Jericho Wall pitch 2 for about 15 feet. Step right and climb the arête via an obvious groove to belay at a good ledge on the right. Scramble off rightwards to finish.

Horseman's Route   355 feet   Hard Severe   (1940)
A rambling expedition with its share of bad rock and vegetation which is somewhat redeemed by its imposing final chimney. Start at the foot of Ivy Sepulchre.

1 75 feet. Scramble up to a ledge and climb a steep crack to a dead tree. Step down to the right until a dirty chimney leads to another vegetated ledge. Climb a chimney to the Ivy Sepulchre ledge.
2 80 feet. Follow the ledge down along to the right stepping low across a damp scoop. Go round the arête and up a broken wall to a poor stance.
3 65 feet. Continue up a narrow rake to the foot of a chimney. Climb this and move along the ledge above to belay between two cracks in the wall.
4 55 feet. Ascend the wall between the cracks of Sexton's Route and Neb's Crawl. Walk up right through vegetation to a grassy ledge, The Haven, below a prominent corner.
5 80 feet. The initial corner proves awkward to the overhung chimney. Climb the chimney with a grandstand view of 'hard men' cruising Atomic Hot Rod until a step out right near the top.

Sexton's Route 215 feet Severe   (1933)
A must for the amateur botanist who detests crowds. This vague and tedious route rambles up through the most vegetated part of the cliff. Start on the rake at the foot of the left-facing gully 30 feet right of Ivy Sepulchre.
1 60 feet. Climb the overhanging chimney to a large spike. Move delicately left with difficulty to a good stance and belay.
2 80 feet. Scramble up to the grassy slopes of The Heath on the right and continue via a heathery glacis and broken rock to a short wall.
3 75 feet. Ascend the left-hand crack with an awkward exit onto a large ledge with trees. Walk left and climb a steep wall above the tree to The Valley, or finish up the right-angled corner immediately behind the trees, much harder.

Pegasus 90 feet Hard Very Severe 5a   (1978)
A worthwhile little route. Start below the last pitch of Horseman's Route. Move right and climb the obvious arête – one hard move over the overlap.

Variation
The steep shattered wall below the arête has also been climbed at E2 5b. Lethally loose.

Neb's Crawl 225 feet Difficult   (1933)
Another rambling route for the botanist, its acres of vegetation almost dwarfing the amount of rock encountered. It takes a diagonal line going from right to left crossing The Heath and ending in The Valley. Start in the gully immediately left of Flying Buttress, or at a vegetated crack, Crockett Crack, a few yards left. Womble vaguely up via the

right-hand crack in a short wall at about 110 feet. Scramble up rightwards then ascend another wall to a sloping ledge and belay. Move round to the left and so to The Valley — variations are legion.

★★★**The Cromlech Girdle**   805 feet   E2   (1956)
A historic expedition of great character. Cruising the airy walls of Cenotaph Corner gives a real adrenalin surge but its other pitches are not without interest. Well worth doing in its entirety on weekdays to prevent traffic jams around Cenotaph Corner. Start at the foot of Parchment Passage.
1 90 feet. Climb up to the holly above Parchment Passage pitch 1.
2 50 feet. 5a. Climb a few feet above the holly stump then traverse right reversing Cobweb Crack for eight feet. Continue right round the arête to belay in Pharaoh's Passage.
3 40 feet. 4c. Climb down and round the next arête to a stance and belay on Pharaoh's Wall.
4 60 feet. Traverse the wall diagonally rightwards to a stance and belay on Holly Buttress.
5 110 feet. Traverse right and downwards to join Dives. Climb this to The Forest and so to a stance and belay on the left edge of the wall of Cenotaph Corner.
6 100 feet. 5b. Step right onto a small ledge. Go up for six feet then traverse right to Left Wall which is climbed to a good flake and nut runner. Descend 10 feet then make several hard moves to a horizontal break leading more easily in to The Corner. Climb up to where the crack widens and a hanging stance. A serious pitch to second.
7 100 feet. 5b. Climb The Corner to a good thread runner around The Pudding Stone. Descend to the start of a narrow rising ledge running across the right wall. Go along this using pockets on the wall above. A hard move gains the wider ledge leading across to the Cemetery Gates belay. Quite a serious pitch for both members of the party.
8 45 feet. 5a. Traverse right round the arête. Descend slightly on brittle rock then move across to the tree on Ivy Sepulchre.
9 50 feet. A descending traverse along ledges leads to the heathery terrace on Jericho Wall.
10 & **11** 160 feet. 4b. As for Horseman's Route pitches 4 and 5.

Flying Buttress Area

★★★**Flying Buttress**   290 feet   Very Difficult   (1931)
A steep and classic route on sound but polished rock with a remarkable degree of exposure. The finest V Diff in The Pass. Start at the foot of the buttress.

1 60 feet. Go straight up the centre of the buttress on large well-worn holds.
2 60 feet. Continue up the centre of the buttress to the pinnacles on its summit.
3 20 feet. Climb over the pinnacles to belay on the left wall of the gully.
4 50 feet. Ascend the large rock steps on the left wall then step round the corner across a little groove (or reach this point from below – harder) to a traverse line and so to the pinnacle ledge. Belay.
5 50 feet. Climb the steep wall behind the flake to a rightward slanting gangway. Follow this to belay on a ledge below a chimney.
6 50 feet. Climb the chimney which is difficult to start.

★**Kamikaze Finish** 60 feet Very Severe 4c   (1978)
6a Climb the slabby wall above the last stance of Flying Buttress to an overhang. Move left and finish direct – a fine little pitch.

Castle Gully 200 feet Difficult   (1892)
The first climb to be done on The Cromlech. It is the gully right of Flying Buttress starting at a big cave. Easy climbing and a little chossy, save for the thrutch up the last 10 feet.

René 100 feet Very Severe 4c   (1948)
A short but steep route of surprising difficulty. Start on the right wall of Castle Gully at about the same level as the summit of Flying Buttress. Climb a groove to a tree. Traverse left to a perched block. Climb the nose between the grooves and move left into a square-cut corner. Climb this awkwardly to an easy finish.

The Puerile Ticker 100 feet Very Severe 4c   (1978)
A pleasant climb. Start as for René to the tree. Follow the obvious groove to the right of René.

The Quaker 100 feet Hard Very Severe 5a   (1978)
Slight but interesting. Start as for René to the tree. Climb the rib on the right to a ledge at 20 feet below the groove of The Puerile Ticker. Climb a slab, then layback diagonally rightwards on a dubious flake to a small ledge below an overhang. Go up moving left under the overhang then pull up onto the arête. Move right then finish direct.

Notanda 110 feet Hard Severe   (1952)
Right of Castle Gully lies the obvious descent gully with a prominent pinnacle on its right wall. Start at the foot of this.
1 55 feet. Climb the corner to a small ledge and high flake belay.
2 55 feet. Step up above the belay then move awkwardly round the arête to the left to gain the foot of a difficult heathery crack. Climb this.

Crampon Route   100 feet   Very Severe 4b   (1989)
Takes the ridge of the pinnacle to the left of Notanda. Start just left of
the ridge on a small ledge. Climb the wall and ridge delicately for
about 80 feet. Traverse below the final crack of Notanda and ascend
a heathery groove with difficulty to finish.

Climbs in and above The Valley

Tributary Crack   40 feet   Difficult   (1939)
The normal escape route. Start a few feet left of Cenotaph Corner
Finish. Pleasantly climb the diagonal crack.

★**Misty Wall**   60 feet   E2 5b   (1979)
A serious little pitch up the wall left of Cenotaph Corner Finish. Start
just right of Tributary Crack. Go straight up the wall to a small
sapling. Step right then continue to reach the short finishing crack.

Cenotaph Corner Finish   50 feet   Severe   (1939)
An enjoyable pitch with its crux in the initial moves. The line of
Cenotaph Corner continues above The Valley as another large
right-angled corner. Start below this. Climb strenuously up the corner
for 20 feet then break out left and traverse steeply to the left edge, or
better still finish directly up the corner at Very Severe 4b.

★★**Overlord**   55 feet   E7 6c   (1992)
The painfully obvious sharp arête just behind and left of the tree belay
at the top of Cenotaph Corner is at the technical cutting edge of
current mountain crag standards and requires razor-honed climbing
skills. Pull directly onto the arête using a suspect flake. Quote,
"Reasonable moves", unquote, enable one to reach a poor peg and
small wire runner. An intricate sequence leads to a second peg,
which is hard to clip, but once passed gains a slight shake out. One
more hard move and a slap for jugs gives an exciting finish.

Gruel   55 feet   Hard Very Severe 5b   (1978)
The finishing crack is particularly stubborn. Start in the corner to the
left of Ivy Sepulchre Crack. Climb the corner crack, then struggle up
the wide overhanging continuation crack to the left.

★**Ivy Sepulchre Crack**   50 feet   Very Difficult
Steep and strenuous and on perfect rock. Good value for its grade.
Start from The Valley at the foot of the obvious crack/chimney
splitting the wall above and left of the finish of Ivy Sepulchre. The Pass
equivalent of Monolith Crack.

★★**Rumblefish**   50 feet   E7 6b   (1986)
The left arête of Grond gives a lonely and vicious lead. Pull onto the

arête from the right and make dramatic moves past two Rock 1s with a long stretch up for a peg (which may prevent a crater). Arrange RP protection behind some suspect flakes; desperate moves up to the overlap precede a wild swing left on sidepulls to the 'safety' of a Thank God hold. Finish more easily with considerable relief.

★★**The Bastard Practice**   50 feet   E7 6c   (1989)
Immediately right of Rumblefish the peg-protected overhanging rib so cruelly cleaned and equipped in the mid-80s, now gives a short but mighty pitch... which as its name implies, may require a lot of BP! Climb the wall, rib, and groove with more than a little difficulty passing three pegs *en route*... the first peg is rather dubious.

★★★**Grond**   50 feet   E2 5b   (1958)
An explosive enough test-piece to put a smile on the face of even the most jaded of gritstone addicts. Right of Ivy Sepulchre Crack is a clean-cut overhanging right-angled corner crack. Climb the crack with either difficulty or ease. Superbly butch.

Grand   45 feet   E5 6c   (1986)
The sharp right arête is climbed dynamically to where the angle eases, the crux is at 20 feet – exit left or right. Unfortunately the two tied-off pegs and the *in situ* wire which protect the route are a bit of an eyesore.

The Mystery   70 feet   E1 5b
The obvious corner 40 feet right of Grond. Climb the technical corner passing an old sling.

★★**The Monster**   70 feet   E1 5c   (1977)
A very good crack pitch; technical, strenuous and insecure. Start at the foot of The Mystery. Gain the crack by a rightward traverse on jams. Difficult moves now lead to an exposed and precarious finish where the crack widens. Exit just left of a perched block. A brute of a route!

Joshua's Traverse   120 feet   Hard Very Severe   (1965)
A boulder-problem wall leads to an eminently forgettable middle section and a fine finish up Horseman's Route. Useful as a finish to Jericho Wall. Start in The Valley from the block belay at the top of Jericho Wall below The Monster.
1 60 feet. 5b. Move down to the right and ascend the fierce little wall below the right arête of The Monster to a ledge. Walk along this round the corner to the right and along another ledge to belay at an impending crack.
2 60 feet. 4b. Continue traversing right below overhangs, good

worm's eye view of Atomic Hot Rod, to finish up the final corner of Horseman's Route.

Awesome   50 feet   E4 6a   (1986)
The poorly protected overhanging groove between Gross Encounters and The Monster is usually dirty and obviously makes a deep impression... so could you if you fail to abseil inspect it. Start from the long ledge on Joshua's Traverse. Struggle up the overhanging groove, a truly awesome experience. Two RP3s and an *in situ* RURP protect.

Gross Encounters   70 feet   E2 5b   (1978)
This takes a direct line up through the crack just left of Atomic Hot Rod. Climb the initial wall to a ledge below the impending crack, rather loose. Glorious jamming up the perfect hand-crack leads all too quickly to an easy finish.

★★**Atomic Hot Rod**   70 feet   E5 6b   (1980)
Once the ultimate, but now perhaps only the penultimate crack pitch; this ferocious finger-ripping test-piece slices the crag as if cut with a scalpel. The advent of Friends has made this a much easier lead nowadays, but the crack still manages to slow down most would-be suitors. Start on The Haven below the final pitch of Horseman's Route. Follow Horseman's Route up the corner then move left to the foot of the undercut and overhanging finger crack, the ascent of which proves to be somewhat trying; unless you're on meltdown.

Valley Crossings   490 feet   Very Difficult   (1931)
A rather vegetated girdle of the cliff which nevertheless takes in some impressive scenery. Start from the top of Spiral Stairs and step across the top of Sabre Cut to hollies. Continue up over large blocks across a wide chimney, then airily across to a delicate step down and so to The Valley proper above Cenotaph Corner. Ramble up and across above Ivy Sepulchre round the corner to below The Monster. Descend the sloping ledge. Either climb or abseil down to trees. Scramble across rightwards to finish up Flying Buttress.

Outlying Climbs

Eggmeat Buttress

Behind the Cromlech Boulders, a wide low relief ridge runs down the hillside to terminate in an overhanging wall which rises from the scree slopes at its foot – Eggmeat Buttress. The wall is breached by short, striking twin corners which in turn are separated by the sharp overhanging Eggmeat Arête (this lies way down and to the right of Cromlech Grooves). Around and up on the lower left side of the ridge is a short overhanging white wall containing a capped central groove; a small rounded globe-like subsidiary buttress just above and beyond this (25 feet to the right across scree from the start of Cromlech Grooves) gives the first of a series of fierce micro-routes.

Sheepcat 30 feet E5 6b   (1987)
Tackle the left to right crack splitting the front face of the globe. Protection is difficult to arrange and the climbing is fierce.

Down on the main section is...

Animal Locomotion 45 feet E7 6b   (1987)
A bold route, said to be "Choppier than the Bay of Biscay." It takes the central groove, flake, then wall up the overhanging black shield left of Eggmeat Arête. With sustained, strenuous and technical climbing above a nasty landing, and only one skyhook for protection, it seems unlikely to become a trade route.

Birdseye 35 feet Very Severe 5a   (1987)
The corner just left of Eggmeat Arête proves to be a trifle tricky.

Eggmeat Arête 30 feet E3 6a   (1987)
A classic little problem which should appeal to 'slappers' everywhere. The superb overhanging arête reserves its contortionate slappy crux for the last move – to slip, is to turn eggmeat into mincemeat... unless you have the correct sized 'Friend' to hand...

Ringsnack 30 feet E2 5c   (1987)
The steep wet dripping corner right of Eggmeat Arête justifiably merits its awful name.

Milk Cow   30 feet   E4 6b   (1987)
Tackle the grooved arête 10 feet right of Eggmeat Arête; direct! Looks a doddle doesn't it.

Pork Trout   30 feet   Very Severe 5a   (1987)
The slim groove and wall just right again is less beefy, thus more amenable, than its neighbours.

Cromlech Grooves   100 feet   Severe   (1951)
Worth doing when one is tired of the slog up to Dinas Cromlech. Dinas Cromlech throws down a long narrow ridge towards Ynys Ettws. The lower end of this tapers sharply into a junction with the stream well above and to the left of the Cromlech Boulders. Sixty feet right of this lower end are two slabby grooves which start a few yards left of the globe-like Sheepcat Buttress. Go up the right-hand groove to a small overhang. Step delicately round the corner into the left-hand groove and continue on doubtful rock. Scramble up the ridge to Dinas Cromlech.

Corky   130 feet   E1 5b   (1978)
The short wall and groove in the arête of the buttress a few yards left of Cromlech Grooves on the other side of the stream. Climb directly up the short wall to the foot of the groove. A hard start leads to easier climbing up the groove and large tape runner around a pinnacle on the left. Undercut right across the top of the groove to gain a sloping ledge, tricky. Finish up the shallow leaning corner, trickier; or sneak off rightwards round the arête.

In the holly filled alcove round behind Corky what feels like a HVS jungle-bashing approach gives access to...

Honking By The Pool   45 feet   E3 5b   (1989)
A route of allegedly great character (building potential) taking (or dismantling) the prominent corner. Climb the corner with difficulty taking care to leave the holds in place as you pass.

Castell Craig (Rock Castle) known as The Thumb

About 200 yards right of Dinas Cromlech and on a level with its base is a blunt needle of rock – The Thumb. This isolated monolith has four ways up it. On the long side is a superb Hard Very Severe crack, 5a. Opposite this on the short side is a wide Hard Severe crack, also the descent apart from abseil. The arête 10 feet right of the Hard Severe crack gives the fingery **Thumbling With My Wicklows**, 35 feet, E3 6a whilst **King Kipper**, 35 feet, E1 5b is the left arête on the short side stepping in from the right.

Never a Dull Moment   60 feet   E4 6a   (1986)
Fifty yards right of The Thumb is a slender buttress reminiscent of
Trevallen Pillar (in Pembroke). Pull up leftwards on a hollow flake to
gain a crack. Move back right (crux) to a hold. Climb boldly up the
right arête to the top – a fine pitch.

Midway between the foot of Dinas Cromlech and The Thumb and at a
slightly lower level is a prominent white wall:

Drury's Drama   50 feet   Hard Very Severe 5b   (1985)
Don't make a crisis out of the steep the central groove.

Esgair Maen Gwyn or Scimitar Ridge

(Spur/Scarp of White Rock)   OS Ref. 635 564

Farther up towards Pen y Pass from Dinas Cromlech, a much-eyed striking
slabby ridge running up the hillside for around 150 yards has a rounded
left flank and an extremely steep east face plastered with hard routes –
this is Scimitar Ridge whose crest gives a rambling but quite testing
traditional Severe which contrasts markedly with some of the sterner
'mind games' lurking down to the right. Once something of a climbing
backwater, the crag now boasts some of the best single pitch climbing
in The Pass, and is much larger close up than it would appear to be from
a distance. Catching the morning sun (when it chooses to appear) and
receiving little drainage, the east face is quick-drying – by local
standards. The rock is blocky and should be treated carefully although
most of the climbs are sound. Some of the harder routes have *in situ* peg
protection, so it is probably advisable to check the state of the pegs prior
to an ascent. The descent is up the ridge, traverse right and cautiously
descend the gully which runs up under the east face. On approach, the
first route one comes to is Artemis, Very Difficult – the tree filled groove
at the bottom left end of the crag. It provides a quick way up to the top.

★★**The Roc-Nest Monster**   80 feet   E4 6a   (1990)
To the right of Artemis, this takes the line of scoops in the wall left of
the flying arête – King Wad. Start as for that route. Climb 10 feet up
King Wad, runners, then span left on undercuts to a peg. Climb
directly up on blind layaway moves passing a further three pegs to
finish up either the groove or arête left of King Wad.

★★★ **King Wad**   100 feet   E6 6b   (1987)

A classic. Superb moves and positions up a detached flake, bulging wall, and stunning flying arête starting right of Artemis and just left of the arête. Layback the hovering flake and climb the groove above to a thread. Continue up and right to a niche, wire, then bridge up to the base of a groove, peg runner. Now swing right onto the arête in a sensational position and bridge thin air for 25 feet passing a peg to a dynamic finish... an electrifying pitch!

★★ **Surgical Lust**   100 feet   E7 6b   (1987)

Up and right of King Wad is a large groove taken by Chreon... this fine severely overhanging testpiece which is quote, "Massively serious!", tackles a line based on the crack in the impending wall left of Chreon's blunt left arête. Follow the line of the crack, two peg runners. The climbing is extremely serious up to the first peg. Switch on the turbocharger... it is possible to 'crater' from 70 feet; one of the most strenuous routes in the Pass... queue here!

★★★ **Tufty Club Rebellion**   90 feet   E5 6a   (1987)

Another excellent pitch based on the blunt arête left of Chreon. Start about 25 feet down and left of Chreon at a tottering flake. Climb up and left to good holds on a doubtful flake. Pull up slightly rightwards to a slot, then go straight up to obvious undercuts. Using these, traverse boldly right around the arête to a peg runner. Move up and left onto the arête proper. The arête gradually eases to finish in a little black groove.

Opposite:

Esgair Maen Gwyn

1. The Roc-Nest Monster	E4
2. King Wad	E6
3. Tufty Club Rebellion	E5
4. Troy	E1
5. Chreon	E2
6. Killerkranky	E5
7. The Kicker Conspiracy	E5
8. Agamemnon	E1
9. Hermes	VS
10. Kitten Versus Pig	E5
11. Achilles	E3

Troy   90 feet   E1 5b   (1979)
Interesting and exposed. The crack in the left wall of the large open
groove of Chreon. From the foot of the groove on Chreon, step left
into the snaking crack and climb it past a few tufts of heather.

★**Chreon**   85 feet   E2 5b   (1979)
This sustained pitch takes the large open groove with a sapling at 20
feet. Climb a square cut groove becoming a thin crack to a fine
exposed finish.

★**Romany Soup**   90 feet   E4 6a   (1987)
One of the more amenable hard routes – good, varied and sustained.
Start five feet left of Killerkranky. Climb straight up into a steep black
groove. Exit left to an area of undercut flakes. Pull over onto a slab,
then move up right onto some blocks. Finish directly up the arête.

★★**Killerkranky**   90 feet   E5 6a   (1986)
The hairline crack, just right of the large open groove of Chreon is
reasonably protected and used to be a Draconian test of one's mettle
until 1987.

★★**The Kicker Conspiracy**   90 feet   E5 6a   (1987)
This takes the big curving line right of Killerkranky by some very bold
climbing. Start at the large pinnacle. Move up, then traverse left
along a slab, then go up into a scoop just right of Killerkranky. Follow
this with interest past two peg runners to finish.

★★**The Trumpet Blowers**   80 feet   E7 6c   (1992)
An outrageous pitch, both testing and technical. Start as for The
Kicker Conspiracy. Follow The Kicker Conspiracy until it moves left
along the slab. Climb boldly straight up past a hidden small wire
placement to arrive at a peg. Move right to a second peg then
ascend direct to a niche below an obvious groove. Swing right
around the arête to gain another groove. Follow this moving
rightwards to the top.

★★★**The 39 Slaps**   70 feet   E7 6b   (1987)
Strenuous, dynamic and dramatic! Start just right of the last route,
below a line of six pegs (not one of which is bombproof, they are
either sawn off or tied off or something equally unreliable). A series of
radical slaps up the leaning wall, allied to a strong sense of
motivation, enable one to reach a large wire placement – quite handy
for protecting the top.

Agamemnon   70 feet   E1 5b   (1979)
Slabby columns lie against the main face forming a central groove

which rises from left to right. Starting from the perched pinnacle, ascend diagonally right to an easy finish. Rather disappointing.

Scabbard 90 feet Very Severe (1953)
The original way up the crag. Start at the foot of a crack about 20 feet up from Agamemnon.
1 45 feet. Climb diagonally along the crack and groove to a spike stance on Agamemnon.
2 45 feet. Traverse right along a sloping ledge and across the rib. Continue diagonally left into the corner which is taken with care to finish.

Hermes 75 feet Very Severe 5a (1979)
Start 40 feet up the gully from the pinnacle of Agamemnon. Follow the shallow ramp up left past a small gorse bush at 20 feet to join Agamemnon at the top.

★**Kitten Versus Pig** 80 feet E5 6b (1987)
Ten feet right of the start of Hermes is a pinnacle of tottering flakes below a dead-straight crack/seam. Climb the stubborn crack direct to finish on the right in an easy but mossy groove.

★**Mutiny on the Mouse Organ** 80 feet E4 6a (1987)
This takes narrow ramps through the steep walls, right of the dead-straight crack/seam, and left of a large bulge with an obvious downward-pointing spike at its top, below which The Bells... starts. From just left of The Bells... start under a mottled black and white ramp. Climb up to, and onto this with some difficulty. From the top of this ramp, move left onto the next ramp and continue up to a ledge at its top left-hand side. Climb up the easier mossy ramp above to finish in the final corner of Kitten Versus Pig.

The Bells, The Bells, The Bells 90 feet E5 6b (1987)
Yet another taxing pitch. Start 30 feet right of the tottering flake pinnacle (Kitten Versus Pig) just left of a prominent bulge with a large hanging spike at its top. Trend up rightwards over the bulge on huge undercuts to gain the spike. Pull over for a rest, then continue up a leftward leaning ramp until it is possible to finish up a vague, steeper groove, stepping left to avoid loose rock at the top.

The next four routes are described from RIGHT to LEFT...

Xerxes 60 feet E1 5b (1979)
At the top right side of the crag is a corner with a sharp right arête. Climb the corner which proves deceptively tricky.

Thermopylae   60 feet   Hard Very Severe 5a   (1979)
The disjointed crack left of Xerxes is followed with interest.

Sparta   70 feet   E3 5c   (1979)
A technical and sustained pitch. About 15 feet left of Thermopylae is
a smooth red scoop which is gained by a traverse from the right and
is finished direct.

Achilles   70 feet   E3 5c   (1979)
Steep, strenuous and serious. About 30 feet left of Xerxes sits a huge
perched boulder, about 30 feet up the face. Start below and just to its
right. Climb diagonally left and across to get established on a
hanging fang of rock. Go up to, and whisper over the Damoclean
block. Continue slightly shaken to the top.

Clogwyn Blaen Coed   (Woods' End Cliff)

OS Ref. 637 562

This area consists of three small buttresses which lie further up the Pass
from Scimitar Ridge, low down, below the level of the road. The first has
a short wall below a grass ledge, and a slabby top, it has one route:

Thor   150 feet   Severe   (1952)
Start at the left side of the crag on a large ledge beneath the
right-hand end of a heathery bay, by a dirty chimney.
1 60 feet. Ascend the chimney, exit on heather, then take the rock rib
towards an oak tree. Huge flake belay.
2 40 feet. The steep wall on the left is climbed to the highest ledge.
Step left into a crack (dubious holds). Go up and round the corner on
the left, then follow a glacis to belay.
3 40 feet. Take the continuation of the glacis then a pleasant slab on
the right, 100 feet of scrambling with an optional slab on the right
remain.

One hundred yards farther along to the right lies the most distinctive and
best of the crags – a huge roof at one-third height on its front face is an
obvious feature. The bay on the left side of the crag has a deep chimney
in the back and a steep right wall sporting two hollies, the lower one
being by far the larger of the two; the first route is on the left wall.

Bryn Rhedyn 60 feet E3 5c (1993)
Start at the lowest point of the steep left wall of the chimney. Take a
central line up the wall, first past good horizontal wires, then across a
bolder central section. Finish leftwards up a good crack.

★**The Berlin Wall** 60 feet E5 6a (1989)
A slight but serious route which takes the wall immediately right of the
deep chimney. Take a direct line up the wall, occasionally using the
arête as required. The only runner is in the horizontal break at around
20 feet, but there is an easing from around 40 feet to the top.

Holly Cracks 90 feet. Very Difficult (1952)
Start at a crack below and right of the lowest holly.
1 60 feet. Go up cracks on the right of the tree (or the wall on its left)
to a crevasse on the edge to the right, then up a 15-foot glacis and a
short wall to a large ledge below an overhang.
2 30 feet. Go awkwardly up the centre of the wall to the overhang.
Pull up to the crack. Traverse left on a small handhold then go up left
by two hard moves.

Codswallop Flobalobalobalob 45 feet Hard Very Severe 5a
(1985)
Climb the prominent, short, sharp arête over to the left of the central
overhang, and just right of the holly, direct.

Berlin Philamonia 60 feet E1 5c (1989)
Start 15 feet left of the trees below the roof at a block below a steep
slab perched on top of a short wall. From the block lasso the spike at
the top of the short wall, then go directly up, via the rib and slab
above (avoiding the right arête) to a large ledge. Another steep 25
feet straight up the groove leads to the finish.

The Sheepwalk 135 feet Very Difficult (1952)
Start on the main wall facing the road, 10 feet left of a large tree
which protrudes horizontally from under the overhang, at an inverted
corner below a thin vertical crack.
1 40 feet (of climbing). Go up the corner pulling out left. Traverse left
for 10 feet, then up the edge for five feet. Move back right and
ascend a cracked V-groove – concealed hold on the right around the
corner.
2 30 feet. Easily up a crevassed ledge to the base of two cracks.
3 30 feet. Climb the right crack (in the corner) leading to the glacis of
Holly Cracks.
4 35 feet. Climb the steep awkward crack directly above the large
block on the right-hand end of the grass ledge (Severe) or finish up
Holly Cracks.

Watts the Crack   60 feet   E2 6a   (1986)
The thin crack in the wall left of the main overhang gives the
substance of the route, succumbing only to an 'electric' jamming
technique.

Libel, Smears, and Slander   70 feet   E3 5c   (1987)
Much more accomodating than its sister. Start under the large roof, as
for Language... Follow Language, Truth, and Logic to the base of the
layback flake. Bridge over left and ascend the diagonal left-slanting
crack.

Language, Truth, and Logic   70 feet   E4 6b   (1987)
Start below the left-hand tree, under the large roof. Climb up to the
tree and take the right-hand crack to the base of a groove/layback
flake. Take this, exiting left at the top, peg, then move right to enter a
shallow groove leading up to the break. Move right to a
peapod-shaped crack, then traverse left to finish on a perched block.

★★**Marlene on the Wall**   75 feet   E4 6b   (1986)
This takes the right-hand side of the overhang above the prominent
tree. Climb the roof with difficulty and continue up the groove for 15
feet. Traverse 20 feet left to a crack, splitting the wall. Ascend this to
its top then traverse left again, for 15 feet, to finish by a perched
block.

Felix the Crack   40 feet   E1 6a   (1986)
The diagonal crack in the short white wall just above and right of the
large overhang gives a pleasant little problem.

P F Putrid   40 feet   Very Severe 4b   (1986)
The slanting crack just right of 'Felix' is short but pleasant.

A further 60 yards up the Pass sits a small outcrop of short walls and
large blocks which although climbed on in the past, has little to commend
it... a prominent arête here is **The Grim Dower Tower,** Hard Very
Severe.

Bryn Gwynt   OS Ref. 639 565

This crag lies on the skyline some 800 feet directly above the previous
crag. It has three faces which form a sort of pillar. The lower section is
a semi-detached plinth.

Ridge Route   130 feet   Very Difficult   (1978)
A direct line up the centre of the cliff. Start at the toe of the buttress at
a crack. Climb the crack for 30 feet to where it eases. Now take a
groove near the left-hand end of the wall. From the top of this a
pleasant scramble leads up to finish.

Bryn Du   (The Black Hill)

OS Ref. 639 569

This crag lies well above and to the right (east) of Dinas Cromlech at
about 2,250 feet, on the ridge Glyder Fawr sends down to Pen y Pass.
It is the only large crag in the area, its white broken south face being
clearly visible from below the Cromlech. The cliff's right-hand face is
steeper and sterner giving several interesting routes. Best approached
from Pen y Pass, 35 minutes walk, crossing the ridge which runs down
from Glyder Fawr above Cwm Fynnon. This cliff is not as marked on the
Snowdon OS 1:25000 Outdoor Leisure Map.

Ragged Wall   280 feet   Very Difficult   (1952)
This lies on the slabby south face of the crag. A pleasant route,
vegetated at first but steepening and becoming more exposed higher
up. Start at a heather depression, 150 feet from the left-hand end of
the south face.
1 100 feet. Go up the depression on heathery rock to a large heather
ledge on the left.
2 100 feet. Traverse right up the rake to where it ends in a corner.
3 80 feet. Climb over the belay block and down a little groove on the
left. Traverse left across the wall, near the end, head for a sharp
notch on the ridge skyline. A fine open pitch.

The following routes all lie on the steeper east face:

Genesis   230 feet   Very Severe   (1973)
Start at the left-hand end of the face below an obvious steep nose of
clean rock. A cairn marks the start, just left of the crack line.
1 90 feet. Climb the grooved rib left of the crack to a small ledge.
Continue up the corner with difficulty to another small ledge. Step left
onto the overhanging wall and make an awkward move up to better
holds. These lead to a good stance.
2 20 feet. Go easily rightwards up the rake to a stance with a flake

belay below a very steep smooth wall.
3 120 feet. Follow the line rightwards to a short corner which is taken to a small ledge below the smooth section of the wall. Climb the wall just left of another corner with several steep awkward moves. Finish up an obvious recess.

Jeremiah 240 feet Very Severe   (1973)
Start 10 feet left of the prominent crack-line (Jonah). A steep route, but a lot easier than it looks.
1 120 feet. Climb the steep wall to a small ledge. Step right and continue on good but slightly mossy holds just left of the rib. Move left at the top onto a shattered ledge. Traverse right on the ledge to avoid an overhang, then back left onto a good grass stance below a very small overhang split by a crack.
2 120 feet. Easily climb the overhang and follow the slabby crack passing a prominent finger of rock on the left of a steeper smoother section. Climb this at the left-hand end to the top.

Jonah 240 feet Very Severe   (1973)
Approximately in the centre of the cliff, this is a prominent crack-line – continuing in the upper section. Start at the foot of the crack in a small bay.
1 120 feet. Climb the crack, strenuous, to a niche. Move right onto the arête and step back left into the crack above an overhang. Stance and belays on the right.
2 120 feet. Gain the foot of the crack via easy slabs and follow the line to the top of the crag.

Joshua 240 feet Very Severe   (1973)
Twenty feet right of Jonah is another crack-line.
1 120 feet. Climb the crack moving left at the top onto a good ledge with twin cracks continuing steeply. Take the right-hand crack steeply on good holds.
2 120 feet. Easily up broken slabs to finish.

The South Side of the Pass

The Teryn Bluffs

These fine little cliffs lie in the upper part of Cwm Dyli, just below and south of Llyn Teryn. The pipe line from Llyn Llydaw runs between the two hummocks. The nearest, on the Pen y Pass side of the pipes, and easily visible from the PyG Track is Clogwyn Pen Llechen. On the far (south) side is Craig Aderyn, better known for the Teryn Slab. Both crags can be reached in less than 30 minutes from Pen y Pass and are useful for a short day or in bad weather.

Craig Aderyn   (Bird Crag)

OS Ref. 639 543

The main feature of this crag is the fine south-east facing slab which gives five routes.

Subsidiary Slab   180 feet   Moderate
1 85 feet. From the foot of the slab, straightforward moves lead up past a sapling to a good rowan tree and belay.
2 95 feet. Climb up leftwards onto the arête. Follow this pleasantly to belay near the top on a large ledge, or better, on a good spike and small stance 25 feet higher at the tip of the arête. From the tip of the arête, make a slightly descending traverse right for 40 feet to reach the top of a low relief rib. Follow this carefully down and round to the left (facing out) then back right below a short rock wall, with a rowan tree and a spiky stump to a slippery slabby step leading to a short grassy gully and the foot of the crag.

The Arête Climb   170 feet   Difficult
A pleasant and popular route. Start at the extreme right-hand edge of the slab.

1 100 feet. Ascend the right-hand arête and go into a small groove at 10 feet. At 25 feet take the groove left under the overhang, then follow the right arête of the slab past possible stances to a better one on the arête at 100 feet.
2 70 feet. Continue easily up the arête to a good ledge at 45 feet, optional belay. Small stance and spike belay 25 feet higher at the top of the arête. Descend as for Subsidiary Slab.

Jacob's Ladder   120 feet   Very Difficult   (1924)
Artificial in line but good climbing. Start 15 feet left of the right arête. Ascend direct to quartzy holes at 45 feet. Continue up parallel to the arête via a weakness leading to two small scoops then join The Arête Climb. Finish up this.

Via Media   160 feet   Very Severe   (1925)
A very good route up the centre of the slab. Most of the difficulties may be avoided at Severe standard. Start in the centre of the slab below an easy gangway.
1 100 feet. 4b. Follow the gangway up right to its apex at 20 feet, then go straight up to reach a heathery break just left of a small gorse bush at 50 feet. Continue direct for about 35 feet until shallow cracks lead to a small ledge on the left in another 15 feet. Belay.
2 60 feet. Traverse right for a few feet then move up to a leftward-slanting crack. Follow this to good holds and ledges. Spike belay at the top of the arête.

★★**Jacob's Media**   160 feet   Hard Severe
The best outing on the slab, a combination of the previous two routes. A 50 metre rope is necessary unless the team is prepared to climb together for a few feet. Start 15 feet left of the arête and go straight up for about 80 feet (as for Jacob's Ladder). Trend left and follow the left-slanting crack to the apex of the slab (pitch 2 of Via Media).

Treasury Climb   160 feet   Severe   (1924)
Similar climbing to Via Media, but a bit mossy and often greasy. Start on the left immediately right of a mossy patch.
1 100 feet. Follow a sloping ledge up to the left, then over a tiny overlap keeping just right of the mossy patch. At 60 feet, make a rightward traverse to easier climbing just beyond a grassy rake, and so to the Via Media belay ledge.
2 60 feet. Finish as for Via Media or, go steeply up grass then break out left after 20 feet to join Ash Tree rib.

Ash Tree Rib   180 feet   Difficult   (1948)
The broken buttress forming the left boundary of the slab. Start at the foot of the rib.

1 60 feet. Keep on the right up broken rock to a ledge at 30 feet. Continue up to a ledge. Traverse 20 feet left then diagonally back right to a spike belay at the foot of a rock section.
2 60 feet. A short overhanging chimney is climbed awkwardly to a shattered ledge. Traverse 20 feet left then diagonally back right to a spike belay at the foot of a rock section.
3 60 feet. Ascend airily up the arête on good holds, steep, to the top.

Broad Marsh   Vegetably Severe   (1948)
This interesting ramble across the left side of the cliff is possibly the most vegetated climb in North Wales with an amazing variety of plants. From the top of Ash Tree Rib walk left across a broad grassy ledge with fallen columns. After a narrowing, stroll across marsh grass below overhangs to reach a narrow undercut ramp. Make a hard move up onto it, then struggle along left through dense undergrowth to the clutching embrace of ancient stunted oaks, The Coppice. Ascend a mossy 10-foot wall on jugs, then a quick move up a mossy slab leads to grassy scrambling.

Clogwyn Pen Llechen

(Crag of the Slabby Top)   OS Ref. 641 545

This little cliff is the nearest of the Teryn Bluffs to the Miners' Track. It has two faces, one looking south which overhangs and the other looking east which lies back. Unfortunately, both are rather scruffy by modern standards, copious amounts of vegetation growing on many of the ledges, with carpets of moss covering the slabby areas; these receive a lot of drainage and require at least a week of good weather to enable them to dry out. However, when dry, the rock offers good friction and sports mainly incut holds. In contrast, the south-east corner of the cliff provides a classic Very Difficult climb which is quick drying, on good rock and with little vegetation... well worth a visit on a short day or afternoon.

The South Face

Ledge Climb   130 feet   Very Difficult   Very Dirty   (1943)
An awkward and unpleasant climb which accepts the vegetable challenge of the left side of the south face. Start 400 feet left of the south-east corner, in a vague corner 25 feet left of a rowan tree

growing 10 feet up the face, directly below an oak tree, 40 feet higher.

1 90 feet. Gain a ledge at six feet, then go left up a little grassy groove to a second ledge. Traverse awkwardly back right for 30 feet to a 10-foot leaning flaky corner. Climb this and gain the ledge on the right. Step back left and climb a heathery slab to a stance. A pitch with more than a smiggot of loose rock.

2 40 feet. Ascend a short overhanging wall on the left, then move left to a whitened tree stump. Continue in the same direction for a few feet, then finish up over grass ledges.

Little Audrey   200 feet   Very Severe   (1953)
This takes the diagonal gangway running up the left edge of the steep wall, on the right-hand side of the south face. Start 50 yards left of Winthrop Young's Climb.

1 40 feet. Scramble easily up heather to a ledge level with the foot of the gangway. Belay on the right.

2 50 feet. Move awkwardly onto the gangway. Step right, then ascend delicately moving back left to an obvious recess.

3 110 feet. Climb the crack on the right of the gangway to gorse. Traverse left and go up diagonally left with difficulty to finish.

Persons Unknown   150 feet   XS   (4 pts aid)   (1972)
About 100 feet left of Winthrop Young's Climb is a reddish rock scar below a lichenous groove. According to an eye witness, four points of aid at least two of which still remain, were used to force this line by an unknown team.

The South-East Corner

★**Winthrop Young's Climb**   230 feet   Very Difficult   (1913)
The best climb on the cliff. The hard section is very short. Start above a prominent quartz boulder at the south east corner of the cliff, by a short grassy chimney on the left of the rib.

1 40 feet. Take the chimney for 15 feet, then make an awkward step left onto a detached block. A pleasant traverse left along a diagonal crack leads to a stance.

2 70 feet. Cross easy slabs on the left to a large detached block on the skyline.

3 50 feet. Surmount the block and go easily up to a broad terrace.

4 40 feet. From the far end of the terrace, climb a short and strenuous flake crack, (much harder than anything else on the route). Continue up ledges to a belay.

5 30 feet. Finish up the clean rib on the right.

Mick Johnstone on *Left Wall* (E2) Dinas Cromlech. Photo: Glenn Robbins

Nigel Riddington making an early repeat of *Right Wall* (E5) Dinas Cromlech. Photo: Paul Williams

Sean Williams and Rusty Baillie on *Flying Buttress* (V Diff) Dinas Cromlech.
Photo: John Cleare

Viv Smith on the top pitch of *Flying Buttress* (V Diff) Dinas Cromlech.
Photo: Ian Smith

The Grey Rib   200 feet   Difficult   (1915)
This goes up the south-east corner on the left side of the mossy slab.
After the first 80 feet, which are taken on the rib, continue up to a
grassy bay. Escape across to the left via some piled-up stones and
scramble up to finish.

Two Tree Route   200 feet   Difficult   (1948)
A mediocre route with an airy finish and only one remaining tree.
Follow The Grey Rib for 80 feet and continue up to the grassy bay.
Climb a steep groove on the right past a small tree and continue in
the same line to the summit.

The East Face

The routes on this face are described as one meets them on the approach
to the cliff... from RIGHT to LEFT. The clean slab seen in profile from the
Miners' Track divides this face which has steep subsidiary cliffs below
it. The crossing between the foot of the slab and the top of the lower
rocks is awkward and hazardous so that it is probably easier to go right
down to the bottom.

East Ridge   80 feet   Easy
The right arête of the East Face shows signs of having been used from
time immemorial.

Lichen Arête   120 feet   Very Difficult   (1955)
A somewhat artificial route on the extreme right of the East Face. Start
left of and lower down than East Ridge. The line follows mossy slabs,
heather, a short wall and a grooved arête.

Anne Cornwall's Climb   80 feet   Severe   (1972)
This climb takes the centre of the recessed wall at the right-hand end
of the face. The left side of this wall is bordered by a large
corner-crack with a block overhang above. The right side is also
bordered by a short corner-crack. Start at the foot of this. Walk along
the ledge to the left for 15 feet, climb a shallow groove, and step
onto the ledge on the left (possible belays). Go up to the right,
moving right then back left to pass over the bulge. Follow the
left-slanting groove and finish up a little wall.

After Eden   140 feet   Very Severe   (1972)
Steep and strenuous. Towards the right-hand end of the crag is a big
block overhang which caps a right-facing corner-crack, the substance
of the middle pitch. Start from large blocks at the foot of a
leftward-slanting grassy break.
1 60 feet. Scramble up the gully for 20 feet, along the upper ledge to

the right to reach an undercut niche holding a perched block, directly below the big overhang. Using the block, surmount the bulge. Vegetated climbing leftwards leads to the foot of the crack.
2 30 feet. Climb the crack to the overhang and a sitting belay by a perched block.
3 50 feet. Cross the ledge to the right and with a delicate step join the finish of Anne Cornwall's Climb.

Tongue and Groove   215 feet   Hard Severe   (1972)
A good route on sound rock taking the right-hand side of the large central slab. Three starts have been made, that described first being the easiest. Above and right of the large slab there is a spreading oak tree. Start at a suspect flake directly below the tree. There is a large hanging flake 30 feet higher.
1 30 feet. Follow the rock ledge to the left until an awkward move gains a steep little corner. Ascend this and move left to awkward nut belays at the foot of the slab.
2 75 feet. Traverse right to a belay-less ledge. Climb the left-slanting groove until it finishes, then cross the right wall on hollow flakes to ledges and a block below the oak tree.
3 60 feet. From the block stride left onto the slab and follow a line of big holds leftwards to the top. From here escape is possible along the terrace to the right; or via the grassy gully on the left. However, the slab above gives the best finish.
4 50 feet. Climb the slab directly or traverse onto the right arête at mid-height.

Variations
Original Start   80 feet   Very Severe
1a From the belay flake climb directly into a short groove and mantelshelf onto a traverse line. Move left to the belay-less ledge of pitch 2, and continue.

Aboriginal Start   Very Severe
1b The stance at the top of the first pitch can also be reached from the start of Pastoral.

Original Finish
3a Climb up through the tree, past a small rowan to the foot of the upper slab.

Pastoral   180 feet   Hard Severe   (1972)
After a heathery and annoyingly indirect start, the route gets onto good rock and a fine finish. It uses the shallow gully-like feature just left of the central slab, reaching it and finishing by leftward

excursions. At the foot of the crag, left of centre, is a hawthorn with a grassy slope above. Start from the ledges at the top right-hand corner of this slope, at a break below and right of the hanging gully.

1 100 feet. Climb up to a leftward traverse across a long narrow heather ledge (beneath the gully) to reach the rib on the left. Climb this via a steep mantelshelf and go up the slab on the left. Traverse back right into the gully and climb this on good holds to a stance 10 feet short of the steeper rocks. Awkward belays.

2 80 feet. Step left into the corner and go up to a big block. Move round the rib on the left and step across onto a bottomless slab with two small incuts before good holds. Finish direct.

Promises, Promises   240 feet   Very Severe   (1972)
Good climbing, spoiled by the evasion of a direct finish. A large hawthorn stands beneath the foot of the crag with a slab above and left of it. Start from the ledge at the top left of this slab.

1 80 feet. Follow the slanting overlap at the left side of the mossy slab and swing right to pull onto the ledge. Continue up the overlap then traverse the slab on the right and ascend the open corner on wedged blocks. From a little pinnacle move right, pull up onto slabs and continue left to the base of the overhangs. Poor thread.

2 80 feet. Move back down and traverse rightwards. Descend and continue the exposed traverse to a grassy ledge. Move down a small open corner and step across the slab onto the large holds of Pastoral. Go up for 15 feet to a stance. Poor belays.

3 80 feet. Finish as for the top pitch of Pastoral.

Carreg Gwalch   (Crag of the Hawk)

OS Ref. 643 554

These little crags lie just above the PyG Track, about 500 yards from Pen y Pass and have yielded several routes over the years, the best of which are fully described. A few scruffy lines remain for the climber to rediscover.

Cul-de-Sac   100 feet   E1 5b   (c1964)
Nearest the path is a sombre looking crag with a steep front face. The climb takes the prominent damp green flake overhang on its left side. Start below and left in the corner. Climb awkwardly up to the

right, normally damp and dirty. Turn the overhang and finish more
easily up the fine corner crack.

Pyg in the Middle   140 feet   Hard Very Severe   (1964)
An interesting climb across the front of the buttress with an airy finish.
Start below the arête on the left side of the cliff, just right of
Cul-de-Sac.
1 100 feet. 5a. Ascend the arête for 25 feet then traverse right into a
V-scoop. Take the diagonal crack in the back of this rightwards and
around the corner. Continue along the crack, below roofs to a
hanging belay at the top of the slab.
2 40 feet. 5b. Pull out over the roof and finish delightfully up the
crack.

★★**Into the Groove**   60 feet   E4 6c   (1989)
A technically precocious and strenuous little pitch. Start to the right of
the previous routes. Enter the large central V-groove, then move left up
the slab to gain its left arête and a good rest by a prominent block.
Thin tape runner and a peg in a recess. Move right along the obvious
crack, and, having clipped another peg, enter a hanging groove
round to the right. Sustained climbing up the groove/crack lead to a
distinguished finishing move.

On the slabby wall to the left of Cul-de-Sac lies a prominent crack; the
old classic climb – **The Gauge** 60 feet Difficult. Immediately on its right,
the wall offers the somewhat lichenous – **Micrometer** 60 feet Very
Severe 4c. About 100 yards farther up the hillside near the crest of the
ridge is a cliff with a very steep wall on its left and a gentle right-hand
flank.

The Green Beam   90 feet   E2 5c   (1992)
A reasonable route which should clean up with traffic. Start just right
of the large flake, below and left of the finishing crack of Shadow of
Youth. Climb direct past a good runner to a sloping ledge, runners. A
bold sloping section for 20 feet up, then rightwards, leads to the top
crack of Shadow of Youth. Finish up this.

★**Shadow of Youth**   90 feet   E2 5c   (1985)
A stiff proposition taking the diagonal crack in the centre of the wall.
Start below this. Attain the ledge at 10 feet. Go steeply up now via
flakes moving left to a layback flake and small ramp. Continue more
easily to finish via a scoop. Excellent strenuous climbing.

Captain's Bluff Direct   110 feet   Very Difficult   (1925)
The original route of the crags, once popular with Pen y Pass
habitués. The line follows the arête of the buttress. Start at the foot of

this. Climb the arête, steep to start. Continue on improving holds in a delightful position easing towards the top. An alternative start up a groove a few feet round to the left.

Well round to the right of the Cul-de-Sac crag is a large but more broken cliff (OS Ref. 641 553) sitting in its own little cwm. The ancients have scrambled here since at least the 1920s, and probably before that. In fact it is possible to climb almost anywhere at V Diff. One route has been recorded:

Moch Up   150 feet   Very Difficult   (1952)
Start well round to the right, at the top of the scree, level with some large boulders.
1 50 feet. Ascend the slab to a small heather ledge with belays.
2 60 feet. Gain a ledge on the right. Continue right and enter a hollow (possible belay). Move up left, and traverse the sloping ledge leftwards. Climb a small groove to an awkward stance and belay.
3 40 feet. Climb up to the overhang line. Move right along to a jutting ledge where a steep move gains easy ground.

Nearer Pen y Pass, and adjacent to the PyG Track are many traditional problems such as The PyG Track Slab, which one of the old pioneers, Geoffrey Winthrop-Young (who had a wooden leg) could only surmount with a flying (hopping!) start.

Clogwyn Gafr known as Craig Fach

(Goat Crag: Little Crag)   OS Ref. 634 554

Please note: the diagram for this crag appears on pages 316 and 317. This impressive little cliff, until recently much neglected, lies on the 1,200-foot contour line, about one mile west of Pen y Pass Youth Hostel just below the PyG Track. It stands about 100 feet high, its steep walls of rough, sharp rock cut at half-height by a line of black square overhangs which enhance its sombre appearance. Facing north-west, the crag only receives the sun in the afternoons and evenings. The climbs all tend to follow features such as cracks or grooves. Some, which were originally done with aid, now go free, to give reasonably well-protected technical problems – these lie in the steepest central area. On the left-flank of the cliff are short amenable climbs, suitable for beginners, though whether they ever become popular only time will tell.

Ruddy Groove 45 feet Difficult   (1955)
Start at the left-hand side of the cliff, 30 feet left of the huge black
overhang. Climb the delightful groove which has runners in its
cracked red right wall.

Alex in Wonderland 45 feet Severe 4b   (1988)
Pleasant climbing up the blunt rib and cracks to the right of Ruddy
Groove.

Preliminary Groove 45 feet Severe   (1955)
Start 10 feet right of Ruddy Groove. Go up to the bulge at about 15
feet. Make an awkward pull round this, then finish more easily up the
slab.

Mur y Fester 60 feet Severe   (1955)
Start between Preliminary Groove and the groove to the right, below
a smooth wall with twin cracks. Climb directly up the wall via twin
cracks which start 20 feet up.

Staircase Groove 60 feet Very Difficult   (1955)
Start just to the left of the huge overhang, below a groove. Go
pleasantly up the blocky groove on good holds to a steep finish.

The Gangway 80 feet Very Difficult   (1955)
Start 15 feet right of Staircase Groove below the centre of the
hanging flake. Step up, then follow the diagonal ramp leftwards to
finish up Staircase Groove.

★★**Satsuma Special** 100 feet E3 5c   (1992)
A fine route at its standard which should become popular. Follow
Diapason up and through the roof, but move immediately back left on
small positive pockets, until a long stretch hopefully gains a large
pocket on the left; peg on the right. Tricky moves up and a foot
change in the aforementioned pocket lead to yet another stretch left,
to a good spike. Finish up the rib. The route can be split at the
Diapason stance 5c, 5c.

Diapason 100 feet E1   (1964/1983)
An intimidating pitch. Start below the huge black overhang, 15 feet
right of Staircase Groove (as for The Gangway).
1 50 feet. 5c. Climb up to the foot of the corner crack which is
followed to the roof. Cross the six-foot roof with difficulty to gain a
sloping ledge on the wall above. Move up to the right end of the
ledge. Nut and Friend belays.
2 50 feet. 5b. Climb the steep crack past a peg at 12 feet, awkward.
Continue up to a small pocket. Trend delicately and diagonally right

to the steep arête. Move right around this 10 feet from the top to finish up a crack.

★**Outspan** 80 feet E5 6b (1988)

A direct start to Diapason leading up to its final crack. Ascend leftwards to a large pocket/hole, then move up right to a hairline crack and peg runner. A difficult section up the crack leads to better holds and the finish of Diapason.

Hanging Flake Route 90 feet Very Severe 4c (1955)

A pleasant climb which follows the right edge of the huge hanging flake. Unfortunately, the lower section is rather dirty. Start from the top of a flake by a rock spike directly below the right end of the flake. Climb the steep dirty slab and pull round into the crack which bounds the right edge of the hanging flake. Follow this awkwardly to a heathery ledge. Continue up the crack to the top.

Variation
More pleasantly, start 10 feet farther right and climb a cracked red wall to a heather ledge, then traverse left to reach the crack.

★★**Satsumo Wrestler** 110 feet E6 6b (1987)

A fearsome outing which utilises the obvious gap between Hanging Flake Route and The Nectarine Run... a fitting companion to the latter. Start left of The Nectarine Run below a crack and climb it to a grassy ledge. Bridge up the groove above and enter the crack, exiting right onto a ramp, crux. Rest! Exit up a crack by bold and tenuous moves to reach another rest and poor wire. Move left and continue up, sustained and serious, to finish.

★★★**The Nectarine Run** 120 feet E5 6b (1986)

Hard, technical climbing up the wall, groove and roof left of the left-facing corner in the centre of the crag. Start just left of the corner and climb the lower wall to a RURP, just below the short hanging groove. Layback into this from the right and ascend with difficulty, exiting left past a peg. Make committing moves back down and right to a foothold just above the lip of the roof. A scary high step and rockover up the wall above gains easier ground, a flake and a good Friend placement just above. Finish direct.

★★**Sacred Idol** 100 feet E3 6a (1966/1984)

A fine pitch which gives thin technical climbing up the left-facing square-cut corner in the centre of the crag – the old aid route Pi. Start below the Corner. Free-climb precariously up the white right-angled corner past three *in situ* peg runners – very sustained, very good.

★★ **Pulsar** 100 feet E3 6a (1974/1983)

Once an A3 peg route, this crack is now a superb jamming
test-piece. Start eight feet right of Sacred Idol at a thin vertical crack.
Ascend to the overhang where the crack becomes difficult. Continue
up, the crack proving more stubborn than it looks, to a ledge at about
70 feet. Traverse right a few feet and finish direct – excellent!

★ **Red Giant** 80 feet E4 6b (1988)

A stiff pitch which takes the wall right of Pulsar before crossing it to
tackle the obvious direct finish. Start up the crack on the right then
move left on the obvious holds. Step up to gain the crack which is
followed on user-friendly holds to a junction with Pulsar. Finish fiercely
up the headwall past one ancient, and two newish, peg runners.

The Slash 100 feet E1 5b (1957/1983)

Yet another aid route that has gone free. The easiest extreme on the
crag. Start 15 feet right of Pulsar and climb the obvious chimney to a
ledge. (The original start came up from the left). At the back of the
ledge on the left is a thin corner crack. Climb this to a small roof and
move left, hard, to another ledge. Continue up the wall above
trending slightly left to finish.

Clingstone 100 feet E3 6b (1988)

The difficulties are short but sharp. Climb the first thin overhanging
crackline right of The Slash... difficult moves up the brown bulge lead
to easier climbing.

★ **Buck and the Noise Boys** 100 feet E2 5c (1988)

An amenable route starting under large flakes, 20 feet right of The
Slash. Climb the flakes to reach a steep wall with a flat-bottomed
crack. Follow this to a ramp, then step left and finish up the pocketed
wall and slabs above.

The Last Outpost 75 feet Very Severe 4b (1975)

A slight and somewhat broken route. Start 20 yards right of Pulsar at
the foot of a steep slab. Easy climbing up the slab leads to a tree and
a grassy ledge. From the left end of the ledge step up onto a large
block. Good jams up the steep crack on the right quickly lead to the
top.

The Craig Fach Girdle 315 feet E3/A3 (1967)

A sustained expedition yet to go free. Start at the left-hand base of the
cliff.

1 70 feet. 4b. Make an ascending rightward traverse to a stance on
Preliminary Groove.

2 45 feet. A1/5c. Move right a few feet and descend slightly.
Continue right to join Diapason (A1). Follow the roof of Diapason,

free, and so to the stance at the end of its first pitch.

3 50 feet. 5b. Make a hard move right and hand-traverse the horizontal crack to the arête. Climb this and the crack of Hanging Flake Route to its top.

4 70 feet. 5a/A3. Stride right to a peg. Move right and downwards to a flake with a peg. Tension right and down for 15 feet to reach a thin traverse line with difficulty. At head level there is a very thin crack formed by a rock overlap. Using thin blades in the crack for fingerholds, and tension from the rope, traverse right to a hanging belay on Sacred Idol.

5 40 feet. 6a. Free climb Sacred Idol to the top of its overhanging section, and an awkward stance.

6 40 feet. 5a. Traverse right along the obvious line then go up to gain the arête. Finish up this. The climb is described in its most free form to date. A completely clean ascent will prove very hard indeed.

Craig Cwm Beudy Mawr

(Crag of the Cwm of the Big Cowshed)

OS Ref. 628 556

This crag is situated on the north-east slope of Crib Goch, high up in the left-hand corner of the cwm. It is most easily approached from Pen y Pass along the PyG Track. After about one mile, just beyond a long flight of steps where the path turns left to cross Bwlch Moch, contour across the hillside for about a quarter of a mile to a small cwm with a broken rib of quartz-marked rock which is Ysgar – The Quartz Rib, a fine 200 foot Moderate. Either, climb this, scramble up for a further 80 feet and traverse round to the upper left side of the crag; or move across at a lower level to a point below it. Alternatively, one can make an excellent day by visiting Dinas Bach first, the Crag of the Cwm, finishing with a pleasant walk to Crib Goch – sadly this itinerary no longer seems very popular. Bounded on the right by a deep wet gully, the cliff rises from right to left parallel to the scree slope, a long tapering mass of rock which loses itself in the hillside on the eastern side. It is about 250 feet high. In the central part the rock is quite clean and solid, but it becomes more broken on either side. The main features are a series of overhangs on the left with a smooth slab on their right. Lower down the hillside is the gently rising V-shaped Dodo Gully which steepens higher up. There is a stream running down it. To its right lie two large broken buttresses, Dodo Buttress and Minor Buttress. Between these is a large expanse of heather and broken rock.

Minor Buttress   180 feet   Moderate
On the extreme right of the cliff, a slabby buttress on the left of a watery gully gives a pleasant enough route. Start at the left edge of the buttress and follow the rib overlooking the gully as closely as possible.

Dodo Buttress   270 feet   Difficult
A pleasant route up the broken buttress right of Dodo Gully, reminiscent of the climbs on the East Face of Tryfan. Start where the buttress meets the scree, a few feet below the gully.
1 50 feet. A short wall leads to a grassy slab. Climb this to a large grassy stance below an overhanging wall.
2 60 feet. Climb the short slab on the left to a ledge at 20 feet. Ascend the rib steeply for a few feet. A small wall at 50 feet leads to a stance below a prominent nose.
3 40 feet. Go round the right of the nose to a grassy ledge.
4 70 feet. Cross heather to the next rock rib. Climb this keeping left.
5 50 feet. Go slightly left over perched blocks into a shallow groove. Good holds abound, and the angle soon eases.

Dodo Gully   250 feet   Difficult   (1909)
A traditional expedition with a good water supply. Keep to the bed of the gully and take the right-hand branch.

Slab Variant   180 feet   Very Difficult   (1910)
At the top of the initial scrambling section of Dodo Gully, move left to grassy ledges below the prominent overhanging corner. Follow the steep grassy crack up the left side of the steep slab on the right, then traverse right on grass into the left-hand branch of the gully. The gully is dirty at first but gives a fine airy finish.

Phoenix Buttress   260 feet   Very Severe   (1925)
Higher up the hillside from Dodo Gully is a large prominent slab with a smooth overhung corner on its right. This route climbs the grassy breaks left of the slab, finishing up a steep arête on the upper buttress. Interesting climbing with a short desperate section when wet. Start about 120 feet up the scree from Dodo Gully at a grassy break.
1 80 feet. Scramble easily up heather and rock to a small grassy platform and twin spike belay at the foot of the slab, or better; take the first pitch of Mortuary Slab to the same spot (4b).
2 45 feet. Move left across the foot of the slab to reach the grassy break on the left. Follow this to a small stance below a slabby groove.

3 60 feet. 4b. The slabby groove is the only break. Awkward when dry, it is a little horror when wet. Belay on the large grass terrace above.
4 50 feet. Move left and climb the steep arête on good holds; care is needed in handling a couple of hollow spikes.
5 25 feet. 4b. A short, tricky, mottled wall provides the final obstacle.

Mortuary Slab   300 feet   Very Severe   (1955)
An entertaining route through the slabs and overhangs on the right of Phoenix Buttress. Start as for Phoenix Buttress, 120 feet up the scree from Dodo Gully.
1 80 feet. 4b. Climb the steep shallow groove and go diagonally right along a slabby ramp to a grassy platform and twin spike belay.
2 80 feet. 4b. Take the left edge of the prominent slab overlooking the grassy break of Phoenix Buttress to reach a diagonal grassy break. Follow this rightwards, then step down onto the slab again and make a semi hand-traverse across to the top of the corner. Belay on a vegetated ledge.
3 80 feet. 4b. Climb the next slab trending back left to easy slabs.
4 60 feet. 4a. From a pinnacle, trend left up a gangway then go back right to the arête and climb easily to the top.

Direct Finish
2a 150 feet. 4c. Follow the left edge of the slab. Instead of traversing right, continue up the slabs in a direct line to the top.

The Ashes Route   220 feet   Severe   (1948)
A pleasant but slight route which works up through the overhangs to the left of the two previous routes. Start 80 feet farther up the scree from Mortuary Slab at a little green gully, the first break on the left of some steep walls.
1 50 feet. Climb the gully for 30 feet. Traverse right along the top of a massive perched block to a deep recess on the other side.
2 30 feet. Climb the right-hand side of the recess and go up the steep crack on the right to the top of a block. Climb easily to join Phoenix Buttress on the large grassy terrace.
3 70 feet. Climb easily up the dirty groove on the right to a pinnacle.
4 70 feet. From the top of the pinnacle, take the short crack on the right to a slab. Move left under steep walls to join the last pitch of Phoenix Buttress.

Burnt Out Buttress   185 feet   Very Difficult   (1955)
A tricky exercise on poor rock and steep grass. Start at the lowest point of a broken-looking buttress left of an unpleasant-looking gully some way up the scree from The Ashes Route.

1 30 feet. Climb the short steep wall at the foot with curious white markings, to heather and a steep chimney.

2 35 feet. Climb the chimney to heather and a spike belay. Loose and interesting.

3 70 feet. Move right behind a large pinnacle and go up until it is possible to traverse out over the gully. Climb into the bed of the gully on very doubtful rock, and pull up to grass over detached spikes; or traverse right into the other branch of the gully, over steep grass (both are exposed). Easily up the gully to a grassy stance.

4 50 feet. Pleasant slabs.

Clinker 160 feet Hard Severe (1955)

Much farther up the scree from Burnt Out Buttress is a large rounded pinnacle (best seen from left of the crag). About 80 feet left of this is a light-coloured slab, surmounted by a grass rake and a reddish, subsidiary slab. Start in the middle of the slab.

1 35 feet. Climb the slab bearing left until a corner chimney leads to a grassy ledge; or go directly up the slab.

2 45 feet. Traverse right over a little slab into a corner crack forming a pinnacle. Climb this to a stance and belay on the pinnacle.

3 80 feet. Traverse right over easy slabs, round a corner and up a difficult crack.

Craig Beudy Bach

(Crag of the Little Cowshed) OS Ref. 631 558

This is the small clean easy-angled crag midway between Dinas Bach and Craig Cwm Beudy Mawr. It has one worthwhile route which gives a pleasant way into the upper cwm.

Yellow Scoop 210 feet Very Severe (1979)

After the initial scoop and the short wall the climbing is about Difficult. Start in the centre of the crag at the foot of a scoop.

1 90 feet. 4c. Friction up the unprotected scoop (which is often greasy) via two good pockets, then scramble up for 40 feet to belay.

2 20 feet. A 20-foot section of steep rocks leads more easily to the foot of the upper area.

3 100 feet. Climb up clean pocketed rock past spikes and tiny ledges keeping as near to the nose as possible. A delightful pitch.

North Face of Crib Goch   OS Ref. 625 553

Below the summit of Crib Goch, the tall clean Crib Goch Buttress rises for 250 feet from the scree slope of the upper cwm (Cwm Uchaf Cwm Glas). It is a pleasant little climbing ground well-known for Reade's Route. The crag is well-positioned, with spectacular views across the Glyders and routes finishing on one of the finest summits in Wales. A visit here may be combined with a trip round the Snowdon Horseshoe to give an enjoyable mountain day. To the right of Crib Goch Buttress lies Crazy Pinnacle Gully with the broken buttress of Crazy Pinnacle next to it. This is flanked on the right by Western Gully, an Easy scramble either up or down – the short chimney near the top is best taken on the left.

Route III   290 feet   Very Difficult   (1946)
A mediocre route on poor rock. Start at the foot of a rib left of Reade's Route, and at a much lower level.
1 100 feet. Ascend the easy rib.
2 75 feet. An easy diagonal line leads up left for 30 feet, then keep left till a move onto a tricky slab. Go up right to belay.
3 40 feet. Climb the rib on the left above the ledge, then cross into a grassy corner.
4 75 feet. Ascend a steep wall on the right for 15 feet then traverse out on the wall for a few feet. Climb the slab above to a grassy recess. Surmount the large capstone and finish easily out to the right.

Route II   325 feet   Hard Severe   (1946)
A parallel line to Reade's Route. Start as for Route III.
1 100 feet. Scramble up the rib to steeper rocks.
2 40 feet. Continue in the same line to an overhanging wall.
3 90 feet. Avoid the bulge by a move round to the right. Climb a crack and a short wall on the left then step onto a slab above the overhang. Go steeply up the slab, then diagonally up right to a stance close to the pinnacle of Reade's Route.
4 45 feet. Climb the slab on the left to a good ledge.
5 50 feet. Step out to the right then go straight up almost parallel to the last pitch of Reade's Route. Move left near the top to finish.

★Reade's Route   220 feet   Very Difficult   (1908)
A classic outing. The stride across from the top of the pinnacle is quite memorable. Start immediately left of Crazy Pinnacle Gully and scramble up broken slabby ground until it steepens. Belay on a stance overlooking the gully.

1 100 feet. Climb easily up the rib past numerous ledges to a large platform below a steep wall. An easy rake leads into the left-hand branch of the gully.
2 20 feet. Ascend the wall with a difficult move on the left and go up to a stance at the foot of a large pinnacle.
3 50 feet. Climb the pinnacle and stride across to a crack in the wall, crux. Ascend the crack to the top of another pinnacle.
4 50 feet. Finish up the rib by a shallow groove.

Reid's Route   80 feet   E1 5a   (1983)
A rather artificial climb up the blank wall right of Reade's Route. Start as for Reade's Route to the first pinnacle, then make an easy traverse right into the gully, at the base of the wall. Climb the middle of the wall with a hard move to gain a pocket on the left. Go up to a horizontal break, then continue diagonally right to reach good holds on the arête. Climb this to another break. Trend up rightwards to the top.

Crazy Pinnacle Gully   180 feet   Moderate   (1887)
Scramble easily up the bed of the gully for 100 feet to where it divides. Take either branch, the left-hand one giving an interesting cave pitch. The rib up the centre of the gully may also be climbed.

Crazy Pinnacle Face   100 feet   Difficult   (1894)
Scramble up for 100 feet to a grassy nook and belays. Ascend to the summit of a minor pinnacle on the left then continue straight up for 50 feet to finish.

Dinas Bach   (Little Fortress)

OS Ref. 632 560

Five hundred yards on the Pen y Pass side of Dinas Mot and 300 feet above the road, this little cliff with its excellent rock gives a few pleasant routes and three hard short pitches. The east wing is clean and steep, with a noticeable flake, Flake Chimney, rising from the lowest point. The west wing is separated from the east by a large grassy gully and is characterised by a smooth slab rising like a house roof above the line of overhangs. The large flake of the east wing forms two chimneys, a short one on the left and a larger one which faces west.

★**The Boys of Summer** 50 feet E4 6b   (1985)
Short but serious! Climb an incipient crack just left of the right arête of
the flake. Continue boldly up the wall to a sloping finish.

Felony 60 feet E5 6b   (1984)
The large peg originally in place has been replaced by a poorer one
so as not to facilitate it as a foothold and the pitch is now finished
direct. Climb a crack in the centre of the flake and continue with
difficulty to a peg runner. Either make a desperate move right to
better holds (E4) or go straight up with even more difficulty.

Body Rock 50 feet E4 6c   (1985)
The left arête of the flake. If you like a hard well-protected problem;
then this is for you. Start at the foot of a small flake just left of Felony.
Climb the flake to a junction with Felony, protection. Step left and
make a desperate move up and left to a jug. Continue for 15 feet to a
ledge on the pinnacle on the left.

Flake Chimney 100 feet Difficult   (1925)
The route takes the long chimney and then the buttress above.
1 50 feet. Ascend the flake, which is similar to Monolith Crack.
2 50 feet. Step across onto the wall and move right to a good ledge.
Finish up the steep crack on the right. The face of the large flake has
been put 'under the microscope' to produce three boulder problem
type routes which are described from right to left.

Right of Flake Chimney is a slabby wall split by three large cracks. This
is Mortlock's Slab.

Route 1 100 feet Very Severe 4c
The left-hand crack, which unfortunately takes some drainage. From
just right of Flake Chimney ascend and move right at 20 feet. Follow
the flaky crack past a grassy central section, tedious, to a cleaner
finish. (Also known as Mortlock's Slab).

Route 2 100 feet Very Severe 4c
The central crack. Start 10 feet right of Route 1. Climb the flake crack
on good holds to join a crack on the right at 60 feet. Finish up twin
cracks – a grim struggle with grass and heather.

Route 3 100 feet Hard Very Severe 5c
Start 10 feet left of the holly and climb a thin crack to a ledge at 15
feet. Move eight feet left and go up the crack to join Route 2 at 60
feet. Finish as for Route 2.

Route 4 90 feet E1 5b
The right-hand crack keeps coming at you. Start just left of the holly.

Climb the crack, awkward at first, then continue up with good protection. At 70 feet, step right to finish up the heathery crack.

Freefallin'   90 feet   E3 5c   (1992)
Start at a holly tree, just up and right from the start of Route 4. Boulder out the shallow groove above the holly – bold. Step right to get the first protection, a chockstone behind the large layback flake. Continue by either laybacking the flake, or by face climbing slightly to the left of it. Ascend to a ledge. Climb up and around the arête to finish via a crack.

The Play-away Flake   85 feet   E1 5c   (1992)
Start a few yards left of Flake Traverse. Climb the right-hand side of the arête to a small horizontal slot. Swing round leftwards to an undercut flake. Continue up the groove above and an 'excellent layback flake'. Delicate and insecure moves up this gain a continuation groove which gives a pleasant finish.

Ash Tree Gully   60 feet   Difficult
Immediately right of Mortlock's Slab a wooded gully rises up from a holly at its base. Climb up via two pleasant flakes then bushwhack and scramble up to finish.

★★**Flake Traverse**   85 feet   Difficult   (1931)
Right of Ash Tree Gully, this is an obvious line of well-scratched flakes up the left wall of the wide central gully. The difficulty can be varied and some care is needed with the rock.

The following climbs lie on the west wing:

Slanting Buttress   140 feet   Very Severe   (1955)
This takes the vegetated buttress which slopes diagonally left of the slab of Crack and Slab. Rather artificial, but adds yet another avenue for masochistic pioneers. Start from the foot of the buttress by scrambling over loose blocks to a grassy platform.
1 40 feet. Ascend easily over rock and heather to a large block. Go left to a light-coloured slab leading to trees.
2 35 feet. Climb the undercut chimney on the right with difficulty to a bilberry ledge.
3 45 feet. Go left over blocks to a layback crack leading to a large ledge and pinnacle belay.
4 20 feet. Climb the rib to the top.

Crack and Slab   135 feet   Severe   (1925)
Start 15 feet left of the wall.
1 60 feet. A series of reddish-coloured ledges lead to a deep crack which is hard but short. It leads to The Annexe.

2 45 feet. Walk up left and climb a fault in the upper wall. Continue to a higher ledge.
3 30 feet. Step round the corner on to the edge of the slab. The right edge provides a difficult finish, or the centre is easier. Scramble up to finish.

Variation
Wall and Traverse Finish   175 feet   Severe   (1925)
2a 60 feet. Walk to the left for 20 feet to an obvious traverse line below the overhangs. A balustrade of large blocks leads to a stance on the left.
3a 30 feet. Follow a grassy rake left to a leaning bollard.
4a 35 feet. Swing across into a groove on the right and go up this for a few feet until it is possible to break out onto the edge. This is the left edge of the roof slab. Follow the edge to a good stance and belay.
5a 50 feet. Traverse back right easily. Above and left of The Annexe is an obvious stone spike. The roof 15 feet left of this gives a 5a problem.

Wall Direct   185 feet   Difficult
An interesting training climb – there are many variations, but this is the best. Start on the right side of the west wing above the wall.
1 65 feet. Climb the steep wall on good holds to a perched block. Ascend a mossy groove in the same line to The Annexe.
2 120 feet. From the back of the grassy area of The Annexe, climb direct via a mantelshelf, a crack and an arête.

Below the crag and only a little way above the road is a small buttress with a stone wall abutting its base. A large 'surfboard' block can be found on the right.

Cut Back Crack   50 feet   Severe   (1993)
Start directly above the stone wall, once past a slimy start the deep jamming crack provides some interest, with one precarious move near the top.

Going Over The Falls   50 feet   Very Severe 4c   (1993)
Takes the obvious flake crack on the right, which gives an entertaining pitch on perfect rock. Layback up to a break, then keep powering up to the top, which eases all the time.

Totally Tubular   50 feet   Difficult   (1993)
The surprisingly easy chimney on the right is partially obscured by a tree.

Midway between Dinas Bach and Dinas Mot is a small crag comprised of jumbled boulders and grassy ledges with a prominent twin spiked overhang at its left edge. In the centre of the crag is a large triangle of grass. Above its apex rises an obvious flake crack, the substance of Dracula Spectacula, the first route starts about 150 feet left of Dracula...

Salem's Slab   60 feet   E1 5a   (1993)
Start at the base of a slender slab, which has a perched block at its top, just right of a wide crack. Step up and right to reach a thread and climb directly up the slab via a couple of juggy breaks to a final, bold, move to finish at the perched block.

★**Dracula Spectacula**   50 feet   E1 5b   (1983)
A worthwhile little pitch in the esoteric vein. Start by scrambling up to the foot of the flake, the bottom few feet of which are green and grassy. Avoid the green section by climbing jammed blocks on the left for 15 feet. Use the left-hand corner to gain the crack (crux), then rapidly layback the 'batwing-shaped' flake to the top.

The Bat Passage   50 feet   Very Severe 5a   (1987)
Start left of Dracula Spectacula and either chimney or bridge the crack using the pillar to the left of that route; or, boldly layback the crack and continue to the top – good protection prevents one from becoming a 'bat-dropping'.

★**Vlad the Arête**   25 feet   E4 7a   (1988)
A mortifying, microscopic morsel for those of a technical bent. The arête left of Dracula Spectacula sports two peg runners. Frustrating on first acquaintance... only 'Rock-Jedi' will succeed.

Dinas Mot   (Fortress of the Giant Mot)

OS Ref. 627 563

Dinas Mot forms the gable end of the north ridge of Crib Goch and it dominates the south side of the valley when seen from almost any direction. It is around 400 feet high and about a quarter of a mile wide, yet is easily reached from the Pont y Cromlech car park in 15 minutes. The cliff has three main facets, the most dominant being the detached buttress of The Nose – the huge triangular slab at its centre. Above this broken rocks arbitrarily divide the main cliff into the Eastern and Western Wings. The Eastern Wing, although bristling with overhangs, has no modern desperates on it – as yet. Routes generally weave their way up through intimidating territory at a relatively modest standard with good protection when needed. This is in marked contrast to the smooth open slab routes on The Nose which has the occasional long poorly-protected run-out. On the two-tiered Western Wing, routes tend to follow devious lines which are difficult to identify on first acquaintance, and there is more vegetation. Farther right, beyond the narrow Groper Buttress, sits Plexus Buttress with its superb climbing on rough compact rock. Western Gully provides the easiest descent from the top of The Nose. For The Eastern Wing the best descent is via a shallow gully and broken rocks, left (east) of Staircase Gully. The normal way down from the top of The Western Wing is via Jammed Boulder Gully, but this needs care.

The Eastern Wing

The Eastern Wing is bounded by Staircase Gully on the left and by Eastern Gully and the steep broken arête above The Nose on the right. Beside the upper part of Staircase Gully is a tower-like buttress split by a groove in its upper half (pitch 2 of The Toad). This tower is well-defined on its right by the sloping slab of The Mole. Right of The Mole, the cliff becomes much longer extending down to the level of Eastern Gully and is divided by an obvious grassy rake which slants up right, Troglodyte Wall. Below the rake are steep mossy walls, and above it, large overhangs and grassy ledges. The structure of the cliff is such that route-finding can be very complicated. Most climbs have been drastically transformed from their original vegetated state, but grassy ledges and lichenous rock are still encountered. This detracts little from the quality of climbing and amplifies the cliff's impressive atmosphere. The following two routes are not on The East Wing proper but lie on a small wall just to its left. It is in fact the retaining wall of the descent gully.

Honky Tonk Corner   120 feet   Severe   (1971)
Interesting but rather dirty. The first prominent feature when coming down the descent gully is a corner on the left. Start directly beneath the corner.
1 90 feet. Climb the corner to a ledge on the right. Possible belay. Step left and continue in the same line as the corner passing an overhang on the left to belay below an overhanging chimney.
2 30 feet. Climb the overhanging chimney.

Tarotplane   140 feet   Very Severe (1 pt. aid)   (1971)
Start a few feet down the gully from Honky Tonk corner at the base of a rib beneath a fine-looking flake crack which leads to the ledge on the right 60 feet up Honky Tonk Corner.
1 80 feet. 4c. Climb delicately up the rib to the foot of an

overhanging groove. Climb the groove (sling for aid) until it is possible to layback into the flake crack above. Follow this to the ledge 60 feet up Honky Tonk Corner.

2 60 feet 4c. Above the ledge is a white tree. Starting from the right climb a leftward-slanting crack to the tree. Climb the groove behind the tree to a horizontal crack leading to the arête on the left. Layback up this and step left into the short groove above the overhang.

Staircase Gully   330 feet   Moderate
A normally damp gully climb which defines the easterly limit of the cliff proper. The fairly sound rock gives an interesting scramble for 150 feet. The gully now steepens to a 20-foot crux wall 80 feet higher, then eases off to finish.

★The Toad   200 feet   E3   (1963)
A serious and technical route on good rock in a fine position. It is up the tower-like buttress just right of Staircase Gully. The peg runner which used to protect the crux has long since gone making this a bold lead as nut protection only exists way down to the right. Start from a small bay in the gully (above the start of The Mole), below a short pocketed wall which leads to a large grassy ledge at the foot of the steep tower.

1 40 feet. 4a. Pleasantly climb the pocketed wall to the grassy ledge on the right.

2 80 feet. 6a. Follow the horizontal crack right to join the short rib of The Mole. Climb this and move left to a badly corroded peg. Continue left to surmount the overhang. Go easily up slabs now to belay by a flake.

3 80 feet. 5b. Climb the shallow groove on the left, soon easing, then finish up short easy walls on the left.

★M P P   200 feet   Hard Very Severe   (1964)
A good climb which starts up The Toad and the crux rib of The Mole. The crux traverse is delightfully exposed and quite bold for its grade. Start in the gully as for The Toad.

1 40 feet. 4a. As for The Toad pitch 1.

2 90 feet. 5a. Climb the horizontal crack to the rib of The Mole. Follow The Mole to a good thread runner in the corner. Hand-traverse sensationally out leftwards, around the arête where a thought provoking move gains a tiny ledge and peg runner. Traverse left again to meet the easy part of The Toad above its overhangs (care should be taken to ease rope drag on this section). Scramble up to the flake belay as for The Toad pitch 2.

3 70 feet. 4c. Move right to the arête, then take the left-slanting crack-line over some bulges to a small ledge. Finish up a short wall.

★★The Mole   275 feet   Hard Very Severe   (1961)
A justifiably popular route on superb rock; often wet and tricky. The
steep tower taken by The Toad has a prominent line of undercut slabs
running up underneath it from left to right. These give the substance of
the route. Start in the gully above the grassy rake of Troglodyte Wall.
1 90 feet. 4a. A small grassy rake leads to a short steep slab. Climb
this to a grassy bay just right of a huge flake.
2 110 feet. 5a. Ascend the huge flake and walk left to a steep rib.
Climb this (crux) and move right to the diagonal slab, thread runner
up in the corner. Move right to the slab edge and go up a corner.
Traverse right below the overhang and go up a short groove to a
ledge and belays.
3 75 feet. 4c. Move into the groove on the left and follow it until an
obvious traverse right to ledges leads to a finish up easier rock – a
pitch which is often wet.

Troglodyte Wall   300 feet   Very Severe   (1955)
Disappointing. The easiest line up The Eastern Wing provides good
views of other routes but has little else to commend it. It follows the
narrow grassy rake winding out of Staircase Gully and crosses Beorn
at the prominent L-shaped block seen on the skyline from the foot of
the crag. Above this it breaks back left to finish near the top of Beorn.

Tales from the Riverbank   240 feet   E3   (1989)
Surprisingly good. Sustained and technical climbing up an impressive
part of the cliff. Start a few feet left of Gollum/The Molehill at a thin
crack leading to a groove, just left of the Molehill groove.
1 80 feet. 6a. Climb the crack and step slightly right to gain a sharp
downward pointing spike below the roof. Layback leftwards to enter
the groove. Move up on the right wall to climb a small groove and
pillar above. Belay on the large ledge.
2 40 feet. 5b. Move left and layback up to gain a small niche. Exit
awkwardly left to reach The Mole belay.
3 60 feet. 5c. Pull directly up the rib on the left and continue right to
the traverse on The Mole. Follow the right-leaning groove above after
a worrying start. Continue to a good handhold then move up
diagonally rightwards to the good thread on The Mole.
4 60 feet. 5c. A very deceptive pitch. Follow the traverse of M P P to
the arête, moving right and climbing the groove direct to a
sensational pull out rightwards. Trend back left over easy ground to
belay on the large thread of The Toad's top pitch.

★The Molehill   310 feet   E3   (1968/1977)
An impressive route up some very steep rock. Technical and bold.
Start as for Gollum.
1 120 feet. 6a. From the belay bold moves lead fiercely up into a

short groove. Climb this and the small easy slab to a flaked wall which funnels into a groove leading to small trees. Trend left up easier rock to belay at the top of The Mole pitch 1.

2 80 feet. 5c. (Mole Direct). Go up the slab into the corner. Boldly negotiate two roofs by agonising bridging, all very technical, then continue via a bulging crack to an awkward exit. Continue up to a stance about 15 feet below the top of The Mole pitch 2. Nut belays.

3 110 feet. 5a. Traverse left along the obvious line of slaty holds, then move up left to blocks on the arête. Climb the arête and eventually finish up the final crack of M P P.

Variations

Molehill Direct Finish   70 feet   E3 5c   (1980)

3a The poorly-protected arête immediately left of The Mole proves to be a serious soul-searching lead.

3b Instead of traversing left under the overhangs to belay near the top of The Mole pitch 2, continue up to the second stance on that route. It is now possible and easier (4c) to traverse left, around the arête (of the Direct Finish) to join M P P and the normal finish.

★**Gollum**   300 feet   Hard Very Severe   (1964)

A fine route with a spectacular overhang on its third pitch which more than compensates for the grassy terrace on its second pitch. The climb takes a shallow groove up the lower walls and the slabby groove under the overhangs of The Mole. Start from a grassy pedestal right of the gully.

1 40 feet. 5a. Go diagonally right up and over a bulge, peg runner. Move slightly left to a stance and belay.

2 60 feet. 4b. Traverse right and climb the clean flake crack to a tree belay on the rake of Troglodyte Wall. Stroll 50 feet left to The Mole pitch 1 belay.

3 110 feet. 5a. Climb the slab diagonally right for 30 feet. Muscle up the overhang on good holds in a sensational position, peg runner. Climb a shallow groove then move left and go up to The Mole pitch 2 belay.

4 90 feet. 4b. Traverse right across a slab to an enjoyable finish up the juggy arête.

★★**A New Austerlitz**   330 feet   E2   (1982)

An excellent route, high in its grade. Sustained and interesting moves in impressive surroundings. Start just left of, and below the huge perched block of Gandalf at a wide shallow groove in a slab.

1 70 feet. 5b. Climb the groove or the crack to its left into a dirty niche, just left of the huge block. Bridge up its left-hand side by a huge protruding spike and pull boldly over the bulge onto a short

Dinas Mot

The Eastern Wing

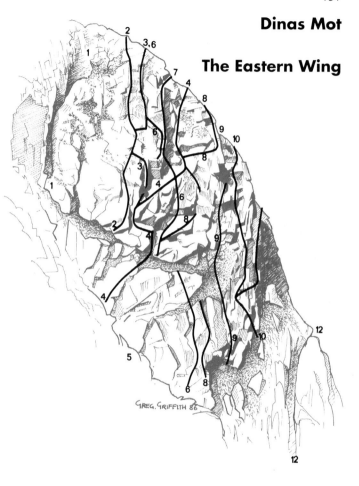

GREG. GRIFFITH 86

1. Staircase Gully	M	7. Direct Finish	E3
2. The Toad	E3	8. Gollum	HVS
3. M P P	HVS	9. Gandalf	E1
4. The Mole	HVS	10. Beorn	E1
5. Troglodyte Wall	VS	11. Mordor	E3
6. The Molehill	E3	12. Eastern Gully	D

slab. Belay at the base of the flake on Gollum pitch

2 60 feet. 5b. Step right round the corner onto a slab. Climb a thin crack to its end and continue direct up the edge of the slab to easy ground. Walk 40 feet left to belay on the right-hand side of the Mole/Gollum flake.

3 110 feet. 5c. Starting five feet right of the flake, pull over the initial roof at a slim groove to gain good holds. Pull up to the next roof and traverse right to a groove at its right-hand end. Climb this to the tapes of Gollum. Step right and surmount the overhang on massive holds to a resting place on a big flat-topped block. Ascend directly up the slab on small hidden holds. Take the short groove above and exit to a grassy ledge. Nut and Friend belays.

4 90 feet. 4b. Move out right along the lip of the roof to finish up the flying arête (as for Gollum pitch 4).

★**Gandalf**   340 feet   E1   (1966)

An excellent climb in the Beorn mould with an intimidating first pitch. Scramble (or rope) up grassy corners to a good flake belay a few feet right of the cave formed by the large overhang.

1 120 feet. 5a. Move left into the recess below the overhang and climb up onto the large protruding block. Step right round a spike, then turn the roof on its right-hand side to good holds. Follow the flaky crack and move left to finish on a grassy ledge. Good holly tree belay 10 feet higher in a grassy bay.

2 130 feet. 5a. Climb the small rib on the right to a ledge. Go diagonally left and pull up into a small corner, good Friend in a horizontal break. Climb diagonally rightwards for 10 feet to a peg runner. Stride left to a ledge. Pull up and step right. Slant up rightwards making for the left end of a diagonal band of overhangs. Pass these on the left, then step right immediately onto the slab. Climb this for six feet then step left and go up into a corner below the uppermost of two large overhangs. Traverse left along the lip of the lower overhang and swing round the arête to belay in a corner (on Gollum).

3 90 feet. 4b. Traverse out rightwards to finish up the airy arête (pitch 4 of Gollum).

The Wobbler   320 feet   Hard Very Severe   (1966)

Not a very good route. Start as for Beorn.

1 110 feet. 5a. Descend a few feet and surmount a line of overhangs to a small ledge. Go left along a ramp to more ledges which are climbed until a step left can be made into a groove. Ascend the groove moving left at the top to a large grassy ledge and tree belay.

2 70 feet. 5a. Climb the rib and grass on the right to poor belays. Climb over creaking blocks on the left to a small ledge, ancient peg runner. Move right and go up a steep groove and the wall above to a small stance and peg belay.

3 60 feet. 5a. Traverse left under a line of overhangs to a groove. Go up this until a mantelshelf move out left leads to a grass ledge.
4 80 feet. 4b. Straight up the rib to finish.

★**Beorn** 230 feet E1 (1964)

A very good route with exciting positions which takes a devious yet logical line up through the overhangs on the right-hand arête of the wall. Start by scrambling up rightwards from the foot of the Gandalf 'cave' to belay in a small corner directly above the start of Eastern Gully, below and just left of a square black overhang with a small white tree above it.

1 110 feet. 5c. Climb a short wall then a 20-foot groove to the roof. Make a hard traverse left from an ageing peg to gain the arête. Move left into the next groove, then back up right and climb the slab to cross the long diagonal overhang at its weakest point. Pull over to a small grassy stance and flake belays.
2 120 feet. 5b. Climb 10 feet to a higher grassy ledge. Ascend a 10-foot wall and pull leftwards over the roof at the top. Traverse left to the big groove and ascend it leftwards to the major overhang. Surmount this and go up airily to the top overhang, avoided by a mantelshelf on the left. A short groove leads to the top.

Mordor 220 feet E3 (1968)

This fierce climb sees very few ascents, and is almost always dirty. It is however, in a good position and has some interesting climbing. A recent ascent has cleaned most of the dangerous loose blocks, but care should still be exercised. Start as for Beorn below the prominent groove which leads to a roof.

1 50 feet. 4c. Climb diagonally rightwards up a heavily vegetated ramp and groove until it is possible to move left at the top of the groove to a grassy ledge and prominent tree above the square, black overhang of Beorn. Belay in a cave (good thread).
2 80 feet. 6a. Move six feet left then climb the blocky wall to an old peg at the foot of a blank V-groove. Move right with difficulty (crux) below the level of the peg to gain a niche below a roof. Move back left under the roof on good holds until below a groove in the vague arête. Climb the groove between two huge, suspect pinnacles to a sloping stance. Belay to any number of rather hollow blocks.
3 90 feet. 5b. Move slightly left and climb an awkward, out of balance groove beneath the loose flaky-looking overhang. Good protection is difficult to arrange. Layback the roof boldly on the flakes (which turn out to be solid), move up and turn the large roof on the right to finish up the arête. Belay well back.

Variation
1a 60 feet. 5c. Follow Beorn until it is possible to break out right to the white tree and cave belay. Cleaner and more in keeping with the route's standard.

East Wing Girdle   360 feet   Hard Very Severe   (1966)
A disappointing climb. Start from the top of The Nose and scramble up to a belay below the steep wall.
1 80 feet. Climb diagonally left just above the lip of the overhangs to a stance beyond the skyline.
2 40 feet. Descend for 25 feet, then move left to a stance and belay.
3 50 feet. Move down a few feet to a slab on the left. Climb the groove on Beorn moving left at the top to a small stance and peg belay on The Wobbler.
4 60 feet. Traverse left under overhangs. Climb a groove until a mantelshelf left leads to a ledge (as for The Wobbler pitch 3).
5 30 feet. Traverse left to belay on The Mole.
6 100 feet. Climb the corner for 10 feet, then move round the arête to finish up the slanting crack and short wall (as for M P P).

Flammarian   200 feet   Very Severe   (1968)
From the top of The Nose, traverse left for 50 feet to a grass-topped pinnacle and then across more grass to a slabby wall.
1 30 feet. Cross the wall, then go up to two trees below overhangs and a large ledge.
2 50 feet. Go left again, then straight up easily to the peg stance of Beorn.
3 60 feet. Step right to take a rightward-slanting crack, finishing in jammed blocks. Climb over these and traverse round the overhangs into a wide easy corner.
4 60 feet. Go up left into a pleasant V-chimney, then up a slab to the top.

Eastern Gully   Difficult   (1901)
The short straight gully defining The Nose on its left side is a quick way up, or a tricky descent from its summit. A rock step near the gully foot may prove to be a 'stopper' in the wet.

The Nose

The smooth slabby face of The Nose, with its good sound rock, is a worthy counterpart to Dinas Cromlech opposite. Above its undercut base are some 50 feet of steep rock with fine holds which merge into smooth slabs at a lesser angle with good, but widely spaced holds. The final steep section, rising from two large recesses separated by a central rib provides cracks and corners. Just to the right of the very foot of The Nose is a large rock scar where part of the initial band of overhangs collapsed during the winter of 1981. This now means that all the climbs between the Direct Route and Diagonal have a common starting point although the Zeta start has been re-climbed at a loose and dirty 5c.

★★**The Cracks**   295 feet   Hard Severe   (1930)

A classic climb. One of the finest at its standard in The Pass. The last pitch has a Very Severe mantelshelf which can easily be avoided. Start just up and left from the lowest point of the buttress, by some blocks above polished slabs in the path.

1 40 feet. Make a steep move up onto a ledge (well-worn), then follow a small corner/groove slanting back left to a ledge. Belay on another ledge six feet higher.

2 60 feet. Step across left for five feet, then continue diagonally left up a slender left-facing corner, finishing up a short crack (hard if wet), to a stance below an overhang and chockstone belays.

3 45 feet. Traverse delicately right below the overhang, often wet, into a chimney which leads to a good ledge and belay.

4 45 feet. Climb the thin crack splitting the slab on the left to a large ledge and possible belay. Step up and walk rightwards to belay on a large pinnacle.

5 60 feet. From the top of the pinnacle make an awkward move right onto a ledge. Climb the crack in the slabby left wall of the corner to another ledge and belay.

6 45 feet. Climb up to the right and make the infamous mantelshelf onto a smooth rounded ledge. Traverse left and climb the arête to the top of the Nose. The mantelshelf, 4c for climbers of average height, and 5a or impossible for those of lesser stature may be easily bypassed. Several inferior variations exist on the left of the main route.

Sombrero Fallout   125 feet   E2   (1984)

A powerful and painful little route. Scramble up left of The Cracks to where a grassy ledge runs right from the foot of Eastern Gully. Start from the right-hand end of the ledge below a steep wall.

1 70 feet. 5b. Climb the thin crack in the middle of the wall past a resting ledge to a stance.

2 55 feet. 6a. There is a thin crack behind the belay (left of the difficult crack on G B H). Attack this, stubborn at the start, and continue without much respite to finish at the final belay of The Cracks.

★**You're Not in Poland Now**   30 feet   E1 5a   (1987)

The delightful pocketed arête left of Sombrero Fallout pitch one.

God Help the Sailors on a Night Like This!   30 feet   E1 5b
(1987)

The thin seam with two pockets next to it, just left of Sombrero Fallout
pitch 1, is climbed using a useful crack for the right hand.

★★**Truncheon Meat**   50 feet   E6 6c   (1987)

The overhanging groove between Sombrero Fallout pitch 2 and G B
H pitch 3 gives one of the most taxing pitches on the South Side of
The Pass. Crank up the desperately strenuous and technical groove to
a rest. The boulder problem cracklet in the even steeper headwall
also proves stubborn – a fitting finale. One poor peg and a rack of
wires protect.

★**G B H**   270 feet   E2   (1978)

A worthwhile route if only for the crack on pitch 3. Start as for The
Cracks.

1 40 feet. 4b. Climb the rib on the right to belay as for The Cracks.
2 130 feet. 5b. Climb straight up between Lorraine Variation and The
Direct to a good ledge. Slant left up a line of shallow grooves,
pockets and cracks to move onto the good ledge at the top of
Lorraine Variation, after a few layaways up a crack. Pinnacle belay.
3 55 feet. 5c. Climb the vicious crack just left of the arête, above the
pinnacle.
4 45 feet. 4b. Finish up the arête on the left of the last pitch of The
Cracks.

★★**Lorraine**   260 feet   Very Severe   (1941)

A pleasant and enjoyable route just right of The Cracks. It is a parallel
line to that route and the stances are shared.

1 40 feet. As for The Cracks. Ascend steeply to a ledge at 10 feet,
then climb a corner groove on the left to a ledge. Belay on a second
ledge six feet higher.
2 65 feet. 4c. Go steeply up and left over a bulge to reach a
left-slanting groove formed by a scarp wall. Follow this past a hard
section, then step left into the short chimney on The Cracks. Belay at
its top.
3 50 feet. 4c. Climb the thin corner crack and a short corner to belay
at a pinnacle on the right, junction with The Cracks.
4 60 feet. 4c. Step right off the top of the pinnacle and move across
a ledge to climb a corner crack to good block belays. This pitch can
be split at the foot of the corner.
5 45 feet. 4c. Climb a series of steps up right as for The Cracks, and
finish via the difficult mantelshelf.

★**Lorraine Variation**   120 feet   Hard Very Severe 5a   (1965)

A superb pitch that is delicate and sparsely protected. Harder, but

better, than the original. From the first stance, follow Lorraine for 25
feet until a steep move across the bulge leads to another slab. Climb
delicately up past a steepening, good runner, and continue onto a
ledge at the centre of the shallow scoop above. Traverse down
leftwards to the foot of a crack in the arête. Climb this to the large
pinnacle on the ledge of The Cracks.

★★★**The Direct Route**   245 feet   Very Severe   (1930)
A superb and popular route which requires a wide variety of
techniques especially on the last pitch. It follows the obvious
light-coloured groove down the centre of The Nose. Start at the lowest
point of the buttress, left of the rock scar.
1 50 feet. 4a. Scramble up to the top of short twin pinnacles.
Continue up for 30 feet then move round to the left and belay on the
first stance of The Cracks.
2 90 feet. 4b. Climb diagonally rightwards crossing a blunt rib to the
base of the prominent shallow groove. Ascend this, steepening at the
top, to good belays in an open bay.
3 50 feet. 4c. Go easily right up steps to the start of a steep diagonal
crack. Hand-traverse this for a few feet, make a long step right, and
ascend easily to a long ledge with huge flake belays.
4 55 feet. 5b. Ascend the smooth polished corner on the left;
layback, bridge or use a shoulder. Continue pleasantly up the flake
cracks to finish up a shallow corner.

★**Famine**   255 feet   Hard Very Severe   (1978)
A surprisingly good eliminate. Start as for The Direct.
1 50 feet. 4a. Climb up and over the twin pinnacles (as for The
Direct Route) to belay on a spike below and left of the huge perched
flake – or step left to belay as for The Direct.
2 150 feet. 5a. Climb across to the flake, then from its top go up into
a scoop exiting onto The Direct. Follow the crest of the rib right of
Direct Route to a bulge. Pull rightwards onto this and follow a crack
for 20 feet to join the end of The Hand Traverse (on The Direct). Go
easily up to flake belays.
3 55 feet. 5b. Walk left to finish up the corner of The Direct Route.

★★★**Superdirect**   245 feet   E1   (1974)
A leisurely slab precedes an overhanging corner which is climbed
with a sense of urgency, very popular. Start as for The Direct.
1 70 feet. 4b. Scramble up over the twin pinnacles, then up a few
feet to a spike. Move down right and traverse the obvious line just
above the rock scar. Move up to belay on a ledge about 20 feet
below a small overhang.
2 130 feet. 5b. Climb up past the overhang to the nut slot on

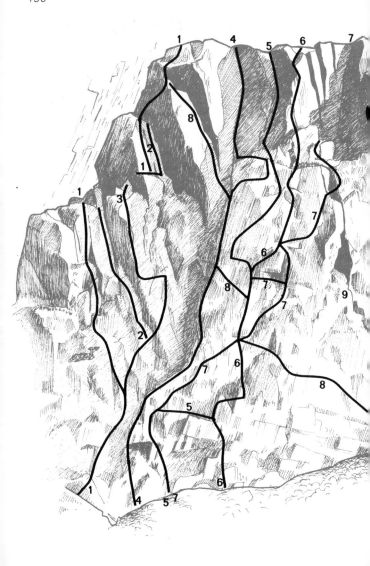

Dinas Mot: The Nose

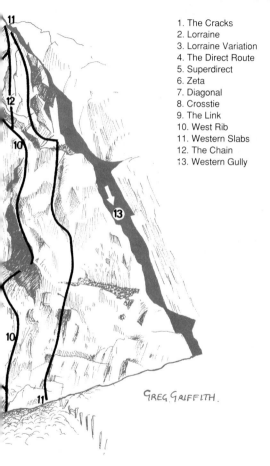

1. The Cracks	HS
2. Lorraine	VS
3. Lorraine Variation	HVS
4. The Direct Route	VS
5. Superdirect	E1
6. Zeta	E3
7. Diagonal	HVS
8. Crosstie	HVS
9. The Link	E1
10. West Rib	HVS
11. Western Slabs	VS
12. The Chain	E1
13. Western Gully	M

GREG GRIFFITH.

Diagonal and continue for eight feet where a short traverse leads left to a thin crack. Follow this up to the long ledge and flake belays on Direct Route.

3 45 feet. 5b. Climb the spike on the wall above then finish up a short overhanging corner crack.

★★**Zeta**   250 feet   E3   (1967)

A fine, sustained and serious climb up the centre of The Nose. Pitch 2 is quite thin and leaders often have epics on it – but pitch 4 is the stopper. The original start has disappeared in a mammoth rockfall, so start as for Superdirect.

1 70 feet. 4b. As for Superdirect.

2 60 feet. 5c. Climb up past the small overhang to the nut slot on Diagonal. Bold moves diagonally right lead to the second stance on that route.

3 70 feet. 5b. Ascend the thin crack above the pegs. An easy flake now leads to a ledge. Step down right to a good ledge and belays.

4 50 feet. 6a. Move left and climb up to the overhanging arête. Ascend this past the remnants of a peg… poor wires offer some spiritual comfort for the crux moves. The scoop is entered from the right, or from the left by the deft. Finish more easily – a frightening pitch.

★★★**Diagonal**   260 feet   Hard Very Severe   (1938)

A magnificent route which wanders boldly across the centre of The Nose from left to right. The third pitch is very delicate and requires finesse for success. Start as for The Direct Route.

1 80 feet. 5a. Climb the groove just left of the rock scar then continue up the left side of a huge perched flake. From the top of this move up a few feet then make a difficult traverse right across the slab to a stance and nut belays under a small overhang – this is more in keeping with the rest of the route. Or, start up the first pitch of Superdirect – easier.

2 40 feet. 5a. Above and slightly right is a large overhang with a bottomless chimney on its right-hand side. This chimney can be reached in two ways; either climb up to the left side of the overhang, good runner slot, then make a hard traverse underneath it, or more easily, climb diagonally right to good holds then step up left into the chimney which leads to a small stance with peg belays.

3 100 feet. 5a. Traverse right into a shallow scoop. Climb this and move right to make the famous mantelshelf onto a small ledge. A long reach to a good pocket leads to an easy sloping crack (possible belays). Follow the crack up into a recess below the steep corner crack.

Adam Wainwright on his own route *The Bastard Practice* (E7) Dinas
Cromlech. Photo: Steve Mayers

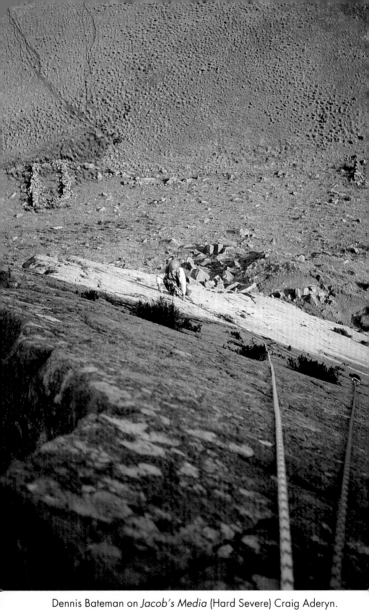

Dennis Bateman on *Jacob's Media* (Hard Severe) Craig Aderyn.
Photo: Terry Gifford

Pete Crew on the crux move of his own route *M P P* (HVS) Dinas Mot.
Photo: John Cleare

William Kyffin making the difficult moves on the second pitch of *Ten Degrees North* (E2) Dinas Mot. Photo: John Darling

4 40 feet. 4c. The strenuous corner crack yields to a determined approach.

★**Crosstie** 235 feet Hard Very Severe (1955)
A good counter line to Diagonal, going from left to right and finishing up the left-slanting groove left of the final pitch of The Direct. Start below the overhanging chimney of The Link.
1 60 feet. 4b. Go diagonally leftwards heading for the small overhang at the Diagonal pitch 1 belay.
2 90 feet. 5a. Follow Diagonal to the slot left of the overhang Step up and traverse left, rising slightly into the groove of The Direct. Climb this to the open bay stance.
3 85 feet. 5b. Ascend the corner groove directly above the scoop to the foot of the final corner of The Direct Route. Step back left into the groove and climb its left wall on good holds to a steepening. A few strenuous moves lead to a good ledge – hard. Junction with The Cracks.

★★**Stairway to Heaven** 230 feet E3 (1978)
This very fine climb, both bold and technical, gives a sustained outing. Start 40 feet left of the stile at the top of some quartz steps, below a break in the initial overhangs, as for Crosstie.
1 70 feet. 4c. Climb directly up to a block stance below the left wall of The Link – 10 feet left of the Blink! Don't! flake stance. Thread belay on the left.
2 50 feet. 5c. Ascend for 10 feet to good runners, then traverse left across the wall and pull boldly around the arête on small holds. Go straight up into the Diagonal scoop. Reverse the Diagonal traverse to belay at the top of its second pitch.
3 60 feet. 5c. From the right-hand end of the belay ledge a thin crack runs up the steep slab parallel to the difficult thin crack on pitch 3 of Zeta. Climb the crack direct trending right near the top to exit on a large grassy ledge. Belay in the corner.
4 50 feet. 5c. Climb the middle one of the three grooves between Zeta and Diagonal top pitches past a peg runner. A technically absorbing exercise which may be dirty.

★★**Stairway Direct** 100 feet E3 5c
A bold but escapable pitch – hard for the grade. Start from the first stance of Stairway to Heaven. Ascend for 10 feet to good runners, then traverse left and pull boldly round onto the slabby arête as for Stairway to Heaven. Climb directly up through the scoop crossing Diagonal to reach a crack up on the left. Avoiding an escape to the right (and last runner), climb the centre of the rounded rib above on small widely spaced holds.

The Link   80 feet   E1 5c   (1954)
The conspicuous overhanging chimney joining West Rib to the upper part of Diagonal, often greasy. Start at the top of West Rib pitch 1. Move up to grapple with the stubborn overhanging chimney/crack. A good continuation pitch (**The Chain** – 5b) can be done up the finger crack between the last pitches of West Rib and Western Slabs.

★★**West Rib**   225 feet   Hard Very Severe   (1931)
The long shallow rib to the right of The Link gives a fine pitch similar to, but slightly easier than Diagonal. Spaced protection make this a 'steady' lead. Start below the chimney/crack of The Link.
1 60 feet. 4b. Climb up towards The Link, then move right to a stance just left of the rib.
2 105 feet. 5a. Traverse horizontally right and up onto the crest of the rib. Climb this with a high step up after 30 feet, good nut, then continue delicately, trending slightly left, then right, up to a flake belay on Western Slabs.
3 60 feet. 4c. Move round the arête on the left to climb a thin crack using some doubtful flakes. Mantelshelf onto the steep arête and move right delicately to finish as for Western Slabs, or better, finish up The Chain.

Blink! – Don't!   210 feet   E1   (1978)
A rather contrived line with some good moves but little new climbing. Start as for Western Slabs.
1 80 feet. 4c. Climb Western Slabs for 20 feet. Break out left and ascend to a small stance on a large spike 20 feet left of West Rib.
2 90 feet. 5b. Make a few moves up the diagonal crack and pull up into the groove just on the left of West Rib. Climb this to a junction with West Rib which is followed for 10 feet. Continue along a flake crack which runs up left to meet a crack above The Link. Climb the thin crack in the slab to a flake belay.
3 40 feet. 4c. Scramble up behind the belay and finish via the corner crack of Diagonal.

★★**Western Slabs**   200 feet   Very Severe   (1931)
A popular and enjoyable route up the right-hand side of The Nose. Start just left of the stone wall.
1 50 feet. 4b. From the top of a quartzy block pull up onto a ledge and climb to a rightward slanting groove. From the top of this go round the arête to a ledge with small belays.
2 90 feet. 4b. Gain the ledge above and ascend to the lower of two small overlaps. Pass this on the right to a small sharp spike (sling). Step right and climb across under the second overlap then follow the groove up to a ledge. Continue up into a shallow groove which leads rightwards to a ledge overlooking Western Gully.

3 60 feet. 4c. Step down left and climb the easy groove to a higher ledge by a large flake. Climb the groove on the right to the top of a block. Make a hard move past a steepening then exit right onto a ledge. Finish easily.

Variation.
1a Start 20 feet left of the wall on a sloping platform and climb diagonally right into the slanting groove – 4b.
2a From the small sharp spike above the first overlap where the original line moves right, step left and ascend directly to the ledge – hard 4c.

Speeding Fine   200 feet   E2   (1978)
A very bold route to the right of Western Slabs. The sustained second pitch although not technically hard has poor protection. Start 35 feet right of the stone wall and eight feet left of a seeping crack.
1 40 feet. 4c. Climb up trending left to the grassy ledge on Western Slabs. Belay on the extreme left as for that route.
2 100 feet. 5b. Go up right into a broad scoop. Bridge this and exit right. The bold and precarious slab immediately left of the arête leads to the second stance of Western Slabs.
3 60 feet. 5b. Traverse left around the corner to finish via a thin finger crack, The Chain.

Spaghetti Western   185 feet   Hard Very Severe   (1982)
This takes the left edge of Western Gully with some poorly protected climbing. It is marred only by the close proximity of the gully – an easier version of Speeding Fine with which it shares some of the climbing. Start five feet left of the leftmost crack of Western Gully.
1 35 feet. 4a. Ascend via flakes and ledges on the rib on the right to join the gully.
2 80 feet. 5a. Go easily up the rib about eight feet left of the arête for 30 feet. Continue up the crest, over the bulge then traverse eight feet left and go up a thin crack to join Western Slabs. A delicate pitch.
3 70 feet. 5a. Traverse five feet towards the gully bed, then climb a crack and its continuation to meet Western Slabs.

The Girdle of The Nose   155 feet   Very Severe   (1931)
A short high-level crossing of The Nose, mainly Severe in standard with the exception of the Hand Traverse on the second pitch. It may be taken in either direction. but is normally climbed from left to right. Start as for pitch 5 of The Cracks at the pinnacle belay.
1 40 feet. 4b. From the top of the pinnacle move across onto the ledge, runner in the corner. Descend a short crack and an easy-angled slab to the open bay above the long groove of The Direct.
2 55 feet. 4c. Follow The Direct Route along its Hand Traverse, crux,

then continue more easily to a large ledge and belay.
3 60 feet. 4b. Traverse on good flake holds to reach the groove of Western Slabs. Finish up this.

★**The New Girdle**   225 feet   E2   (1978)
A pleasant open route which crosses The Nose at half-height. Start on ledges on the left-hand side of The Nose, level with the 'undercuts' traverse on pitch 3 of The Cracks.
1 30 feet. Step across the gap and traverse round and down to the stance on The Cracks.
2 85 feet. 5c. Step down and cross easily to a rib. Go up to a flake then move down across The Direct to some spikes on the arête. Reverse Crosstie to Zeta, which is followed with interest to the Diagonal stance.
3 50 feet. 5a. Traverse the obvious line onto West Rib. Move round to a pocket and climb the wall rightwards to a large ledge overlooking Western Gully.
4 60 feet. 4b. Finish as for Western Slabs.

Western Gully   200 feet   Moderate   (1901)
The easiest way to the top of The Nose. Start up either of two short cracks or more pleasantly by a traverse across slabs from the right. Continue up on excellent holds. This is also the normal descent, trickiest at the bottom.

North Ridge of Crib Goch   Difficult   (1901)
The upper rocks of Dinas Mot are weakest directly above The Nose and provide a useful exit for parties wishing to continue the day by a walk along Crib Goch or by a climb on one of the higher crags. On a wet day this tricky line is not obvious and great care should be taken whilst following it. From the top of The Nose cross the quartz-veined rib above Western Gully and go up a mossy chimney, then a smooth corner. Traverse left to a pile of large blocks about 60 feet above the rib. Scramble leftwards over blocks into a small cave, then traverse left to a large grassy avenue where the angle eases.

The Western Wing

This area, between Western Gully and Jammed Boulder Gully, gives long rambling climbs with inter-changeable finishes owing to the cliff being split horizontally by a series of grassy ledges, The Great Terrace. Below the terrace are steep open slabs of compact rhyolite similar to The Nose, while above the terrace the rock is similar to that of The Eastern Wing, giving complex route-finding.

Approaching from Western Gully the first feature is an area of steep black slabs, often wet which are taken by the fine 'Black' routes. This is bounded on the right by a dirty gully, Dolerite Dump. Below this gully is a tall pear-shaped flake which marks the starts of both Tremolite and Bluebell Cracks. Right of the flake, the compact slabby rock of the lower tier continues to the top of the crag. The Great Terrace is the line of The Western Wing Girdle. It also provides a way of escape either into Jammed Boulder Gully or to the top of The Nose by Moderate scrambling.

★ **Slow Ledge Climb**   205 feet   Severe   (1934)

A delightful route which cleverly finds a way through the many overhangs of the upper tier. The climbing is continually interesting and the rock is sound. A good continuation to The Cracks or a better finish to Dolerite Dump. Start from the top of The Nose. Slow Ledge, a severely undercut sloping shelf, protrudes from the cliff face dominating the right skyline. Cross the quartz rib above Western Gully and scramble 50 feet right to a flake belay.

1 75 feet. Climb easy ledges moving right. A short wall with a tiny tree leads to a good stance. Move right up the slab and semi hand-traverse across to the Slow Ledge (a person sitting on this ledge would slowly slide off...). Step right and go up a small groove to make another short traverse to a grassy rake. Belay at the top of this.

2 130 feet. Go straight up to a mossy groove. Cross the rib on the left into a cleaner groove. Climb this moving left or right to avoid difficulties. Scramble up slabs to finish.

At the base of the cliff right of Western Gully is:

★ **Black Shadow**   430 feet   E3   (1969)

A delicate and sustained climb up the edge of the black wall which overlooks Western Gully. It dries faster than its neighbours. The peg runner which used to protect the entry into the finishing groove on pitch 5 is no longer in place, making this the crux pitch. The E3 grade is given for a complete ascent. A rightward escape at the end of pitch 4 along Slow Ledge Climb for the sane and the faint-hearted reduces the grade to E2. Start 30 feet right of the foot of Western Gully.

1 50 feet. Climb the wet wall to a dirty terrace below the slabs.

2 70 feet. 5a. From the left-hand end of the ledge move left across the slab and climb a thin crack near the arête until it peters out. Step left and go up the arête and onto a slab below a large overhang. Nut and peg belays.

3 120 feet. 5c. Move right up the slab and step left onto the lip of the roof. Climb 15 feet to the foot of a blank groove and move right to a rib. Climb the short blank wall past a peg (hard) then step left into a slabby groove which leads to a grassy ledge. Ascend the groove above the right end of the ledge until a pull left onto the quartz rib leads to easier climbing and so to a belay on The Great Terrace – a pitch which has stopped many leaders.

4 80 feet. 4a. Scramble up across The Great Terrace over broken rock to the left of two small trees to reach a flake belay just left of the foot of the rightward-curving groove with a crack in it (junction with Black Spring).

5 110 feet. 5c. Traverse left for 10 feet, move up to a good hold, then go back right into a slabby groove directly above the stance. Follow this, heading for the wide shallow groove which breaks through the capping overhangs. Enter the groove boldly and continue on better holds to a large ledge (or scuttle off right along the obvious break). Nut belays 30 feet back on the left. Scramble up to finish.

Black and White   240 feet   E3   (1978)

A worthwhile addition to the 'Black' wall. Start as for Black Shadow.

1 50 feet. As for Black Shadow to the dirty terrace.

2 80 feet. 5c. Climb the wall left of Black Spring then traverse left to a line of shallow pockets which lead up into a shallow groove. Exit left at the top to belay on Black Shadow.

3 110 feet. 5c. Climb the overhang on its gully side by a long hard pull. Climb the groove on the left to an overhang below a grassy crack. Step round right below the square cut roof, then move out right and up to a grassy ledge (on Black Shadow). Finish more easily up the obvious quartz ramp/groove.

★★Black Spring   580 feet   Hard Very Severe   (1965)

An excellent route which gives delicate climbing up the steep black slabs right of Western Gully. The second pitch is unfortunately often wet. Start 30 feet right of the gully, as for Black Shadow.

1 50 feet. Climb the wet wall to the dirty terrace below the slabs.

2 90 feet. 5a. Climb a prominent crack for 30 feet, then move left for 10 feet until pockets lead up the steepening slab to a bulge. Pull around this and ascend delicately left and up to gain a cave stance a few feet right of Black Shadow. Peg and nut belays.

3 110 feet. 5a. Climb the overhang just right of the stance and swing round right onto a steep slab. Ascend the shallow groove for a few feet then trend diagonally left to a quartz groove. Climb this to The Great Terrace.

4 90 feet. 4a. Scramble over broken rocks past two little trees to a steep wall and huge flake belay on Slow Ledge Climb.

5 120 feet. 4c. Go up a crack on the left to below the big roof. A long easy traverse right leads to a belay on Slow Ledge Climb.

6 120 feet. Fine open slabs lead to the top.

Variation

3a 120 feet. 5b. Follow pitch 3 over the overhang to the shallow groove, then take an obvious diagonal line up right with difficulty. Regain the main line up easy ledges to the left.

★**Coon's Yard** 470 feet E2 (1974)
A fine technical route with a superb third pitch under the diagonal band of quartz overhangs which break out rightwards from the Black Shadow cave. Start 30 feet right of Western Gully.
1 50 feet. As for Black Shadow up the wet wall to the terrace.
2 90 feet. 5a. As for Black Shadow to the cave, then traverse right to the cave belay of Black Spring.
3 140 feet. 5c. Climb diagonally up right under the overhangs with increasing difficulty until a hard move leads round the arête on the right. Move up to grass and scramble up to a flake belay 15 feet below a small tree.
4 70 feet. Climb easy rocks and move up into a square niche. Swing left onto a prow. Climb the wall to the roof of Slow Ledge. Move right and climb the groove to a good belay.
5 120 feet. 5b. Climb the roof above the short groove with difficulty, then step right to the foot of a groove. Climb this with slightly less difficulty to a small sloping ledge where the groove narrows. Step right to jammed blocks. Finish up easier rock.

Variation

3a 140 feet. 5b. It is possible to pull through the quartz overhangs and traverse along the lip – much easier.

Black Foot 510 feet E2 (1965)
A serious and technical route. Start right of Black Spring below a large grassy pillar.
1 80 feet. Climb easy rock then go up a grassy crack on the left side of the pillar. Move right then climb to a stance and good belay 15 feet below the apex of the pillar.
2 85 feet. 5a. Climb the groove formed by the pillar and the wall, then the wall above on pockets to the overhang. Traverse right to a grassy stance. Peg belays.
3 120 feet. 5b. Climb the arête behind the stance for a few feet. Traverse left across the steep wall to a quartz ledge on the lip of the overhang. The steep crack above leads to easy ground.
4 75 feet. 5b. Scramble up left to a large detached block. Traverse right to a large flake, go up this then step right into the bottom of a groove (the large round overhang of Slow Ledge Climb is just on the right). Climb the groove with a very hard finish. Move right to belay. A serious and poorly protected pitch.

5 150 feet. Move right to below an overhang. Traverse under this to the foot of a long broken groove. Climb this to the top.

Variation

The Black Page   70 feet   E1 5b   (1979)
A direct alternative to Black Foot pitch 2. Start on the other side of the pillar.
2a Climb the grey walls, a groove and the overhang above.

Dolerite Dump   540 feet   Very Difficult   (1944)
Below The Great Terrace is a large corner facing left which gives the line of this poor route. Above, the climb deteriorates into a grassy scramble. Best done as a start to Slow Ledge Climb. Start 60 feet right of Western Gully.
1 65 feet. Easy rock leads to a short overhanging crack. Avoid this by traversing left then go up to another steep crack.
2 60 feet. Climb the crack direct or more easily by excursions onto the slab on the right. From a grassy ledge, go up a path below steep walls and traverse left round the corner to a grassy bay.
3 45 feet. Ascend the long mossy groove.
4 60 feet. Go easily up the gully to The Great Terrace. It is possible to scramble up leftwards to join Slow Ledge Climb from here.
5 60 feet. Climb up on heather to the foot of a smooth slab, overhung on the left.
6 70 feet. Climb up broken rocks on the right of the slab then up a short steep corner.
7 80 feet. Scramble up a subsidiary groove on the left until one is forced further away to the left by an overhanging wall. Continue in the same line to the base of the final groove.
8 100 feet. Continue up the long wide groove straight ahead. Where the scrambling becomes awkward near the top, break out right and finish on clean rock.

Tremolite   400 feet   E1   (1963)
A varied and interesting climb. Start at the pear-shaped flake which marks the start of Bluebell Cracks.
1 60 feet. 5a. Climb the difficult bulge and go up on good holds to the top of the flake.
2 50 feet. 5b. Move right across wet sloping ledges to a tree. Climb the strenuous overhanging crack onto a slab. Good thread belay.
3 100 feet. 5a. Traverse from the belay across a slab to a thin crack, hard to start, but soon relenting, into a shallow groove. Climb this exiting left at the top onto The Great Terrace.
4 130 feet. 5a. Climb the arête left of an open corner leading up to a huge overhang. Move right above the overhang then zigzag up the

wall to avoid difficulties. Follow Dolerite Dump to a belay below a large overhang.
5 60 feet. 4b. Climb the arête left of the roof and go up a cracked groove to join Boulder Buttress just below the top.

Dole-ite Variation   120 feet   E1 5b   (1983)
Scramble rightwards from the top of Tremolite to belay below the second pitch of Sych at a holly tree.
2a Climb up to the two large pockets and step left onto a small ledge. Traverse left a few feet then follow a rising line to reach the base of the groove on Tremolite. Finish up the shallow groove as for Tremolite pitch 3.

Bluebell Cracks   185 feet   Very Difficult   (1948)
Pleasant but hard for its grade. Thirty five yards right of Dolerite Dump is the only other easy break below The Great Terrace, a cracked groove facing in the opposite direction. This is reached by a long traverse from the pear-shaped flake at the foot of the crag.
1 40 feet. Climb the corner right of the flake by a series of shallow caves to the passage between the flake and the cliff.
2 40 feet. The quartz-veined slab leads right into an overhung recess. Traverse right to a ledge below a holly tree.
3 65 feet. Traverse right along a narrow ledge then go slightly up to a grassy niche at the foot of a corner. Climb the steep corner to a ledge with a tall flake leaning against a corner.
4 40 feet. Climb the flake then the crack or the slab on its left. Escape rightwards along The Great Terrace.

Sych   470 feet   E2   (1976)
A steep line on the right of Tremolite. The name is Welsh for 'drought'. Start as for Hiawatha.
1 70 feet. Scramble up grass and heather to a small holly.
2 150 feet. 5c. Climb up to the two large pockets and step left onto a small ledge. Make a series of difficult moves, first left then straight up to a good handhold. Swing right to the thin crack and climb this via a very hard move to reach The Great Terrace; the crack can be climbed direct – easier, 5b.
3 130 feet. 5b. Above is a huge overhang. Climb onto the steep slab below the overhang and traverse right for 15 feet to the arête. Climb up, peg runner, to pass the roof on the right and follow a groove until a step left over loose blocks leads onto Tremolite. Follow that climb to a flake belay in a large grassy bay.
4 120 feet. 5b. Climb up behind the belay then step right and climb over detached blocks to below a small roof. Make a hard move over the roof then take a crack and easier rock to the top.

Dinas Mot: The Western Wing

1. Western Gully — M
2. Black Shadow — E3
3. Coon's Yard — E2
4. Black Spring — HVS
5. Black Foot — E2
6. Slow Ledge Climb — S
7. Dolerite Dump — VD
8. Tremolite — E1
9. Bluebell Cracks — VD
10. Sych — E2
11. Hiawatha — HVS
12. Jubilee Climb — HVS
13. Boulder Buttress — VD
14. Jammed Boulder Gully — M

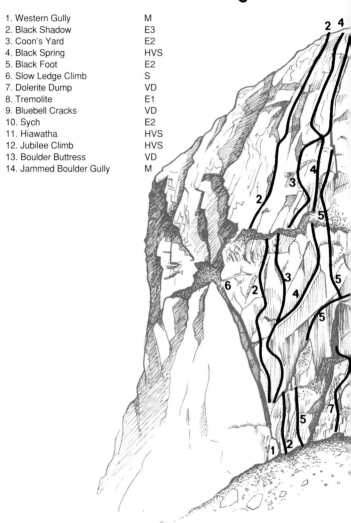

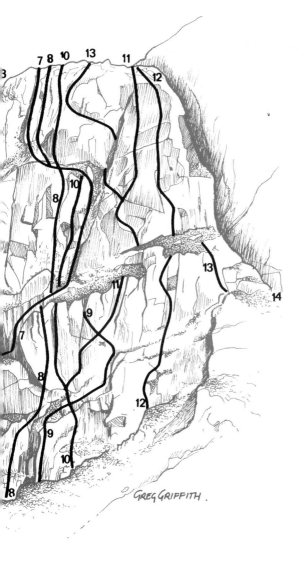

GREG GRIFFITH.

★**Sidewinder** 550 feet E2   (1983)
Interesting and varied climbing up some impressive rock. Start as for
Hiawatha.
1 60 feet. Scramble up grass and heather to belay at a small holly,
as for Hiawatha.
2 120 feet. 5b. Climb the first 10 feet of Hiawatha/Sych to the
pocket then traverse left along the obvious line until it is possible to
move up and reach the base of the groove on Tremolite (Dole-ite
Variation). Move 12 feet left and go directly up the wall to a good
small pocket. Continue steeply to reach a crack which is followed to
good belays on a terrace.
3 40 feet. Climb easily up heathery rock to a small tree and good
belays below the upper part of Tremolite.
4 110 feet. 5b. Move left and climb various ribs and bulges heading
for a roof below a prominent triangular slab below a larger roof. At
the level of the first roof traverse left, peg runner, passing a
precarious-looking flake with difficulty. Step round the arête onto a
steep wall and continue to a comfortable exposed ledge below
Damoclean blocks. An exhilarating pitch .
5 70 feet. Climb over blocks up to a short chimney. Follow this
steeply until a move left to a stance on Slow Ledge Climb.
6 150 feet. Finish up Slow Ledge Climb.

Hiawatha 350 feet Hard Very Severe   (1961)
The lower section is a series of variations on Bluebell Cracks. The
upper section takes the left-hand side of the well-defined slabs, just left
of the top part of Jammed Boulder Gully. Start below the cracked
groove of Bluebell Cracks.
1 70 feet. Climb quartz and heather moving right at the top to belay
on the right-hand of two trees.
2 100 feet. 4c. Ascend the steep awkward crack then move right
near the top to the tall flake of Bluebell Cracks. Make a rising traverse
right then go up a shallow groove (just in front of the skyline) to the
heather terrace.
3 50 feet. 5a. Climb the stepped groove in the steep wall to the
grassy rake of Boulder Buttress (hard). Cross this and continue to a
good spike belay.
4 130 feet. 5a. Layback into the heathery groove in the wall above.
Climb the slab and heather grooves to the line of overhangs. Flake
Traverse Variant crosses here. Traverse 10 feet right and go over the
overhang to an obvious foothold. Either traverse left, thin, to the
corner groove and go up to another overhang or, pad up the slab
'Red Indian' style then traverse left to the same point – harder.
Traverse left and continue up the left edge of the main slab proper to
a large ledge. Scrambling remains.

Intruder   430 feet   Hard Very Severe   (1965)
A vague route. Basically it is a harder variation on Hiawatha. Start
30 feet right of Hiawatha, just right of a grassy corner.
1 60 feet. 5a. Climb over a bulge to the right. Step left and go
straight up to a grass ledge and peg belay.
2 120 feet. 5a. Climb up to the left and follow the prominent groove.
Scramble up broken rock and belay below a deep groove above the
terrace.
3 90 feet. 5a. Climb the groove and step left at the bulge. Climb this
to a ledge and belay.
4 70 feet. 4c. Climb a short slab to the right then go up a crack to a
roof. Belay on the right.
5 90 feet. 5a. Traverse left and over a small overlap to a peg.
Continue up to the next small overlap then finish up Jubilee Climb.

★ **Jubilee Climb**   280 feet   Hard Very Severe   (1959)
This fine climb takes a parallel line up the slabs to the right of
Hiawatha. The lower section goes via an obvious square-cut niche,
the crack above being 'a bit of a brute'. Start at a large flake directly
below the square niche.
1 100 feet. 4b. Go up easy slabs for 60 feet then climb difficult twin
heather grooves to a small holly tree in the niche.
2 30 feet. Traverse left to a good flake then go up easily to the
heather terrace.
3 50 feet. 5b. Above is a steep little wall with a crack near its
right-hand end. Move up right round the corner of the wall and
ascend on spikes until a move back left leads onto the front wall.
Climb the crack to a good spike belay. The coffin-shaped recess on
the left of the lower wall also leads to the same point.
4 30 feet. 4a. Follow the crack up a mossy slab to a huge belay at
the end of Flake Traverse Variant.
5 70 feet. 5a. Make a difficult rising traverse left up the slab to the
central scoop. Regain the crackline above a small overlap and climb
it – a fine exposed finish.

Boulder Buttress   310 feet   Very Difficult   (1934)
A scrappy route up the grassy break left of the final slab of Hiawatha
and Jubilee Climb. Start by scrambling up Jammed Boulder Gully to
grassy ledges at the foot of a few steep outcrops. The first section of
the buttress lies on the left.
1 70 feet. Go pleasantly up rough slabs to the heather terrace.
2 60 feet. Move left under the steep walls. The break on the left is
ill-defined at first. Climb a short corner to a grassy rake which is
followed left round the steep buttress into the groove.
3 30 feet. Scramble up keeping close to the rocks on the right.

4 60 feet. Follow the groove until one can break away left to a heather ledge below a wide rock bay.
5 40 feet. Ascend to a holly tree, bear right and go up split blocks to a maze of belays.
6 50 feet. Traverse 20 feet left and finish up the arête on excellent rock.

Variation
4a 120 feet. Go straight up the groove. It is now better defined. At 100 feet is a short steep bit above which the vegetation can be avoided on the right.
6a 40 feet. Instead of traversing left to the arête, cross the slab on the right and ascend a steep corner (about Severe).

Flake Traverse Variant 210 feet Very Difficult
A dry alternative to the top of the boulder. Despite vegetation, the traverse is worth the diversion. Start at the foot of the gully and scramble up to the heather terrace on the left, or this can be reached by Boulder Buttress pitch 1.
1 120 feet. As for Boulder Buttress. Go into the large grassy groove up on the left via a short corner and grassy rake. Scramble up to the left end of a horizontal crack under a small overhang.
2 30 feet. Hand-traverse right along the crack finishing awkwardly on a heathery ledge with belays.
3 60 feet. Scramble across right into Jammed Boulder Gully.

Western Wing Girdle Difficult (1934)
A vegetated scramble needing little technique, but which gives views of the other routes. From the top of The Nose it follows the vegetated terraces across to the foot of Jammed Boulder Gully. Scramble up Eastern Gully to the top of The Nose. Cross the quartz rib above Western Gully and continue for 100 feet or so, descending slightly to an excellent belay. Descend a grassy rake to the right for 50 feet then continue along the heather terrace to the foot of Jammed Boulder Gully.

★**Jammed Boulder Gully** 200 feet Moderate (1900)
A typical gully with good rock and an interesting cave pitch. It is the obvious wide recess in the centre of The Western Wing where a massive boulder has become wedged about 200 feet above the screes. A tricky descent when wet.
1 100 feet. Scramble to the cave below the boulder, or climb the harder slabs on the right which are often wet and not so pleasant.
2 20 feet. Enter the cave and struggle through a narrow hole in the roof, the cause of much amusement.

3 80 feet. Continue up the main gully-line starting via a shallow groove on the right.

The Lymph   230 feet   E2   (1968)
A poor route up a groove and slabs on the small buttress between Jammed Boulder Gully and Black Cleft. Essentially a left-hand variation of Groper. Start below the buttress by scrambling up to belay below the obvious groove.
1 110 feet 5c. Climb up and step right into the foot of the groove. Start this by hard moves, peg runner, and continue up to the big roof. Step right onto the slab and go straight up to a heathery way.
2 60 feet. 4b. Ascend easily rightwards to the Groper peg belay.
3 60 feet. 5b. Finish as for the Groper pitch 3, or escape left along a ledge to reach vegetation, up which it is possible to finish.

Groper   260 feet   E2   (1965)
A varied route on the same buttress as The Lymph. Start at the left-hand end of the big roof above the base of the buttress, as for The Lymph.
1 150 feet. 5c. Climb the groove until it forks. Peg runner high in the right-hand groove and another peg runner on the wall. Traverse right to a slab and move up right to a shallow scoop. Climb the steep crack past a hidden spike to a ledge on the arête. Move left then go up to a stance and belay.
2 50 feet. 4b. Follow the rib to a sloping ledge and peg belays.
3 60 feet. 5b. From the right-hand end of the ledge, climb a crack past a peg runner until level with an overhang on the right. Hand-traverse left to a layback crack. Ascend this to an overhang, move right and continue up to a good stance. Scrambling remains.

Variation
1a It is possible to climb the thin crack in the arête of pitch 1 at the same standard. Finish up The Lymph.

★**Zyklon 'B'**   85 feet   E4 6a   (1984)
A bold route which follows the centre of Groper Buttress over its initial roof. Start below the centre of the buttress. A crack on the right leads to a steep wall below the roof, peg runner on the left. Climb the wall and thug across the roof on large holds, peg runner. Finish up the centre of the wall to the top, about 150ft in total. A spectacular pitch.

Runnymede   250 feet   E2   (1977)
An exposed and poorly protected route up the right arête of Groper Buttress. Start below the right end of the big roof.
1 30 feet. Scramble up to a field just left of Black Cleft.
2 90 feet. 5b. Ascend a short groove in the right arête of Groper

Buttress and move left to join Groper just above the big roof. Climb the scoop of Groper to two obvious pockets. Move right round the arête and climb to a horizontal crack. Follow the arête mainly on the right to a spike belay. A fine exposed pitch.
3 60 feet. 5a. Move down right and go up a steep ramp. Trend slightly left and go back up right to reach the pitch 2 belay on Groper.
4 70 feet. 5a. Traverse left 10 feet, climb an open scoop for 20 feet then move right to the layback crack of Groper. Ascend this, then surmount the overhang to finish up a short groove.

Runnymede Easy Variation   200 feet   Hard Very Severe   (1978)
Slight but entertaining. Start at grassy field above start of Runnymede.
1 70 feet. 5a. Climb a line of flakes to join Runnymede.
2 60 feet. 5a. As for Runnymede pitch 3.
3 70 feet. 4c. Climb the smooth slab on the left of the upper wall.

★**Black Cleft**   390 feet   Severe   (1897)
This classic gully, usually wet and repulsive, is the exclusive preserve of masochists and is generally deemed to be 'a fine climb in the traditional idiom'. It is the deep rift right of Jammed Boulder Gully.
1 80 feet. Scramble up into a wide bay.
2 40 feet. The narrowing gully passing a chockstone on the left.
3 60 feet. Crux. Climb the steep waterworn bed of the gully.
4 60 feet. Another interesting gully pitch.
5 150 feet. Scramble to the top.

Plexus Buttress

On the right of Black Cleft is a large area of slabby rock split at two thirds height by a line of huge overhangs – the continuation of The Great Terrace fault line. This is the magnificent Plexus Buttress, which has a high concentration of top quality routes.

★★**Sexus**   420 feet   E4   (1965/1977)
A difficult and sustained excursion up the left-hand side of Plexus Buttress. The roof on pitch 4 looks innocuous enough from below, but when tackled, proves to be a ferocious obstacle. Start 20 feet right of the arête.
1 100 feet. 5a. Climb the leftward slanting flakes to a shallow groove which leads up to a grassy ledge. Move left to nut belays by a tree.
2 100 feet. 5c. Traverse 20 feet right and go up to a thin vertical crack in the arête. Climb this, very hard, trending left up a steep ramp. Move right at the top of the arête to the cave belay of Plexus.
3 70 feet. 4a. Traverse left under the roof to a thread belay at its left end.

4 150 feet. 6b. Power over the roof, or more usually siege it, onto the slab. This transition from the strenuous to the delicate has bamboozled many leaders, giving them a chance to bump up their 'flying hours'. Traverse right on the slab to a prow, peg runner. Step down right and go up a hidden groove. Traverse left a few feet and climb a short groove to the slabs above. Possible belay. Eighty feet... for the connoisseur of 'haute cuisine'... some tasty scrambling remains.

Variation
Direct Start 190 feet Very Severe   (1965)
The original start follows the left arête of the buttress.
1a 100 feet. 4c. Climb the left arête of the buttress overlooking Black Cleft moving right up the face until a swing down to a tree stance and nut belay on the arête.
2a 90 feet. 4a. Climb the crack, step left, and continue to the huge roof.

★★**The Red Ring** 310 feet E5   (1966/1981)
A bold, intimidating and sensational route freeing The Grinder, which required seven pegs to force its way through some airy territory. The line follows Sexus for two pitches to the big roof, surmounts this, then moves right to finish via a prow, a second roof and a groove.
1 & 2 5c. As for Sexus to belay under the roof.
3 30 feet. 6b. Launch out across the massive roof, which sometimes succumbs to technical thuggery, and pull round the lip to climb an easy slab – not a pitch for the faint-hearted. Belay below the biggest roof.
4 80 feet. 6a. Take the eight-foot roof direct, an anticlimax after the previous pitch. Above this step right into a groove which leads to a hard exit onto easy slabs.

★★★**Perplexus** 330 feet E5   (1989)
A tremendous eliminate based on Plexus with some sensational climbing in its upper reaches. Start right of Sexus, directly below the first groove of Plexus.
1 60 feet. 5b. Climb up to an obvious vertical crack, and use layaways on the left to gain height. Continue to reach slabs and a belay in the first groove of Plexus at a peg.
2 110 feet. 6a. Follow Plexus to stand on a flake where it moves right on to the slab. Make a move left into a groove, and bridge up it to a sloping shelf on the edge of the arête gained by a mantelshelf. Take the crack above to a ledge. Trend first right, then left, continuing directly up the arête. Belay just below the overlap.
3 50 feet. 5b. Move across a grass ledge on the right to reach the groove leading up to a belay, below the crux groove of Plexus.

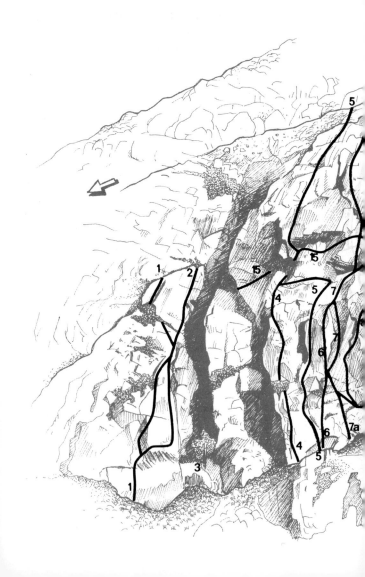

Dinas Mot: Plexus Buttress

1. The Lymph — E2
2. Groper — E2
3. Black Cleft — S
4. Sexus Direct Start — VS
5. Sexus — E4
6. Perplexus — E5
7. Plexus — HVS
8. Ten Degrees North — E2
9. Nexus — E1
10. The Windmill — E3
11. The Smodge — E4
12. Nexus Direct — E5
13. Gardd — VS
14. Hornets Attack Victor Mature — E2
15. Plexus Girdle — E3

GREG GRIFFITH 86.

4 60 feet. 6b. Climb the crux of Plexus (high Friend ½), then traverse right along the lip of the overhang whence a high step up gains a nick in the slab. Follow the faint depression above to stand on a rounded boss. Move right to a crack on the edge of the arête and belay at the end of the Nexus traverse.
5 50 feet. 6b. Layback the arête above to easy ground. (Friend ½ up and left, and a hand placed peg in a slot half-way up the arête may give some comfort).

★★**Plexus**   450 feet   Hard Very Severe   (1962)
The superb original route of the buttress provides delicate climbing in exciting positions on sound rock. Start at the right side of the buttress where the lower wall relents.
1 70 feet. Climb the easy groove to a large ledge. Traverse easily left above the lower wall to a stance and flake belay below the long scoop which runs up to the large overhang; or start direct, 5a.
2 150 feet. 5a. Climb to a bulge, peg runner. Go over it into a groove. Step right on to a slab, thread runner. Move left and climb a crack and the groove above until it steepens. Traverse left to the arête. Climb slabs to the big overhangs. Peg belays.
3 120 feet. 5b. Traverse right to where the overhang is smallest. Climb up, peg runner, and step left into a corner. Ascend for a few feet then traverse right and up a delicate slab to a ledge beside a large detached block. Move left over the block into a scoop and leave this on its right side by an awkward mantelshelf. Traverse diagonally left to a stance and belay.
4 110 feet. 4b. Shallow grooves and slabs lead to the top.

★★**Ten Degrees North**   400 feet   E2   (1974)
This excellent groove and slab between Plexus and Nexus gives sustained delicate climbing with well-spaced protection. A modern classic.
1 70 feet. As for Plexus pitch 1 to a flake belay.
2 50 feet. 5b. Climb a short wall then move right to a peg runner. Go up to the groove, step left and ascend with difficulty to a nut belay on a slab.
3 90 feet. 5c. Move right and balance up the open groove to a roof. Step right then go up to a peg runner. Step left then climb the slab to a small overhang. Continue up right to the huge roof and move right to belay on the flakes as for Nexus.
4 60 feet. 5b. Climb the crack on the left side of the flake to join the Nexus traverse. Follow this left to a belay on Plexus.
5 110 feet. 4b. Climb the groove and slabs as for Plexus pitch 4.

★★★**Nexus**   420 feet   E1   (1963)
A companion route to Plexus, but slightly harder and better. It takes

the right-hand arête of the crag overlooking Garden Groove.

1 30 feet. As for Plexus to the first ledge. Belay.

2 150 feet. 5b. A magnificent pitch. Climb the slab on the right of the corner to the overhang. Hand-traverse left to a thread runner on the arête. Layback round the roof, small wire, to the foot of a narrow gangway slanting up right. Follow this in a superb position and where it steepens make a difficult move up to a sloping ledge on the right. Climb a short overhanging crack on good holds and continue up a shallow groove to a stance and belays at the right-hand end of the big overhang.

3 40 feet. 4b. Climb the slab on the left till it steepens to a ledge with a perched block on the left. Peg belay.

4 50 feet. 5b. Traverse left along a horizontal crack. Swing round the arête to join the upper part of Plexus pitch 3. Belay in the scoop.

5 150 feet. 4b. Climb shallow grooves and slabs as for Plexus.

The Texas Start   150 feet   E3 6a   (1987)

2a A boulder problem arête left of the usual start leads to a junction with the parent route at the thread runner. The purist will continue as for Nexus.

★★**Nexus Direct**   80 feet   E5 6b   (1966/1977)

Despite its benign appearance, this is a fierce and technical pitch with little in the way of protection, which still sees many failures. Very dry conditions is only *one* of the prerequisites required for a successful ascent. Start from the Nexus belay, above pitch 3. Climb up into the foot of the groove. A small wire provides the only protection. The blank groove above is climbed direct and yields to the 'Technical Master' with a cool head.

The Windmill   360 feet   E3   (1974)

An intricate first pitch up steep rock. Start as for Nexus.

1 150 feet. 5c. Climb the slab and the overhang above. Ascend the groove and move up to the roof. Go right on undercuts then layback round and up to a small stance below a slab. Go delicately across the left wall and round the arête on to Nexus. Move up a few feet to the overhangs and go right under these to a hidden flake in a groove. Move up to a ledge then go right to easy ground. Nexus pitch 2 belay.

2 40 feet. 4b. As for Nexus up the slab to the perched block.

3 80 feet. 5b. Follow the crux of The Girdle (pitch 5) to easy ground. Go right and up to large blocks, then move right across a slab to a peg belay in a niche.

4 90 feet. 5a. The overhanging crack above leads to a ledge. Continue up the wide crack to finish.

★★The Smodge 210 feet E4   (1989)
A surprisingly good mirror-image line to the right of The Windmill.
Start at the foot of a groove immediately right of The Windmill start
(from the ledge at 30 feet).
1 120 feet. 6a. Climb up into the groove exiting left at its top to a
junction with The Windmill. Trend precariously right across a slab
below the obvious groove. More tenuous moves gain a solid handjam
in a pod (Friend 1½). Move up the groove with interest then cross
easier ground and climb a slab to a peg belay below the arête, by a
block.
2 90 feet. 5c. From the top of the block, climb directly up the arête to
reach the last pitch of The Plexus Girdle. Step left and follow the
upper arête.

★★The Plexus Girdle 420 feet E3   (1965)
A brilliant route never unduly difficult, which throughout its length
gives sustained and delicate climbing in an exposed position. Start up
grassy terraces on the left of the buttress to below a small roof. A
better start is up Sexus.
1 80 feet. 4b. Traverse right under the roof to wet slabs. Cross these
high, passing a large spike to reach a grassy ledge. Climb onto a
slab above large spikes and descend to these.
2 60 feet. 5a. Traverse the slab to a prow and go up the groove as
for Sexus, peg runner. Move out right below the roof until a descent
to a sentry-box stance. Nut belays.
3 40 feet. 5b. Step down and traverse right on a steep slab to the
arête. Ascend to a stance and belay in the scoop of Plexus.
4 50 feet. 5b. Descend the Plexus blocks, go round the arête and
reverse the Nexus traverse. peg belay.
5 140 feet. 5b. Climb the steep slab under the overhang, peg runner,
to the arête on the right. Climb this, stepping round right then back
left (or direct, 5c) to easy ground.
6 50 feet. Ascend easily to the top.

Right of Plexus Buttress the rock degenerates considerably but
immediately to the right is the attractive slab of Gardd.

Garden Groove 305 feet Difficult   (1944)
The shallow groove which defines the right-hand side of Plexus
Buttress. The rock is still appearing from the vegetation.
1 50 feet. Avoid the first steep bit by a detour on the left.
2 50 feet. Climb to the first overhang and pass it on the right.
Continue up vegetation to a stance.
3 90 feet. Follow the groove till it widens into a heathery bay below
an outcrop of quartz, then continue up to the slab below the second
overhang.

4 35 feet. Climb the slab to a ledge on the right level with the overhang. Thread belay.
5 80 feet. Climb the short slab then go left up a loose groove.

Variation
The left-hand exit makes the route independent of Twin Groove.
4a 45 feet. Go up the left side of the bay using a slab and some blocks and gain the edge of the buttress.
5a 50 feet. Finish up the easy arête.

Gardd 150 feet Very Severe 4c   (1962)
A pleasant little route with many variations. It takes the long narrow slab with a prominent Z-shaped crack at its top, right of Garden Groove. Start at the bottom left-hand corner of the slab. Traverse right and go over the bulge to the easy-angled slab. Climb straight up keeping slightly left on the clean parts (crux in the middle). Go up left then back right into the wide crack to finish. Continue up Garden Groove or abseil off.

Hornets Attack Victor Mature 110 feet E2 5c   (1983)
An enjoyable pitch. Start 20 feet right of Gardd by scrambling up about 20 feet to a grassy boulder below a small square overhang. Climb a short groove to the overhang and surmount it using a good jam crack. Follow this to a small triangular overhang which is skirted on the left up easy ground to the slab above (much harder direct). Make several lonely and delicate moves on small edges and ramps for 20 feet culminating in a long thin reach for a flat hold on the arête. Finish up the arête to belay as for Gardd.

Twin Groove 320 feet Difficult   (1935)
Much better than Garden Groove. It is the groove on the right of the Gardd slab. Start at the foot of the groove.
1 80 feet. The slabby bed of the groove leads to the foot of the square-cut chimney.
2 65 feet. Climb the chimney and the steep crack above it. A wider crack leads to the grassy terrace above Gardd.
3 60 feet. Scramble across to the junction of two grooves.
4 35 feet. As for Garden Groove. Climb the slab on the right to a ledge level with the overhang.
5 80 feet. Ascend the short slab and a loose groove on the left.

Right of Twin Groove the cliff is very vegetated. Several very poor routes have been recorded, all of them struggling to achieve mediocrity. Fifty yards right of Gardd is a prominent pillar split by a wide crack on its left.

Calluna   180 feet   Very Severe   (1968)
A vegetated outing for those of the gardening ilk which seems to be
cleaning up. Start below the pillar about 50 feet up the heather slope,
in a jungly gully with a large jammed block.
1 150 feet. 4b. Trend left and go up to a rowan tree. Ascend right
up the slab to a steep crack. Jam this to a crevasse. Traverse left and
grovel up the chimney to the top of the pillar.
2 30 feet. Escape rightwards through the jungle.

The Lectern   240 feet   Severe   (1949)
A route of sorts if you can find it. Start near Calluna below a
lectern-shaped rock above a wall.
1 40 feet. Climb the wall to the lectern.
2 50 feet. Traverse into a grassy groove and then out onto the face
along an obvious line.
3 50 feet. Move round the rib on the left. Hand-traverse onto the
face, then go up to a large recess.
4 60 feet. Climb the right-hand of four grooves.
5 40 feet. Go easily up to finish.

The Blade   200 feet   Hard Very Severe   (1965)
At the right-hand end of the crag is a vegetated gully with a steep
clean tower high up on its right. The route takes a crack splitting the
tower, 5a.

Ettws Isaf   OS Ref. 624 564

This buttress lies some 200 yards right of Plexus Buttress where the path
from Dinas Mot to Cwm Glas passes above Little Benjamin Buttress. It is
in fact the spur thrown down from The Blade on the right-hand side of
the wide vegetated gully. The tip of the spur is dominated by a square
cut overhung corner.

Wimpey Pa   400 feet   Very Severe   (1983)
A rather disjointed route with some pleasant pitches broken by large
grass ledges. Start about 30 feet left of the overhung corner at the
second groove left of its arête; large polished spike. This can be
reached direct by a 20-foot rock pitch.
1 100 feet. 4c. Climb up left for 10 feet to gain the groove. Follow it
for 30 feet then go across left and ascend past a loose sapling to a
heathery ledge. Traverse this for 25 feet to its right end, then

hand-traverse right and down to an obvious corner. Climb the crack/groove on the left to finish on a grassy terrace marking the top right-hand limit of the crag.

2 60 feet. Scramble up to a large terrace with a cave at its top right-hand end.

3 60 feet. 4b. Twenty feet right of the cave is a 15-foot leaning pillar on the arête. Climb this and the two steps above then walk across the grassy ledge.

4 80 feet. 4a. The Delaminated Wall. This excellent pitch lies left of the smooth arête of the buttress and in between two heathery grooves.

5 100 feet. Pleasant scrambling leads to a surprise view. Walk off down to the right.

Although the three following routes are only single pitches, they are worth a visit being of similar quality to those routes found on Plexus Buttress.

★**Silent Thunder**   120 feet   E4 5c   (1983)

Superb bold climbing on excellent rock – may need cleaning prior to an ascent. Start just left of the left arête of the overhung corner below a square cut overhang and just right of Wimpey Pa. Make a difficult move over the overhang and go up into the corner on the right which is followed to a large block. With difficulty move right to a sloping ledge on the arête proper, poor peg runner above. Pull up onto a small slab on the left and a good hold. Make a committing traverse right around the blunt rib across the slab to a poor foothold on the arête. Follow the arête by long reaches to a hidden easy groove. This leads to good holds and easier climbing.

Gorty's Triangle   120 feet   E4 6b   (1983)

A desperate roof problem with extreme bridging, unfortunately often wet. Start a few feet right of Silent Thunder. Climb the left edge of the triangular-shaped bay and slab below the overhanging left wall with increasing difficulty, passing two peg runners near the top. Make a difficult move up the slab to the foot of the overhanging crack. Climb this crack (two wire runners were pre-placed on the first ascent) with a good finishing hold out to the left.

★**Stalling Out**   130 feet   E2 6a   (1983)

Extremely good climbing although escapable in two places. Well-protected. Start below a steep wall and rightward-trending flake crack. Climb the steep wall via the flake crack to a large ledge below a roof; this can be reached from the right by a difficult traverse. Move right from the ledge and climb the very steep superb finger crack to a good flake hold, wire runner *in situ*. Move up right, around the arête to the large roof and a peg runner. A delicate traverse right leads to a cracked block. Pull over the roof and go up the surprisingly exposed slab above to the top.

Huge Frog   100 feet   Hard Severe   (1970)
Above the three previous routes and farther up the spur is a large grassy pasture below a short wall. This is reached via a gully on the right. Start just left of a 10-foot chimney which leads to a heather terrace on the right.
1 60 feet. Climb delicately up a short open groove until it is possible to mantelshelf up right. Traverse left to a cannon of rock. Follow short twin cracks behind the ledge to a small cave.
2 40 feet. Climb out of the cave to a small slab on the left. Take the wall above to an obvious traverse line leading to an arête on the right.

Little Benjamin Buttress

This is the two-tiered buttress split by grassy bays, and with a chimney to the left of its upper half, sitting directly below Ettws Isaf, about level with the top of The Nose. The climbing is clean and steep.

Jacob   80 feet   Very Difficult   (1979)
On the left flank of the buttress is a big central overhang. This route takes the break on the left and above the overhang making for a bilberry ledge and a chimney. Start at an arête 12 feet left of the line of the chimney. Follow a cracked scoop then go slightly right and up into a small V-groove. Traverse right to a bilberry ledge and finish up the chimney.

★**Loves-A-Scent**   130 feet   Very Severe   (1990)
Start 10 feet left of Little Benjamin at the base of a steep slab.
1 60 feet. 4c. Climb straight up the slab to reach the bay left of the arête and a ledge on the left.
2 70 feet. 4b. Step off the block and climb the rib to reach the rightward trending groove/rampline, which is followed to the top of the pyramid.

★**Little Benjamin**   115 feet   Severe   (1925)
An entertaining climb. Start on a boulder below the buttress.
1 65 feet. Step off the boulder, climb a crack to a ledge, then traverse left and go up the edge via a crack to a bay.
2 50 feet. A crack on the left leads up a pinnacle. Ascend this and step off the pinnacle to finish steeply over a nose.

Zimmer Frame-up   100 feet   Hard Very Severe   (1990)
Slight but pleasant enough. Start 10 feet right of Little Benjamin under a wide crack in the wall.

1 70 feet. 5a. Problematic starting moves lead up to the crack, then a shallow groove. Ascend this exiting right onto a slab. Move back left to belay at a vertical crack near the centre of the wall.
2 30 feet. 4a. Womble up the delightful crack.

Piggy's Arête 60 feet E2 5c   (1990)
An unbalanced, bold route. Start at the base of the arête 40 feet up Little Benjamin. The prominent arête left of Little Benjamin pitch 2 is unprotected to begin with. Fortunately, the difficulties are short-lived. Finish easily up Little Benjamin, or preferably traverse right a few feet to join and finish up...

Accept For Access 50 feet E2 5b   (1988)
The wall right of Little Benjamin, left of the Zimmer Frame-up finishing crack. Start just right of the belay of Little Benjamin. Go up slightly leftwards via vague flakes to a small ledge. Finish direct up shallow scoops – pleasant.

Ettws Buttress

Lying 150 yards right of Little Benjamin, this slabby buttress comprises a sheet of rough red dolerite, with a stone wall abutting it. Routes are described from RIGHT to LEFT.

Bon Mot 700 feet Very Difficult   (1979)
A discontinuous mountaineering route. Start up to the right of the wall.
1 100 feet. Start up grass on the right for 40 feet until a line of pockets, scoops and cracks leads up and diagonally left for 50 feet to a large heather ledge. (A direct VS variant starts from the top of the stone wall and is delicate).
2 200 feet. Go left and up to a rowan tree, then slabs. Climb the intermittent arête which is like easy gritstone in places. Arrive at an enormous field.
3 200 feet. After walking across the field a slab leads to a scooped arête which starts with a smooth corner/groove.
4 200 feet. The rib soon peters out so cross a grassy trough on the right and continue up slabby humps and grooves.

Chilli Willie and the Red Hot Peppers 130 feet E1 5a (1990)
Makes the most of the rock between The Glass Flipper and the grassy gully on the right, escapable. Ten feet right of the stone wall, start steeply up, as for The Glass Flipper, but move right to pockets (Bon Mot), and the first shallow groove on the right. Climb the groove then go directly up the rib past a loose flake to cracks. Finish direct (to the right of The Glass Flipper).

★**The Glass Flipper**   140 feet   Hard Very Severe 5a   (1989)
An eliminate on Bon Mot which saves its crux for the top section. Start
10 feet right of the stone wall direct to Bon Mot. Climb the steep slab
to reach a vertical crack. Easier climbing, Bon Mot, leads to a tiny
flake. Follow a groove up right to a steep tower of slabs with a
shallow crack leading up leftwards to finish.

Cinderella Penguin   130 feet   Very Severe 5a   (1990)
An escapable route taking the slabby left arête of the buttress. Start
just right of this at a crack. Climb the awkward crack to a scooped
area. Pad up to the upper scoop and step left onto a block pedestal.
Ascend the parallel cracks above.

Craig yr Ogof

About 300 yards left of Craig y Rhaeadr is a buttress with a large cave
on its right-hand side. Well worth going up to, good clean rock and fine
views.

The Wrath of Grapes   240 feet   E1   1990
Start on the leftward side of the buttress at some slabs 30 feet below
a downward pointing, slabby finger of rock.
1 110 feet. 5b. Climb the slabs to reach a roof, surmount this and
ascend the continuation slab and grooves to a belay.
2 130 feet. 4c. Follow the grooves up the left-hand side of the
buttress with some hardish moves towards the top.

Cave Buttress   260 feet   Very Severe   (1965)
Not an obvious line. Start at the lowest point of the rocks below and
to the left of the cave.
1 130 feet. 4c. A vegetated groove leads diagonally left for 30 feet,
then cross a slab rightwards above the overhanging wall to the
prominent central groove. Climb this (crux) and the rocks above to a
ledge and belays.
2 130 feet. 4b. Ascend steeply and follow the shattered crack.

Anturiaethau Dic Preifat   260 feet   Hard Very Severe   (1990)
Two very good pitches. Start at the right of Cave Buttress at some
slabs under a diagonal crack slanting leftwards.
1 130 feet. 5a. Climb the slabby rib to reach the crack, climb this
(crux) to reach a groove. Follow ribs on the left above the groove to
belay (down and left of the Cave Buttress belay).

2 130 feet. 4b. Traverse left above an overhang to reach a series of grooves in the centre of the buttress. Follow these to the top.

Craig y Rhaeadr

(Diffwys Ddwr – Precipice of Water)   OS Ref. 622 562

Low down on the left side of Cwm Glas, this prominent, wet, reddish-black crag rises steeply for some 350 feet. A waterfall cascades over a line of black overhangs near the top onto The Pedestal, a massive sail-shaped block at the foot of the cliff. Way over on the far left is a large pillar – Cwm Glas Pinnacle. Right of the waterfall a steep nasty-looking gully runs the full height of the crag. The buttress on its right is at a slightly easier angle and rather more broken. A vertical furrow marks it on the right. The main cliff routes are worth doing for their fine positions and unusual atmosphere; the rock is compact and protection can be difficult to find and arrange.

Cwm Glas Pinnacle Difficult   (1935)
A short entertaining climb. Back-and-foot up behind the flake until the chimney becomes too wide, then swing across and climb the edge to the top.

Verglas Slab 245 feet Very Severe   (1955)
Very grassy and not recommended. An artificial and indefinite line starting just left of Cwm Glas Pinnacle.

There are other lines farther left at Very Difficult/Severe in standard.

★**Ghosts** 240 feet E3   (1980)
Good climbing up the open face to the left of The Wall. Poor protection but the rock is perfect. Start as for The Wall.
1 90 feet. 5b. Climb fairly directly to below a small overhang at 35 feet. Move up to the left with difficulty then climb up rightwards for 30 feet and move up into an obvious groove. Restricted stance and good belays.
2 150 feet. 5b. Move left and climb the steep scoop to better holds. Continue up and slightly left to more featureless terrain and climb easily to the top, or finish at the left edge of the crag… more or less the same finish as 'T'ouse Wall.

Craig y Rhaeadr

1. Verglas Slab   VS
2. Ghosts   E3
3. The Wall   E1
4. 'T'ouse Wall   E2

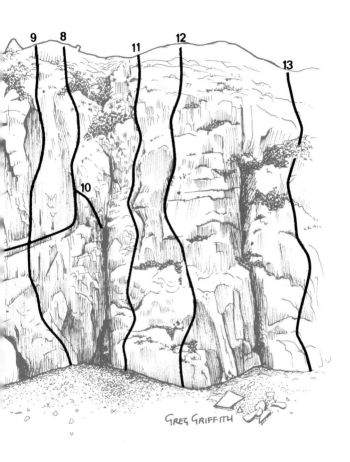

GREG GRIFFITH

5. Red Wall	HVS	11. Mushroom	VS
6. Chequered Wall	HVS	12. Botany Climb	VS
7. Lung Fish	E3	13. Grooved Slab	S
8. Waterfall Climb	S	C Cwm Glas Pinnacle	
9. The Sewer	E3	P Pedestal	
10. Waterfall Climb Direct Start	HS		

'T'ouse Wall   360 feet   E2   (1969)
A fairly direct line (save for a 30-foot traverse) up the area of steep
rock between Ghosts and The Wall. The climbing is pleasant enough,
despite what the name implies. Start as for The Wall.
1 100 feet. 5a. Follow The Wall up to where it traverses right. Take
the groove directly above to a stance and belay.
2 90 feet. 5b. Traverse left for 15 feet, then climb a thin crack.
Traverse delicately left for another 15 feet to a groove. Follow this to
a good stance.
3 120 feet. Ascend uninterestingly to a grassy ledge.
4 50 feet. Continue easily to the top.

★**The Wall**   350 feet   E1   (1959)
A fine steep route with moderate protection up the obvious white wall
half-way between Cwm Glas Pinnacle and the red walls in the centre
of the crag. Start below the wall.
1 140 feet 5a. Go steeply up right on an obvious traverse line then
back left along another traverse to the foot of a smooth groove. Climb
this for 20 feet, crux, then trend steeply right making for the left end
of some grassy ledges. Move diagonally left to a small grassy ledge
and peg belay directly above the crux groove.
2 150 feet. 4c. Traverse left for 10 feet then ascend on good holds to
a shallow V-chimney which leads to grass and rock. Continue more
easily to a good grass ledge.
3 60 feet. 4c. Climb the awkward corner from the ledge then ascend
direct to the top.

Red Wall   290 feet   Hard Very Severe   (1953)
A direct line up the red walls in the centre of the crag passing a minor
set of overhangs on the right. It is easier but more grassy than the
other routes. Start from a large terrace midway between The Pinnacle
and The Pedestal.
1 110 feet. 5a. Climb a shallow groove for 20 feet then traverse
right to a grassy ledge at the foot of a smooth groove. Climb on the
right of the groove until a step left leads into it. Follow the groove to a
ledge on the right. Go up to a stance and peg belays.
2 90 feet. 4c. Climb left up a series of awkward ledges. Go up a
short crack and step left onto a steep slab. Trend right up the slab to a
small ledge underneath and at the extreme right edge of the
overhangs. Step round the corner on the right, then go straight up to
a stance and belay on the edge of the overhang.
3 60 feet. Step right and climb direct to the top.

Chequered Wall   400 feet   Hard Very Severe   (1959)
A wet but clean route up the centre of the crag. Start below and on
the left of The Pedestal.

Nick Wharton on *Nexus Direct* (E5) Dinas Mot. Photo: Bob Wightman

The final pitch of *Main Wall* (Hard Severe) Cyrn Las.
Photo: Malcolm Creasey

Steve Hartley on the final hand-traverse pitch of *Lubyanka* (E3) Cyrn Las.
Photo: Huw Perkins

Martin Crook on *Pretty Girls Make Graves* (E6) The Gravestones.
Photo: Ray Wood

1 70 feet. Ascend the groove to a large grassy ledge.
2 30 feet. 4c. Climb the obvious crack on the left of the flake.
3 120 feet. 5a. Climb the wall for 20 feet then go up the obvious groove trending left to an awkward corner. Go up this to a stance and peg belay 20 feet higher on the left.
4 80 feet. 5a. Traverse 15 feet left along the ledge, then go up to enter a steep shallow groove with difficulty, and onto a tiny ledge with a rickety block. Climb delicately up to a tiny grass ledge at the right-hand end of an overhang. Awkward thread belay.
5 100 feet. Go round the rib on the right and traverse 30 feet to a white slab – finish up this.

Variation Finish
4a 60 feet. 5a. From the stance stride across and go steeply up right to a grassy ledge at the end of the enormous overhangs.
5a 100 feet. Go left and ascend directly up the white slabs.

Lung Fish   330 feet   E3   (1974)
A good route when dry. It takes a very direct line above The Pedestal. Start near the right-hand side of The Pedestal below some pockets.
1 40 feet. 5c. Climb up and left to a tiny spike on an arête. Move up with difficulty and go right to the pockets. A difficult rising traverse leads to the edge of The Pedestal.
2 100 feet. Scramble easily up to the apex of The Pedestal.
3 60 feet. 5b. Climb directly up the wall making for a deep V-groove. Go up this and exit left to a small stance and peg belay.
4 80 feet. 5c. Continue in the same line up to the overhangs. Climb through these past one peg runner and go up to a grassy stance.
5 50 feet. Finish easily.

★★**Silent Spring**   350 feet   E3   (1980)
An excellent route on perfect rock taking a central line up to, and through, the overhangs. Start as for Lung Fish.
1 140 feet. 5c. Climb diagonally left for 30 feet to a good runner below a shallow groove. Climb this to reach a horizontal line of handholds. Step right then go straight up the face to easy ground. Climb to the top of The Pedestal, then ascend obvious grooves above as for Waterfall Climb to a good spike.
2 110 feet. 5c. Above is a smooth black groove. Climb to the base of it, then move left and climb steeply to gain the slab. Go up left slightly to the apex of the slab, then move back right across the top of the black groove. Climb for a few feet then go up left on improving holds until a slight groove leads up to the right to some ledges below the main overhangs (and just left of the obvious way through them). Good belays.

3 100 feet. 5c. Climb out to the right through the roofs then go up a clean white slab to an easy rib leading to the top.

Waterfall Climb   415 feet   Severe   (1932)

A unique and serious expedition which is seldom dry as the line traverses along the obvious terrace under the waterfall. Although technically straightforward, some care is needed in handling the loose rock. Start from the foot of the easy chimney which leads up the right-hand side of The Pedestal.

1 50 feet. Climb the chimney to a rock rake leading to the pedestal top. Good stance.

2 40 feet. Descend a few feet and traverse right into a steep groove. Climb this to a small ledge on the right then continue easily to the left-hand end of the terrace. Consider retreat!

3 35 feet. Follow the terrace easily, under the waterfall (which provides a brisk cold shower) to a rock bay beside the gully.

4 40 feet. The wall on the right bulges but soon has good holds. Traverse into the gully as soon as possible to a grassy stance on the right.

5 60 feet. Keep to the right over broken rocks and grass.

6 40 feet. Go straight up then trend left to a prominent white rock.

7 150 feet. Climb broken indefinite rocks with stances etc.

Variation

The Direct Start Hard Severe

The lower easy section of the gully is climbed direct. Difficult at 40 feet.

The Sewer   290 feet   E3   (1967/1983)

This endurance test follows the drainage line up the wet wall just right of The Pedestal. The grade is given for an ascent when the waterfall stops running, but this will only occur when 'Llyn Padarn dries up', according to the first free ascensionists. In its normal state, slime, seaweed, dirt and streaming rock will be encountered making this a strong contender for 'The Most Unpleasant Route on the South Side of The Pass Award'. Start 15 feet left of The Direct Start to Waterfall Climb.

1 80 feet. 5a. Climb the steep wall just right of a wet flake. Traverse left along an obvious ledge to belay at its end.

2 30 feet. 4c. Ascend the groove on the left to the terrace of Waterfall Climb.

3 60 feet. 5c. Climb the precarious and technical slimy groove directly below the right-hand end of the overhang past a rotten peg (crux) to a small stance. Peg belay about 30 feet below the roofs.

4 120 feet. 4c. Move diagonally rightwards onto the rib and follow it, keeping left, to the top.

Mushroom   300 feet   Very Severe   (1967)
A steep line with reasonable holds on the buttress just right of the
chimney of The Direct Start to Waterfall Climb. A groove capped by
an overhang 100 feet up is an obvious feature. Start at the left corner
of the buttress.
1 90 feet. 4c. Climb the arête or easy cracks to a grassy terrace.
Layback up the prominent undercut flake, then go diagonally left over
an overlap to a ledge. Continue to a belay on the left of the groove.
2 150 feet. 4c. Climb the groove moving left at the overhang, then
ascend an easy arête and grassy slabs.
3 60 feet. Finish easily up vegetated rock.

Sphagnum   330 feet   E2   (1981)
Start midway between Mushroom and Botany Climb.
1 40 feet. 4c. Pull over a slight bulge onto the wall and climb to a
large mossy ledge. Belay on the left.
2 90 feet. 5b. Ascend the middle of the steep wall to an obvious
undercut. Make hard moves to reach a block where the angle eases.
Continue up the slab keeping left of a shallow groove to gain the
left-hand end of a large grassy ledge. Climb short cracks above to a
small stance and high spike belay near the foot of the groove on
Botany Climb.
3 140 feet. 4b. Climb the right-hand edge above, then move out left
onto the slabs and continue to a stance and spike belay.
4 60 feet. Easy rocks lead to the top.

Variation
3a 140 feet. 5b. Above and left of the belay is an undercut flake. Reach
this and go left to easier ground. Climb the slab to join the original line.
More in keeping with the grade.

Botany Climb   370 feet   Very Severe   (1955)
A rather grassy route up the long shallow groove right of Sphagnum.
Start at the lowest point of the buttress.
1 50 feet. 4b. Climb a steep wall to a rowan tree. Easy slabs on the
left lead to a grassy terrace.
2 75 feet. 4b. Layback a short crack; steep walls and grassy grooves
lead to ledges below and to the right of the main groove.
3 135 feet. 4a. Take the obvious line left up pleasant slabs into the
groove and climb this to grassy ledges.
4 110 feet. Walls and grassy scrambling lead to the top.

Grooved Slab   300 feet   Severe   (1955)
Right of Botany Climb is a slabby light coloured buttress flanked by
grassy grooves. Shallow grooves are followed up the slabs bearing
left to a grass gangway, then trend leftwards to the top.

Rhaeadr Girdle   750 feet   Hard Very Severe   (1955)
Start up a little grassy gully just right of Botany Climb. Follow Botany
Climb pitch 2 then traverse left into the Direct Start of Waterfall
Climb. Go up this and traverse easily across the terrace swept by the
waterfall. Continue in the same line until a line of weakness ascends
diagonally left to an awkward corner (junction with Chequered Wall).
Above the corner traverse left to an area of grass on Red Wall, and
then ascend diagonally across a wall to a poor stance. Traverse left
to a spike on the skyline then climb diagonally up to finish on an
obvious terrace with a cave.

Sunshine Breakfast   150 feet   Very Severe 4c   (1968)
A steep little route. Start at the foot of a pink wall in the descent gully
at the right-hand side of the crag. Climb straight up to a flake crack
and follow this until it is possible to stride right to a sloping ledge.
Finish directly up the wall.

West End   120 feet   Very Difficult   (1960)
On the right of the crag is a steep little buttress of excellent rock
separated from the main cliff by the descent gully. Start near the
centre of the buttress at a gangway trending left.
1 65 feet. Ascend the gangway to an awkward mantelshelf, then
traverse 10 feet right to a narrow ledge. Climb flakes to a large
grassy ledge on the left.
2 55 feet. Climb the steep slab trending right and finish direct.

Little Jim   75 feet   Very Severe 4b   (1960)
Start 15 feet right of West End at an arrow on the rock. Climb the
bulging wall to a narrow ledge on the left. Climb a vague crack right
to a ledge under an overhang. Pleasant slabs lead up leftwards to the
top.

The Intermediate Slabs   (Cwm Glas)

On the eastern side of Cwm Glas, between the two streams to the left of
Cyrn Las, is an outcrop called Castell, with a clean stretch of slabs up to
250 feet high. The main slab lies between the right-hand edge and a
prominent black chimney on the left.

Spring Chimney   195 feet   Very Difficult   (1949)
Start at the foot of a continuous buttress well to the left of the black
chimney. An overhanging chimney starts half-way up.

1 50 feet. Scramble to a heathery ledge.
2 75 feet. From the right-hand end of the ledge go diagonally up right towards the chimney, to a small ledge below a groove. Climb the groove to a recess below the overhangs.
3 70 feet. The steep chimney splitting the overhangs is hard to start. Above the chimney finish up a wall.

Intermediate Chimney 130 feet Very Difficult   (1949)
Start in the black chimney.
1 70 feet. Climb the groove right of the overhanging chimney. Bear left near the top to a stance in the chimney.
2 60 feet. Keep in the right-hand corner and go up steeply until a pull out right; or finish up the chimney direct.

Tradition 200 feet Severe   (1949)
Start to the right of the black chimney at the foot of a groove leading up to an overhang.
1 60 feet. Climb the groove for 30 feet until it becomes awkward. Swing out right, go over a rib and across a short steep slab to a detached block. Climb up above the block to a grassy stance.
2 50 feet. Step out left onto a slab. Ascend this to a broad ledge, a good pitch.
3 90 feet. Walk along the ledge to the first break on the right. Ascend a few feet then go diagonally left, underneath a poised block to the top.

Conway Climb 180 feet Difficult   (1949)
Start at the lowest point on the right-hand end of the slabs.
1 50 feet. Climb the shallow groove and then the slab.
2 40 feet. Go diagonally left with ease.
3 90 feet. Climb the steeper rocks ahead and continue up in the same line to finish.

Clogwyn y Person and Clogwyn y Ddysgl

From the ridge of Crib y Ddysgl a rocky promontory juts out into upper Cwm Glas dividing it into two cwms each having a tiny llyn. The crest of the ridge is called Crib y Person or the Clogwyn y Person Arête. The western flank of the ridge is a steep rock face, Clogwyn y Ddysgl. At the extreme end of the ridge a prominent nose of rock, some 150 feet high is separated from the main cliff by a vertical break. This nose is Clogwyn y Person and the clefts defining it are Eastern Gully and Western Gully. Clogwyn y Ddysgl is an extensive cliff varying in height from 200 feet to nearly 500 feet. On the left towards Clogwyn y Person the rock is clean and solid. As one moves right, the quality deteriorates until the main cliff ends in a mass of broken ground, unstable 'organ pipes' and scree-filled gullies. Along the base of the cliff is a wide rake, The Parson's Progress. Most of the climbs start from this rake. One hundred and fifty yards from Western Gully is a huge fallen block with a prominent crack above it. On the left of this is a large recess with a broken chimney. To the right of Fallen Block Crack is a large area of partially explored rock; the main lines have all been climbed, but there may yet be some scope for the pioneer. The lower section of the cliff here is very steep for 150 feet but above it is broken and loose. To the right a V-shaped stone shoot marks the line of Waterslide Gully. The cliff ends with the large triangular Infidel Buttress. Beyond this is a jumble of broken rocks and scree. The best descent from Clogwyn y Ddysgl is down the Clogwyn y Person Arête, and then down Western Gully.

Clogwyn y Person   (Cliff of the Parson)

OS Ref. 617 555

Square Gully   195 feet   Severe   (1949)
Start at the foot of the first break left of Eastern Gully.
1 100 feet. A wet rake slanting up left leads into the gully. Continue up over grass to a stance below an overhang.
2 45 feet. Go over the interesting overhang to good holds. Step left and over the rib to a good stance and belay.
3 50 feet. Scramble up grass to a stance. Climb the angular chimney on the left, over a loose flake, then climb the right-hand branch. Scramble up to finish. The rocks on the left of Square Gully are more broken, but odd interesting routes up chimneys can be worked out.

Eastern Gully   160 feet   Moderate   (1879)
The left-hand boundary of The Parson's Nose gives a loose scramble with two small cave pitches. From the summit of The Parson's Nose the Clogwyn y Person Arête gives a fine ridge scramble. The route is well-marked and the standard can be varied by climbing the various obstacles direct.

The Eastern Edge   220 feet   Severe   (1879)
An interesting route up the left side of The Nose on poor rock. Start at the foot of a grassy slab slanting up leftwards below the front of The Nose.
1 60 feet. Scramble up the slabs to a band of quartz.
2 55 feet. Climb the quartz to an awkward sloping shelf. Step across to a chimney which leads to a stance and belay.
3 45 feet. Ascend the corner, first left then right almost to the foot of another chimney. Follow a natural traverse line right, then climb steeply to a grassy break.
4 60 feet. Finish easily up grass or more pleasantly up the rib.

★**The Parson's Nose Direct**   130 feet   Very Difficult   (c.1900)
A fine climb with airy situations but poor protection which is best done in one runout. Start 80 feet above the foot of The Nose. Easy scrambling over loose rock leads to a sloping triangular ledge. Step out to the left and go up towards an arête on the skyline (possible stance on the arête below a small overhang, shaky belay). Climb the steep gangway on the right of the arête for about 35 feet then swing over onto the arête. Good holds lead to a grassy corner near the top of The Nose.

★**The Parson's Nose**   250 feet   Difficult   (1884)
A delightful route with fine exposure on good holds. Start at the lowest point of the rocks at some easy slabs.
1 80 feet. Ascend easy-angled slabs.
2 70 feet. The slab continues to steepen but good holds still arrive. The route curves over slightly towards Western Gully. Stance and belay at the foot of a shallow groove.
3 50 feet. A rising traverse along a faint crackline leads to a large ledge overlooking the gully.
4 50 feet. Easy scrambling leads to the final section of The Right-Hand Edge.

The Right-Hand Edge   150 feet   Moderate   (1892)
A short route which pleasantly follows the western edge of The Nose. Start just left of Western Gully. Numerous stances etc.

Western Gully   150 feet   Easy   (1879)
A useful descent. The top pitch is about Moderate and can be taken on the right wall or up through the cave.

Clogwyn y Ddysgl

(Cliff of the Dish)

OS Ref. 615 554

Gargoyle Route   270 feet   Very Difficult   (1948)
An entertaining climb. Start at an obvious V-chimney about 100 feet
right of Western Gully.
1 50 feet. Climb the chimney and exit left onto the slabs above.
2 50 feet. Broken rock leads to the foot of an overhanging chimney.
3 40 feet. Traverse across the right wall to another chimney.
4 60 feet. Ascend the chimney then climb the corner on the right over
immense piled blocks.
5 70 feet. Step off the quartz-topped block on the left and climb the
crack above. Cross grass below the gargoyle, to the foot of the
left-hand crack. Ascend this to join the arête.

Choristers' Cleft   215 feet   Very Difficult   (1939)
A pleasant route, artificial but worthwhile. Start between the
V-chimney of Gargoyle Route and the start of The Gambit Climb, at a
vertical corner the first main break left of The Gambit Climb.
1 50 feet. Climb the corner on good holds to an awkward exit onto
the slabs above. Continue easily to a large bollard.
2 40 feet. Step off the bollard into a shallow scoop in the right wall
and go up to a small stance. Climb a difficult groove, then an easy
slab to belay in the right-hand corner.
3 50 feet. The overhanging crack leads to a grassy ledge. From a
higher ledge climb the right wall to a large grassy ledge (The Green
Collar of The Gambit Climb).
4 75 feet. Climb the interesting flake crack on the left to a stance.
Ascend the crack on the right to a grassy bay. Finish up the left wall.

★ Hooded Crow   395 feet   E3   (1983)
A good route with much varied and interesting climbing. Start as for
Choristers' Cleft.
1 100 feet 5a. Climb a right-slanting groove to an overhang. Pull
round this into a vertical groove. Go up the groove exiting right after
a few moves, then climb up to ledges (on The Gambit Climb).
2 50 feet. 4b. Trend easily up and rightwards until a step right can
be made round a corner to reach a crack. Climb this to grassy ledges.
3 85 feet. 5b. Ascend to a grassy ledge at 15 feet, then go up the
middle of the slabby wall above, finishing by a short right-facing
corner. Superb climbing.

4 60 feet. 5a. Climb cracks direct to a grassy ledge.
5 100 feet. 4b. Follow a crack, move right to a corner and up this to easy rock.

★★★**The Gambit Climb** 325 feet Very Difficult (1910)
An excellent route of its standard, sustained and interesting with the crux on its first pitch. Llanberis's answer to Grooved Arête on Tryfan. Sixty yards to the right of Western Gully is a curious pock-marked wall. Start 15 feet left of this at a flaky crack.
1 75 feet. Climb the flaky crack until a step onto the left edge. Traverse left onto a slab, and after a short descent, step across the base of the slab into a corner crack which leads to a good ledge. Ascend the short awkward crack above to belay on broad ledges.
2 55 feet. A short traverse right leads to an easy chimney. Climb this to a broad grassy ledge, The Green Collar.
3 45 feet. Traverse right with difficulty for a few feet then climb a short chimney to gain a good ledge.
4 70 feet. In the far corner, an impressive chimney is taken to the top of a pinnacle. A short hand-traverse right leads into a corner crack. Climb this easily; or the wider crack on the left to a scree ledge.
5 80 feet. Climb a sloping ledge on the right to a right-angled corner. A strenuous finger crack up the corner gives a fine finish. A short scramble up leads to the arête.

Variations
4a The 'He-man' Variation is a 50-foot Very Difficult slab starting on the right, at the top of pitch 3. It leads to a ledge below a quartz-mottled corner.
5a Longland's Variation. From the top of the 'He-man' slab, and a few feet left is a steep arête. Climb this to a small platform and large belay. Traverse up and across the wall to the left to finish level with the mottled recess, Very Difficult. Many variations can be made above pitch 3. The arête direct on Longland's Variation is Severe.

★**Nunc Dimittis** 350 feet Very Severe (1957)
A pleasant and sustained series of variations on The Ring, hard for its grade. Start five feet right of The Gambit Climb below a clean cut groove which is higher up the crag.
1 40 feet. 4c. Climb the layback crack 10 feet up to a grassy recess at the foot of the groove.
2 55 feet. 5a. Climb the deep V-groove moving right at the top; crux.
3 75 feet. 4b. Ascend 10 feet and move left to a spike on the arête. Climb the wall trending slightly right, then go straight up steeply to a stance and perched block (junction with The Ring).
4 60 feet. 4a. Above is a steep wall. Climb it on the right by cracks

in a groove above an initial slab to a large bay.

5 120 feet. 4b. Climb the left arête, then move right to join the last cracks of The Ring. Ascend easily to the ridge.

★**My Best Friend**   380 feet   Hard Very Severe   (1991)
Essentially a direct start to The Ring. Start 10 feet right of The Gambit Climb at a cracked slab.

1 70 feet. 5a. Jam the crack in the slab to a spike belay – a superb pitch reminiscent of gritstone.

2 20 feet. Move up leftwards to join Nunc Dimittis at its second stance.

3 75 feet. 4c. Ascend for 10 feet then move left to a spike. Take the wall above, finishing steeply, to join The Ring at a perched block.

4 70 feet. Traverse left and go up the cracked corner to a spiky stance. Climb a short wall to a corner slab which leads in turn to a ledge below a corner with twin cracks (The Ring – pitch 5).

5 120 feet. 4b. Climb the left-hand crack to a ledge. Step right into the corner and jam steeply up the twin cracks. Broken rocks lead up to the ridge (The Ring – pitch 6).

★**The Ring**   380 feet   Very Severe   (1948)
A steep, pleasantly exposed and somewhat rambling route. Start midway between The Gambit Climb and Fallen Block Crack at a steep groove just right of two chimneys.

1 50 feet. 4a. Climb the awkward groove for a few feet then move left round the corner. Ascend to large perched blocks at 30 feet. Continue for 20 feet to a ledge with belays on the left.

2 40 feet. Step up and traverse left into a corner. A series of three large steps lead to another corner.

3 50 feet. 4b. Ascend the corner for 15 feet then step out left. The wall above has small holds and an awkward mantelshelf. Traverse right to a small stance and belay beside a tiny slab.

4 50 feet. 4c. A small fingerhold on the left enables an awkward traverse to be made across the slab to its far edge. Ascend to a shallow chimney and the crack above it. Stance at a perched block.

5 70 feet. Traverse left and go up the cracked corner to a spiky stance. Climb a short wall to a corner slab leading to a ledge below a corner with twin cracks.

6 120 feet. 4b. Climb the left-hand crack to a ledge. Step right into the corner and jam the strenuous twin cracks. Broken rocks lead up to the ridge.

Ribbon Route   300 feet   Difficult   (1910)
Loose and not recommended. A very broken route which is ill-defined in its upper reaches. Start a few yards left of Fallen Block Crack by a pock-marked block. Climb direct, zigzagging to avoid difficulties. At

100 feet a prominent quartz ribbon is crossed after which the route deteriorates into scrambling.

Fallen Block Climb 290 feet   Moderate   (c.1900)
The obvious but disappointing gully left of the Fallen Block.
1 90 feet. Scramble up into the bed of the gully and climb the broken crack in the left corner of the chimney on the right. Ascend the upper part of the chimney.
2 200 feet. Loose scrambling up the gully line leads to the arête. Numerous stances and belays.

Bad Moon Risin' 120 feet   E3 6a   (1984)
A fierce route which gives good climbing up the imposing crack in the wall left of Simulid. Start just left of Simulid. Climb directly up the wall to the detached flake/pillar on Simulid. Continue up the crack to finish.

Simulid 140 feet   Hard Very Severe 5b   (1981)
A short but worthwhile climb. Start just left of Fallen Block Crack. Climb left up a series of flakes to the top of a detached flake/pillar. Traverse right and down along the obvious line to the foot of a steep groove. Climb this, past a ledge, making a difficult move out right just below the top. Step back above the groove to belay.

★**Fallen Block Crack** 290 feet   Very Severe   (1927)
Interesting and enjoyable. The wide crack may prove to be slightly easier in boots, the traditional footwear for this esoteric outing. Start from the Fallen Block.
1 30 feet. 4a. The strenuous crack leads to a chockstone belay.
2 85 feet. 4c. The crack is very steep to a resting place at 30 feet on some loose blocks. The middle section of the crack can be avoided by the harder, thin crack on the right. The crack eventually eases and leads to a large ledge shared by The Black Gates.
3 175 feet. As for The Black Gates. A chimney on the left for 30 feet and then scrambling up to the arête.

★**Route of Knobs** 175 feet   Hard Very Severe   (1952)
An exposed and technical route which takes the right wall of Fallen Block Crack.
1 30 feet. Climb the crack as for Fallen Block Crack.
2 95 feet. 5a. Use a hold on the right wall to reach the outer edge. Climb the arête for 15 feet to a ledge. Traverse right past a thin vertical crack to a groove/crack on the right. Climb this for a few feet then move back into the centre of the face. Ascend trending right till a crack leads to the arrival ledge of Fallen Block Crack.
3 50 feet. 4b. Traverse left across the crack and climb the left wall.

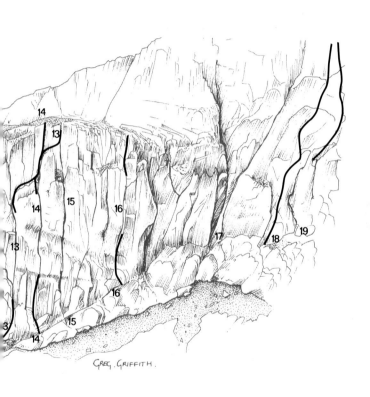

GREG. GRIFFITH.

Clogwyn y Ddysgl

Variation
Direct Start Hard Very Severe
1a 5b. Follow a steep crack on the right to join the main line.

★**The Black Gates**   220 feet   Very Difficult   (1915)
A little known gem. Start 50 feet right of Fallen Block Crack at a
shallow groove in a steep wall.
1 30 feet. Ascend the groove to a stance below large boulders.
2 50 feet. 'The Black Gates'. Go over the boulders to a niche below
a leaning pinnacle. Leave the niche strenuously and climb the crack to
the top of the pinnacle. Belay 15 feet higher in a corner.
3 40 feet. Climb the chimney in the corner for 20 feet, till an exposed
step round the corner on the left to a small ledge. Climb the wall to a
larger ledge, 10 feet higher is one with a belay.
4 35 feet. From the left end of the ledge climb the chimney (the upper
part of Fallen Block Crack). Thirty feet of scrambling leads to a
chimney on the right.
5 65 feet. Climb the chimney with a chockstone at 10 feet, then go
up 10 feet to a ledge. Finish up a fine steep slab.

Genesis   395 feet   Hard Very Severe   (1970)
A well-protected climb up entertaining cracks. The exact line is quite
hard to find. Start as for The Black Gates.
1 130 feet. 5a. Follow The Black Gates for 30 feet then go right up a
wall at a leaning block. Corner cracks, then steep thin cracks lead to
a good belay ledge.
2 100 feet. 5a. Traverse 20 feet right into a right-angled corner. Go
up the strenuous corner-crack and the continuation chimney.
3 75 feet. 4b. Step right and climb a groove to a ledge. Step right to
a short crack and ascend to a huge crevasse below thin water-worn
cracks in a prominent steep wall.
4 90 feet. 5a. Ascend the steep left-hand crack on good jams.

★★**Rectory Chimneys**   430 feet   Very Difficult   (1925)
An excellent route, one of the best of its standard in The Pass. Start
30 feet right of The Black Gates, at a narrow chimney guarded by a
leaning flake
1 60 feet. Use the flake to climb the chimney then go up a groove in
the steep wall. Easier than it looks.
2 70 feet. Ascend a short steep wall on the left, then a short crack
with a mantelshelf to a niche below a pinnacle. The crack above is
strenuous but can be avoided by crafty deviation. Step round to the
left and enter the crack from behind. Fifteen feet of easy climbing
above the crack leads to a good stance.
3 40 feet. Step up in the corner, then traverse a narrow ledge to a
large chimney. Climb this to a ledge.

4 60 feet. From the ledge at the top of the chimney climb over broken rocks to the right by a grassy gully.
5 120 feet. A grassy rake traverses up right above a huge crevasse, stances etc. This leads to an immense cairn of bollards, The Vestry.
6 80 feet. Traverse a further 20 feet right into a broken chimney which leads easily up to the arête.

Quintet Route   350 feet   Severe   (1935)
This vague route is right of Rectory Chimneys. Start 20 feet right of the line leading to a conspicuous recess near the foot of the crag. A 30-foot crack leads to a stance. Traverse left and go up a vertical corner with a rib in it to a broad platform. Above this is The Grey Chimney, difficult to start which is climbed for 45 feet to a belay. Move left onto an arête to a stance after 40 feet. Traverse right onto a steep exposed slab which is followed pleasantly to a perch on its left edge. Continue up in the same line to finish.

Duet Chimneys   320 feet   Hard Severe   (1935)
A worthwhile route despite some dubious rock. Immediately right of Rectory Chimneys is a steep buttress, the right-hand side of which is defined by this route. Start by scrambling up to a quartz-topped bollard below a smooth V-chimney.
1 30 feet. Go easily up to the chimney to a ledge. Belay on the left.
2 45 feet. The smooth chimney is difficult up to a stance. Work up into the roof of the chimney and swing round to a higher ledge using good holds well up on the left.
3 45 feet. Climb up behind the perched block and traverse diagonally up to a stance beside a chimney. A good pitch.
4 30 feet. The narrow dirty chimney leads to a cave in the wider cleft above, loose. Belays in the cave floor.
5 60 feet. The chimney is strenuous and the flakes forming the roof are difficult to get round. Continue more easily then leave the chimney to reach a stance at a long finger of rock.
6 60 feet. Continue in the same line to the foot of a steep wall. The piled bollards of The Vestry are above and to the right. Climb the wall to a stance and belay.
7 50 feet. Descend slightly left and go up a break in the wall until it is possible to move round onto the face. Follow the right edge and finish in a niche just below the ridge.

Hexagonal Phase   305 feet   E1   (1984)
A direct line on Quartet Wall. Interesting but disjointed climbing. Start 30 feet left of Three Cave Gully.
1 70 feet. 5b. Climb thin cracks in the front of the buttress to a grassy ledge.

2 130 feet. 5a. Climb a wide flake crack above the belay and cross broken rock to avoid the overhang on the right. Continue directly up the wall to a stance.

3 105 feet. 5a. Scramble up for 20 feet, then follow a crack in the thin slabby buttress left of the gully.

The Quartet Wall 180 feet Very Difficult (1935)

This pleasant and exposed route leads directly to The Vestry, via the loose wall of Three Cave Gully.

1 35 feet. Climb to the floor of the cave, then climb up a pinnacle on the left wall to a ledge.

2 45 feet. Traverse to the end of the grassy ledge and climb the wall on a diagonal line of holds to a good stance.

3 50 feet. Traverse diagonally up right below the overhang into a shallow groove. Climb the right edge of the groove, then cross to the roof of the overhang. Pinnacle belays.

4 50 feet. Take a direct line up the wall to The Vestry.

Three Cave Gully 225 feet Very Difficult (1937)

A poor route on bad rock. Right of Duet Chimneys is a steep broken buttress with an obvious overhang about half-way up. The route follows the prominent chimneys on the right. Start by scrambling up to the foot of the gully.

1 65 feet. Climb the gully to a cave. Ascend the right wall and traverse to a stance on the edge. Climb a small corner near the edge to a slab on the right, then traverse back across a smooth slab into the second cave.

2 90 feet. Ascend the deeply-cut chimney to the third cave.

3 70 feet. Climb out of the cave and follow the gully continuation to join Rectory Chimneys at the crevasse. The final easy chimney of this leads up to the arête.

Lectern Grooves 170 feet Hard Severe (1962)

The walls to the right of Three Cave Gully are smaller but very steep and split by some impressive cracks. About half-way between the gully and the large triangular buttress on the right is an inverted V-chimney. The route follows twin grooves up the wall on the left. The escape above the route is exceptionally loose. Start by scrambling up to ledges at the foot of the steep upper walls.

1 100 feet. Step left onto a rib and go up to the foot of the first groove. Move left immediately and onto the wall on the left. Climb this on small positive holds to the second groove and ascend this steeply to a good ledge.

2 70 feet. Climb the easier continuation of the groove for a few feet then move right to a grassy ledge. Scramble up with caution to finish.

★Russet 170 feet E3 (1971)

An excellent crack pitch, well worth the walk. Towards the right-hand end of the cliff is a well-defined and steep red groove. Start below this.

1 140 feet. 5c. Climb the overhanging groove, very fierce at the start. Continue more easily up the groove and past the overhang. Belay.

2 30 feet. Scramble easily to the top.

The Curate's Egg 220 feet Very Severe (1967)

A poor route. Start left of Waterslide Gully at the lowest point of the buttress.

1 80 feet. Climb easily to grassy ledges and belays below a large detached pinnacle.

2 40 feet. 4b. Ascend the pinnacle and groove above on dubious flakes. Move right to a stance and belays.

3 100 feet. 4b. Climb the flake cracks behind the belays, then traverse left across a slab for 15 feet and finish up the wall above.

Waterslide Gully 400 feet Moderate (1908)

The left side of Infidel Buttress is defined by a scree-filled gully running the full height of the cliff. In the lower half it gives typical gully climbing for about 100 feet to the steep waterslide, a tricky pitch which leads out of the main gully to the right. The rock then deteriorates. Not recommended.

The Organ Route Easy (1908)

From below the waterslide one can break out left over loose rock to a subsidiary gully on the left. Follow this to the upper sills of felstone, which seem like stacks of organ pipes when viewed from the cwm. Care should be taken as the rock is very loose here.

Sedilia 210 feet E2 (1968)

The first pitch is steep and on rotten rock. Start below and left of The Infidel, some 10 feet right of a short chimney which defines the edge of the buttress.

1 100 feet. 5b. Climb up to a sloping ledge and continue with difficulty into a shallow scoop below a diagonal overhang. Move left and up a hidden flake crack. A short loose groove on the left leads to a good ledge and peg belays. Serious.

2 70 feet. 5a. Climb a shallow green groove behind the stance and traverse six feet below an overhang. Step across a groove and ascend to easier ground.

3 40 feet. 4b. Traverse right across a slab and go up a short rib to a grassy terrace.

★★**The Rosy Crucifixion**   200 feet   E2   (1963)
A fine open route which accepts the challenge of the wall left of The
Infidel. Start as for The Infidel at a grassy ledge below the flake crack.
1 120 feet. 5c. Climb diagonally up left to a tiny ledge level with the
foot of the flake crack. Move up in the same line and layback a blind
flake crack (hard) to a small loose spike. Traverse right to a ledge in
the middle of the wall. Move up 10 feet then follow a thin diagonal
crack, peg runner, which leads to the foot of a bottomless groove on
the right. Climb this (good small nuts) via a very hard move to a small
roof and move left to a long narrow ledge. Belays on the left.
2 80 feet. 5a. Move back right and ascend the steep crack-line on
good holds moving left near the top. Continue up easily to ledges and
belays near the top section of The Infidel, 150 feet of scrambling
leads to the top.

The Infidel   390 feet   Very Severe   (1963)
An interesting climb with some enjoyable moves. At the right-hand
end of the cliff is a large triangular slabby buttress. The route follows
a flaky crack up the right side of the buttress. Start by scrambling up
the easy slabs for 100 feet to a ledge 40 feet below the flake.
1 140 feet. 4c. Climb a thin crack then the flake or the wall on the
right. Move right at the overhangs, crux, to a ledge on the arête. A
short steep groove round the corner leads to a ledge. Belays.
2 100 feet.4a. Climb the short diagonal flake crack in the wall
above, then trend left up rough slabs to a huge flake belay in a
grassy bay.
3 50 feet. 4a. Climb either crack in the steep back wall.
4 100 feet. 4b. Move up left to a huge spike at the foot of the
prominent arête. Step left off the spike and climb the arête to a ledge
near the top. Move left again to finish up a steep and very loose
groove.

Right of The Infidel the rocks are very broken and give no scope for
continuous routes. Well up in the cwm, Grey Gully gives a good Easy
scramble to the crest of the ridge.

Clogwyn y Ddysgl Girdle   Difficult   (1913)
An arbitrary outing which can follow a variety of lines in either
direction.

Cyrn Las

(The Blue Horn)

OS Ref. 614 561

At the head of Cwm Glas, Cyrn Las rises challengingly some 600 feet above the scree. It is a lower off-shoot of Cyrn Las proper, the prominent great step in the ridge between Cwm Glas Mawr and Cwm Glas Bach. The cliff is known locally as Diffwys Ddu (The Black Precipice), but the earliest climbers for no very good reason bestowed the name Cyrn Las upon the cliff. Seen from low down the cwm, the cliff appears as a huge dome, with large and impressive overhangs forming the final nose. The most obvious feature is the huge vertical gash of Great Gully which is deeply cut and divides near the top. Left of Great Gully the rock is more broken and on the lower sections the structure is similar to that of Lliwedd. The Upper and Lower Chasms are two obvious vertical rifts separated by a broad terrace of scree and heather. Left again the cliff breaks away into the stream which runs down from Llyn Bach below Clogwyn y Ddysgl. Right of Great Gully is Great Buttress, which sweeps up from the screes to end in a large overhang. The first vertical feature right of the gully is the curving crack line of Subsidiary Groove and part of Main Wall. Right again is a short black cleft in the shape of a curved L. This is part of The Great Buttress climb and the girdle connections. Right of this are the prominent leftward-slanting cracks of The Grooves which lead up to the grassy area right of the final nose.

The right-hand section is defined by the deep vertical chimney of Schoolmaster's Gully. The rest is broken. Two gullies; the first ill-defined, and the second of yellow rock, run up to the right of Schoolmaster's Gully and then Gwter Fawr, an easy gully which gives the best descent on that side, marks the end of the cliff. The rock is not always perfect and a good deal of competence is needed even on the easy routes. The major routes are long, exposed and as good as any in Wales.

The Chasms   700 feet   Moderate   (1903)
A pleasant scramble, useful as a way of descent.

The Lower Chasm is left of Great Gully and just above the stream. It is an obvious inverted L-shaped cleft. Scramble 100 feet from the scree into the bed of the chasm. A 40-foot pitch up the cave is taken as a through route or on the outside. From the cave ascend the left wall and go up to the slab on the left; or this can be avoided on the right. A short 20-foot chimney leads to a broad ledge of red scree.

The Upper Chasm starts with a scramble of 60 feet into the gully and goes up a short chimney finishing on the right. Continue for 60 feet up to the cave. From here make a delicate traverse across the wall on the right and go up over doubtful blocks, 45 feet. It is possible to traverse the left wall, but this is more difficult; 300 feet of easy scrambling up the scree-filled gully leads to the top.

Central Route   450 feet   Hard Severe   (1903)
A long and intricate mountaineering route with its share of both good and bad rock. The lower pitches are the hardest part of the climb. Start on the heather band below Great Gully.
1 60 feet. Climb the rib on the left, then move left below a large flake to an awkward groove which leads to a good ledge on the left.
2 65 feet. Climb the large block above and step left. More grass and a short traverse right lead to a short steep wall. Ascend this and the groove above to a stance below an overhang.
3 50 feet. Move left at the overhang and climb easily to a belay below orange-coloured slabs.
4 80 feet. Ascend the clean slab on small holds to an open chimney on the right. Good holds on the left of the chimney are the key to the problem. Exit on jugs to reach a large terrace.
5 75 feet. Follow an easy gangway up right to a good stance below a chimney.
6 50 feet. Climb the chimney and move out right to a sloping ledge.
7 70 feet. Move back left and ascend a steep exposed wall. A crack on the left of a big flake leads steeply up to finishing cracks.

★**Great Gully**   440 feet   Very Difficult   (1904)
One of the best gully climbs in the valley. Much harder when wet. Stances should be arranged beneath overhangs to protect the second from loose scree. Start by scrambling up the bed of the gully until it steepens about 350 feet above the scree. Keep to the right, on a heathery rib, to a heathery band which runs across the gully at the same level as a triangular-shaped cave and about 40 feet to its left.
1 80 feet. Descend slightly and follow the heathery gangway to the centre of the gully. Go steeply up the bed to a stance
2 50 feet. Start the slightly overhanging wall on the right. It leads strenuously to a short chimney
3 90 feet. Ignore an easy leftward rising traverse. Keep in the main gully line up the right-hand chimney to a large chockstone forming a cave. Good belays.
4 40 feet. Turn the cave on the left and scramble up to where the gully divides.
5 120 feet. Follow the central line up a chimney to grass at 60 feet, stances etc. Continue to a cave below a capstone.

6 60 feet. Ascend the chimney until a step onto the right wall. Climb to a good belay above the capstone.

Variation
The left-hand branch of the gully gives 150 feet of less interesting climbing. The rising traverse above pitch 2 can be taken and the gully regained by a rising traverse to the cave.

Trauma Grooves 350 feet E1   (1962)
A disjointed line of grooves on the left of Main Wall with some dangerous blocks which need trundling. Start as for Main Wall.
1 100 feet. 4a. As for Main Wall for 30 feet then continue left to belay at the foot of the first groove.
2 60 feet. 5a. Climb the grassy groove on the left then make a difficult traverse right to reach a small ledge. Pass the large loose flake jammed in a crack, to the short chimney beyond. Go up this to a grassy ledge and belays.
3 100 feet. 4c. Climb the groove on the left to a long narrow ledge overlooking the gully. Move left and go up the shallow vertical groove to a ledge on the left. Move up a little and traverse right to a grassy ledge. Flake belays below overhangs
4 40 feet. 4c. Traverse diagonally back left and go up the groove over the overhangs to a ledge below the Main Wall final slab.
5 50 feet. 4a. Ascend the final slab of Main Wall.

Druid's Dilemma 400 feet Severe   (1956)
A rising traverse which meanders up the left-hand part of the cliff; not really recommended. Start as for Main Wall, and from the top of pitch 1, traverse the top of the slabs up left across grass to a stance in Great Gully 40 feet above the overhanging wall. From here, go up 30 feet and traverse left to a grass ledge on the edge of the gully. Continue up insecure grass to another grass ledge about 60 feet away. Traverse right on grass to a stance on the edge of the second rib going left from the gully (40 feet). Continue the traverse across on easy slabs to a stance on the edge of the gully, above its pitch 4. Take the steep rib for 30 feet. Traverse left awkwardly past a spike to a narrow ledge (belay at its left-hand end). Go straight up the flake and finally up the overhanging crack to easy ground (40 feet).

★★★**Main Wall** 465 feet Hard Severe   (1935)
One of the most enjoyable expeditions in Snowdonia – a great Welsh classic. This exposed and serious route for its grade zigzags up the steep wall between Great Gully and Subsidiary Groove. Start about 350 feet above the scree near a conspicuous triangular shaped overhang with a grassy field above. From the scree fan on the left

scramble to a slab left of the overhang and at a lower level.

1 70 feet. 4a. Climb diagonally left up the well-worn slab to a vegetated ledge at 30 feet. Ascend a short corner for 10 feet. Move right across a slab and round a rib, then go up to a pulpit stance.

2 80 feet. 4b. Make some difficult moves up the rightwards sloping gangway on the right of the pulpit to the chimney of Subsidiary Groove. Climb this for a few feet then traverse back left along a ledge to a corner overlooking the gully. Peg belay.

3 45 feet. 4a. Ascend the arête above then go diagonally right to a large triangular platform in the corner.

4 90 feet. 4b. Descend slightly and climb a flaky pinnacle on the left. From its tip step left onto the steep wall and pull up into a niche. Go round the corner on the left and up a steep arête until a step leads across a chimney to a short slab, stance and belays. A fine pitch.

5 80 feet. 4a. Go up to an overhang then move left across a broken chimney to the foot of a large slab overlooking Great Gully. Climb the left edge of the slab on excellent holds to a good stance at its top – delightfully exposed.

6 100 feet. Climb up left to a ledge then ascend a slab to the right. Scramble to the summit.

Main Wall Eliminate   280 feet   Hard Very Severe   (1973)
The left-hand arête of Subsidiary Groove. Start as for Main Wall to the stance just before the crevasse.

1 60 feet. 5a. Climb the crevasse until a difficult step leads out left onto the nose, which is climbed to reach good ledges. Move right onto the wall and climb direct to a stance and belay on Main Wall.

2 120 feet. 5a. Traverse left a few feet and climb the steep wall on fragile holds to a shallow depression leading to a short wide crack. Climb this to reach the top of the pinnacle on Main Wall and step right from it onto the wall. Follow a shallow groove then a crack to a loose finish onto easy slabs. Main Wall belay.

3 100 feet. 4b. Follow the edge of the slabs then the grooved arête. Move left near the top onto easy-angled slabs.

★★ **Subsidiary Groove**   370 feet   E1   (1953)
A very fine route which unfortunately has some doubtful rock. Sustained climbing and an exacting final corner crack make for an invigorating outing. It is the obvious line of curving chimneys defining the left side of The Great Buttress.

1 90 feet. 4a. As for Main Wall to the stance above pitch 1. Move across to the foot of the chimney/groove.

2 50 feet. 4b. Ascend the chimney/groove joining Main Wall part way up. Step out right at the top to a crevasse stance.

3 135 feet. 5a. Climb the crack in the same line on doubtful rock, hard if wet, to a junction with Main Wall. Make a rising traverse across a steep wall for 20 feet, then go back right up a small gangway to a resting place higher up the corner. Climb the steep wall above moving left at the top, stance. Last possible escape.

4 45 feet. 4c. Ascend the groove to the overhang. Step round the corner on the right on poor rock, then climb easily up the slab on the right to a stance and belay.

5 50 feet. 5b. Ascend the crack on the left of the slab to the bottom of the steep corner. Climb this strenuously to a stance and belay. Scramble up to finish.

★★★**Lubyanka** 390 feet E3   (1976)

An excellent and varied route which is very popular. The climbing is sustained, technical and in a dramatic situation, particularly on the top pitch. The climb follows a series of grooves and corners between Subsidiary Groove and The Skull before breaking out onto the headwall above the top pitch of the latter.

1 90 feet. 4a. As for Subsidiary Groove.

2 50 feet. 4b. As for Subsidiary Groove to the crevasse stance.

3 60 feet. 6a. Above the stance is an obvious groove. Enter this with difficulty from the left and climb it without much respite to a large bay. Peg belay.

4 50 feet. 5b. Climb the corner behind the belay then exit right and descend the slab for a few feet to a spike and peg belay.

5 70 feet. 5b. Climb directly up the slab, over an overlap, and enter a short open corner. Climb this and exit left at the top, hard, then continue up the short slab to a small ledge. Peg belays.

6 70 feet. 5c. An exposed pitch. Hand-traverse to the right along the quartz band above the roof for 10 feet, until a fingerhold enables a standing position to be attained. Climb the groove (good holds round to the left) until it curves round to form a roof. Layback boldly through the roof and continue easily up the slab to nut and spike belays.

The Left-Hand Finish 70 feet E4 6a   (1987)

Harder, though not as exposed as the original way. Hand-traverse the quartz band for six feet to an awkward step up. Pull out leftwards on to the wall. Sustained climbing up and leftwards on small holds leads to a slab, six feet above the roof – a bold pitch.

★★★**Long Kesh** 430 feet E5   (1985)

A climb of tremendous exposure which crosses above the top pitch of The Skull. Pitch 5 is one of the most 'out there' trips in The Pass. Start as for The Great Buttress.

1 & 2 190 feet. As for The Great Buttress pitches 1 & 2.

3 60 feet. 5c. Follow The Skull pitch 3 to its belay, then go up 10 feet to a larger ledge. Belay.

4 40 feet. 5c. From the right end of the ledge step up right onto the wall. Climb a thin crack for six feet then move right to the arête. Follow this to a peg belay.

5 140 feet. 6b. Climb directly up the slab and over an overlap to enter a short open corner (as for Lubyanka). Step right, then go up to a peg runner, traverse right to a second peg runner and climb up onto a slab on the right (crux). Ascend to the roof, two peg runners, pull boldly over this and continue to the top. Belay on a flake at the top left of the easy angled slabs.

★★The Skull   420 feet   E4   (1966)

A thrilling and spectacular climb with a memorable top pitch. It is the arête right of Subsidiary Groove and the prominent slanting groove left of the final overhanging nose. Start as for Great Buttress.

1 & 2 190 feet. 4c. As for The Great Buttress pitches 1 and 2.

3 50 feet. 5c. Step down left, then climb awkwardly left using a dubious flake to reach a thin crack. Climb this strenuously to a stance.

4 50 feet. 6a. Move right to a shallow groove in the overhanging arête. Ascend this with difficulty then continue up a slab to a peg belay.

5 130 feet. 5c. Climb the slab above trending right to the foot of the obvious slanting groove, peg runner. Make a hard step right and climb the right wall of the groove to a small ledge. The groove above is very technical, but well-protected, and is best climbed by wide painful bridging which somewhat amplifies the exposure. The groove now eases and an easy slab and block belay are soon reached. A superb pitch in a magnificent position. Scramble up to finish.

★Hindenburg   400 feet   E5   (1979)

Sustained hard climbing with protection which is both difficult to find and arrange, particularly on the first pitch. It is a direct and independent line between The Skull and Great Buttress.

1 & 2 190 feet. 4c. As for The Great Buttress pitches 1 and 2.

3 50 feet. 6a. From the top of the pinnacle step left onto the wall, and climb up to enter an open groove. Ascend this and continue a further few feet to a sloping ledge. A worrying pitch. Nut belays over on the right at a poor stance.

4 40 feet. 5c. Climb up and slightly left to obvious undercuts and using a crack on the left go up to a sloping ledge. Nut and peg belay in place under the bulge.

5 120 feet. 5c. Climb the problematical groove above which is hard to enter and continue to a junction with The Skull part way up its last pitch. Finish as for The Skull. N.B. A belay is possible at the top of the groove so that the second can be better protected.

Cyrn Las

1. Great Gully	VD		9. Sunday School Outing	E4
2. Main Wall	HS		10. The Prune	E2
3. Subsidiary Groove	E1		11. The Overhanging Arête	E2
4. Lubyanka	E3		12. The Grooves	E1
5. Long Kesh	E5		13. The Edge of Time	E4
6. The Skull	E4		14. Times Past	E3
7. The Great Buttress	E2		15. Pedants Buttress	VS
8. The Green Caterpillar	VS			

★★The Great Buttress 460 feet E2   (1963)

A superb and varied route on good rock. It takes a line up the centre
of the buttress finishing up a series of overhanging grooves right of
the final nose. Start as for Main Wall.

1 90 feet. 4c. Climb a steep slab and a short strenuous chimney to
the field at the foot of Subsidiary Groove.

2 100 feet. 4c. Climb a steep flake crack on the left of the arête.
Descend slightly and move right round the arête to a wall. Trend left
to the foot of the L-shaped Helter Skelter Chimney. Go up this to a
stance level with the crevasse of Subsidiary Groove.

3 80 feet. 5b. Traverse right to the arête and move up, hard, to a
small ledge. Step right to a shallow vertical groove/crack. Climb this
and move left along a narrow ledge for 10 feet. Go steeply up to a
diagonal flake and follow it right to a niche.

4 40 feet. 5c. The strenuous overhanging crack leads to a niche. Exit
right. Fierce jamming/laybacking sometimes leads to a stance on the
left and a well-earned rest.

5 150 feet. 5a. Trend right and climb a steep cracked wall, a
rightward-slanting groove and the final groove of The Grooves.

The Green Caterpillar 400 feet Very Severe   (1949)

A grassy route connecting the lower part of Subsidiary Groove with
The Grooves and finishing up to the right of the latter. Some
interesting ground is covered and the grade of the route is open to
debate depending on one's attitude to grass climbing. Start as for
Great Buttress.

1 60 feet. Scramble up rightwards and climb the short strenuous
chimney to the grassy field. Move right and ascend a grassy crack in
the same line to a stance with a thread belay on the right.

2 60 feet. Above and on the left another grassy crack leads to a
gangway which is followed to the left. Pull out on grass and climb a
few feet to a small corner and belay.

3 60 feet. Ascend diagonally rightwards into a grassy chimney which
leads up to a wall. Traverse 10 feet to a large flake below a corner.

4 40 feet. Climb the overhanging corner on good holds to a stance
at the top of the blocks. Descend the crack on the other side and
traverse to a good grassy ledge and belay. Junction with The Grooves.

5 90 feet. Ascend the rib above the stance for a few feet, then step
across the corner to a ledge with an overhang above. Make a difficult
traverse to a mossy slab on the right, then traverse the slab with even
more difficulty to a grassy ledge. Go straight up over a mossy bulge
and continue to the grassy slab, keeping near to the corner when
difficulties appear. A small rock stance is thankfully reached above a
short corner. Twin flake belays.

6 90 feet. Easier climbing up to the right gains the top of Schoolmaster's Gully.

The Prune   425 feet   E2   (1966)
Essentially a direct start to The Great Buttress, but harder and not so enjoyable. Start at a 10-foot block 30 feet left of The Grooves.
1 80 feet. 5a. Traverse left a few feet to a steep groove with a loose block forming part of its right wall. Move right at the top of the groove. Climb a steep wall to a peg runner where an awkward move leads to a wide crack. Follow this to a pinnacle belay.
2 80 feet. 4c. Traverse awkwardly right to good holds then climb the wall trending slightly left at first, to a junction with The Grooves at a grassy ledge. Scramble up grass to a block belay.
3 75 feet. 5c. Descend the far side of the block to a ledge below an obvious line leading up to the niche of The Great Buttress. Step left and climb a thin crack leading to the foot of a corner. Ascend this with difficulty past the bulge to a ledge below the crack on The Great Buttress.
4 & 5 190 feet. 5c & 5a. As for The Great Buttress pitches 4 & 5.

Sunday School Outing   380 feet   E4   (1989)
A good climb on sound rock taking the inverted V-groove between the second pitches of The Prune and The Grooves.
1 140 feet. 5b. As for The Grooves pitch 1. Scramble across leftwards, over the prominent pinnacle, descending its far side to a secluded stance.
3 120 feet. 6a. From the top of the pinnacle, climb the crack and groove with increasing difficulty to the roof. Pull over this and exit rightwards to a sloping ledge. Friend belays.
4 120 feet. 5c. Climb the crack above to a grassy ledge. Finish as for the final part of Great Buttress and The Grooves.

★★★**The Grooves**   370 feet   E1   (1953)
One of the best mountaineering routes of its standard in Britain. It follows a series of impressive grooves which slant up leftwards just right of the centre of the cliff. The climbing is strenuous and the difficulties sustained, though at no point excessive. Start at the foot of the prominent groove line with an overhang at its base.
1 140 feet. 5b. Go up easily to the overhang. Pull round this (hard if greasy, and it generally is) and enter the groove above. Follow the groove, frequent runners, to a small bay. Climb a short wall on the left to a large platform.
2 120 feet. 5b. Climb a rib on the right to a little groove. A hard move up this and awkward jamming lead to an impending wall. A tricky step left leads to the foot of the main groove. This is sustained

but well-protected and soon leads to a ledge. Continue more easily up a short corner to a larger ledge.
3 110 feet. 5a. Step up right then traverse left easily along a narrow ledge to an overhanging groove. Climb this on large holds until an awkward move right gains the easier finishing groove.

Variations

★★**The Overhanging Arête** 120 feet E2 5b (1958)
This sensational pitch is the arête right of the last pitch of The Grooves. Start at a square cut corner 10 feet right of the last stance.
3a Climb the corner direct to a good runner at about 30 feet. Traverse left to the arête and grasp a huge jug. The rock above now overhangs alarmingly, the view below is impressive and the weight is on one's arms, so quickly pull up to a second huge jug. Continue past an old peg runner where a delicate step right gains good holds and easier-angled rock. Finish via the easier top part of The Grooves pitch 3.

The Right-Hand Finish 140 feet E2 (1959)
A fierce and exposed piece of climbing. Start at the foot of the Overhanging Arête corner.
3b 80 feet. 5b. A thin awkward crack in the right wall leads to a slab below the overhanging corner. Climb the slab and corner with a difficult finish on flat holds right of the bed of the corner. Climb more easily to a stance and belay.
4b 60 feet. 4a. Make a rising traverse left below the overhangs.

★★★**The Edge of Time** 380 feet E4 (1989)
A classic expedition with breathtaking situations, which tackles the prominent right-hand skyline arête of the crag, starting as for Times Past, and continuing up where that route moves right. Start just right of The Grooves. Spike Belays.
1 90 feet. 5c. Climb up to the overhang as for Times Past. Undercut leftwards to enter the groove. Continue up this until just below the overhang, where a move up and right brings a good spike to hand. Stand on the spike, then move left, pulling round the overhang on huge holds. Thread and nut belays below the overhanging arête.
2 90 feet. 5b. Climb directly up the right-hand side of the arête to good runners in a horizontal break. Pull up on the edge of the arête and continue in the same line until a small left-slanting groove leads onto the slab above. Go left to belay below the hanging prow – or descend further to a more comfortable belay on The Grooves.
3 100 feet. 6a. Climb up to the overhang (Times Past takes the right-hand twin cracks). Pull around left to gain and follow a thin crack just right of The Grooves. Layback into the groove above and

bridge up to a good spike where it finishes. Stand on the spike and pull up to a pancake flake and small spike just to the left, line runner. Move left and down to a foothold on the arête, and using pinch grips, move down again to reach a rest in the groove near a curious hole. Go left again and move up to stand on the huge fin. Climb the crack above to good belays on the terrace. BEWARE ROPE DRAG.
4 100 feet. 5c. Climb directly up the true line of the Overhanging Arête, entering from the left. Gain the spike of that route and finish as for Overhanging Arête.

Times Past 390 feet E3   (1969/1977)
A challenging line which follows the old aid route Black Mamba. Start a few feet right of The Grooves, below two bottomless grooves.
1 80 feet. 5c. Climb to beneath the large overhang. Move left to the groove, climb up into it passing an old peg, then make a bold move into the right-hand groove. Ascend this and go left to a good spike. Continue up to the overhang and surmount it to a belay.
2 80 feet. 4c. Climb the overhanging groove and move left to an arête. Go up this and move left to a slab. Belay.
3 90 feet. 6a. Traverse 10 feet left to a bottomless groove. Start this with difficulty, then continue up to belay as for The Right-Hand Finish to The Grooves.
4 & 5 140 feet. 5b & 4a. As for The Right-Hand Finish to The Grooves.

Caterwaul 320 feet Very Severe   (1969)
Very steep and vegetated. Start as for Schoolmasters' Gully.
1 70 feet. Climb the left-hand branch of Schoolmasters' Gully to a stance on top of a rib.
2 80 feet. 4b. Descend 15 feet and follow ledges out left above the overhang. Climb diagonally left to the arête. Go up to a ledge, step right round a rib and climb a groove. Stance and belay. Specimens of the rare Malampyrum Sylvaticum should not be disturbed on this pitch.
3 60 feet. 4a. Move easily out to the arête on the left and go up a slab to join The Green Caterpillar.
4 50 feet. 4a. Climb The Green Caterpillar to a wide corner.
5 60 feet. 4c. The tricky crack in the right wall of the corner leads to a ramp. Follow this to the top.

Schoolmasters' Gully 280 feet Severe   (1906)
A good route of its type, fairly serious and with some loose rock. The upper chimney of this well-defined gully can be seen from low down in the cwm. Start on the heathery band below the gully. Scramble up to the foot of the gully.

1 70 feet. Ascend the left-hand branch to the top of the broken rib in mid-gully.
2 30 feet. Easy grass leads to The Croquet Ground, an easy platform.
3 40 feet. Climb the wall some feet left of the corner crack and go up for about 10 feet. Traverse left to a stance on the edge.
4 40 feet. Go diagonally back right and traverse to the foot of the duplicate Plaster Chimney. Stance on the opposite side.
5 50 feet. Face right to climb the dirty chimney to an awkward grassy landing. Belay high up on the left wall.
6 50 feet. Scramble up to a short chimney, then ascend to the top.

Variation
The Original Start
1a 80 feet. Climb to a tiny cave then the wall on the right. Move back into the gully after a few feet to a larger cave with a dubious flake. Climb out of the cave to a grassy ledge on the right (The Bowling Green) stance etc. Step left and ascend a short groove on good holds to the top of the mid-gully rib.

Pedants Buttress   250 feet   Very Severe   (1968)
A scrappy route up the narrow buttress right of Schoolmasters' Gully. Start at the top of the buttress.
1 70 feet. 4b. Climb an easy groove to a big spike then step left to a slab. Climb this and traverse right along a ledge. Swing round the arête and go up to a grassy ledge.
2 70 feet. 4a. Climb the obvious crack on the left. Step right at the top to a ledge below a corner.
3 70 feet. 4c. Go up the corner past a bulge and step right onto the arête. Climb this easily to a ledge and a big block belay.
4 40 feet. 4a. Step off the block and climb the wall above, avoiding the overhanging chimney, into Schoolmasters' Gully. Scrambling remains.

Double Cave Gully   Difficult   (1906)
Right of Schoolmasters' Gully is a shallow and ill-defined vegetated break. The main feature is a two-storied cave 150 feet up. A mediocre scramble.

Yellowstone Gully   Difficult   (1906)
The poor gully on the right of the main cliff is easily identified by its yellowish rock. The first section, up the yellow chimney by its left wall is steep and intimidatingly loose. After two pitches the gully deteriorates into a stone-shoot.

The Green Necklace   605 feet   Very Severe   (1949)
A rambling expedition which girdles the cliff, pleasantly sustained. It

traverses into Great Gully at about one-third of its height, then across and down the hardest part of Main Wall before joining The Green Caterpillar. Start above the main pitch of The Upper Chasm where a heather band runs along the cliff. Follow this to a stance overlooking Great Gully.

1 120 feet. Traverse down into the gully via a large detached block. Climb above the cave and cross the gully to a large stance on the right wall.

2 100 feet. Follow the obvious quartz-marked traverse to the far edge. Descend for a few feet then step right round the corner and down into a scoop. Continue the line of descent to a flaky pinnacle, then down again to a large triangular platform in the corner (most of this is pitch 4 of Main Wall in reverse).

3 45 feet. Abseil down to the crevasse on Subsidiary Groove, or reverse Main Wall to the same spot.

4 20 feet. Move down and across to a flake at the top of Helter-Skelter Chimney.

5 40 feet. Descend the smooth curving chimney and traverse across to a grassy corner.

6, **7**, **8** & **9** 280 feet. Finish as for The Green Caterpillar pitches 3, 4, 5 and 6.

The High Level Girdle 315 feet Very Severe   (1958)
A route with some interesting positions, though rather pointless. Probably best used as an approach to The Overhanging Arête or The Right-Hand Finish. Start from the top of pitch 3 of Main Wall.

1 45 feet. As for the top half of Subsidiary Groove pitch 3. Up the steep wall on the left then back right up a small gangway to a chockstone belay and stance six feet from the corner.

2 60 feet. Step right across the groove onto an easy angled ramp which leads to a stance.

3 50 feet. Cross to the far end of the grassy ledge on the right. Step down and make a short traverse to a small ledge in the corner; junction with The Grooves. Climb the crack on the right to another large ledge.

4 40 feet. Walk across the ledge.

5 30 feet. Make a 15-foot abseil, a short ascent now leads to a good ledge on The Green Caterpillar.

6 90 feet. As for The Green Caterpillar.

★**Crossbones** 740 feet E3   (1977)
A lengthy and sustained expedition on good clean rock which meanders diagonally up the cliff from left to right. Start as for Great Gully.

1 150 feet. Climb easy rock as for Great Gully to a grassy ledge.

Move right to belay as for Trauma Grooves pitch 1.

2 130 feet. 5a. Go up the groove on the left for 15 feet as for Trauma Grooves pitch 2, then traverse right across the steep wall round the lip of the ledge to a crack. Climb this to a ledge. Go up a groove on the left then traverse horizontally right at the obvious fault to the peg belay of Main Wall at the top of its second pitch.

3 70 feet. 4a. Climb diagonally right as for Main Wall pitch 3, then go right to belay as for The Skull on the lowest ledge.

4 80 feet. 5a. Descend 10 feet down pitch 3 of The Skull. Traverse right to a rib. Cross this, then hand-traverse across a quartz break to The Great Buttress. Continue in the same line to a foothold stance on the arête. Belay.

5 100 feet. 5a. Ten feet up on the right is a small spike. Abseil 20 feet down The Prune. Traverse right along an obvious overlap into pitch 2 of The Grooves. Climb this for 20 feet. Belay in slings at a flake.

6 70 feet. 6a. Descend the groove (or abseil) and exit right to an overhanging groove. Climb the right arête past two peg runners. Climb out into the left-hand of two grooves above. Go up this to a ledge and climb the crack above to a block belay. Walk right to The Right-Hand Finish of The Grooves.

7 & **8** 140 feet. 5b & 4a. The Right-Hand Finish.

The West Buttress   140 feet   Very Difficult   (1903)
A pleasant little climb with an interesting finish. West of the main cliff a broken buttress on Cyrn Las proper bounds the right side of Gwter Fawr, the easy gully. A curiously-streaked slab with a broken chimney on the right is the most obvious feature. Start by scrambling up 200 feet, first right then left, to the foot of the chimney.

1 40 feet. The chimney is entered by a mild layback. Climb up past a large block to a good stance.

2 40 feet. The chimney is very broken. So pleasantly climb the rib on the right to a stance above a pile of boulders.

3 60 feet. After a traverse right which bulges awkwardly, ascend to a large pinnacle. Climb this then step into the corner on the left. The finish is just below the Cyrn Las ridge.

Equator Walls

The Equator Walls lie to the right of Cyrn Las, and right of The West Buttress. They are the much-eyed, golden brown, slabby walls about 150

Nick Wharton on *Weasels Rip My Flesh* (E4) Craig Cwm Glas Bach.
Photo: Bob Wightman

Nick Dixon on his modern desperate *Beginner's Mind* (E8) Dinas Mot
Boulders. Photo: Andy Hall

feet high divided into two sections by a easy grassy gully running down their centre. The left-hand wall is split at half-height on the right-hand side by an obvious overhang with pockets forming a line out below it, and back across to the right, above. On the left side are two water streaks (one of which rarely dries) down a superb-looking crackline. Across the easy grassy gully lies the right-hand wall which from below appears to be the more unbroken and larger part of the cliff. In its centre sits a prominent grass ledge which marks the belay of Preamble. The rock here is quick drying and extremely compact, particularly on the left-hand wall similar in texture to a pocketed Clogwyn y Grochan. There is a good terrace at the base of the walls for dumping gear. It is reached from the right. The descent is down a gully on the right.

New Era and Steel Appeal, the first really modern routes here were originally done with three bolts for protection on their common crux section, a controversial act which caused a stir in the climbing world. The bolts were soon replaced by three pegs and the routes re-led, thus maintaining the unwritten code of 'no bolts in traditional areas'. Traverse easily along a terrace below the walls, up a short groove, then leftwards up grass ledges to the base of the left-hand wall.

★★**Steel Appeal** 160 feet E6 6b (1983)
A poorly protected line with exceptionally good face climbing, much steeper than it looks, and often wet. The pegs which once protected the crux have all but corroded or gone – hence the E6 cachet. Start at the foot of the left-hand wall just left of New Era, below and right of a pillar and a flaky groove. Climb to the top of the flaky groove, move up leftwards, past a small wire to a foothold below a crack sporting the remains of a peg (wire runners in pockets down on the left). Ascend the crack with difficulty to a thin ledge on the right. Traverse right to a poor peg on New Era. Climb up as for New Era to the remnants of the top peg and a poor foothold. Using a small hold make a very hard move left, quickly easing to a larger hold and the easier angled slab. Ascend first leftwards then back right, and go up to the grassy terrace. Easy ground on the left or the right leads to the top.

★★**Alchemy** 160 feet E6 6c (1988)
The stunning rightwards trending hairline crack running the full height of the left-hand wall is a modern masterpiece. Stamina, technical ability and a cool head (failing that, a damn good leader), Friends 2 & 3, a good rack of small wires, plus a week's dry weather should fulfill the necessary criteria for a successful ascent. Start by Steel Appeal. Climb up to a poor peg runner at about 20 feet and pass it by difficult moves, then trend slightly right and go up to the pocket of

New Era. Move left and clip what remains of the first peg of that route. Layback into the obvious niche. Bridge up this to clip an ancient peg. Stand on the good incut hold next to the peg and step right to a reasonable rest. Make desperate moves up and slightly leftwards to (hopefully) grab the huge pocket at the end of New Era. Continue, still quivering, to finish as for New Era... a route for 'Rock Ninjas' only.

★★**New Era** 160 feet E6 6b   (1983)
Another superb but serious wall pitch. Like Steel Appeal, the route has been upgraded to E6, reflecting the current state of the pegs. Start on the right side of the left-hand wall at the foot of a grassy gully. Climb easily up the grass-filled gully on the right to a large block at 15 feet. Traverse out leftwards on amazing pockets across the very smooth wall. At the end of the pockets move up to a small flat topped flake, then make a series of difficult moves left past another pocket and go up to the remnants of a peg. With increasing difficulty climb up past another peg, in similar condition, to reach a poor resting foothold and a third poor peg. Make a huge reach up right to a poor small pocket. Swing right in a crucifix position across a very smooth wall to a large pocket. Gain the right-hand pocket and go up to a broken groove and easy ground. Climb up leftwards to a grass terrace, belay on the right. Climb the corner on the right or the smooth slabby wall above.

Mild Steel E6 6b – a combination of the New Era Start and the Steel Appeal finish is also noteworthy.

Across the grassy central gully lies...

★**Preamble** 200 feet E1   (1965)
An excellent well-protected route. Start below an obvious flake crack on the left-hand side of the right-hand face.
1 150 feet. 5a. Climb the flake to a small grassy ledge. Step up right to large holds. These lead right to a spiky block. Step right onto a long ledge below a short slab. Traverse right and balance around a rib to reach broken ledges. Ascend the small right facing corner to a thin crack which leads up the slabby wall to a groove. Climb the groove to a grassy terrace which crosses the buttress.
2 50 feet. Climb the loose rock to an overhang. Traverse left and ascend to the top.

Flicker of Hope 130 feet E5 6c   (1988)
In the centre of the buttress, right of Preamble, a smooth leftward-slanting groove, sporting an old peg at 20 feet, gives relatively safe yet technically desperate face climbing. Lasso the peg.

Using this as protection, climb directly up the water stains left of the groove to gain flakes on the left and a good incut left of the peg runner. Continue up and left to a groove leading to a ledge on the right. Move about 10 feet right then climb straight up the face following various cracks to finish.

Cyrn Las Fach

(Little Blue Horn)

OS Ref. 615 563

This fairly broken cliff lies on the western side of Cwm Glas Mawr, at the same level as the foot of Cyrn Las. Several routes have been done here involving scrambling, grass and some loose rock, before petering out near the ridge of Chwarenog (Lumpy – as with swollen glands) which leads to a pleasant scramble up the ridge of Cyrn Las proper.

Tiercel 275 feet Very Difficult   (1954)
Helps to make the walk over to D'ur Arddu more interesting. Start near the left-hand end of the crag, some 30 feet right of the foot of a grassy gully which slants gently leftwards.
1 120 feet. Climb the steepish open groove to a small ledge. Follow the groove and finish up the heathery gully; belay on the rib on the left.
2 60 feet. Scramble in the same line over broken ground to the foot of a corner/chimney, thread.
3 35 feet. Climb the corner/chimney.
4 60 feet. Follow the slabs trending left to the top of the cliff.

Impromptu Buttress 270 feet Difficult   (1954)
The steepest buttress on the Cyrn Las ridge, about half-way along to the right of a clearly marked col and immediately left of a deep gully, is split from right to left by a diagonal groove. Start a few feet right of the groove and almost at the lowest point of the buttress.
1 40 feet. Climb the wall to the right of the groove for 15 feet, traverse left and climb the groove on its left edge.
2 75 feet. Take the steep crack in the wall above and continue up it to quartz ledges. Scramble up a grassy ledge for 30 feet to the left and climb blocks to the top of the rake to land on a prominent nose.
3 35 feet. Swing right into a chimney and climb it to a ledge followed by a mantelshelf to a large spike belay.
4 70 feet. Traverse left along a quartz ledge into a chimney. Climb

this escaping on its flaky right edge. Ascend diagonally right to a grove of bollards. The steep wall above leads to a grassy rake which can serve as a finish, but better is...

5 50 feet. The slab above gives pleasant climbing for 20 feet, then scramble to the crest of the ridge.

There are two other routes recorded on this cliff; **Ochre Buttress**, 275 feet, Severe; and **Asphodel**, 275 feet, Severe, whose descriptions, despite the diligent efforts of the guidebook writer to trace them, still remain 'lost'.

Cwm Glas Bach Area

This is the area of broken mountainside opposite Clogwyn y Grochan and behind Cwm Glas Cottage. The cottage, partially hidden by trees, is best reached by walking along a grassy track from the two wooden bridges near Blaen Nant. Another, although damper, approach can be made from the upper of the two laybys below Clogwyn y Grochan; crossing the river and following a faint path up to the cottage. Cwm Glas Bach can be broken down to represent a number of differing crags. Commonly called 'Bumhole Buttress' this area offers a selection of gritstone type climbing with good landings. The first climbs are immediately above Cwm Glas Cottage where some rocks form the back wall of a large sheep-fold. Close to the right hand wall of the fold is a slim coffin shaped slab, with a holly tree at about half height on its right.

Back in the Fold   50 feet   Very Severe 4c   (1991)
A smart little pitch, which may have been done before. Start below a stained crack. Ascend the crack system, with some difficult moves to start, to a heathery ledge. Continue up a final crack to a large ledge.

Raging Thesaurus   50 feet   E2 5b   (1991)
A nice way to finish off a day in this area of the Pass. Start at some pockets to the right of the crack system. Climb up to a horizontal crack, move up right to a vertical crack, continue directly to gain a second horizontal break and the final slab. Precarious moves gain a scoop and a ledge. The belay is a few feet above the ledge.

Clogwyn Llo known as Cwm Glas Facet

(Calf Crag)   OS Ref. 619 568

This is the first proper expanse of rock to be encountered. Approach along a track, from behind Cwm Glas Cottage, to where it passes round a ruined building and then becomes walled. At an old wire fence, bear up and left to reach a stone wall below a broken area of clifflets. Above is Clogwyn Llo, this is split in two by a grassy gully. High up on the right-hand buttress is a Y-shaped tree and the prominent pinnacle of The Dolemen.

Left Buttress

This is bounded on its left by a short gully slanting up leftwards from a damp and grassy bay, 40 feet to the right of three stone walls perched on ledges on the left-hand side of the bay. Two heather ledges run across the buttress, the lower one is about 30 feet up, below which lies a seeping red wall.

Aratnerphobia 140 feet E2   (1991)
Quite enjoyable but escapable climbing. Start in the gully on the left of the buttress about 10 feet below a grotty grotto at a boulder.
1 100 feet. 5c. A difficult start to gain a flake leads to a slabby rib, follow this to the perched block. Step off the block, and climb the wall via thin cracks to reach a large ledge. Walk off, or:
2 40 feet. 4c. Ascend the flake and crack above the ledge to reach a heathery terrace.

Catflea Massacre 80 feet E3 5c   (1993)
Start on a vegetated ledge below a slim groove, reached by climbing the first secton of Aratnerphobia. Ascend the groove and easy wall to a break, move up again to an overlap. Climb the wall above (bold) to a sloping ledge then swing up left to a further ledge and teeter up the final arête.

Foxglove 135 feet Severe   (1949)
A poor, vegetated route, although the final corner gives it some reason for existence. Start down and to the right of the gully where a heathery strip reaches the base of the cliff, a little to the left of the seeping wall.
1 70 feet. Scramble diagonally right up heather, then up into a little

Cwm Glas Bach Area

a. Clogwyn Llo Left-Hand
b. Clogwyn Llo Right-Hand
c. The Gravestones
d. Twll Tin Bottom Tier

e. Hidden Wall
f. Twll Tin Middle Tier
g. Twll Tin Upper Tier
h. Yr Ochr Wen

Cwm Glas Bach Area

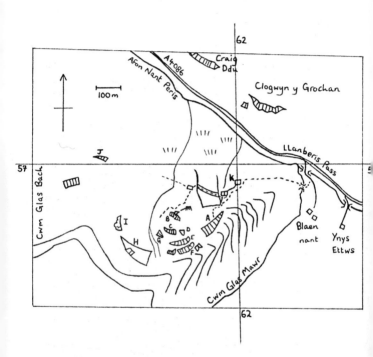

A. Clogwyn Llo
B. The Gravestones
C. Hidden Wall
D. Twll Tin: Bottom Tier
E. Twll Tin: Ribble Wobble Area
F. Twll Tin: Top Tier
G. Yr Ochr Wen
H. Clogwyn Mawr
I. Craig yr Hwntw
J. Craig Cwm Glas Bach
K. Cwm Glas Mawr (CC Hut)

hollow. Take the wall behind starting up a flake. Continue for a few feet to the foot of a heathery corner containing a holly.

2 25 feet. Climb the corner past the holly to gain a heather ledge with a gnarled yew tree.

3 40 feet. Ascend the short steep wall via the tree to another ledge. Finish up the clean steep corner crack.

Of Mice and Men   170 feet   E3   (1991)
The route ascends good clean rock and the final pitch is quite tough. The normal start is as for Inoculation Wall, although the wall just to the right of the reddish wet streaks has been ascended at about 5a to give an independent start.

1 50 feet. Move left as for Inoculation wall, but continue leftwards to belay behind a holly tree below two cracks, one straight, the other ragged and vegetated.

2 60 feet. 4a. Ignore the heathery crack and follow the left-hand and straight crack to a heathery stance below the upper wall.

3 70 feet. 5c. Ascend to a ledge, then gain the shallow groove in the centre of the arête, climb this to its top, step right and climb the wall just left of the corner to easy ground. Belay in the corner above.

Tafod y Gors   160 feet   Very Severe   (1989)
A good varied route in a fine position. Start on top of the rock steps to the right of the wet streaks, below a leftward slanting slab, the start of Inoculation Wall.

1 110 feet. 4b. Climb up to a leftward trending slab to reach cracks, 15 feet to the right of the holly, leading up to a shallow left-facing corner. Go up cracks and layback into the corner, then swing out right and ascend the wall, crux, to some jugs and a heathery ledge. Move left to belay as for Of Mice and Men at a crack.

2 50 feet. 4a. Gain the ledge above, strenuous cracks then lead up and right to the base of a leftwards facing corner with a spike at its base, swing up and right to finish at a ledge. Belay in the corner above.

★Thema   150 feet   E1   (1989)
Pleasant climbing leads to an excellent final pitch. Start just right of the steep, seeping wall, directly below a small holly.

1 40 feet. 4b. Ascend the bulging wall to a slabby area just right of the holly.

2 40 feet. 5b. Attack the vertical crack about five feet right of the shallow corner. The crack peters out, but good holds through a bulge bring one to a large ledge below some flakes, and the final wall.

3 70 feet. 5b. Climb past the flakes to reach a thin crack, leading up with one entertaining move to a small ledge. Strenuous laybacking up the continuation crack brings one thankfully to a jug and easier climbing above.

Inoculation Wall   300 feet   Severe   (1949)
A captivating route though not in the modern idiom. Start to the right of the seeping wall above a rock step, a short wall leads to leftward slanting slabs.
1 90 feet. Climb the slabby wall trending slightly left, then move up right onto a heather ledge at 50 feet. Take the short steep corner above, past perched blocks near the top, to reach a large ledge with a holly. Belay behind this at the foot of the obvious chimney.
2 60 feet. Ascend the chimney to belay on the short wall at the top.
3 100 feet. Climb the wall and scramble up to reach the right-hand of two chimneys.
4 50 feet. Finish up the right-hand chimney.

The Wrath of Grapes   100 feet   Hard Very Severe 5b   (1991)
A steep start leads to easier climbing. Start to the right of Inoculation Wall at the base of a slim groove in a steep arête. Ascend the groove until forced out left onto a ledge at 25 feet. Continue up the slabby arête to a blocky overhang, surmount this and follow easy rock to a belay on a ledge overlooking the gully that splits the crag.

Right Buttress

This section of the crag is to the right of the obvious gully slanting up leftwards and can be used as a means of descent.

Lore and Hors D'Oevre   160 feet   Very Severe   (1992)
An entertainig trio of pitches. Start at the foot of the slanting gully at a small perched pillar leading up to the left end of the ledge system of Band of Hope.
1 60 feet. 4b. Gain the start of the ledge, step back left past a block to gain a steep juggy wall. This leads to slabs right of a holly-choked groove, and a grassy belay ledge left of a sharp arête – at the left end of a rectangular wall.
2 40 feet. 4c. Climb the flaky rib behind the stance to a small square roof, just right of a prominent crack. Layback the crack and step left to gain the broad terrace. Belay below the wide right-hand chimney of Inoculation Wall.
3 60 feet. 4c. From just below the chimney, step up and right onto a wide ramp running up rightwards to the foot of a corner. Take the corner past a hollow-sounding flake, laybacking up to slabs. Belay well back.

The Band of Hope   250 feet   Difficult   (1951)
An interesting rambling route of sorts which traverses across the face
to reach the pinnacle (The Dolemen). Start about 25 feet left of the
prominent corner with a holly, just left of a narrow slanting groove.
1 90 feet. Climb diagonally up the wall left of the groove via a hard
mantelshelf at 10 feet making for the left-hand end of a heather
terrace. Belay at its right end.
2 90 feet. Mainly parkland walking, reached on the right by a
mantelshelf half-way up a 10-foot wall, then the chimney behind the
pinnacle.
3 70 feet. Cross into, and climb the groove on the right of the grass
shelf. Avoid the exit – then go right and climb the groove to finish.

Beta   170 feet   Very Severe   (1989)
Fine and varied climbing. Start to the right of the slanting gully just
below a vertical crack that curves over to the left, below an area of
slabs.
1 60 feet. 4c. Pull up and layback the crack, large gear, until it
disappears at a flake. The slab above is easier. Belay at the base of a
steep crack slanting up to the left.
2 50 feet. 4c. Ascend the slanting crack to a large spike, further
flakes and spikes lead up to a move right, just below the broad
heather terrace. Belay well back.
3 60 feet. 4c. Climb the third pitch of Lore and Hors D'Oevre to finish.

★★**Far from the Madding Throng**   240 feet   E2   (1989)
A good clutch of pitches. Start immediately right of Beta, under a
vertical crack system on the left-hand side of a brownish rippled slab.
1 80 feet. 5a. Go up the crack, steep at first, or, the faint rib on the
right for 15 feet. The line leads to grassy ledges and a belay below
the prominent left-facing corner.
2 60 feet. 5b. The steep corner is climbed with well-maintained
interest to a wide ledge.
3 50 feet. 5c. To the right of the largest corner (The Tryptych – pitch
3), is an arête, then a steep wall with two shallow scoops at
half-height. Step off a block below the left-hand scoop and gain a small
overhang. Traverse until it is possible to layback into the right-hand
scoop. Trend up left to a grassy stance; scramble off to finish.

Variation
3a The left arête of the steep scooped wall goes at E2 5c.

★**The Tryptych**   135 feet   E1   (1973)
An obvious line comprised of three cracks. Sadly it is rather
overgrown. Start 15 feet left of the corner and 10 feet right of the
previous route.

Clogwyn Llo

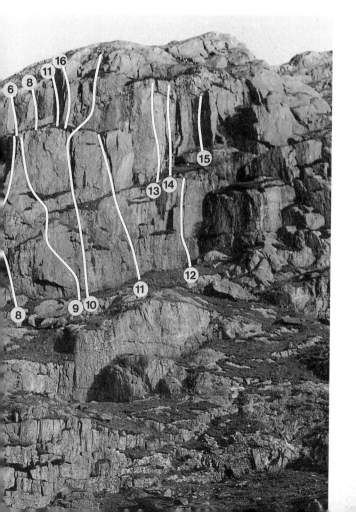

1 45 feet. 5a. Take the vegetated groove to a grassy stance.
2 45 feet. 5c. Continue up the difficult, overhanging and somewhat heathery crack to gain a broad ledge.
3 45 feet. 4b. Continue in the same slanting crack line, the crack now being wider and easier.

Whiplash Smile   70 feet   E3 6a   (1988)
To the right of The Triptych is a corner with a holly tree 10 feet up. Start just left of the corner beneath a damp crack. Climb moistly past a peg to reach a horizontal break, move left and continue up the upper crack to finish at the ledge of The Band of Hope.

The Fun Before the Storm   40 feet   Hard Very Severe 5c   (1987)
Start a few feet right of Whiplash Smile at the base of a small V-groove. A hard start leads to a holly tree, easier climbing and the safety of a heather ledge.

The only other route to start from the base of the cliff is to be found down and to the right of pinnacle of The Dolemen near a damp area of rock, a clean white groove rises up just left of a swathe of moss. This is:

Llysiau'r Gwlith   260 feet   Hard Severe   (1991)
The difficulties are short and hard, all in the first pitch in fact, but the route is safe if somewhat escapable. The top two pitches can be done for their own sake at about Difficult. Start directly below the white groove at some grassy ledges.
1 60 feet. 4b. Gain the base of the slabby groove, the climbing now becomes progressively harder until a monster jug, above the right wall of the groove, can be grasped.
2 50 feet. The obvious wide chimney above is easy, the jam crack on the right a little harder.
3 150 feet. Climb up a little to the right of two large and hollow flakes, then go diagonally rightwards to gain and finish via a delightful rib.

The following routes all start from the horizontal ledge that traverses the face at about half-height to the pinnacle of The Dolemen. The easiest approach is to follow The Band of Hope, which traverses this ledge, to the base of the route required.

★Spanking For Beginners   50 feet   E5 6b   (1986)
A good pitch, high in its grade now that a protection peg *in situ* on the first ascent has disappeared. It takes the square wall above the point where Band of Hope arrives on the heather terrace, just right of the slanting grassy gully which splits the crag. Climb the thin crack in the centre of the wall until it peters out at a sloping ledge. Move up

and slightly left to a shallow groove, crux. Finish up this via good holds on the left at its top.

Eager Submission 50 feet E3 6a   (1988)
A fine little pitch. Start on the wall round to the right of Spanking... at a short corner. Climb the short corner to reach thin crack, move left to ledge near arête and mantelshelf this to gain better holds and the top.

★★**Melancholony** 80 feet E7 6b   (1987)
A desperate test-piece taking the obvious rounded arête behind the rowan trees, passing a flake to reach the hanging groove. Start below the arête, about 25 yards along from the left end of the terrace. Move up and right via a crack to reach a downward pointing and hollow flake on the arête proper, the peg seems to have disappeared. Climb straight up past the 'Cyclops Eye' to a hanging groove past a gnarled and rusty *in situ* wire to reach a ledge. Go up leftwards to finish.

Doleful 75 feet E4 6b   (1988)
Decidedly tricky. Start at the base of the groove behind the tree to the right of Melancholony. Ascend the groove and then the corner on the left, with a hard move at half-height.

The Dolemen 40 feet E2 6a   (1986)
About 20 feet right of Melancholony is a prominent free standing pinnacle, this route climbs the side facing that route. Climb the left arête for 15 feet, pass a peg to gain a spike. Move right to the centre of the narrow face and 'span' this to the top. Abseil off.

★**The Bed of Nails** 60 feet E2 5c   (1992)
A fine pitch. Start at the foot of an arête to the right of the largest corner on this tier – the corner is Trytych pitch 3. Climb the arête using cracks on either side for 15 feet. Swing round rightwards to reach a crack. The ledge above is gained by a hard move. The arête above becomes progressively slabbier and easier.

Doldrums 280 feet Very Difficult   (1955)
A broken rambling climb with some interesting pitches which is difficult to locate. The foot of this buttress lies above a band of broken rocks on a broad grass rake, on the right-hand section of Clogwyn Llo. About 100 yards up this, a ridge of boulders comes down to meet it, and there is a cracked one below. Start down between this and the next one by a rowan at its foot.
1 20 feet. Go up on the left corner. Traverse right behind the tree and finish up a wide crack. Scramble for 20 feet to a belay.
2 40 feet. Go left from under the overhang, then follow the ridge

after a step back right. Large thread belay.

3 30 feet. Better than it looks, up the left edge of the ridge.

4 50 feet. Go down to the left to find and climb a chimney, crux. Scramble 20 feet to large grassy ledges.

5 30 feet. The slabs just left of the heather groove lead to a ledge and belay on the wall above.

6 110 feet. Straight up the slab, soon easing to a scramble.

The Gravestones   OS Ref. 618 568

To reach the next area of rock, continue along the walled track above and behind Cwm Glas Cottage to the second small ruin. Here, the track peters out into open hillside. On the left is a small rectangular crag with a stone wall abutting its left-hand side; this has an excellent landing pad/picnic area. To its right, the stone wall leads up to the base of a short tapered wall. Behind this is a cracked tower with a slanting chimney to its right, Pretty Girls Make Graves takes the crack in the tower. Hidden Wall is approached via the broad and grassy scree fan to the right.

Tapered Wall

⋆**King of Rumpy**   35 feet   E6 6a   (1988)
A short route which is both delicate and very bold, landing on either the wall or the emasculatory fin, is not to be recommended. Start at the stone wall. Step up to a short groove, follow this to a shallow scoop, a series of precarious moves lead to the top.

⋆**The Moose's Toothpaste**   25 feet   6a   (1987)
A tough little number, redolent of gritstone. Start below a line of flakes to the right of the stone wall. A hard start leads up past some layaways to an easing in the rock angle and the difficulty.

Nick's Sexual Problem   20 feet   7b   (1987)
An even harder problem! Start 10 feet right of Moose's... Move past a small pocket in the rounded rib to a slab – if you can... probably the hardest move west of Derbyshire.

⋆⋆**Pretty Girls Make Graves**   60 feet   E6 6b   (1986)
Powerful climbing up the innocuous looking crack splitting the left-hand side of the buttress with a sloping top. Start on the broad ramp, below some overlaps, down and to the left of the obvious

vertical crack. Span up the dank cracks to the overlap, difficult moves sometimes allow one to establish a position at the base of the vertical crack. A sustained sequence needs to be completed in order to gain 'terra horizonta'.

To the right is a holly choked chimney, slanting up to the right; right again is a steep little wall with a sloping ledge at half-height. To the right of this, a flat wall left of a rounded rib gives the desperate Melondrama, but first is...

Ring My Bell 50 feet E6 6b   (1993)
A bold route which starts down, and to the right, of the chimney. Ascend the seam in the wall past a 'buried' peg to reach a pod (Friend 1). Pass this with difficulty to gain the half-way ledge. Continue straight up, then slightly right, to the top.

★★**Melondrama** 50 feet E7 6c   (1992)
Powerful and fingery. The tricky little wall past two pegs is only 6c every move for the first 15 feet.

Espasmos 80 feet Very Severe 4b   (1987)
A slight but steep route. Start on the right-hand side of the rib. Climb up to a quartz topped ledge, move up the front face of the rib to a heather break; easier ground above leads to slabs and a belay.

Variation.
Crook's Direct 6a. Boulder out the left side of the rib, to finsh up, or even down, the original.

Directly above Pretty Girls Make Graves is a small grassy hollow with a pile of boulders grouped together at its base. Above is a small rib leading up to a Rowan tree.

Buhlermaniac 80 feet Very Difficult   (1991)
The short jamming crack proves to be the crux, but is well-protected. Start at the base of the rib leading to the tree. Follow the rib to the Rowan, jam up the crack behind the tree then step right to a further rib; this leads to a large grassy ledge and spike belay.

Peter Panic 120 feet Hard Severe   (1991)
There are some bold and intricate moves, particularly above the scoop. It only just merits the grade. Start about 30 feet to the right of Buhlermaniac, at the base of a slabby area of rock with a prominent scoop up and to the left. Ascend the lower slab and step left in to the scooped area, climb this directly via some bold moves to gain cracks. A series of mantels up ledges leads one to the belay blocks.

The Gravestones

Round and up to the right of Pretty Girls Make Graves and roughly half-way up to Hidden Wall is a slender rib with a holly tree near its base.

Xmas Dinner   280 feet   Very Difficult   (1978)
A pleasant route requiring a blinkered approach, as it is easy to escape at many points along the way. The 'old' third pitch, was quite a long way off and on a different cliff. This is now described as a separate route Xmas Dinner II. Start at the base of the rib below the holly.
1 120 feet. Climb up past the holly, step right and ascend the slabby rib, keeping to the left, to reach ledges.
2 60 feet. A steep cracked wall is at first rough and juggy. An easy angled slab leads to a broad grassy crest.

Hidden Wall

Although this area of rock is directly above The Gravestones, it is very difficult to pinpoint the crag until one is almost upon it. From The Gravestones, simply ascend the open and fairly grassy scree cone to the right and therefore up the left side of a large 'bay' of boulders. After about 100 yards one reaches flatter ground with a steep lozenge shaped wall of rock to the left and white slabs to the right. Descent is via the gully to the left of the wall, there is a huge chockstone at its top.

★**What A Difference A Day Makes**   70 feet   E4 6a   (1987)
A cracking route, much steeper than it looks and with a bit of a sting in its tail. Start up on the left-hand side of the crag below a dark groove, a crack leads up to a narrow ramp. Climb the crack to the sloping ramp, move up leftwards to a short wall, surmount the wall to reach a small slab below the groove. The groove is followed on surprising holds to a wide crack, large Friend, layback up leftwards to the top.

Lasagne Verdi   85 feet   E5 6b   (1987)
An obvious rising line going from left to right, with some very technical climbing. Start as for What a Difference... ascend What a Difference.... for 15 feet, move rightwards to reach the flake on Melon Transplant, crux. Step down and right to reach a crack slanting up diagonally right, follow this to a slab, and so the top.

Hidden Wall

1. What a Difference a Day Makes	E4
2. Melon Transplant	E5
3. Rimsky Korsakov	E5
4. El Guide Direct	E3
5. Rambo	E1

★**Melon Transplant**   90 feet   E5 6b   (1987)

A desperate, but well-protected, start leads to slightly easier but bolder climbing. Start 15 feet down and right of What a Difference... at a white scoop. Climb the scoop past two pegs to reach the obvious traverse line. Move left to arrange protection, then climb the wall to reach a crack, follow this to the top.

★★★**Rimsky Korsakov**   80 feet   E5 6a   (1987)

A fine sustained climb, with only just adequate protection. Start in the centre of the wall, 15 feet right of Melon Transplant, below a slanting crack-line. Move up to the crack, follow this leftwards to a shallow open groove and leaning flake/crack-lines. Continue up the flakes then go boldly up the wall above to a wide crack, large Friend useful. Follow the crack in to the large groove and finish easily.

★**El Guide Direct**   100 feet   E3 5c   (1987)

A good pitch. Start just right of Rimsky Korsakov by a rock step at the base of the cliff. Climb up to the diagonal crack, go up to a small spike, then move left, then up to the undulating weakness of the girdle. Shimmy rightwards to the arête, good Friend 1½ slot, then ascend the wall boldly to a difficult step up on to a wide white slab. Climb directly up the cracked tower above. Scramble up easily to the descent gully.

El Guide   120 feet   E3 5c   (1987)

This has the benefit of attempting to follow the line of the arête throughout. Start as for Rambo, below the rock step. Follow Rambo up to the flakes, swing out on to the wall, to the Friend slot; continue as for the above to the wide slab and cracked tower.

Wagner's Ring   180 feet   E3   (1987)

A delightful girdle that scamanders its way along the undulating weakness from right to left. Start as for Rambo.
1 60 feet. 5b. Climb Rambo to its flake traverse right, belay.
2 120 feet. 6a. Swing left on to the wall and follow the snaking ripple or weakness across the wall to quartz seams and the end.

Rambo   240 feet   E1   (1973)

A good route. Start at the lower right-hand end of the wall, a flake crack leads up to a ledge at the base of a recessed rectangular slab. It is usually damp underfoot, hop along stones to the base of the crack.
1 120 feet. 5b. Ascend the crack to the slab then keep to its left edge. The step left round the rib to reach some good holds proves to be the crux. Gain the obvious line of flakes leading back right to a short corner. Move up the corner past a hollow flake to the slab above, belay beneath a wide crack.

2 120 feet. 4a. Follow the vertical crack to reach easy vegetated slabs, belay well back, almost in the chockstone gully.

Variation
Buck Warren Meets the Headmonsters   120 feet   E2 5c
(1987)
Start as for Rambo. Instead of swinging left up the rib to reach the flake traverse, continue directly up the white slab on the right of the rib to gain the flake rampline and corner.

Yr Ochr Wen

The right-hand side of the crag is white and slabby.

Y Lon Wen   240 feet   E2   (1989)
Reasonable climbing on clean rock, however, the crux is difficult to protect. Start at the lowest point of the buttress, beneath a flake crack, 20 feet right of Rambo.
1 120 feet. 5b. Climb the crack and flakes to reach the base of a slender rectangular slab. At the top left-hand end of the slab, at a short wall, make a bold swing out to gain a flake crack and pull up to a larger slab. Belay at its top, junction with Rambo.
2 120 feet. 4b. Move up diagonally rightwards through a bulge and finish easily up slabs.

Pererindod   240 feet   Very Severe   (1988)
The route weaves a clean path through some heathery slabs. Start at the base of a stepped rib to the right of Y Lon Wen.
1 120 feet. 4b. Ascend the rib to a heathery ledge, follow a series of small slabs, aiming for a vertical crack below a large ledge, with a small dead sapling directly above.
2 120 feet. From the stance follow a groove direct, then move up leftwards, over slabs, to reach belays.

'Sgwd'   250 feet   Hard Very Severe   (1988)
A rather wandering route. Start 10 feet right of Pererindod at some cracks.
1 120 feet. 5a. Climb the cracks to the rightward leaning groove just to the left of Rembrandt's wall. Follow the groove to a vertical crack, climb the crack to a rib, belay at its top.
 2 130 feet. Easier climbing leads diagonally leftwards to belays.

★**Rembrandt Pussy Horse**   70 feet   E2 6a   (1988)
A sparkling pitch. Start to the right of 'Sgwd' at some cracks just
down and left of a clean tower split by a prominent leaning crack.
Climb the cracks to a ledge, hand-traverse right to a peg, step up
delicately to a downward pointing flake. A further move gains the
base of the crack; swagger up the crack. The last sequence of moves
awaits, the scene of many a flying lesson. Spike belay backed up by
a poor set of gear in a crack high up to the right.

Variation.

The Pinnochio Start The direct start is 6c even for the tall, a damp
landing pad awaits for all.

Twll Tin Area

To the left of Hidden Wall is a gully with a huge chockstone near its top;
the following routes are to the left of this gully on a series of short walls.
The Bottom Tier is best reached by descending a little way down the gully
and through a sheep hole in a small wall and turning right (facing out).
Whilst the mid-section is roughly level with the top left-hand end of Hidden
Wall. The routes are described as they are best approached.

Bottom Tier

A grassy rake slants up leftwards, the first wall contains:

★★**Return To Melancholony**   50 feet   E6 6b   (1987)
Only feasible for those with very strong fingers. Start down and left of
a peg at a very thin seam. Move up and then right to the peg with
difficulty. Continue boldly past the peg to finish in a very short easier
groove slightly on the right.

6B Melonoma   30 feet   E5 6b   (1993)
Sustained climbing which starts as for Return To Melancholony but
goes straight up. Climb a thin seam past two peg runners, the first
being very poor. From a good break near the top go right and up to
finish at a notch. (Peg on Return... not clipped).

Higher up the grassy rake is:

The Damp Squib   40 feet   E1 5a   (1988)
A poor wet and vegetated pitch. Start up to the left of Return to
Melancholony. Squirm up the odious drainage line/crack.

To the left of the base of the grass rake, and level with Return to
Melancholy is a large easy angled slab of perfect rock, easily seen on
the top descent from Hidden Wall. The slab is seamed with horizontal
veins of quartz. A small rock step lies below the left edge of the slab.
The slab can be climbed anywhere, however, for those with a wish to
tick, there are the following routes available.

Strap Me to a Nubile   100 feet   Difficult   (1991)
Only just merits the grade if the easier alternatives are not taken. Start
10 feet left of the rock step. Climb directly to some shallow scoops,
move left to some quartz veins and follow the left edge of the slab.
Belay to blocks well back on the rounded top above.

The Gas Man Cometh   100 feet   Difficult   (1991)
Quite pleasant. Start at the rock step. Go straight up to a crack, then
gain a small gangway leading rightwards to a vertical crack. Follow
the crack to belay as for Strap Me to a Nubile.

★**Zirhalee**   100 feet   Very Difficult   (1991)
Probably the best of this quartet. Start at the lowest point of the slab.
Ascend the slab past grassy ledges to a short crack; a hard move
gains a ledge at the top of the slab. The angle now eases as does the
climbing. Belay on the blocks.

New Model Arm   100 feet   Difficult   (1991)
Start a little up and to the right of Zirhalee. Climb the slab to a tiny
overlap and then a grassy ledge, an easier slab gains the blocks.

The top of the grassy rake reaches an area of rock with numerous quartz
ledges, this is the location of the following routes.

Rim with a View   40 feet   E3 5c   (1987)
An interesting pitch, best gained from the bottom tier. Start 40 yards
up and left of Damp Squib at some quartz ledges. Ascend a crack to
an obvious flake and a tiny groove, step left round the flake and finish
directly.

★**Ribble Wobble**   35 feet   Hard Very Severe 5a   (1987)
Short but succulent. Start below a crack to the left of Rim with a View.
Climb the airy crack in the rib on the left edge of the wall.

Middle Tier

Crack and Slab   45 feet   Hard Very Severe 5b   (1987)
An unimaginative and incorrect name for a good little route. Start at
the left end of a heathery ledge, gained from the gully capped by the
chockstone left of Hidden Wall, below an overhang split by an
obvious wide crack. Move up to the overhang, pull through this, and
climb the continuation crack above on jugs, well-protected.

Celynen   80 feet   Very Difficult   (1991)
A rather unusual little route. Start on the right-hand end of the Middle
Tier where a ragged crack leads up to reach an obvious traverse line
leading off leftwards to a corner. Ascend the quartzy cracks and to
reach the right-hand end of the undulating traverse. Follow this to the
holly tree. A fairly interesting little corner leads to a flake belay above.

Vampire Butterfly   60 feet   Hard Severe   (1991)
A nice pitch on good rock, but with sparse protection. Start as for the
previous route. From the quartz cracks, move boldly up and
rightwards to gain a small scoop in the arête. Continue up the arête
to ledges and a flake belay. Walk up the easy slab above.

Allegrophobia   60 feet   Severe   (1991)
The route only just merits this grade due to a hard starting move and
then the paucity of good protection above. Start just right of a short
corner below the arête of Vampire Butterfly. Difficult starting moves
lead to a delightful slab, climb this direct to gain the easy angled
slab. A flake belay is found down and to the left, or walk a long way
up the slab to the ledge above.

Xmas Dinner II   120 feet   Very Difficult   (1978)
The upper section or the sequel of the original route; perhaps it should
be called 'Cold Turkey'. Start in the gully directly below the small
rowan at a wide crack under the chockstone. Follow the wide crack
to a vegetated ledge and the rowan sapling, continue up the crack
then move right on ledges. Follow a second crack to the easy-angled
slab. Belay at the grassy ledge up and to the right.

Bjorn Again   90 feet   Very Difficult   (1991)
A little filler in. Start to the right of the wide crack. Move up and then
right to a horizontal break, continue up the slab just left of the massive
chockstone, or bridge up the groove formed by the slab and boulder.

Top Tier

Above the chockstone is a broad flat terrace, with another short tier above. On the far left is a small 'bottom' shaped craglet. The left cheek is taken by:

Mini Ha Ha 25 feet E5 6c   (1987)
A micro-route packing a macro-punch. The smooth buttock is ascended by means of a thin seam. The right cheek contains a thin crack, with no route as yet, further to the right is a scooped area of rock below a slab (unprotected).

The Real Scoop 40 feet Severe   (1987)
Gain the scoops easily, follow these with a high step to reach slabs.

To the right is a distinct right-angle corner with a flat grassy platform beneath, on the left edge of the platform is:

Cyfrifiadurwyr 65 feet E1 5b   (1990)
A hard start, after which it soon eases. Start at a quartz ledge at the left-hand end of the corner's left wall. Follow the vertical crack to where it curves over leftwards, move up to slabs and follow these to the top.

Rim at the Top 60 feet E2 6a   (1987)
A cracking little pitch. Start beneath a vertical crack leading up to a quartz seam in the wall just left of the corner. Boulder out the first crack to reach the horizontal quartz band, step left and continue up the second vertical crack, soon easing to slabs. Follow the slabs to the top.

Y Gornel 50 feet Hard Very Severe 5b   (1988)
A pleasant route which is occasionally damp. Start at the foot of the obvious corner. Climb the corner by a series of jams, layaways and bridging moves.

★**Ring Ouzel 2** 50 feet E5 6c   (1992)
A complex and strenuous little number. Start at the obvious crack, a few feet right of the corner. A series of difficult contortions up the initial crack may sometimes lead to an apparently juggy ledge. Move right to the arête for a rest. Move back left to finish direct.

To the right of Hidden Wall is the large 'bay' of screes, and boulders, above which is a huge area of broken slabs, ledges and walls; this is Clogwyn Mawr. However, on the far side of the screes, to the right of Clogwyn Mawr, is a broken escarpment of shorter crags. This is Craig

yr Hwntw, and can be best approached by contouring round from
Hidden Wall. On the left is a short steep and undercut craglet cleft by
two cracks.

Craig yr Hwntw

The Mild Very Hard Hand Jam Crack   35 feet   E2 6a   (1987)
A well-protected route that feels much bigger than it looks. Start
beneath the left-hand crack. An awkward start leads to a difficult
crack and a desperate finish.

Yr Hwntw Bach   40 feet   E3 5c   (1987)
Low in the grade, but with some good climbing. Start beneath the
right-hand crack. A hard start leads to a rest at the point where the
crack becomes horizontal. Finish up the wider section above.

The Stain   45 feet   E3 5c   (1987)
Start beneath the right arête of the block. Climb up the arête and
follow it until a swing rightwards can be made to gain an easy slab.

Rumblecock   50 feet   E3 6a   (1987)
Rather friable. Start 30 yards right of The Stain at an arête. Ascend
the left side of the arête until it is possible to make a difficult move
round on to the right-hand face by a flake. Follow the wall above to
easy ground.

A route has been climbed up the broken and rounded arête down to the
right, at about Hard Severe.

Clogwyn Mawr   OS Ref. 616 566

Apart from the most obvious feature, the straight wide crack high up on
the right-hand side of the crag, this, the main cliff, is the most
disappointing in the whole area. The wide crack is the line of an unique
route for the Pass, The Fear of Infection. To approach this area of rock,
one must scramble up the central gully/ramp or climb Hogia Tyn'Llan to
a traverse line back left.

The following route is gained by following a broad gully to the left of Craig yr Hwntw, this leads to a rounded slab with a dog-leg crack on its top right-hand side and a rib above.

Hogia Tyn'Llan   240 feet   Hard Very Severe   (1987)
Two contrasting but interesting pitches. Start at the very toe of the slab.
1 120 feet. 5a. Climb directly up the centre of the slab, past a loose flake, to reach belays at the base of the rib.
2 120 feet. The rib above is fairly straightforward.

★**Fear of Infection**   50 feet   E4 6a   (1987)
A fierce and painful feature, this route has defeated a number of strong teams. A couple of Friend 4s and two six inch Tubes or Titons are required for protection. Start at the base of the obvious off-width about half-way up the broken face of Clogwyn Mawr. Starting the crack is tortuous, difficulty then increases in proportion to height gained, until at half-height, the climbing becomes slightly easier.

Jargon Speaker Creature   45 feet   E5 6a   (1987)
Another fine little route. Start 40 feet up and right of Fear... at a groove with an undercut flake. Follow the groove to a jug, then move right to a rest, go back in to the groove then climb up on undercuts to the top.

In the area above Fear of Infection, ending up at the very top of Clogwyn Mawr, are the following.

Er Cof   120 feet   Very Severe 5a   (1987)
Start at a steep crack in a rib, which itself forms the left-hand edge of an area of easy angled slabs. A couple of difficult moves, another crack to the right is easier, gains the easy angled but bold rib above. Delectable climbing leads to the top.

Iachad   120 feet   E3 5c   (1987)
A bold route. Start 100 left of Er Cof at the foot of a steep slab. Climb the smooth slab to reach a wide flake-crack beneath a short wall. Step up to the next slab and trend up rightwards to gain a crack leading up to the top of the crag.

Craig Cwm Glas Bach

(Crag of the Small Green Cwm)   OS Ref. 613 568

The rock here, in general, is very good, being very rough and in some places peppered with pockets. Heavy winter drainage is conducive to moss growth, however, this detraction is steadily disappearing. Much of the cliff dries out faster than is initially thought, and some of the best routes are also the first to dry out after rainfall.

To reach the cliff it is best to approach as for The Gravestones, from here contour round in to Cwm Glas Bach. On reaching a 'col', just before a large stone wall, the crag comes in to view.

The cliff is split into two sections by a grassy rake, coming down to reach the top of a triangular rock rib forming a step. The left part of the cliff has a fine blunt arête, the location of Weasels Rip My Flesh; then to the right, starting at half-height is the prominent bow shaped chimney of Skid Alley. The crack splitting the fine tower to the right again is Spitting Image. After the grassy rake comes the other part of the cliff. The first feature is a recessed and reddish wall, which contains the hardest routes, at present. Further right is a large wall of rough rock and then a series of gradually descending overhangs. The routes are described from left to right.

On the far left of the crag is an obvious cleaned corner with a holly at its base. Down and right is a slab cleft by a wide crack.

Cornel Celyn   130 feet   Hard Very Severe   (c.1987)
Start as for Stuff the Stoat, below the wide crack in the slab.
1 70 feet. 4a. Follow the crack until it is possible to belay directly below the corner; rather prickly.
2 60 feet. 5b. Climb up the corner past an ancient 'nut'. The difficulties soon relent once the angle eases.

Stuff the Stoat   120 feet   E1 5c   (1988)
Reasonable climbing in general, however, the crux is problematical. Start at the foot of a slab with a wide broken crack leading up to flakes below a steeper wall. Gain the crack, follow this up to where it kinks left, go left then back a little rightwards. The corner on the left is not therefore reached, move up to gain some thin cracks in the wall

(immediately to the right of the corner) above a spike. Bolder but easier climbing leads to the top.

Sheik Yerbooties   120 feet   Very Severe 4c   (1988)
Pleasant enough, large protection is required at some points. Start as for Stuff the Stoat. Go up the crack as for the previous route, where it steepens, move right to a large flake at the bottom of a corner/groove. Layback the corner to gain slabs and easier rock.

★★★**Weasels Rip My Flesh**   115 feet   E4 6a   (1987)
A superb pitch, one of the best in The Pass. Start at the base of the pocketed rib/arête down and right of the previous climbs, at the very base of this section of the cliff. Go straight up to a peg, difficult moves up and right gain a jug and another peg. Climb up and leftwards to reach a thread. Sustained and bold climbing leads up to easier ground and a crack. Swing right in to a slim groove and follow this to the top.

Skid Pan   110 feet   E1 5b   (1990)
A good route, though often damp. Start down and left of the obvious Skid Alley chimney. Steep starting moves and a step right enable one to reach the base of a zigzag crack. This is followed as directly as possible to the top of the crag.

Skid Alley   110 feet   Hard Very Severe 5b   (1973)
A route for the connoisseur (or perverted) – always wet. Start at the left-hand side of the crag below the clearly defined chimney, the bottom of which is at half-crag height. Climb the steep wall trending leftwards onto the damp section. Traverse horizontally right to gain the base of the chimney. Continue directly up the strenuous and greasy chimney to finish – a mammoth thrutch – the difficulties escalating as the height increases.

★**Spitting Image**   90 feet   Hard Very Severe 5b   (1984)
A fine pitch. Start just right of Skid Alley chimney, below the prominent crack. Climb straight up to the foot of the crack – usually wet. The crack above gives a razzling finish.

★**Beasts of the Field**   90 feet   E5 6a   (1988)
Curious rock with some hanging gardens. Start to the right of the grassy rake and the rock step, just down and left of the recessed wall beneath a sapling growing out of the cliff. Climb up to the sapling, thread runner above, then move right and up to another thread runner. Continue directly to a slab and then the overhang to reach easier climbing above.

Craig Cwm Glas Bach Left-Hand

1. Cornel Celyn — HVS
2. Stuff the Stoat — E1
3. Sheik Yerbooties — VS
4. Weasels Rip My Flesh — E4
5. Skid Pan — E1
6. Skid Alley — HVS
7. Spitting Image — HVS
8. Beasts of the Field — E5
9. Noah's Ark — E6

Runner Up   120 feet   Very Severe   (1989)
Takes the left-hand corner of the recessed wall starting from a ledge
at 40 feet. Start under the wall, a little to the right of centre.
1 40 feet. Climb clean rock, moving left on the ledge to belay at the
foot of the corner.
2 80 feet. 4c. Ascend the corner crack, wide at first, then continue up
the groove above.

★★Noah's Ark   70 feet   E6 6b   (1988)
A bold but excellent route up the rubescent wall. Start at the left-hand
side of the ledge, below a crack in the recessed wall; this is gained
by climbing up the first pitch of Rufus. Climb the crack past two
threads to reach a good hold. Difficult moves then lead up to and
past a peg to attain a further good hold, stand on this and move up
leftwards to finish.

★★Over the Beach   75 feet   E6 6b   (1988)
Not as bold as Noah's Ark, but the moves are harder. Start in the
corner to the right of Noah's Ark. Climb up, swing right, and then
move up past two pegs to reach a good hold and a tape runner.
Move up to a flake and then a good pocket, layaway up a groove to
reach another flake. Easier ground and scrambling remains.

Pan Alley   120 feet   Hard Very Severe   (1989)
This is the right-hand corner of the recessed wall. Start as for Runner
Up on the ledge at 40 feet.
1 40 feet. As for Runner Up, but walk right to the foot of the corner.
2 80 feet. 5b. The steep corner is varied and interesting.

Rufus   150 feet   Very Severe   (1973)
Start below and slightly right of the large heather ledge at one-third
height. A small cairn marks the start.
1 45 feet. Take the steep wall, trending left to a good stance on the
ledge, at the right-hand end, below the obvious steep slimy groove.
2 105 feet. Move out right onto the steep wall. Climb this delicately
via a faint weakness to the top.

★The Stebbing   130 feet   E3 5c   (1989)
A clean route on good rock and one of the first to dry. Start a little to
the right of Rufus at the base of a slim groove with a small overlap at
40 feet. Climb the groove to the overlap, surmount this to reach a
series of ledges leading up to a line of weakness trending diagonally
up rightwards (the line of Rufus). Once at a steep crack-line below a
small 'tower', step left and climb the crack, then the 'tower' above to
easier slabs.

Mr Stiff   130 feet   E4 5c   (1989)
A harder, though indirect, version of The Stebbing. Start at the next narrow groove to the right. Follow the slim groove to reach the ledges of Rufus; climb up The Stebbing to finish.

Ecover   130 feet   E1 5b   (1989)
A pleasant pitch which wends its way up the wall. Start 20 feet to the right of The Stebbing at yet another groove, wider this time, just to the left of Rocky. Ascend the groove, difficult at its top, to trend leftwards up the slabby wall then back right up a faint groove. Once at the slabs near the top, trend back left once again to finish near The Stebbing.

Rocky   120 feet   Very Severe   (1973)
This follows a series of insidious cracks up the rough pocketed wall to finish as for Rufus. Start 30 feet right of Rufus. Climb a steep rib just right of an obvious section, then follow a line of thin cracks leading up to an open corner, left of a large brown recess – delicate. Finish as for Rufus.

Belv-Eddie-Ere?   120 feet   Hard Very Severe 5b   (1988)
A good route on rough rock, with the crux at the top. Start to the right of Rocky directly below the large V-shaped recess. Climb the wall boldly, but on good holds, to reach the base of the V-shaped recess. Climb the recess, moving out left at the top.

Slab and Groove   110 feet   Hard Very Severe   (1989)
Not the most original of names, but a good first pitch. Start to the left of a large flake directly beneath a holly-choked groove.
1 60 feet. 5a. Go up the left-hand side of the flake. Traverse right to reach the base of a slim groove. Ascend this for a few feet to a steepening. Trend diagonally leftward to gain slabs and a ledge sporting some hollies.
2 40 feet. Continue up the groove behind the hollies moving left to finish.

The Booze Brothers   120 feet   E2 5c   (1989)
A fine pitch with a surprising roof section. Start at a large flake directly under a holly choked groove with a large triangular overhang to its right. Climb up to gain a clean groove then slabs above to reach the roof. Pull through this from left to right, much easier than it looks. Go directly up the slabby arête, rejecting the easier but dirty line rightwards.

Outside Left   100 feet   Hard Very Severe 5b   (1992)
Takes one of the few weaknesses in this part of the cliff. Start at a

Craig Cwm Glas
Bach Right-Hand

1. Runner Up   VS
2. Noah's Ark   E6
3 Over The Beach   E6
4. Pan Alley   HVS
5. Rufus   VS

clean corner, directly below a downward pointing flake at a breach
in the overhangs. Climb the corner to a ledge, step left to the
Damoclean flake at the base of the groove (it is allegedly quite sound)
left of the large triangular overhang. Continue steeply up, exiting right
at the top of the groove.

Outside Right   100 feet   Hard Very Severe 5b   (1992)
This route should improve with traffic. Start directly beneath the large
triangular overhang. Climb the obvious flake crack and continue up
the slab above to a possible stance, left of a group of Hollies (music
in the background?). Traverse right into a short corner which rises up
to the short triangular roof. Pull out right to a good rest. Traverse
awkwardly right to a thin crack which proves stubborn. Continue to a
stance and greasy slabs above.

Hairway to Steven   160 feet   E1   (1988)
Fifty yards to the right of The Booze Brothers are some vegetated
slabs. Start at the foot of a clean curving flake leading up to a roof.
1 100 feet. 5b. Climb the flake, stand on its top to pull through the
overhang, and so reach parallel cracks. Climb these to reach slabs
and a belay.
2 60 feet. Easy slabs lead up leftwards; belay a long way back.

Chunders Revenge   80 feet   Very Severe 4b   (1988)
On the far right of the crag, a series of pocketed slabs lead up to a
short wall. Start below the slabs. Climb the slabs to reach parallel
cracks, use these to surmount the wall. Finish by scrambling leftwards.

The following routes lie round and up to the right beyond Craig Cwm
Glas Bach and a broad grassy gully in lower Cwm Hetty (derived from
Hetiau – the hats which were blown from the heads of trippers riding the
original open carriages of the Snowdon Mountain Railway to land in the
cwm). The first two are on the dome shaped crag down and left of the
prominent dark, dank cleft of Simdde Sian (Sian's Chimney), whilst the
third is much lower down, directly beneath the chimney itself... the
chimney carries a waterfall that is prone to being blown upwards during
periods of high wind, thus creating a 'smoke' effect.

Famous Grouse   50 feet   E4 6b   (1988)
Needs a prolonged dry spell. Start below the obvious crack in the
middle of the crag below and on the left of Sian's Chimney. Climb the
crack which increases in difficulty to a frustrating crux at the
steepening – a well-protected pitch.

Bunghole Buster   50 feet   Hard Very Severe 5a   (1988)
Almost worth half-a-star. This is the central rib 10 feet right of the
previous route.

★**Beavering in Obscurity**   70 feet   E1 5a   (c.1988)
A bold little route, with only marginal gear. Start at the base of a
narrow rib leading up to a slabby area, to the right of a steep little
wall. Climb the rib to the rounded slabs. Ascend these with some
delicacy. Belay well back.

Llechog   (The Slabby One)

OS Ref. 606 567

Not to be confused with the crag of the same name in Cwm Clogwyn.
This is the impressive squat wedge-shaped crag high up on the
west-bounding ridge of Cwm Glas Bach. From a distance the crag seems
to be broken, but the few routes that have been done here are surprisingly
continuous and reminiscent of the East Face of Tryfan (though with
superior situations). Escape is virtually always possible leftwards along
the terraces which cut the face, making individual pitches
interchangeable on all of the routes. There is probably scope here for
some short extremely fierce little climbs. The cliff is most easily
approached up the Snowdon Mountain Railway although purists will
prefer to scramble up the low-profile rib/spur which runs down from the
cliff towards the valley floor and the cottages of Gwastadnant.

★**Jug Handle**   400 feet   Very Difficult   (1954)
Approach up the ridge to where it steepens. On the left is a large
grass rake. The route is approximately centrally placed, starting from
a large pointed block.

Slab and Tower   290 feet   Severe   (1954)
Start by a pinnacle at the foot of a large steep quartzy slab, bounded
on the left by a dirty groove. The climb heads for the prominent tower
outlined against the sky from the ledge at the foot of the crag

Nice Chimney   280 feet   Very Difficult   (1980)
Start below the steep mossy slab on the left side of the main area.
1 50 feet. Go up the slab to a grassy platform and spike belays.
2 80 feet. Continue up a slab on small holds making for a crack on
the right. Traverse right just below this and go up round the corner.

3 80 feet. Make for the obvious chimney (more pleasant than it looks). Above this is an easy step where two ledges converge.
4 70 feet. Go up left of a pinnacle by small cracks, then left under the overhang above to tackle the final steep wall.

Below the spur thrown down from Llechog are several short crags with some interesting short routes if one can find them.

About 400 yards up the hillside, across the road from Humphrey's Bunk-house, is another collection of walls which contain the following...

Hat Shoe 25 feet E2 6b   (1987)
The right-hand line up a small wall facing Llanberis.

Boot Coat 25 feet E2 6a   (1987)
The line left of the previous route.

Aesthetes Foot 60 feet E1 5b   (1987)
This lies across the hillside (up The Pass) and faces the opposite way to the previously described wall.

Surprisingly Goute 30 feet E1 5c   (1987)
Left again is a slimmer wall facing the road. The line is marked by quartz.

Quantum Dump 90 feet E1 5b   (1987)
This climbs a curving wall up and left, behind the previous route.

Conway Crags   OS Ref. 593 588

Well down The Pass towards Llanberis are several more rocky spurs running down on the north flank of the Snowdon ridge. The largest of these is in a small cwm overlooking Llyn Peris and opposite the slate quarries. The crag consists of rocky ribs protruding from a heathery hillside. Several 300 foot routes have been put up here. Descriptions seem to have been lost, along with the old Wendy's Cafe new route book – however, the main rib gave a fairly good outing at about VS/HVS.

About 500 yards back up The Pass, towards Nant Peris, on the right, as the road crosses the valley floor, a small outcrop sits at the foot of the hillside offering a few problems, the best of which is a 35-foot 'Left Wall' type crack – 5b; the arête to the left is 6c. ALL the other obvious lines have been climbed.

Creigiau'r Cadeirydd

(Chairman's Rocks)   OS Ref. 584 591

These pleasant little outcrops lie on the north-west face of Derlwyn overlooking the Coed Victoria. They consist of a series of three grey ribs running down the hillside, parallel to each other and offer problems of between 25 and 45 feet in height. The area is rich in plant, bird and animal life and climbers are requested to disturb this environment as little as possible. The rocks are best approached from a point on the Snowdon footpath, about 100 yards beyond the top of its initial hill. Contour around to the left, well below a small quarried face (which also has the odd problem) and across boggy ground to reach the top end of the nearest rib. This is the prominent group of high slabby rocks split by two wide cracks.

Original Route 35 feet Difficult
Take the wall to finish up the right-hand crack.

Mini Botterill 25 feet Very Difficult
The small heathery slab immediately left, neat.

Cracked Spur 30 feet Very Difficult
This is the short shattered buttress a few feet to the left split by the second wide crack. A hard pull up right leads to jugs.

One other route is perhaps worthy of recording to date; going down onto the open grass below the trees, continue left for perhaps 50 yards, beyond the second rib, below broken rock and a heavily vegetated gully. There is a large nose of rock left of the gully. Twenty yards left of this is another nose split by:

The Big Groove 40 feet Very Difficult
Scramble up broken ground to the cluster of small trees at its foot. Climb directly up the groove – a short excursion to the right may be necessary half-way up.

Bouldering

Although the area cannot offer the scope or quality of problems associated with sandstone or grit, there are nonetheless several venues well worthy of a visit, where one can find micro-routes of sufficient difficulty to tax even the most gifted of rock athletes.

Fachwen

This is the name generally used to include all of the Padarn Country Park which overlooks the north-west tip of Llyn Padarn. From the Caernarfon end of Llyn Padarn take the minor road to Fachwen, past a long layby and so to a steep little wall by the blind bend, as the road narrows and starts to climb up the hillside.

Electrocution Wall

So called because a telephone cable is suspended about three feet from its crest, although one is more likely to end up in hospital through being hit by a 'mad motorist' rather than by being 'fried'. All the vertical lines, including the 'impossible-looking' (6c/7a) ones have been done, courtesy of Littlejohn, Perrin and Trower. A slanting crack at the right-hand side of the face is 5a. Just left, the classic **Electrocution Wall** 5c, via a small right-facing groove, thin face holds, a sloping ledge then a precarious finish is a real gem. The girdle either way is 5c.

Above the layby just beyond Electrocution Wall the groove on the right is 5b, difficult to enter, and the towering finger crack above is a classic and bold 5b, **Pure Genius** courtesy, respectively, of Harris and Perrin.

Pine Tree Boulders

One hundred yards up through the trees, just before one reaches Electrocution Wall, lies an isolated clump of rocky pinnacles with an obvious crack splitting the side facing the road. Left of this crack, the buttress is undercut, forming a cave. Following the crack out from the very back of this cave gives an 8-foot roof problem – **The Fachwen Overhang** 5c, which finishes up the crack. **Perrin's Arête** just to the right is a hospitalising 6a, while the pillar right again is a similar 5b. The undercut wall left of the Fachwen Overhang is 5b, direct, with the famous **Shorter's Overhang**, a 6b 18-foot traverse going along the lip of the low undercut boulder 25 feet to the right. Round the back and to the sides many other short problems lie waiting to be re-discovered. The complete girdle of these pinnacles and boulders is very entertaining, and quite strenuous.

Lion Rock

This, the most prominent feature in the Fachwen area, is a dome of hard white quartzy rock with black streaks running down its short overhanging west face. There are three good problems here, a ramp on the right side of the face (without the small flake as a starting foothold) is 6b. An optional finish can be made up the airy crack above to a hard finish, 5b, if one can find the crucial hold. The flake crack just left of the ramp is 5c – the best finish goes right along the sloping ledge. The right-to-left girdle of the face finishing up a slab on the left also gives food for thought at 6a. The large slabby face around to the right gives three pitch routes in the Moderate/Very Difficult range.

In the amorphous wilderness behind lies Witches' Hollow, whilst the classic **Harris's Arête** 6b, well worth seeking out by the connoisseur of the obscure, is the obvious feature on the conglomerate bluffs above Fachwen village. Dating from the '60s it was Al Harris's party piece on which he rarely bothered to even dry his EBs. Just below the television mast on the summit is **Accomazzo's Wall** – 6a, a desperate and committing problem.

Yellow Wall

This is situated by the old Llanberis road on the north-west face of Craig yr Undeb (Union Crag) across from Lion Rock on the opposite side of the lake. The super-low girdle coming in from the right is 6b. Several 15-foot problems from 5b – 6b lie up the wall just left finishing on a juggy traversing ledge. A longer and more serious problem (5c), takes the wall on the right.

Cwm Glas

The steep walls and corners of the small outcrop on the opposite side of the stream from Clogwyn y Grochan give long problems with nasty landings, the obvious 25 foot slab left of the two problem cracks being a noteworthy 6a/b. Further over, in a field below Cwm Glas Mawr Cottage sits an enormous boulder, a favourite for many years. The wide crack in the east face is a splendid little Very Severe, 4c. The left-to-right traverse of the face is also very entertaining, especially on the last 10 feet. The traverse of The Puddingstone, on the same side of the river and slightly higher up The Pass, is also a classic problem, whilst **Boysen's Roof**, 6a, is in the field by Ynys Ettws.

The Cromlech Boulders

The huge boulders by the Cromlech car park have amused climbers for years. Problems, and variations on problems are legion, and normally well-chalked up. There are several very good traverses, one of which involves lying horizontally below an overhanging prow, heel-hooking above one of the smelliest boggy landings in the area – fail at your peril. Down towards Llanberis, an isolated boulder next to the road presents a chalked-up overhang – **Jerry's Roof**, a 6c (Fr 8b) problem.

Dinas Mot Boulders

These outcrops lie just up and across the road from the Cromlech Boulders. There are many steep problems, yet of a slabby nature, the hardest of which appears to be a short 'holdless' wall at the right-hand end. The prominent arête next to the bend in the road has been regularly ascended since the '50s, at about 5b. No more claims please. There is one route however, in the modern idiom, which justifies description. Left again past the prominent arête are a series of broken walls and corners, which are bounded by an obvious overhanging arête with a thin crack to its right. The arête is taken by:

★★**Beginner's Mind**   35 feet   E8 6c   (1993)
Climb the obvious and vicious arête past two poor peg runners and an RP2.

Barrel Buttress

This large, long, low-relief boulder lies just above the approach path, to the left of the stone wall, about 100 yards below the foot of The Nose of Dinas Mot. The side facing the road is overhanging, and presents some mortifying problems – all 6b or harder. The low level girdle is 7a (Fr 8b – without using the obvious off route holds). Some climbers have spent an entire summer on/off it. Of the dozen or so vertical problems, the hardest would seem to be the one that goes directly over the right end of the prominent overlap, 7a... unless you know differently.

Outlying Crags

Whilst clearly not in the Llanberis Pass, there are some good small crags above the road between the Pen y Gwryd Hotel and Capel Curig, they have found a home here.

Craig yr Haul

After a mile (or so) of driving from Pen y Gwryd to Capel Curig park at a layby, go through a grey gate and start walking. The crag is high up on the side of the mountain, note, not the lower broken buttress. The rock is superb, there is currently scope for more routes. A perfect place for the seeker of solitude, or those with a distaste for the rest of the human race.

In the centre is a slabby tower, with some easy angled slabs to the right. Left of the tower is a prominent rib with an obvious corner at two thirds height. Left again are some short walls, one with a small corner at its top. The first route takes this.

Partially Obscured by a Tall Sheep 40 feet Very Severe 4b
(1993)
Start at the base of the vertical crack, a series of mantels, layaways and other forms of climbing leads to the corner, up this to jugs. Smile a lot.

Fermat's Last Theorem 35 feet Hard Very Severe 5b (1993)
A well-protected route with some fun moves. Start about 30 feet right of Partially Obscured... at a vertical crack in a 'pebble dash' wall. Ascend the wall to reach the base of the upper crack, positive holds and crystals lead to a flake and small blocks. Continue up, the difficulty easing all the time.

Ossum 75 feet E1 5a (1993)
Start at the base of the obvious rib with the prominent corner at two thirds height. Easy climbing leads up to the corner, place some good

gear before the corner before tackling it. A final easy slab leads to belays.

Annie Get Your Oakleys   90 feet   Very Severe 4c   (1993)
Start as for Alexandra Technique. Ascend the crack for about seven feet then traverse left to a perched flake. Climb the cracks and flakes above, very enjoyable, to finish the escapable arête. Belay well back.

Alexandra Technique   90 feet   Hard Very Severe 5a   (1993)
Takes the central crack system in the slabby tower. Climb the crack to a short 'chimney', step left to gain the middle cracks. Bridge up (monkey-up-a-stick fashion) or layback the cracks, with some good protection, to a ledge and a breather. The final moves past an obvious flake are also entertaining. Belay well back.

Round to the right are the slabs, the first route on these starts at a scoop below some quartz.

Belbin's Bull   90 feet   Very Severe 4c   (1993)
A delightful pitch. Start as for Alexandra Technique but take the crack curving up rightwards to reach a flake. Semi-layback the crack to reach a ledge. Continue up the upper crack.

Further down and right, at the base of the buttress, are two vegetated corners with a stepped arête, the next route follows this.

Shed's Arête   60 feet   Hard Severe 4a   (1993)
A bold little route. Start at the base of the arête, ascend the knobbly rock to reach the base of a steepening. Good holds and a spike (thin sling) leads to a ledge and the upper section of the arête.

Matt's Pad   120 feet   Very Difficult   (1993)
Climb the scoop, then the rib above to the quartz, past this to a large ledge. Ascend the bulge/overhang using a block to finish up the slab. More fun if done without using the edge of the block which forms the slab.

Down and right of Matt's Pad is a pool/pond, a natural jacuzzi, at the base of the slab. The next route starts just left of this.

Herbie the Cat   165 feet   Severe   (1993)
1 75 feet. Climb the slab to a rib, then go up this to some heather. Belay above the heather at the base of an open quartzy groove.
2 90 feet. Ascend the quartz streaked groove and go up the right-hand crack on the slabby finishing block.

Ejectamenta 60 feet Severe (1993)
A nice filler-in. Start just to the right of the natural jacuzzi. Ascend the slab to the base of a short groove, awkward moves lead up to the easy slab above, climb this past quartz and various bits of ejectamenta. Round and right again are some more slabs, split by a broad heather ledge.

The first route starts at the very toe of the slab.

Llados 135 feet Severe (1993)
1 75 feet Climb the pale slab, with great interest but no protection to the heather ledge.
2 60 feet Take the diagonal crack in the upper slab, but after about 15 feet go up the slab direct to the top.

The next two routes are on either side of the top pitch of Llados.

Bistromaths 60 feet Very Difficult (1993)
Slab left of Llados, past flakes and up the clean strip of rock.

Stu the Rabbit 60 feet Very Difficult (1993)
Start 15 feet right of Llados where there is another area of clean slabs with some interesting moves.

The R.A.C. Boulders

Two in number, these pocketed blocks lie in the field below a 50-foot crag, Dyffryn Mymbwr, about a mile and a half west of Plas y Brenin, at a layby on the A4086. The boulders give brilliant sport, but unfortunately sit on private land. The owner, who lives in the house, just above and to the left of the crag, seems tolerant of climbers as long as they ask for permission, keep a low profile, and leave no litter. The crag is divided by an area of broken rock on the left and a grassy gully on the right. All the easier lines have been ascended; other harder lines were first pegged in the '50s. But, with the 'Munich Mechanics', and 'Steeplejackers' long since departed, the crag now sports several desperate routelets to tax the steel-fingered 'wall-creature'.

The left-hand buttress is:

Atom Art Buttress

This is split by an off-width dog-leg crack, and capped by a large tree.

★Jiggit   30 feet   E6 6c   (1989)
Sustained climbing on minute holds up the well-tried wall and
groovelet left of the off-width crack, passing a peg, to finish just right
of the tree.

The off-width itself is a painfully obvious traditional Hard Very Severe...
a detailed description seems superfluous.

★★Atom Art   30 feet   E6 6b   (1986)
Wrongly referred to as Atom Arm in the previous guide, this
carnivorous little horror takes the pocketed wall and crack, starting six
feet right of the dog-leg off-width. It is reputed to be the safest of the
three hard routes here.

★Pygmy Passion   25 feet   E5 6c   (1987)
The thin crack and tiny arête just right of Atom Art are sustained, but
with good protection.

A few feet right is:

Central Buttress

This is by far the widest and highest of the three sections of the crag.
There are three main lines.

★Swcad   50 feet   E1 5c   (1984)
The central groove finishing over the roof gives a fine pitch.

★Stor Klumpe   45 feet   E4 6a   (1984)
The immaculate crack right of Swcad, does not yield without a
struggle.

Spanish Bomb   40 feet   E1 5c   (1984)
On the right-hand side of the buttress, this is the groove right of Stor
Klumpe, with a finish up the arête.

Across a wide grassy gully, to the right and set back, lies the final small
buttress, cut by a slim right-facing corner.

★Retchus (The Longer Reach)   30 feet   E5 6c   (1987)
Climbs the wall with a faint crackline left of El Groove. From the
central flake, swing left and finish up the arête – dynamic and
strenuous with one very hard move.

El Groove   30 feet   E1 5c   (Sixties)
The slim right-facing corner is short, but cute.

Craig Garth

A series of small buttresses on the opposite side of the valley to The R.A.C. Boulders. The following routes lie on the left-hand crag, where a steep and undercut wall faces towards Capel Curig. Approach by passing Garth Farm on the lake side, then cross the boggy valley. Worth a visit if one is going... well... very well.

Just before the undercut wall, the first small cliff one reaches, has a prominent crack in the arête – **Come to Hughie's and See the World** – 30 feet Very Severe 4c.

The Call of the Raven   40 feet   E5 6b   (1987)
This takes the left-hand of two prominent cracks. Climb ledgy ground to a peg runner, then jump for the jug in front of it. Continue up the crack to finish over stacked blocks.

★★**The Big Bird**   30 feet   E6 6b   (1987)
An excellent route taking the right-hand crack past four peg runners and finishing direct.

At the right hand end of the crag sits an obvious undercut arête bounded by a mossy corner...

★★**The Beast Beneath Me**   45 feet   E6 6b   (1987)
Start below the mossy corner, then rock up onto the wall. Traverse left on pockets to gain the arête with hard moves leading to a grassy ledge. Follow the arête on its left side, two peg runners, to a rounded hold on its edge. Pull out right past a peg and continue to the top.

The Ricks and Racks

These crags, suitable for an evening's entertainment only, lie above the A4086 on private land, a few hundred yards west of Plas y Brenin. Unfortunately, the farmer who owns the land is extremely sensitive and has now banned all climbing on these rocks in an attempt to gain payment for their use. You are advised to keep clear.

There are several outcrops scattered along the hillside, the cleanest also being the smallest, and nearest – The Blocks, which have a hard pocketed wall, a steep technical arête, a masochistic chimney and about a dozen or so easier problems. Across the hillside to the left, and at the same level, the next cliff has VS/HVS routes up to 50 feet high.

Climbing Walls

There are four climbing walls in the area, all very different, and each worthy of a visit: the largest and most varied of these is at Plas y Brenin, Capel Curig (06904 214) which actually sports two walls, one an ultra-modern limestone climb-a-like with steep bouldering and leading/top roping, and the other, available for group use, consists of the 'old wall' with modifications; the next largest is built of natural stone, and is slightly polished and slippery (beware – there are no crash mats... though it is handy for the hospital) at Plas Menai (0248 670964) midway between Caernarfon and Porth Dinorwig, on the Menai Straits; fourthly the wall at The Heights (0286 871179) is the smallest of the four, but it is well-thought out with a superb roof to traverse – any more than six is a crowd here.

First Ascents

1879	**Western Gully, The Arête & Eastern Gully** (Clogwyn y Person) R Pendlebury *'...behind them is a V-shaped nook, 15 feet high, peculiar attitudes are often seen here'.*
1884	**The Parson's Nose** A H Stocker
1887 July 30	**Crazy Pinnacle Gully** E R Kidson
1887 July 31	**Western Gully** E R Kidson
1892 April 2	**The Right-Hand Edge** H B Dixon, Mrs Dixon, Mrs Commelons, F W Gamble, A M Marshall
1892	**Castle Gully**
1893 March	**South West Arête** G W H Tunzelmian
1894 Dec 9	**Crazy Pinnacle Face** J M A Thomson, H W Hughes, H Edwards
1897 March 16	**Black Cleft** J M A Thomson *Considered for some time the hardest route in Wales.*
1899	**Bryant's Gully** G B Bryant and party *'A brief lunch was disposed of in a small hollow. We shared it with a well-nourished and contented-looking toad, living there in apparent freedom from all family cares. The general verdict was that, whilst containing nothing to attract the seekers after glory, yet it was an excellent gully'.*
1900	**Jammed Boulder Gully** J M A Thomson, R Williams *'The exit is narrow, and the arrival of corpulent or clumsy followers will be watched with amusement by those who have gone before. A commodious theatre is provided for the spectacle'.*
1901	**Eastern & Western Gullies** (Dinas Mot) W H Price, C G Brown, P A Thompson, P S Thompson *A cairn above The Nose showed that at least one of these had been climbed before.*
1901 Easter	**North Ridge of Crib Goch** C G Brown, P A Thompson
1902 Sept 6	**Thompson's Routes** J M A Thomson, T Williams, D Hunter *In the region of Square Gully. Long since lost.*
1903 April 3	**The West Buttress** J M A Thomson, M K Smith, R F Blackwell
1903 Sept 13	**The Chasms** R F Blackwell, S Tetley, E R Turner
1903 Sept 13	**Central Route** J M A Thomson, T Williams, R Williams *'...and the removal of earth with a penknife disclosed a succession of excellent niches; with the aid of these the ascent was accomplished with an unexpected ease. Strange sounds caught at intervals, and previously accredited to sheep, were now recognised as human voices. Our flanking column under Blackwell's guidance had reached their goal*

and were raising the paean. This was an attempt on Great
Gully, the difficult pitch being avoided by a detour out to the
left. The route described was probably first done on 22
April 1949 by G Dyke, P R J Harding.

1904   **Great Gully** J M A Thomson, M K Smith
'At a point about a yard higher, a half turn was
necessitated, and I found myself looking straight outward,
with my back to the rock. The distribution of the holds lent
themselves to this attitude...'

1904   **Crib Goch Buttress** G D Abraham, A P Abraham
Long since lost, but was near Route III.

1906   **Easter Grey Gully** J M A Thomson

1906 Aug 6   **Yellowstone Gully** A E Barker, G T Atchison, W J Drew,
H Mitchell

1906 Aug 9   **Double Cave Gully** H Mitchell, G T Atchison, A E Barker,
W J Drew

1906 Aug 12   **Schoolmasters' Gully** H Mitchell, A E Barker, W J Drew,
G T Atchison
A remarkable climb for the period. 'Each of us insisted that
the man before him made a ridiculous fuss and spent an
absurdly long time over it. Criticism and advice flowed
freely, but each of us modified his opinion when his own
turn came'. J M Edwards, J N Mahler repeated it on 2
April, 1934 added the left-hand start and considered it new.
Fittingly it was called Plaster Chimney.

1908 Aug   **Reade's Route** W R Reade, G L Bartrum
'A few feet higher is a conspicuous pinnacle 12 feet high.
The leader stands upon it, and, bestriding the gulf like a
Colossus, makes contact with the vertical wall above'.

1908 Sept   **Waterslide Route & The Organ Route** J M A
Thomson, H O Jones, K J P Orton

1908 Sept   **Ribbon Route & Fallen Block Climb** J M A Thomson
'I narrowly escaped being trepanned by a rock chisel'.

1909   **Dodo Gully** G Winthrop Young

1910   **Slab Variant** J M A Thomson

1910 Sept   **The Gambit Climb** J M A Thomson, H O Jones, K J P
Orton
'The discovery, by means of this intricate and difficult route
that these crags so formidable in aspect, were not wholly
unassilable, encouraged the hope that a second breach
could be made'. J L Longland's variation: 2 April 1931.

1913   **Clogwyn y Ddysgl Girdle** G Winthrop Young, C
O'Brien

1913   **Winthrop Young's Climb** (Clogwyn Pen Llechen) G
Winthrop Young, H E L Porter

1913   **The Arête Climb** (Craig Aderyn) S W Herford

1915   **The Black Gates** G H L Mallory

1915 Aug 17   **The Grey Slab** (Clogwyn Pen Llechen) J I Laycock, C T
Lehmann, T B Burnet, Sir J B Farmer, Miss R Farmer

1924 Oct 7   **Treasury Climb, Jacob's Ladder** (Craig Aderyn) F
Graham

1925 Aug 20	**Captain's Bluff Direct, The Gauge** C F Stoehr, W K McMillan, H R C Carr
1925 Aug 21	Two scrambles on the right-hand and largest of the Grey Cliffs.
	'...20 feet of almost holdless slab which can just be climbed in nibbers'. The last two climbs were done by W K McMillan, C F Stoehr and Mrs Stoehr, who, though in the lightest of walking attire, succumbed to temptation.
1925 Aug 23	**Wall and Traverse** H R C Carr, M W Guinness, W K McMillan
	'The party is still under the impending Wall of the nose, and it is necessary to scramble a few yards along the ledge, upwards and to the left, before a weakness in this formidable bastion is discerned'.
1925 Aug 24	**Via Media** F Graham, M W Guinness
	A little-known gem.
1925 Aug 27	**Rectory Chimneys** M W Guinness, W McNaught, H R C Carr
	The Finish as described (The Vestry Variant) was first done by M W Guinness, H R C Carr, 30 Aug 1925.
1925 Aug 27	**Crack and Slab & Flake Chimney** (originally called Tower Chimney) H R C Carr, M W Guinness
	'...climbing is of an exposed nature and of more than moderate difficulty for 30 feet'.
1925 Aug 27	**Phoenix Buttress** M W Guinness, H R C Carr
	'The groove proved to be a vexatious little problem... '
1925 Aug 30	**Little Benjamin** M W Guinness, H R C Carr
	'On the final section, the leader runs out 50 feet of rope'.
1925 Aug 30	**Intermediate Slab Routes** M W Guinness, H R C Carr
1927 Sept 11	**Fallen Block Crack** I M Waller
	A fine lead taken straight out in one pitch.
1930 Easter	**The Cracks** (4pts. aid) B L Bathurst, H C H Bathurst
	First explored in 1926. The party traversed in from the foot of Eastern Gully and climbed the heather-filled crack direct to the twin cracks by means of two pitons, a bolt and top rope. C F Kirkus led the first free ascent later in 1930. The top pitch was done by the arête on the left, 23 June 1938 by A D M Cox, J L Longland.
1930 June 22	**Direct Route** C F Kirkus, J B Dodd
	A Kirkus classic. Much of the route had been done earlier in the year by C F Kirkus, C J A Cooper, G G Macphee. 'Time taken 4 to 5 hours – should long remain a record. A ladder would make the final crack suitable for others than a few rock gymnasts'. A shoulder was used on the final pitch, but Kirkus later climbed it without. Groves Variation (now pitch 3 of Crosstie) climbed by P Hampson, A Cowburn, B Usher on 26 July 1952.
1931 May 30	**Flake Traverse** P L Roberts, R D Crofton
1931 Aug 6	**Western Slabs** J M Edwards, A R Edge, A M D'Aeth

The direct start was climbed 8 June, 1946 by P R J Harding, R E Meyer.

1931 Aug 6 **Girdle of the Nose** J M Edwards A M D'Aeth

1931 Sept 13 **West Rib** C F Kirkus, I M Waller
Another brilliant lead by Kirkus.

1931 Oct 13 **Holly Buttress** J M Edwards, S C R Walmsley
The first real attack on the north side of The Pass. An easy variation to the last pitch was done on 18 Dec 1931 and the modern start, 9 June 1931, both by J M Edwards.

1931 Dec 6 **Spiral Stairs & Valley Crossings** J M Edwards, S B Darbishire
The former route was initially very vegetated.

1931 Dec 18 **Flying Buttress** J M Edwards
A fine classic discovery which has become exceptionally popular. Originally named Sodom. This shocked the CC guidebook Editor who persuaded him to change the name.

1932 Sept **Waterfall Climb** J M Edwards, A B Hargreaves
The Direct Start was taken on 12 July, 1945 by J Campbell. The upper line was slightly different from the original and the whole climb thought to be new. It was called Heather Climb.

1933 Feb 2 **Nebuchadnezzar's Crawl** J M Edwards, C F Kirkus
Crockett Crack start; 21 April 1956 by M H J Baylis, J F Pagella.

1933 March 27 **Parchment Passage & Pharaoh's Passage** J M Edwards, O S Bell
Variation Finish to Pharaoh's Passage 2 Sept 1951 J Brown, M T Sorrell.

1933 April 17 **Pharaoh's Wall** J M Edwards, A B Hargreaves
Direct Finish; 26 March 1946 by M G Hughes.

1933 May 13 **Dives** J M Edwards, T E Davies
Pitch 1 was climbed on l8 Dec 1931 by J M Edwards as a variation on Spiral Stairs. The original finish was as for Spiral Stairs; the Better Things finish was climbed by T D Bourdillon, J W T Tomlinson, M J Bell on April l8 1949.

1933 June 17 **Sexton's Route** J M Edwards, G G Macphee, R W Stallybrass
The hard variation to the last pitch had been led on 13 May 1933 by J M Edwards.

1934 March 30 **Slow Ledge Climb** J M Edwards, J Gask
The long groove, now part of Dolerite Dump was taken as a finish. The final section was added by G W S Pigott, H A Carsten on 29 May 1948.

1934 March 30 **Boulder Buttress** J M Edwards, J Gask
H A Carsten added the modern finishes on 28 May 1948.

1934 March 30 **Western Wing Girdle** J M Edwdrds, J Gask

1935 Jan 20 **Ledge Way** J M Edwards, B Mckenna

1935 Feb 17 **Hazel Groove** J M Edwards, B Mckenna
The left-hand finish was led by P R J Harding in Aug 1948 and the Direct Start was added by P R J Harding, P R Hodgkinson on 12 April 1949.

1935 March 9	**Cwm Glas Pinnacle** R V M Barry, J R Jenkins
1935 April 20	**Scrambler's Gate & Long Tree Gate** J M Edwards, C W F Noyce
1935 April 20	**Dead Entrance** J M Edwards, C W F Noyce

1935 April 20   **Dead Entrance** J M Edwards, C W F Noyce
The easy way of reaching Green Park was discovered by R Hind on Good Friday 1940.

1935 May 5   **Bluebell Traverse** J M Edwards, M Glynn, I Corrie

1935 May 7   **Main Scoop Route** J M Edwards, B Mckenna
Koala Finish; 27 July 1969 by M J Bell, J D Griffiths.

1935 June 9   **Quintet Route** J K Cooke, E Holliday, W S Webb, E Pentir Williams, A Burns

1935   **Sabre Cut** E Pentir Williams, R G Williams
The first of the big Cromlech corners to fall.

1935 June 22   **Twin Groove** C H S R Palmer

1935 July 14   **Shadow Wall & Crackstone Rib** J M Edwards, J B Joyce
At the time Crackstone Rib was thought to be more technical than Shadow Wall. The five holly trees on Crackstone Rib are now no more. 'A stern test of anyone's vocabulary. Amid festoons of cowardice, the leader called upon ethereal beings for strength, and assuming sundry copulative postures eventually clawed over the manelpieces' – 1954 ascent of Shadow Wall.

1935 July 25   **West Buttress Arête, Tweedledum, Tweedledee, The Rattle & Central Buttress Arête** C H S R Palmer, H E W R....

1935 July 27   **Main Wall** P L Roberts, J K Cooke
A bold route on a buttress previously dismissed as impossible. First pitch added by the same party plus E Holliday on 16 March 1937, the original start having been made from Great Gully.

1935 Sept 8   **Duet Chimneys** J K Cooke, P L Roberts

1935 Sept 21   **The Quartet Wall** P L Roberts, G A Duckett, J K Cooke, L Milner

1937 May 16   **Three Cave Gully** P L Roberts, J K Cooke

1938 Aug 10   **Diagonal** A Birtwistle, G F Parkinson
A remarkable route, well ahead of its time. It was not repeated for 10 years. The final crack was climbed by P R J Harding, A J J Moulam in May 1946. The original route took the upper part of West Rib.

1939 March 17   **Choristers' Cleft** G K Hodgkin, R C Evans

1939 Oct 21   **Cenotaph Corner Finish** R Hind, J E Q Barford

1939 Oct 21   **Tributary Crack** R Hind
It was believed to have been done before.

1940 Aug 5   **Brant** J M Edwards, J E Q Barford
J M E after farming at Harlech for some days was in extremely good form and produced a climb considerably harder than any of the others which have so far been done on these cliffs, with the possible exception of Long Tree

Gate. 'The Brant – Very Severe, strong arms required and a just appreciation of the value of loose holds'.

1940 Aug 8 **Slape** J M Edwards, G F Peaker, R G Donaldson
A superb addition, thought to be easier than Brant at the time, 'Standard: Severe'.

1940 Oct 20 **Horseman's Route** J M Edwards, J E Q Barford (AL)
'Edwards failed on the middle pitch which Barford led without effort'.

1941 Sept 7 **Lorraine** J E Q Barford, N E Morin (AL)
All but the slab pitch had been done previously by J M Edwards on 9 Sept 1931. The variation was climbed by D E Alcock, C E Davies on 7 June 1965.

1941 Sept 10 **Nea** N E Morin, J M Edwards
Shoulder Connection (joining the main little square gully from the right where Nea joins it from the left) by J M Edwards, G Dyke on 8 Aug 1949. The finish is a grade harder since a rockfall in early Spring 1984.

1943 May 11 **The Ledge Climb** A W Bridge and two Commando stalwarts: Cpl. J Kenny, Cpl. J Lynn of No. 4 Commando.

1944 June 26 **Dolerite Dump** J E Q Barford, D Pepper
The corner and final groove had been climbed previously by J M Edwards in conjunction with Slow Ledge Climb. The continuation above the terrace was worked out by H A Carsten on 28 May 1948.

1944 June 30 **Garden Groove** J E Q Barford, R M P Hartog, M P Ward
The left-hand exit was led by H A Carsten, P R Hodgkinson on 1 April 1948.

1946 Aug 26 **Route II** B L Bathurst, E D Carr, H R C Carr
1946 Aug 27 **Route III** B L Bathurst, E D Carr, H R C Carr, W Fahie
1947 May 4 **Spectre** P R J Harding, E H Phillips
'Not feeling like The Slape, a new climb was done: The Spectre (The Grochan Spectre)'. Harding had made the second ascent of Brant the previous day. The route originally finished up Nea. The present finish was added on 12 March 1949 by P R J Harding, K A W Herbert. First solo ascent by P R J Harding in 1948. The Goat Start 100 feet Very Severe (up Goats Gully for 60 feet, then steep grooves out left over the bounding rib to join Spectre) added by C M G Smith, B L Blake, J H Swallow, 21 July 1949.

1947 Whit **The Crevice & Wrinkle** M P Ward, J E Q Barford, B Pierre

1947 Aug 29/30 **Ivy Sepulchre** (2pts. aid) P R J Harding, E H Phillips
The second of the three big Cromlech corners to fall. 'Operation Garden was commenced on Ivy Sepulchre, P R J H abseiling down complete with trowel etc: the top 60 feet was found to be climbable, involving an all-in wrestling match with a rotten holly tree, which despite its age, still knows how to deal with would be climbers'. '...reinforced by E H P, the party again visited this cliff – this time meaning business. The first ascent of Ivy Sepulchre was made; 200 feet. 120 feet of rope required. Exceptionally

Severe – Rubbers or Kletterschue are advisable for nail fans...'

1948 April 24   **Trilon** (1pt. aid) P R J Harding, N L Horsefield

1948 June 12/13   **The Old Girdle** P R J Harding, P R Hodgkinson
A two day expedition, split at the yew trees.

1948 June 19   **Pedestal Route** P R J Harding, K A W Herbert
The first route on the crag.

1948 July   **Overlapping Wall** M G Hughes
A bold and outstanding lead. Pitch 1 on 18 June 1949 by P R J Harding, F A Smith. Pitch 3 in Nov 1951 by J Brown, R Moseley. Soloed by P R J Harding in 1949.

1948 Aug   **Ash Tree Gully** A J J Moulam

1948 Aug 2   **Bluebell Cracks** H A Carsten, P R Hodgkinson

1948 Aug 18   **The Ashes Route** P R J Harding, A J J Moulam

1948 Aug 20   **Ash Tree Rib, Broad Marsh, Two Tree Route** P R J Harding, A J J Moulam

1948 Aug 23   **The Ring** P R J Harding, J I Disley
An attempt to find an earlier route, The Clasp.

1948 Aug 24   **Gargoyle Route** A J J Moulam, D Thomas

1948 Aug 28   **Kaisergebirge Wall** (7pts. aid) P R J Harding, J I Disley, A J J Moulam
'Nothing was barred; pegs, knotted bootlaces... the leader went up again as last man to remove the attachments'.
'Much harder now. All the tiny flakes in the groove on which it was possible to hook a nail, have disappeared – it's as smooth as a baby's bum!' – Joe Brown 1985.

1948 Aug 30   **Cracked Wall, Little Sepulchre & Holly Gate** J I Disley, P R J Harding, A J J Moulam (AL)

1948 Oct 14   **Rene** R Thomas, A J J Moulam

1948 Oct 29   **Rib and Slab** V J Wiggin, D R Meldrum

1949 Jan 30   **Crown of Thorns** P R J Harding, C W F Noyce (AL)

1949 March 6   **Tradition & Spring Chimney** J I Disley, P R Hodgkinson

1949 March 19   **The Eastern Edge** P R J Harding, J B Nicholson

1949 April 9   **Phantom Rib** G W S Pigott, M Kennedy-Frazer, W H Stock

1949 April 11   **Short Tree Chimney** P R J Harding

1949 April 13   **Delphos** P R Hodgkinson, P R J Harding (AL)

1949 April 17   **Unicorn** (1pt. aid) P R J Harding, P R Hodgkinson, M G Hughes
Pitch 1 had been led two weeks earlier by J B Lawton.

1949 April 18   **Intermediate Chimney & Square Gully** P R J Harding, P R Hodgkinson

1949 April 22   **The Green Caterpillar** P R J Harding, G Dyke
'...boots in preference to rubbers'.

1949 April 22   **The Green Necklace** P R J Harding, G Dyke

1949 April 23   **Little Buttress Climb** J B Lawton, F A Smith, D P Davies, P Dellow, J S Stafford

1949 April 24   **Fa** J B Lawton, F A Smith, D P Davies

1949 April 24   **Brant Direct** P R J Harding, J I Disley, P R Hodgkinson, G Dyke

'This pitch is definitely harder than anything else on The Brant. It is 75 feet long with no respite, strenuous and technically hard all the way – fine pitch'.

1949 April 25 **Garlic Groove** P R Hodgkinson, J I Disley (AL)

1949 April 26 **Halan** P R J Harding, G Dyke

1949 June 6 **Terra Incognita** H A Carsten

'A scramble to the right of Staircase Gully – soloed in filthy weather. This is loose, full of overhangs and plants. The woods in the middle can be reached by way of either of two traverses from the bend of Staircase Gully. These lines are about 30 feet apart and obvious, with massive jug-handles – Flowers! Beyond Staircase Gully there is no coherent rock'.

1949 June 12 **Conway Climb** P R Hodgkinson, R W Beard, M Bosworth, B Meveen

1949 June 25 **Inoculation Wall** F A Smith, P R Hodgkinson

1949 June 26 **Lion** P R J Harding, A J J Moulam

Most of it had been soloed before by P R J Harding.

1949 July 8 **Fatha** A J J Moulam, D Thomas

1949 July 10 **Foxglove** G W S Pigott, A J J Moulam, J Walmesley

1949 July 14 **The Black Belt** A J J Moulam, B L Blake, C M G Smith

1949 July 15 **Goat's Gully** C M G Smith, B L Blake

1949 July 17 **The Lectern** P R Hodgkinson, R W Beard

1949 July 23 **Central Gully** J M Edwards, R W Beard

Long thought to be impossible. 'Menlove led... turning the cave pitch on the right wall though we thought a strong and confident climber might take it direct'. Left Hand Variation: 14 Oct 1951. J M Edwards, M R Loewy – a shoulder was used to start. The strong and confident climber appeared in the shape of W Hurford, who, with M Parker, led the Superdirect Variation, 8 June 1975.

1949 July 27 **Babel** C M G Smith, J H Swallow

Pitch 3 Variation: 8 March 1969 by M T Taylor, A Booth.

1949 July 27 **Rift Wall** J M Edwards, K N Davies, F J Monkhouse

'...up the steep crack at the back, over a perched block (traveller, treat this jug with care, for other travellers travelling here)...' 'We climbed in rubbers, used slings for safety on the perched block and on the top traverse. Standard. Perhaps just into the Severes!' Re-discovered by J Brown in 1952 who called it 'Anthropology'.

1951 March 22 **Ribstone Crack** (2pts. aid) J I Disley, A J J Moulam (AL)

1951 May 12 **Bole Way** A J J Moulam, G W S Pigott, A Hyde

Direct finish added in 1958. Left-hand finish by J Brown, C E Davies, June l984.

1951 May 18 **Hangover** J Brown, R Greenall, M T Sorrell, F Ashton

'Since the removal of the large flake in the final groove on pitch 3 the character of the route has altered considerably. The final 10 feet is now the crux of the climb'. CC hut book 21 Oct 1955.

1951 May 26 **Unicorn Direct** J Brown, M T Sorrell, P Hampson, R Greenall

1951 Sept 2	**Cobweb Crack** J Brown, M T Sorrell
	So-called, because a spider had spun its web across the crack, ensuring that there were 'no flies on Joe that day'.
1951 Sept 3	**Noah's Warning** J Brown, M T Sorrell
	A classic find. Direct finish by C J S Bonington, G Francis 20 July 1954.
1951 Sept 29	**Cromlech Grooves** G W S Pigott, R M Viney, G P Hample
1951 Sept 30	**Cemetery Gates** J Brown, D D Whillans (AL)
	A major discovery up fierce rock. 'I led the first pitch and took a stance just above the holly tree and hung on to slings attached to poor spikes sticking out of the rock. This was the first stance in slings that we had taken. The position on the face was very sensational and frightening. I brought up Don and he was flabbergasted. "Christ this is a gripping place", he muttered hoarsely. Neither of us seemed able to move. Then it started to rain... all the way up it, little flakes of rock broke off when we pulled or stood on them'. 'Definitely E5 1b' – John Allen, gritstone guru. 1985.
1951 Nov 10	**The Band of Hope** A J J Moulam, A Francis
1951 Dec 16	**Leesled** J R Lees, A J J Moulam, D Fisher
	'...* Leesled across the mossy slab... '* To Leesle – a leaning gliding mantelshelf.
1952 April 7	**The Sheepwalk & Holly Cracks** P Carr, R A Brown
	Holly Cracks was later ascended as President's Climb by A B Black, R Mann on 25 May 1953.
1952 April 13	**Skylon** R Handley, E H Phillips
1952 June 16	**Canol** J Brown, D Belshaw
	The same team added the Direct Start on the same day. Variation: T I M Lewis 1965.
1952 June 17	**Zig-Zag** D Belshaw, J Brown
1952 July 30	**The Black Braces** D McKilvey, R Hughes
	This started along The Black Belt and finished up Zig-Zag.
1952 Aug 1	**First Boulder Bounding Contest**
	Held on the stream opposite the Grochan. D McKilvey beat R Hughes – 1 footbath to 1 hipbath!
1952 Aug 24	**Cenotaph Corner** (2pts. aid) J Brown, D Belshaw
	One of the great milestones in Welsh climbing. 'I was climbing in socks and vainly tried to hook my feet onto rugosities below a large patch of moss, oozing with water. Until then I had forgotten that the conditions on the cliff were bad and the corner was very damp'. 'By 1961 Cenotaph Corner was being described as a trade route'. 'There's no doubt about it; it's a polished horror' Mark Pretty 1986.
1952 Aug 26	**Route of Knobs** J M Edwards, H C Bryson
	For many years a greatly under-rated route, originally graded Mild Severe. Direct Start: Aug 1975 by R Newcombe.
1952 Sept 7	**Notanda** E Marshall, M Ridges, D Penlington
1952 Sept 7	**Moch Up** A J J Moulam, S Fry

1952 Sept 17	**Eve's Crack** (4 pegs. 2 stirrups) J F Adams
	The crack on the north side of the boulder on the east of the Ynys Ettws Field is now a 6b boulder-problem courtesy of M Boysen 1959.
1952 Sept 28	**Thor** A J J Moulam, W R Caister
1952 Sept 28	**Jericho Wall** J Browan, D Cowan
	Pitch 1 was added as a direct start in Summer 1958 by J Smith, D Gray.
1952 Oct 11	**Ragged Wall** P Hampson, Miss J Coates (AL)
1953 March 1	**Surplomb** (1pt. aid) J Brown, D D Whillans (AL)
	Rumoured for many years to have been done wearing big boots during a snowstorm. That attempt failed. First free ascent P Gordon 1959.
1953 March 22	**Subsidiary Groove** J Brown, D D Whillans (AL)
1953 April 25	**Aimless Wall** (artificial) R Hughes, P Hampson
	This climbed the Sickle wall up to the overhangs, and an abseil point. So-called – because it went nowhere. This appears to be the line taken by S.S. Special.
1953 April 26	**Erosion Groove** (1pt. aid) D D Whillans, J R Allen, D Cowan, P White
1953 May	**Millwood's Wall** G J Millwood, A Taylor
1953 June 1	**Yew Link** (2pts. aid) P Hampson, A Kopczinski
1953 June 20	**The Scabbard** A Kopczinski, Fraulein R Ohrtman
1953 July 3	**The New Girdle** H I Banner, D J Abbot, B G N Page
1953 July 6	**Cornix** H I Banner, D J Abbot
1953 Aug 22	**Little Audrey** M H Westmacott, A Alvarez
	The leader called for a top-rope on the last pitch to negotiate an unstable block.
1953 Aug 30	**Sickle** J Brown, D Cowan
1953 Sept 13	**The Grooves** (1pt. aid) J Brown, D Cowan, E Price
	'...the rock was decorated with rosettes of a thick, brown, blubbery fungus growth that one imagined only flourished in a primaeval jungle. Both Don and Eric fell off the second pitch and neither of them wanted to continue'. For a long time the hardest route on the south side of The Pass.
	Right-Hand Finish by J A Austin, D G Farley on 4 Oct 1959 – the team got lost. Overhanging Arête (1pt. aid) climbed by H I Banner, J O'Neill on 15 June 1958 who approached along the first ascent of The High Level Girdle. Soloed on sight by R A McHardy c.1970.
1953 Oct 11	**Red Wall** D D Whillans, T Waghorn
	The first hard route on this formidable cliff.
1954 May 7	**Ochre Buttress & Asphodel** G W S Pigott, K K Hartley, M Hartley
1954 May 16	**Ochre Groove** (1pt. aid) H I Banner, G W Wilson
	First free ascent C E Davies 1964. Pitch 1 by P H Hill, M W Harvey, P C Henry on the day.
1954 May 30	**Tiercel** G W S Pigott, J M Barr
1954 July 22	**Sunset Boulevard** (1pt. aid) C J S Bonington, A C Cain, G G Francies
1954 Aug 5	**Gryphon** A C Cain, C J S Bonington (VL) S Lane

*'Warning: The large rectangular block at the top of the
layback flake on the crux has suffered during the winter.
Since last Sept it has moved about ¼" away from the
parent rock – it will now take a line, or maybe ¼ weight
sling in lieu of the piton, which was removed. One hopes it
will continue to function as a hold, or the climb may become
very hard indeed'. P H Biven 9 May 1955 – it didn't, and it
is.*

1954 Aug	**Black Wall** (1pt. aid) D D Whillans, J Brown
	Variation to pitch 4 c.1986 by F Hall and I A Jones
1954 Aug 22	**The Link** (Several pts. aid) J Brown, E Price, D Roscoe
1954 Sept 8	**Impromptu Buttress** C Fishwick, D J Hewitt
1954 Sept 19	**Jug Handle & Slab and Tower** F A Smith, R Summers (AL)
1954 Sept 23	**Slape Direct** (1pt. aid) M W Harvey, D J Abbott
1954 Nov 7	**Broad Walk** D D Whillans, J Brown (AL)
1955 Jan 3	**Staircase Groove** A W Killingback, B Summers
	The crag had been climbed on before but no records were kept.
1955 Feb 5	**Troglodyte Wall** R Moseley, D T Roscoe
1955 March 19	**Verglas Slab & Grooved Slab** D T Roscoe, T Waghorn
1955 March 19	**Botany Climb** R Moseley, D E Shortall
1955 May 28	**Question Mark** P H Biven, H T H Peck
1955 June 26	**Doldrum** A J J Moulam, Miss P D Chapman
1955 July	**The Gangway** A W Killingback
1955 July 17	**Scrog & Yellow Groove** J Brown, D D Whillans
	A similar line to Scrog was climbed on 21 Aug 1959 by H Smith, C E Davies, M Tweed and called The Mantis.
1955 July 22	**N'Gombo** J Brown, D D Whillans
1955 July 27	**Crosstie** H I Banner, G W C Wilson, P H Hill
1955 Aug 3	**Slanting Buttress** A D Baker, A W Killingback
1955 Aug 5	**Mortuary Slab** A W Killingback, A D Baker
	Direct Finish; W F Hurford, C B Fitzhugh on 10th July 1971.
1955 Aug 10	**Burnt Out Buttress & Clinker** A W Killingback, A D Baker
1955 Aug 11	**Preliminary Groove, Ruddy Groove & Mur-y-Ffester** A D Baker, A W Killingback (AL)
1955 Aug 17	**Erosion Groove Direct** D D Whillans, J Brown
	For some years considered by many to be the ultimate in seriousness and difficulty, and as such it was given a wide berth until modern protection techniques improved. It is still no pushover.
1955 Dec 24	**Hanging Flake Route** (some aid) A W Killingback, A D Baker
1956 Feb 11	**The Thing** J Brown, D D Whillans
	'Extremely strenuous. A short vicious climb of great technical difficulty. Possibly the hardest problem in the valley. Difficulty is sustained, protection poor, retreat beyond the crux uninviting and the ground below nasty to land on'.

One of two routes to be given the Exceptionally Severe grade in the 1964 guide.

1956 April 1/2   **The Cromlech Girdle** (3 pts. aid) D D Whillans, J Brown
A technical masterpiece, done in two stages. 'Had we relied too heavily on modern techniques, such as rope tension moves, and moral support from ropes arranged above and behind us, for crossing the Corner? One of the old guard thought so. "By Jove", he spluttered, "you should have seen it. Any of the old-timers could have done it with the gear that those young fellows were using."' The initial section across to the Forest had nearly all been climbed in reverse as Twisters Traverse by R Hope, P Walsh (AL) of the Creag Dhu on 11 July 1953.

1956 April 15   **Little Whizzer** P H Biven, H T H Peck

1956 April 26   **Rhaeadr Girdle** R Moseley, J R Sutherland

1956 May 6   **Left Wall** (Several pts. aid) R Moseley, J Smith, J Sutherland
Cunning chockstoning on the first ascent. The present start was added later by D D Whillans. The route was climbed free by A Garlick on 21 Sept 1970. 'Watch your language, there are MEN down here!' – unknown climber below the route, upon hearing a string of four letter expletives from an attractive girl who had just fallen off the crux.

1956 Aug 6   **Druid's Dilemma** R C Evans, C J Simpson, E J Clegg

1956   **Swcadd** R Orgill
Re-discovered and named by L Clark on 28 June 1984.

1957 April 25   **Grey Wall** P H Biven, H T H Peck (AL) C Fishwick
Originally climbed as part of two separate routes, Black Magic (VS) and The Dark Horse (HVS). These were revised and amended at a later date by the first ascent team.

1957 June 1   **Nunc Dimittis** G J Fraser, M J O'Hara (AL)

1957 June   **Strapiombo** (2 pts. aid) J Smith, J Brown

1957 July   **The Slash** (S & A2) T Panther, R Stephens
Direct finish (VS & A1). T Panther, C Langley – in very poor conditions, May 1971. Direct Start – S Mathewson (solo) 26 May 1974. First free ascent (including the direct finish) done by D Pycroft, D Lancely, 14 July 1983.

1957 Oct 6   **Rameses Wall** C T Jones, A Beanland, J R Sims

1958 April 2   **Rackstone Crib** H I Banner, K Judy, L Brown

1958 May 18   **Dinas** – wall left of overhanging prow pegged at A2 by N Williamson.
Others had pegged here before and climbed some easy lines. The overhanging prow and hand traverse were both soloed by D Ellison who developed the crag c.1963/64.

1958 June 14   **Boston Spa Climb** J M Scarr, N C Peacock, H B Carslake

1958 June 15   **The High Level Girdle** (Cyrn Las) H I Banner, J O'Neill
The last two pitches had been previously climbed by H I Banner, B Barlow, J Sutherland, so the route was finished up the Overhanging Arête.

1958   **Yellow Crack** H I Banner, C T Jones
Possibly climbed previously.

1958 Aug 1/2   **Karwendel Wall** H I Banner, J O'Neill, R Beesly

1958 Sept 14	**Reluctant** P Bell, G Stumock
1958 Sept	**Grond** D D Whillans, J Smith, D Gray, J Brown
	All four led the route.
1959 Jan 18	**The Thumb** C E Davies, C T Jones, W A Trench
1959 April 23	**Jubilee Climb** C J Mortlock, P M Hutchinson
	The finish has been changed with that of Hiawatha. The upper slabs were done by J Brown, D D Whillans. The route was thought to be new when climbed by J A Maguire and E C Townsend on 14 June 1964. They called it The Mekon.
1959 June 27	**Route 1** (Dinas Bach) C J Mortlock, A Tayler, W Wycherley
	Also known as Mortlock's Slab.
1959 Aug 31	**The Wall** (1pt. aid) J Brown, A C Cain, C T Jones
1959 Sept 6	**Chequered Wall** A C Cain, C T Jones (AL)
1960 May 19	**West End & Little Jim** I Clough, J A Bennet, D Cooknell, R Pottage
1961 March 6	**Petite Fleur** C E Davies, G D Verity
1961 April 8	**The Mole** J Brown, E D G Langmuir
	A route which revealed the potential of the wings of Dinas Mot.
1961 July 2	**Hiawatha** D Turner, D Kerr
1961 Nov 18	**Slime Wall** P Crew, C T Jones
	The first new route from a very powerful climber. It was originally called Mank Wall.
1962 May 20	**The Tickle** M J Cummington, J S Hobhouse
1962 May 26	**Trauma Grooves** (1pt. aid) B Ingle, P Crew (AL)
1962 June	**Grooved Rib** J Robson, D Cook
	Also climbed as Mellow Yellow on 17 April 1968 by P Donnelly, S Ashley.
1962 July 16	**Yellow Wall** D Yates, D Potts (AL)
	A Direct Finish was added by J Harwood, R High on 3 July 1965.
1962 Oct 6	**Lectern Grooves** B Ingle, P Crew (AL)
1962 Oct 8	**Epitaph** (Several pts. aid) R James, M Petrovsky
	Top roped first but nontheless, a bold and serious lead. Climbed free by J Ewbank, T Murphy on 9 Aug 1965.
1962 Oct 14	**Plexus** (2 pts. aid) B Ingle, P Crew (AL)
	Major gardening altered this route considerably.
1962 Dec 2	**Gardd** P Crew, V N Stevenson, B Ingle
	Barford and Moulam both led routes on this slab.
1963 Feb 23	**Ensis** R G Wilson, W H Smith
1963 Feb 24	**The Bearded Crack** R G Wilson, J H Russell (AL)
1963 March 23	**Pholidomya** R G Wilson, J H Russell
1963 March 23	**Solen** R G Wilson, B Hendrickson, J H Russell (AL)
1963 March 24	**Ampyx** R G Wilson, J H Russell
1963 April 20	**The Infidel** P Crew, B Ingle (AL)
1963 April 28	**The Castle** R G Wilson, J H Russell, B Hendrickson (AL)
1963 May 4	**The Great Buttress** (1pt. aid) B Ingle, P Crew (AL)
	A bold impressive line. First free ascent R Barley, A Barley c.1964.
1963 May	**Old Holborn** (1pt. aid) P Crew, B Ingle, D Potts

1963 May 21	**Nexus** (1pt. aid) M Boysen, P Nunn
	A brilliant discovery.
1963 Aug 29	**Tremolite** (1pt. aid) P Crew, B Ingle (AL)
	Pitch 3 was gardened then climbed on 14 Sept.
1963 Sept 20	**The Rosy Crucifixion** P Crew, B Ingle
	B Ingle, D Potts had previously done the top pitch.
1963 Oct	**The Toad** (2 pts. aid) M Boysen, A Harris
	A sling was used to place the peg as high as possible. First free ascent J Moran 19 July 1977.
1963 March 27	**Gollum** (2 pts. aid) B C Webb, A Harris, V Cowley
	First free ascent J Perrin 1966.
1964 April 3	**Beorn** (1 pt. aid) B C Webb, B C Ruby
	First free ascent A Harris 1965.
1964 June 21	**Elidor** J Harwood, R High
	Unrecorded at the time but climbed and named in 1977 by M E Crook.
1964	**Quasimodo** R James, A Earnshaw
c. 1964	**Cul-De-Sac** 1st ascensionists unknown
1964 Aug 23	**Diapason** (3 pts. aid) T Panther, P Sorrell, J Fisher
	Climbed free by D Pycroft, D Lancely on 14 July 1983.
1964 Aug 25	**Micrometer** W Hurford, D Moore
1964 Aug 26/27	**Pyg-in-the-Middle** W Hurford, D Moore
1964 Oct 4	**M P P** P Crew, C Boulton
	The 'micro precision product' which gave the route its name was the camera of either John Cleare or Ken Wilson.
1965 March 27	**Sexus** (3 pts. aid) M Boysen, A Williams
	Climbed free by D Hollows on 29 May 1977. Pitches 1 and 2 first climbed (2 pts. aid) as part of The Grinder (qv); pitch 2 free by J Moran, G Milburn 28 May 1977.
1965 April 3	**Black Spring** M Boysen, A Williams
	Variation: J Moran, G Milburn 24 April 1976. A similar variation was done in July 1969 by D Cowans and B Goodwin.
1965 May 1	**The Plexus Girdle** (1 pt. aid) M Boysen, D Little
1965 May	**The Blade** M Boysen, A Williams
	A similar line, Wild Grass was climbed by D Keeling, G Young on 13 June 1971.
1965 June 14	**Intruder** D E Alcock, B A Fuller, A Williams (AL)
1965 June 19	**Preamble** D E Alcock, B A Fuller, J Fuller
	Re-discovered by S Cathcart on 8 Aug 1983. He named it Black Eyes.
1965 June 20	**Cave Buttress** D E Alcock, B A Fuller, J E Todd
1965 June	**Goldcrest** (2 pts. aid) J Harwood, B Burns
	They did not record the route. Climbed free by A Sharp, J Harwood on 6 Sept 1983.
1965 July 3	**Black Foot** (1 pt. aid) B A Fuller, D E Alcock (AL)
	Pitch 3 by D E Alcock, P Crew in Sept 1965.
1965	**Groper** (2 pts. aid) R Evans, T Hurley (AL)
	First free ascent with a variation, P Whillance, D Armstrong, 26 Aug 1978.
1965 Aug 9	**The Mystery** J Ewbank, T Murphy

A whodunnit? – solved at last.

1965 Oct 4   **Spectrum** (4 pts. aid) R Edwards, D Mellor, M Boysen
First free ascent, G Regan 1975.

1965 Oct 7   **Perygl** (3 pts. aid) R Edwards, D Mellor
During the first ascent a huge trundled block created havoc by blocking the road for some time. Brede Arkless came out of her house nearby thinking that The Pass had fallen down. Brilliantly freed by S Haston, M E Crook in 1982.

1965 Oct 23   **Joshua's Traverse** S Wroe, A Howard (AL)

1966 March   **The Wobbler** R Evans, T Hurley (AL)

1966 April 29   **Corruption** (3 pts. aid) J Costello, D J Southall
Freed by L Brown c.1969.

1966 May 1   **The Skull** (6 pts. aid) M Boysen, A Williams, J Jordan
A tremendously impressive line. Climbed completely free by R Evans, H Pasquill (AL) c.1974.

1966 May 17   **The Crucifix** L T Brown, E Jones
At the time it was thought to be the last great problem. The quote, 'Lew should be given a special pat on the back for his clean lead of this outstanding problem' (1974 guidebook) is perhaps the most embarrassing compliment ever foisted on a climber in the history of guidebooks.

1966 July 17   **Fever** (1 pt. aid) D Yates, K McLoughlin, P Donnelly

1966 Aug   **Pi** (VS & A3) T Panther, R Stephens
Direct Finish (VS & A2) T Panther, N Bradburn (AL) Aug 1976. Both were transformed into a fine free climb by M E Crook, P Norton – Sacred Idol on 9 May 1984.

1966 Aug 24   **Gandalf** R Evans, J Esplin

1966 Aug 26   **Nexus Direct** (4 pts. aid) P Crew, D E Alcock
'Climb the groove until the angle eases, 4 pegs (1st native, 2nd and 3rd American – difficult to position'. First free ascent D Roberts, 20 June 1977... on sight. 'It didn't look too bad from below, so I gave it a blast. Suddenly, I found myself committed above a dodgy wire, I was too gripped to fall off. There was no chance but to go for it. I reached a tiny hold on the left and pulled like mad. The gods smiled – I made it'. – Dave Roberts.

1966 Sept   **The Grinder** (HVS A3) M Boysen, W Birch, J Jordan (VL)
Five poor pegs were used to cross the roof. Free climbed as The Red Ring by S Haston, L K McGinley, Easter 1981. A magnificent achievement. 'Man, its just the wildest' – Steve Haston describing the ascent.

1966   **East Wing Girdle** R Evans, A Kellas

1967 April 30   **The Mushroom** M R Sinker, R J Isherwood (AL)

1967 May   **Zeta** (3 pts. aid) A Willmot, J Tooke (AL)

1967 May   **The Craig Fach Girdle** (HVS & A3) T Panther, R Harpley, – plus B O'Connor, T Bartlett, J Malcolmson, R Stephens, P Sorrell.
The route is still graded E3 & A3.

1967 June 8   **Castor** C J Phillips, R I C Kirkwood.

1967 June 13   **Orpheus** C J Phillips, R I C Kirkwood, J Arthy

1967 June 17 **The Sewer** (2 pts. aid) M Boysen, R J Isherwood
Free climbed on 10 July 1983 by S Haston, C Brear, P Norton – a gruelling effort.

1967 July 9 **The Curate's Egg** C H Taylor, R J Isherwood

1968 June 2 **The Flammarian** C T Jones, T Lewis

1968 June 24 **Mordor** (1 pt. aid) P Johnson, G R Birkinshaw
On the traverse, a block came off; the team now thought two pegs would be needed. The climb repulsed many would be ascensionists. It was finally free climbed in 1985 by M Campbell and I Fox. During the ascent, a huge tottering block peeled off 'I thought I was going for a monster'– Malc Campbell.

1968 July 7 **Pedants Buttress** F A Wedgewood, C H Taylor, J J Wedgewood (AL)

1968 Aug 10 **The Lymph** (1 pt. aid) G J Gilbert, B R Whybrow (AL)

1968 Aug 18 **Jawbone** (2 pts. aid) M Kosterlitz, D Cook
Freed by J Moran 21 July 1977.

1968 Sept 14 **Sedilia** L E Holliwell, L R Holliwell

1968 Nov 3 **Calluna** K Cartwright, P L Gerby
The line described is not the original route.

1968 Dec 14 **Sunshine Breakfast** S Johnson, R Perry

1969 June 14 **Black Shadow** (1 pt. aid) D E Alcock, M Boysen (AL)

1969 July **'T'ouse Wall** J Brown, P Crew
The Baron was finally prevailed upon to name this route late one night in the Padarn. The two apostrophes do seem to be necessary to record the route name in print. For 33 years, the route description described the line as going up right of The Wall...'It does in fact go up to the left. The guidebooks have put it in the wrong place and it's about time the record was straightened' – Joe Brown Nov 1992.

1969 July 27 **Fester** M J Bell, J D Griffiths (AL)

1969 Aug 10 **Carlos** (1 pt. aid) R Perry, S Johnson

1969 Aug 24 **Caterwaul** M J Guillard, J L Carley

1969 Sept 27 **Black Mamba** (XS & A1) C Foord, M J Guillard
Free climbed by J Moran, D Hollows (AL) on 31 May 1977. They controversially re-named the route Times Past – an act which stimulated much ethical debate at the time.

1969 Sept **Last of the Summer, Whine** T Rolfe, N Phillipe
Re-discovered and named by J R Peart, J L Hardy 19 Sept 1979.

1970 June **Huge Frog** D Keeling, M Carter

1970 Aug 29 **Genesis** (Clogwyn y Ddysgl) B Cooper, E Lawther

1971 Feb 20 **Original Route & Cracked Spur** P C Shone, M Knowles, P Knowles
The first of several probings on Chairman's Rocks by the Chester Climbing Club.

1971 March 26 **The Big Groove** E D Summers, P C Shone

1971 Sept 11 **Honky Tonk Corner & Tarotplane** (1 pt. aid) D Keeling, P Clein (AL)

1971 Sept 14 **Roll On** R Evans, C Rogers

1971 Sept 19 **Russet** (2 pts. aid) J Brown, D Alcock

Climbed free by A Sharp, P Lewis, June 1983.
c. 1972 Several routes on Clogwyn Mawr by various local climbers. Exact details as to what was done, recorded in the old Wendy's Cafe New Route Book, have disappeared, along with the book.

1972 July	**Speedfreak** B Molyneaux, R Schneider
	A bold lead for its time.
1972	**The Monster** M Boysen, E Volar
	Not recorded at the time. It was climbed in 1977 by M E Crook, D Roberts, who named it.
1972 Autumn	**Persons Unknown** (4 pts. aid)
	An unknown party sieged the line over 3 or 4 days, trundling a monstrous block in the process.
1972 Sept 20	**Tongue and Groove** H Drasdo, Miss A Cornwall
	Aboriginal Start by A J J Moulam, H Drasdo c.1968.
1972 Sept 23	**Pastoral** H Drasdo
	Led on a long rope; the second did not follow owing to darkness.
1972 Oct 1	**Promises, Promises** H Drasdo, Miss A Cornwall
1972 Oct 24	**Anne Cornwall's Climb** Miss A Cornwall, H Drasdo
1972 Nov 1	**After Eden** H Drasdo, Miss A Cornwall
1973 April 26	**Rufus, Rocky & Rambo** J Brown, C E Davies
	Three fine additions to a hitherto neglected part of The Pass.
1973 April 27	**The Tryptych** (1pt. of aid) & **Skid Alley** J Brown, C E Davies
	The Tryptych now goes without the aid, first free ascent unknown.
1973 May 18	**Genesis** (Bryn Du) J Brown, C E Davies
1973 May 19	**Joshua, Jonah** J Brown, C E Davies
1973 May 27	**Main Wall Eliminate** B Wyvill, R Evans
1973 June 9	**Mini Botterill** A Mitchell, N Owen
1973 June 16	**Jeremiah** J Brown, C E Davies
1974 April 20	**Lung Fish** (2 pts. aid) D Pearce, N Estcourt (AL)
	Freed by G Tinnings, D Greenald in May 1980 after a very dry Spring.
1974 May 7	**The Windmill** A Sharp, B Hall, S Humphries
	The first of Sharp's fine trilogy of climbs on the West Wing of Dinas Mot.
1974 May 26	**Pulsar** (HVS & A3) T Panther, P Warner, J Jiggins, S Mathewson (VL)
	An excellent pitch free climbed by P Davidson, D Pycroft 20 July 1983.
1974 June 15	**Right Wall** P Livesey
	A new concept and a major step forward in Welsh climbing. Possibly sharing a place with Cenotaph, as the 'most celebrated Welsh rock climb' it had become a trade route by 1980.
	'6b – terminal' – Mountain Magazine 54 March/April 1977.
	'I got halfway up your Right Wall and just ran out of gas' –

American Rick Accamozzo 1977.
'It's only 5c — eee' – Chris Gore taking a 60 footer from just below the girdle ledge in 1979. Soloed twice by P Davidson in 1982, 1983 (the second time for photographs). 'An easy and outdated crag' – Jerry Moffatt after soloing Right Wall, Left Wall, Foil, Memory Lane, Cenotaph Corner – and down Ivy Sepulchre, one afternoon in 1983.

1974 June 27	**Ten Degrees North** A Sharp, J J Zangwill
1974 June 28	**Superdirect** R Evans, H Pasquill

Variation in 1976 by A Dilger, N McKenzie.

1975 May	**Jayway** C J Phillips, M Barnicott
1975 May	**The Last Outpost** T Panther, S Mathewson, N Bradburn
1975	**Resurrection** (4 pts. aid) R Edwards, N Metcalfe

A magnificent discovery. First free ascent, including the Right-Hand Finish, (climbed by mistake) P Livesey, Ms J Lawrence in Sept 1975. Left-Hand Finish, described as original way, free climbed by R Fawcett. Redhead's Finish by J M Redhead in the 1980s.

1975 July 5	**Blackguard & Flying Trapeze** K Bentham, D W Shaw (AL)
1975 July 6	**Sheep in Situ** (1 pt.aid) K Bentham, D W Shaw

Free climbed by P Williams, D Pycroft 1981.

1976 May 5	**Stroll On** R Fawcett, P Livesey

The first of many additions to The Pass by a very talented climber. 'Comparable to one of the harder moves on the Bradford Wall' – – the first ascent team, commenting on the crux.

1976 May	**Crucifix Direct** P Livesey, R Fawcett

Still a bold and serious lead, not to be underestimated.

1976 July 1	**Foil** P Livesey

A gem of a pitch; steep, sustained and well-protected.'When the going gets tough, it is possible to throw oneself into Sabre Cut'.

1976 July	**Memory Lane** P Livesey, Ms J Lawrence, Ms G Price
1976 Aug 19/20	**Sych** (1 pt. aid.) J Wincott, R Robson

Free climbed by D Howard-Jones, J Brown in 1979.

1976 Aug 21	**Lubyanka** E Cleasby, J Eastham, R Matheson (AL)

A superb route which was 'put up' on sight. Soloed by G Tinnings 1980. Left-Hand Finish climbed by A Smith, A Millsom in July 1987.

1977 May 8	**Mural** (1 pt. aid) R Newcombe, D Blythe (VL)

Previously known as Stone Child after an ascent by J Moran, M E Crook on 30 May 1977. Pitch 1 by J Moran on 21 July 1977.

1977 May 26	**Wind** M E Crook, J Moran
1977 May 31	**Times Past** J Moran, D Hollows (AL)

See also Black Mamba 27 Sept 1969.

1977 June 12	**Quasar** J Moran, A Evans, E Marshall
1977 July 2	**Zangorilla** A Sharp, C Dale

A route put up 'to sort the men out from the boys'just before Sharp left for America – suicidally undergraded at E1. The rattling block on the top wall has long since gone.

1977 July 16   **The Molehill** J Moran, G Milburn
Pitch 2 was climbed in Aug 1968 as Mole Direct (2 pts. aid) by A Willmot, D Johnson. This was freed by D Roberts, P Williams in May 1977. The Direct Finish was added by C Gore, D Greenald in 1980.

1977 July 19   **Curfew** J Moran, G Milburn
Pitch 1 was climbed on 4 May 1957 as a Direct Start to Sabre Cut by D T Roscoe, A C Cain, P Shotton, H McInnes.

1977 July 20   **S S Special** D Roberts, P Williams, B Dunne
'Going round the top roof is like stepping out of an aeroplane' – Anthoine Le Menestrel.

1977 Aug 6   **First Test** A Green, G Shanks (AL)
1977 Aug 17   **'C' Minor** C Brooks, P Harrop
1977 Sept 9   **Leftover** J Moran, S Horrox
Pitch 1 was climbed on 13 Sept 1965 as Hangover Direct (4 pts.aid) by G Homer, J M P Jones. First free ascent by G Regan 1975.

1977 Sept 9   **Sun Valley** J H S Ashton, J G Jackson
1977 Sept 17   **Crossbones** (3 pts. aid) R E Millward, A Dilger (AL)
First free ascent by J Moran, A Evans 21 May 1978.

1977 Oct 14   **Vanishing Point** M E Crook, P Sowter
1977 Oct 26   **Runnymede** J Moran, G Milburn
1977 Oct 28   **Peeping Tom** J Moran, R D Sykes, G Milburn
1978 Jan 5   **Xmas Dinner** P Martin, K Martin
1978 April 28   **The New Girdle** (Dinas Mot) P Burke, I Canton (AL) W Parker, D Hilling

1978 May 10   **First Amendment** D Roberts, P Williams (AL)
So called because it put the newly published Pass guide out of date. The top pitch had previously been climbed by C Gore, Summer 1975 – in mistake for Slape pitch 2. Also climbed as Walk on By – T Mitchell, M Dennis 1981. The Right-Hand Variation to pitch 1 was ascended by P Thomas, Summer 1983.

1978 May 17   **Strapiombo Direct** W Hurford, D Pycroft (AL), P Williams.
1978 June 5   **The Pump** R Fawcett, C Gibb
Direct Start: J Silvester, 4 Aug 1984.

1978 June 18   **Runneymede Easy Variations** M G Mortimer, M G Allen
1978 July 15   **Gross Encounters** D Roberts, P Williams
So called, because it lies next to The Monster.

1978 July 15   **Kamikaze Finish** D Roberts, P Williams
1978 July 15   **Pegasus** P Williams, D Roberts
N Shepherd and party made a serious start, Flying Fish, up the lethal wall below, in Autumn 1978.

1978 July 29   **Speeding Fine** G Gibson, R Hewitt
The leader also recorded a new route, Tank, at Tremadog on the same day. A keen effort.

1978 July	**Too Hard For Jim Perrin** P De Mengel, P Thomas
1978 July 31	**Advert** A Sharp, S Lewis
1978	**Summer Famine, Speeding Fine** G Gibson, R Hewitt
1978 Aug 18	**The Heretic** J Moran, P Williams
1978 Aug 26	**Black and White** G Gibson, J Perry
1978 Aug 26	**Blink! Don't!** G Gibson, J Perry
1978 Sept	**Stairway to Heaven** S Cathcart, T Curtis

Direct Start by A Jones, T Carson 2 June 1985.

| 1978 Oct | **Ridge Route** P Martin, Mrs F Martin |
| 1978 Oct 7 | **The Puerile Ticker** W Hurford, P Williams |

The Scoop, Strone Ulladale was supposedly put in 'Hard Rock' by Ken Wilson to stop 'peuerile ticking'. The leader had done all the routes – bar one.

| 1978 Oct 13 | **The Quaker** P Williams, W Hurford |
| 1978 Oct 22 | **Corky** P Williams, W Hurford |

Named in honour of the leader's pet parrot!

| 1978 Oct 22 | **The Nubian** P Williams, T Walkington |
| 1978 Oct 22 | **Gruel** P Williams, T Walkington |

'The finishing holds were sloping and slimy, and with my gear a bit below, I was too gripped to fall off'.

| 1979 April 24 | **Zimbabwe** P Williams, D Pycroft |
| 1979 May 12 | **Brute 33** D Roberts, P Williams (AL) |

After watching Williams 'thug' round the roof, Roberts pronounced him to be a 33 year old brute – amongst other things.
'7a youth! Overhangs the road' – J M Redhead finding the roof a struggle to second in 1981.

| 1979 May 15 | **Misty Wall** L K McGinley, P Williams, M Brett, D Roberts |

For the third man, this was his first time out.

1979	**The Black Page** G Griffiths, P Waters
1979 June	**Artemis** G Gibson
	Thermopylae, Sparta G Gibson and party
	Xerxes, Troy J Walker and party
	Achilles, Hermes P Wilson and party
	Chreon M Walton and party
	Agamemnon M Walton, P Wilson

The honours were shared equally during the rapid first phase of development (two days) of this long neglected crag.

1979 June 17	**Yellow Scoop** K Martin, P G Martin
1979 June 22	**Bon Mot** K Martin, P G Martin, Mrs F Martin
1979 June 25	**Golgotha** L K McGinley, P Williams

During cleaning operations, a huge flake, 'soundly' attached to the rock became airborne with surprising ease. It flew down, crashing through the trees to land in a vast cloud of dust on the scree. 'You bastards!', came a cry from below.

| 1979 June 26 | **Lord of the Flies** R Fawcett, C Gibb |

A tremendous pitch which stunned the locals. Filmed on the first ascent for a TV programme. 'Come on arms, do your stuff' – the now famous comment by Ron Fawcett on the first ascent. The climb originally finished on top of an unstable

boulder, '...but that night, armed with crowbars, car jacks and brute strength, the expatriate Englishmen proved that the gentle art of trundling is not yet dead. Apparently the boulder made quite a bang, obliterating the path below The Corner, and actually causing one party to fail to reach the start of Spiral Stairs' – Crags 20 Aug/Sept 1979. 'Christ, it's the size of an asteroid' – an expatriate Englishman watching the boulder float 140 feet down Right Wall before it exploded on the ledge below.
On a significant, subsequent ascent, 'Holy Shit' from Louise Shepherd as she peeped over the edge and saw Graham Livingstone 15 feet from the top seconding her in trainers. Soloed by D Thomas, Summer 1990, a superb achievement.

1979 Aug 18	**The Vendetta** M E Crook, M Griffiths

Made the best of some previously climbed though unrecorded pitches.

1979 Aug 30	**Hindenburg** E Cleasby, R Matheson

A major cleaning effort was needed. Pitch 2 was climbed on 8 July 1979 by E Cleasby, I Greenwood. The route was originally named Superskull. 'Must be at least E5'. 'How do you know, you only got three feet up it'. 'Well you didn't want to lead it'. 'True!' – an exchange from the Plas y Brenin new routes book, 1985.

1979 Sept 9 **Jacob** P Martin, K Martin

1979 Oct **Quantum Jump** R Fawcett unseconded
An often tried, ferocious route. Originally graded E2 5c. 'I couldn't understand why it hadn't been repeated' – Chris Gore on the second ascent in 1982.

1979 **Pus & Pus in Boots** S Haston, I Johnson
'Both have claimed several notable scalps' – Steve Haston 1982. Right-Hand Finish done in 1982 by S Haston, L K McGinley.

1980 Jan 13 **Precious** R Fawcett unseconded
Another powerful route. Done in a spell of freak sunny weather. The belayer, C Thomas, had never met Fawcett before, until he was asked to hold the ropes. The original way traversed in from Right Wall: the Direct Start (now the described way) was climbed by J M Redhead in 1980... only a few feet of new climbing, but probably the technical crux. 'Precious, the best route on the Cromlech because there's a bolt in it' – Mark Pretty referring to the old bolts left from the MacInnes artificial attempt in the '50s.

1980 April 11 **Hall of Warriors** R Fawcett, P Williams
'Some strenuous and technical moves lead to an impasse at 80 feet, where upward progress is made by utilising "the dreaded flying leap."'

1980 April 11 **Atomic Hot Rod** R Fawcett, P Williams
One of the first three Welsh routes to be given a technical grade of 7a – - it still warrants a 6b rating.

'Ron landed on top after an almighty struggle with the roof,involving a long heel hook out left, all his gear had dropped out save for a MOAC under the roof, and a Friend which had walked. He lay on the top gasping for breath. "That's the hardest crack I've done, makes *Crimson Cringe look easy", he said. Now I'd heard of Crimson Cringe, and knew that it was 5.12. My mouth suddenly went dry and my hands started sweating – fear; an adrenalin fix for the climbing junkie. "If you can take in, just a little faster than the speed at which I'm seconding, it would be appreciated."' – Paul Williams on the first ascent.
* *A desperate Yosemite crack climb.*

1980 April 12   **J R** R Fawcett, P Williams, C Shorter
'It would have eight bolts in it, in France, and it would be twice as good'. – Martin Atkinson 1985.

1980 April 18   **Ivory Madonna** R Fawcett, P Williams
'It was a superb day. The sun had come out, beating down on the walls with an almost tropical intensity. The wet streaks running down Lord of the Flies were rapidly drying up. The crux involved an exceptionally fingery 20-foot section to reach the sanctuary of The Corner. We wondered if it was a "Desmond Decker" for a leader to slip off from the last move into it...'
A climber fell off this self same move in 1982... and missed the ground by five feet before his swing took him on an airborne inspection of Cemetery Gates. '... good 6a at *Pex'. – Joe Healey commenting on the crux sequence during the second ascent.
* *A notorious finger-wrecking sandstone quarry.*

1980 April 19   **True Grip** R Fawcett, P Williams
On a very cold morning, Fawcett climbed and reversed a shallow ramp three times before he worked out the crux move into Left Wall. Done with freezing fingers and a long way above protection, the route name well reflects the leader's feelings on the first ascent.

1980 April 19   **Nice Chimney** P Martin, K Martin

1980 May 9   **Sea Panther** D J Roscoe, B M Roscoe
The reappearance of a familiar face after a long absence.

1980   Y Glocsyn
A prominent erratic boulder behind Pen y Pass was trundled, apparently, by two visiting Americans. This act aroused the anger of conservationists throughout Wales. Despite a £100 reward for information, the culprits were never caught.

1980 May 18   **Ghosts** P Littlejohn, S Lewis
A good start to the day before...

1980 May 18   **Silent Spring** P Littlejohn
...all in an afternoon's work; another major addition to a much neglected cliff – a fine finale to a busy day.

1980 May 23   **Venturi Effect** R Fawcett, P Williams

'It was an extremely windy evening, and on the painfully wide bridging move, the updraft was so fierce that it whistled up our shorts, chilling certain parts of the anatomy that aren't mentioned in polite circles – hence the name'.

1980 June **Wang** M Boysen, J Brown, D Potts, S Haston
Put up by a team of 'golden oldies' and a 'young rooster'.

1980 Aug 25 **Cockblock** J M Redhead, C Shorter, K Robertson
'The arête had been fancied for years. A brilliant effort from an inspired climber'.
Soloed by P Davidson in 1984: 'You've got to be off your rocker to solo that' – Ron Fawcett on hearing the news.

1980 Summer **King Kipper** A Williams
Re-discovered and named by S Howe, T Birks 11 Oct 1986.

1981 March 26 **The Grim Jim** S Haston, P Williams (AL)
Direct Start by J M Redhead 27 March 1981.

1981 April **Divertimento** C Shorter, J M Redhead (AL)

1981 Easter **The Red Ring** S Haston, L K McGinley (AL)
See also The Grinder Sept 1966.

1981 May 9 **Rolling Stone** P Simkiss, J Pitts

1981 May 9 **Wounded Knee** J Pitts, P Simkiss

1981 May 9 **The Black Pig** C Shorter, P Williams (VL)

1981 May 10 **Blackhead** C Shorter, P Williams (VL)

1981 June 1 **Sphagnum** C Jones, W Parker (AL)

1981 June 27 **Simulid** W Parker, N Raeside
The first new route on the cliff for 10 years.

1981 June 27 **F B Madonna** J M Redhead, C Shorter
A desperate start. Last pitch previously climbed by M Boysen, J Brown.

1981 July 29 **Tess of the D'Urbevilles** D Jones, G Mclleland
A route with an infamous and controversial past. According to eyewitnesses (closely questioned by the guidebook writer at the time) there seems to be a heavy element of conceptualisation on the part of the first ascensionists as to the the line that they actually climbed. Climbed as described by P Jenkinson 7 Aug 1989.

1982 May 9 **Scarab** W Parker, S Reid

1982 June 7 **Spaghetti Western** K Martin, P Martin
The right arête of The Nose; certainly done before.

1982 June **Wimpey Pa** K Martin, P Martin

1982 Summer **Gizzard Puke** M E Crook, S Haston

1982 **Wardance** R Potter, B Moon
A similar line, Wet Behind the Ears (HVS) was climbed by H Moss, M Saunders around the same time.

1982 June **Sheepslayer** S Haston, M E Crook
'A pinnacle came right out from the rock with Haston hanging on to it. He belayed, brought up Crook, and together they trundled the rocky spear. It floated down the hillside like an Exocet missile, colliding with an unfortunate sheep'.

1982 July **A New Austerlitz** G Gibson, N Harvey

> *A great find which has some of the best climbing on the East Wing.*

1982 July 21   **Jupiter** C Jones, S Reid (VL)
A bold and overlooked quality route.

1982 July 23   **The Scapegoat** S Reid, W Parker (AL)

1982 Aug 7   **Fear and Loathing** C Jones, W Parker (AL)

1982 Aug 7   **The Despicable Act** (1 pt. aid) C Jones, W Parker
Aptly named – the first aid to be used on a first ascent in The Pass for many years. Honour was restored on the first free ascent by M E Crook, A D Newton, S Haston, P Norton on 21 June 1983.

1982 Aug   **Spectrological Arête** S Lewis, R Williams

1982 Aug 20   **Dill** W Parker, J Gibson (AL)

1983 April 30   **Hornets Attack Victor Mature** P Waters, G Griffiths
Named after a Los Angeles punk band. Also claimed two months later by G Gibson as Slab and Arête. A similar line, White Lightning (4 pts. aid) was done by D Keeling, B Moore, M Carter in Autumn 1970.

1983 June 5   **Rootorooni** M Lynden, J Silvester (AL)

1983 June 16   **Reid's Route** S Reid, S Martin

1983 June   **Dole-ite Variation** M E Crook, B Schmidt, S Glowacz

1983 June 21   **What a Jump** C J Phillips, solo
Mostly climbed before.

1983 June 21   **Hit the Basement** C J Phillips, solo

1983 June 30   **Silent Thunder** S M Cathcart, P Waters
A surprising find.

1983 July 4   **Twisted Sister** M E Crook, D Towse

1983 July 10   **Gorty's Triangle & Stalling Out** S M Cathcart, D Gale
The completion of a trio of excellent routes on a small but impressive buttress.

1983 July   **China Girl** Ms E Masson, P Gomersall (AL)

1983 Aug 8   **New Era & Steel Appeal** S M Cathcart, D Hale
Three bolts were placed – a dastardly deed. Rumour has it, that on hearing the news, the CC President fainted. The bolts were chopped by N Dixon and A Popp who both led, starting up New Era and finishing up Steel Appeal owing to wet rock. The name Mild Steel was mooted. Three pegs were used to protect the crux wall common to both routes.

1983 Aug 13   **Hooded Crow** A Sharp, J Harwood

1983 Aug 19   **Cunning Stunts** P Gomersall, Ms E Masson
Cunning punning?

1983 Aug 29   **Sidewinder** J Brown, C E Davies, P Nunn
Joe's first route in The Pass for over a decade.

1983 Nov 17   **Dracula Spectacula** A Brown, solo

1984 May   **Little Groover** R Fawcett, solo
Probably done before.

1984 May 9   **Sacred Idol** M E Crook, P Norton
See also Pi, Aug 1966.

1984 June   **Thumbling With My Wicklows** A Williams, solo

1984 June 13   **Swcad** L Clark, P Waters
Possibly done before.

1984 June 23	**'Zyklon B'** J Moran, J Sonczak
	A fearsome roof problem.
1984 June 23	**Sombrero Fallout** M E Crook, A D Newton
1984 June 28	**Stor Klumpe** L Clarke, C Waters
1984 July	**Spanish Bomb** L Clark, solo
1984 July 3	**Felony** H Stuart, W McKee, C Guest
	Finished direct (a grade harder) by J Dawes in Aug 1985.
1984 Aug 19	**Hexagonal Phase & Bad Moon Risin'** A Sharp, J Harwood
	A fine double on a neglected crag.
1984 Oct	**Featherlight, Barnstormer, Left-Hand Crack, New Form, Right-Hand Crack & Unison** W Todd, Miss S Clark
	All of these were probably climbed before.
1985 March 10	**The Three Cliffs** M E Crook, C J Phillips
1985 March	**Tom's Plums & Bell Fruit** J M Redhead, M E Crook, A D Newton
1985 April	**Telegram Sam** R Griffiths, M Roberts
1985 April 26	**Overhanging Deckchair** W Todd, B Evans
1985 May 2	**Mabinogion** W Todd, J Silvester
	A classy little problem.
1985 May 3	**Tombstone Wall** J Silvester, solo
1985 May 3	**Masochists Mambo** W Todd, J Silvester
1985 June	**Stumpy the Dragonslayer** S Quentin, N Craine
1985 June	**Dried Voices** J M Redhead, R Drury
	'A couple of small wires were placed from Cockblock to protect the initial section'.
1985 June 20	**Shadow of Youth** R Wood, L Hardy
	'A very good route on a small buttress that had been climbed on for over 60 years'.
1985 June 20	**The Boys of Summer** R Drury, P Thomas, M Thomas
	A bold and technical micro-route by a team of young hot-shots.
1985 July 1	**Long Kesh** S Boydon, S Cardy
	A brilliant and major discovery; one of the most exposed routes in The Pass.
1985 July 7	**Ryley Bosvil** J M Redhead, unseconded
	Still one of the hardest technical problems in The Pass taking several days to accomplish. 'The rock in Wales doesn't lend itself to any technical move harder than 5c'. – P Mitchell c.1979.
1985 July 19	**Body Rock** R Drury, unseconded
	Once the ultimate in 'one move wonders'.
1985 Sept	**Drury's Drama** J Dawes, R Drury (both solo)
1986 May 18	**Atom Art** J Silvester, unseconded
	Short, fingery, and very powerful.
1986 June 5	**Pretty Girls Make Graves** C Smith, I Jones
	This hidden gem provided a fearsome fight and pointed the way for future development on Cwm Glas Bach area.
1986 June 18	**Rumblefish** C Smith, unseconded

A 'lonely and vicious' lead: very technical and serious – a long outstanding problem solved at last.

1986 June 21   **Grand** N Dixon, unseconded
Dismissed by some as 'impossible', this was a fine achievement, but slightly tarnished by the placing of an in situ wire – an unsavoury ethic on so traditional a crag.

1986 June 25   **The Nectarine Run** J De Montjoye, Miss H Sharp
One of THE classic hard Llanberis routes.

1986 June 25   **Marlene on the Wall** T Hodgson, J Dawes
A long-standing problem solved on sight.

1986 Aug 6   **Awesome** N Dixon, J Dawes
A RURP was pre-placed for the ascent.

1986 Sept 10   **Melancholony** N Dixon, S Britain
The second really hard route to be added to the Cwm Glas Bach crags.

1986 Sept 11   **The Dolemen** S Britain, A Popp
1986 Sept 11   **Spanking for Beginners** A Popp, S Britain
1986 Sept 29   **Felix the Crack** M E Crook, A D Newton
1986 Oct 4   **Killerkranky** M E Crook, N Thomas
Done on a tip-off from the guide writer; this route triggered a new wave of interest which was to transform Scimitar Ridge into a major crag for hard climbing.

1986 Oct 11   **Never a Dull Moment** S Howe, T Birks
1986 Oct 13   **Watts the Crack?** M E Crook, N Thomas, C J Phillips
1986 Oct 13   **P F Putrid** C J Phillips, N Thomas
1987 Feb 17   **Eggmeat** P Pritchard, solo
1987 Feb 21   **Pork Trout** N Harms, solo
1987 Feb 24   **Ringsnack** N Harms, P Pritchard
1987 Feb 28   **Milk Cow** P Pritchard, N Harms
1987 April 21   **Sheepcat** P Pritchard, unseconded
1987 April 23   **Animal Locomotion** P Pritchard, N Harms
The previous few routes set a trend for micro-development.

1987 April 24   **Language, Truth, and Logic** T Hodgson, M Wragg
1987 April 24   **Birdseye** P Pritchard, solo
1987 April 25   **The Mild Very Hard Hand Jam Crack, Yr Hwntw Bach** E Jones, I A Jones
1987 April 26   **Jargon Speaker Creature** G Smith, P Hawkins
Paul Williams in full flow.

1987 April 27   **Satsumo Wrestler** J Dawes, A Popp
1987 April 28   **Black Mike** P Harrison, M Snell
1987 April 29   **Black Letter Day** P Harrison, M Snell
1987 April 29   **The Bog of the Eternal Stench** P Pritchard, unseconded
1987 April   **Return to Melancholony** N Dixon, J Dawes
1987 April   **Espasmos** I A Jones, R Griffiths
1987 April   **Rim With a View** J Dawes, N Dixon
1987 April   **Ribble Wobble** A Popp, solo
1987 May 6   **Buck Warren Meets the Headmonsters** I A Jones, E Jones
1987 May 6   **The Texas Start** P Pritchard, S Howe
1987 May 19   **The Bat Passage** F Hall, A George
1987 May 20   **Truncheon Meat** P Pritchard, unseconded

1987 May 20	**God Help the Sailors on a Night Like This** A Popp, P Pritchard	
1987 May 20	**You're Not in Poland Now** P Pritchard	
1987 May 22	**Fear of Infection** G Smith, D O'Dowd	

A classic off-width crack.

1987 May 24	**Hat Shoe, Boot Coat, Aesthetes Foot, Quantum Dump, Surprisingly Goute** J Dawes, solo
1987 May	**Play Safe, Be First** P Hawkins, M Raine, S Long
1987 May	**Rimsky Korsakov** J Dawes, unseconded
1987 May	**Hogia Tyn 'Llan, Er Cof, Iachad** I A Jones, E Roberts
1987 May	**Cariad Dic** I A Jones, solo
1987 May	**Wagner's Ring** J Dawes, A Popp
1987 May	**Mini Ha Ha** J Dawes, solo
1987 May	**Rumblecock** P Hawkins, I A Jones
1987 May	**Chopping Block** S Long, P Hawkins, M Raine
1987 May	**Rim at the Top** A Popp, solo
1987 May 24	**Pygmy Passion** G Smith, A George
1987 May 24	**Tufty Club Rebellion** A Popp, M McGowan
1987 May 26	**El Guide** A George, I A Jones

In memory of local activist John Pitts.

1987 May 26	**Libel, Smears and Slander** P Barbier, N Harms

Climbed direct by G Hughes, A Popp 1988.

1987 May 27	**Surgical Lust** P Pritchard, I Jones

Due to its overhanging nature, much of the route was cleaned and brushed on lead.

1987	**Crook's Direct** M E Crook, solo
1987 June 16	**Kitten vs Pig** A Popp, C Waddy
1987 June 16	**The Bells, The Bells, The Bells** C Waddy, A Popp
1987 June 18	**King Wad** P Pritchard, unseconded

'As physically hard as Indecent Exposure'. – J Dawes.

1987 June	**Romany Soup** C Waddy, A Popp

A similar line, 'Hot Worm' was climbed by A Hughes on 23 April 1991.

1987 June	**Friday Night Beaver** A Wells, R Lyon
1987 June	**My Mum's Slabby Arête** P Pritchard, solo
1987 June	**The Moose's Tooth-paste** M Thomas, solo
1987 June	**Weasels Rip My Flesh** S Howe, I A Jones

A Frank Zappa Album.

1987 June	**The Stain** T Thomas, F Hall
1987 July	**Unleashing the Wild Physique** D Holmes unseconded
1987 July 4	**Fred** A Wells, G Turner
1987 July 6	**What a Difference a Day Makes** S Howe, I A Jones

A local activist once ascended a route after a 24 hour yo-yo.

1987 July 16	**Melon Transplant** N Dixon, P Pritchard
1987 July 16	**Lasagne Verdi** P Pritchard, N Dixon
1987 Summer	**The Barrel Boulder**

Some of the hardest bouldering in The Pass, discovered and developed mainly by J Dawes. The low-level traverse F8b is by J Moffatt.

1987 Aug 16	**The Call of the Raven** P Hawkins, G Smith

1987 Aug 16	**Mutiny on the Mouse Organ** A Popp, C Waddy	
1987 Aug 17	**Health and Efficiency** J Dawes, solo	
	Claimed as 'Dragon the Stumpie Slayer' by P Johnstone and party 22 May 1988.	
1987 Aug 17	**Buoux in a Tin (Without the Tin-opener)** P Pritchard, solo	
	Saussuave *(Direct Start) soloed by J Dawes on the second ascent 17 Aug 1987.*	
1987 Aug 17	**The 39 Slaps** J Dawes, unseconded	
	Climbed peg to peg then 'redpointed' on the first ascent.	
1987 Aug 29	**The Revenge** C Devonshire, G Pearce	
1987 Aug	**The Kicker Conspiracy** C Waddy, S Chesslett	
1987 Aug	**Nick's Sexual Problem** N Dixon, solo	
1987	**The Fun Before the Storm** S Andrews, solo	
1987	**Cornel Helygen** D Lampard or J Brown	
1987 Sept 28	**The Big Bird** G Smith, P Hawkins	
1987 Sept	**The Beast Beneath Me** P Hawkins, G Smith	
1987 Sept	**Come to Hughie's and See the World!** M E Crook, solo	
1987 Oct 4	**Beavering in Obscurity** I A Jones, S Howe	
1987 Oct	**Retchus** J Silvester, solo	
1987	**The Real Scoop** A Shepherd and party	
1988 April 10	**Beasts of the Field** S Howe, D Blenkinsop	
1988 April 14	**Noah's Ark** S Howe, P Hawkins	
1988 April 18	**Over the Beach** S Howe, G Hughes	
1988 April 26	**Stuff the Stoat** D Lampard, R Lampard, I A Jones	
1988 April	**Pererindod, Lleu Llanber** I A Jones, T Mitchell	
	The first name means – 'wanderings'.	
1988 May 12	**Flicker of Hope** P Littlejohn, J de Montjoye	
1988 May 13	**Hairway to Steven** I A Jones, E Roberts	
1988 May 14	**Sheik Yerbooties** I A Jones T Mitchell	
	Previously climbed – c.1986 J Brown, C E Davies but not recorded.	
1988 May 14	**Chunder's Revenge** I A Jones, T Mitchell	
1988 May 16	**Rembrant Pussy Horse** G Hughes, A Wells, A Amos	
1988 May 25	**Nappy Brown and the Red Hot Pokers** P Hawkins	
	Climbed with the Direct Start by P A Targett, C Davies as 'Maxines at the Bistro' 21 Feb 1990.	
1988 May	**Belv-eddie-ere?** I A Jones, G Griffiths	
1988 June 1	**Fists of Fury** P Jenkinson, E Stone	
	Possibly climbed in the '50s.	
1988 June 1	**Rediscovered** N Dixon, E Stone, P Jenkinson – all solo	
1988 June 9	**Alchemy** P Littlejohn, J de Montjoye	
	One of the best lines in The Pass.	
1988 June 9	**Big Brother is Belaying Me** D Hawkins	
	Big Brother, Perry, made the second ascent straight after. Also rope-soloed around this time by N Dixon as 'The Old Lemon Squeezer Strikes Back'.	
1988 June 10	**Accept for Access** W McKee, solo	
1988 June 22	**Outspan** A George, P George	
1988 June 24	**Whiplash Smile** S Howe, P Baxter	

1988 June 24	**The Damp Squib** P Jenkinson, unseconded
1988 June 24	**Crack and Slab** P Johnstone, P Jenkinson
1988 June 30	**Red Giant** S Howe, P Baxter
1988 July 1	**Times Laughin' Stock** P Jenkinson, solo
1988 July 18	**Eager Submission, Doleful** S Howe, P Baxter
1988 Aug 8	**Clingstone** A George, P George, I A Jones, S Andrews, A Krolick
1988 Aug 8	**Alex in Wonderland** P George, A Krolick
1988 Aug 8	**Buck and the Noise Boys** I A Jones, A George
1988 Sept 5	**King of Rumpy** A Popp, solo
1988 Sept	**Vlad the Arête** N Dixon, A Brown
	Very short! Very powerful! Very technical!
1988 Oct 21	**Bang Utot** A Leech, C Vegoda
1988 Oct 22	**Corridors of Power** D Jones, F Butler
	Little original climbing, but another way of enjoying the left arête of Cenotaph Corner.
1988 Oct	**Queer** M E Crook, unseconded
	A strange route.
1988	**Into the Groove** G Smith, unseconded
1988	**Famous Grouse** M E Crook, J Tombs
1988	**Bunghole Buster** D Holmes, M E Crook
1989 Jan 1	**Honking By the Pool** M Turner, R Rust
	The team had just left a party at Joe Brown's house where a local climber was sprawled across a picnic table vomiting into the ornamental fish pond.
1989 May 13	**Jiggitt!** N Dixon
	Redpoint ascent! Hard on the fingers!
1989 May 21	**Cyfrifiadurwyr** J Brown, C E Davies
	Re-discovered and named by I A Jones, K W Robertson on 7 Aug 1990.
1989 May 27	**Scroll** P Greening, solo
	Certainly done before but not recorded.
1989 May 27	**Far From The Madding Throng** J Brown C E Davies
	Arête Variation by I A Jones.
1989 May 28	**Tafod y Gors, Thema, Beta** J Brown, C E Davies
	The first route name means Tongue of the Marsh, ie Butterwort, and was originally called Gamma.
1989 May 29	**Back to Trivia** N Dixon
	The name refers to the fact that Dixon had climbed the very hard and bold route, 'Face Mecca', on Cloggy the day before.
1989 June 17	**The Smodge** D Lampard, A George (AL), I A Jones
	Pitch 2 previously climbed by L K McGinley same year.
1989 June 18	**The Edge of Time** D Lampard et al
	Pitches 1 – 3 D Lampard, N Bonnett (AL), D Gleeson, climbed on 10 June 1989. Pitch 4 by D Lampard, A George, B Brewer 18 June 1989. All led on sight. A big, bold route with mind-blowing situations.
1989 June 18	**Slab and Groove, Runner Up, Pan Alley** J Brown C E Davies

1989 June 24	**Toots Direction** S Holmes, P Knight
1989 June	**Indoor Bowling Here I Come!** M E Crook, J Irvine
1989 June	**House of God** P Pritchard, unseconded
	Named by G Farquahar who thought it to be new, during
	an abortive attempt on what was to become 'Nightmayer' –
	the line that Pritchard also tried.
1989 June	**The Stebbing, The Booze Brothers** I A Jones, T Mitchell
	The first name is an Essex village, and also, 'the erection
	you cannot conceal because you are not wearing a jacket
	or jumper'.
1989 June	**Ecover** D Green, I A Jones, F Hall
1989 June	**Mr Stiff** D Lampard, A George
1989 July 13	**Perplexus** D Lampard, M Turner
	The fourth visit by Lampard when all five pitches were
	climbed. Pitch 1 by I A Jones, D Lampard, A George, in
	June 1989. Pitch 2 by D Lampard, I A Jones, A George.
	Pitch 3 D Lampard, D Green. A worthy companion to 'The
	Red Ring'.
1989 July 16	**Sunday School Outing** D Lampard, A George
1989 July	**Y Lon Wen** I A Jones, F Hall
	The White Road or Shining Path.
1989 Summer	**Tales From the Riverbank** D Lampard, A George (AL)
	A major new route climbed on sight.
1989 Summer	**El Guide Direct** A Popp, G Hughes
1989 Aug 4	**Owain's Arête** O Jones
	The result of weeks of effort.
1989 Aug 7	**The Bastard Practice** A Wainwright, unseconded
	After top rope inspection. Fiercely cleaned in the mid'80s,
	the line was protected by three pegs and a glued bolt
	sheath – the latter was not used during the ascent.
1989 Aug 7	**Tess of the D'Urbevilles** P Jenkinson
	The first true ascent. With numerous supporters, witnesses,
	hecklers, and loafers. See also 29 July 1981.
1989 Aug 20	**Bog Trotting** P Reilly
1989 Aug 20	**Grochanspiel** M E Crook
1989 Aug 20	**The Yuppification of Deiniolen** D Holmes
	You have to walk along the village's main street on a sunny
	afternoon to really appreciate the problem.
1989 Aug 30	**The Glass Flipper** I A Jones, T Mitchell
1989 Oct 1	**Crampon Route** G Steele, R N H McMillan
1989 Nov 19	**Slipstone Slab** A Green, B Preston
1989 Dec 10	**Berlin Philharmonia** S Davies, C Davies
1989 Dec 10	**Codswallop Flobalobalobalob** C Davies, S Davies
	The above two routes had been climbed before on several
	occasions.
1989 Dec	**The Berlin Wall** C Davies, M Wells, S Davies
1990	**Piggy's Arête** O Jones, P Reilly
1990 Feb 21	**Four Horsemen of the Apocalypse** P A Targett, C Davies
	Possibly done earlier.
1990 Feb 22	**Too Late to Hesitate** C Davies, P A Targett

1990 April 1	**Loves-A-Scent** A Brown, P Jefferson *Pitch 2 climbed previously as 'Skidmaster' by T Mitchell, I A Jones 30 Sept 1989.*
1990 April 4	**Cinderella Penguin** I A Jones, P Logan, T Glynne
1990 April 27	**The Wrath of Grapes** A George, I A Jones (AL)
1990 April 27	**Anturiaethau Dic Preifat** I A Jones, A George (AL)
1990 April	**Al Fresco** E Stone, M Turner *Climbed on sight.*
1990 May 23	**Zimmer Frame-up, Chilli Willie and the Red Hot Peppers** I A Jones, J Green
1990 Summer	**Skid Pan** J Brown, C Davies
1990 May	**Pink Puffins on Rock** M Turner, C Goodey
1990 Aug 7	**The Roc-Nest Monster** E Stone, G McMahon, D Goodey *Cleaned and equipped by G Hughes in 1988.*
1991 April 27	**Samson Too** C Davies, G Davies, C Jex
1991 July 4	**My Best Friend** P Baxter, M Neil
1991 July 18	**Eager Submission, Doleful** S Howe, P Baxter
1991 July	**Back in the Fold, Peter Panic, Buhlermaniac, Strap Me a Nubile, The Gas Man Cometh, Zirhalee, New Model Arm** I A Jones, solo
1991 Summer	**Second Wind** M Turner, R Wills
1991 Sept 5	**Celynen** I A Jones, B Hughes
1991 Sept 8	**A Touch of Class** R Newcombe, C Becker
1991 Sept 12	**Vampire Butterfly; Allegrophobia** I A Jones, B Hughes, C Cartwright *The leader had written off two Allegros in 12 months.*
1991 Sept 13	**Bjorn Again** I A Jones, C Cartwright, B Hughes
1991	**Stand Proud** O Jones, unseconded
1991	**No More Queensway Sales** A Hughes, solo
1991	**Penal Colony** A Hughes, O Jones
1991	**The Wrath of Grapes, Raging Thesaurus** I A Jones, J Green *The second route name describes Neil Kinnock in full flow.*
1991	**Aratnerphobia** I A Jones, I McNeill *Commemorates G Ratner's 'crap jewellery' remark.*
1991	**Of Mice and Men** R Wightman, J Harrison, I A Jones
1992 April 20	**Sound as a Trout** P A Targett, solo *Previously inspected on abseil.*
1992 May	**Freefallin'** I Lloyd-Jones, C Stephenson
1992 May 5	**Outside Left** J Brown C E Davies
1992 June 10	**The Trumpet Blowers** A Wainwright, unseconded *Outstandingly bold and technical.*
1992 June 16	**Nightmayer** S Mayers, G Lovick *Top-roped prior to the ascent. The biggest plum left in The Pass had been previously looked at by several accomplished climbers who .were put off by the technical, strenuous and committing run-out up the final headwall.*
1992 June 23	**Satsuma Special** P A Targett, C Greatwich
1992 June 26	**Outside Right** J Brown C E Davies
1992 June	**Overlord** S Mayers, unseconded

A much fancied and improbable-looking arête.

1992 June	**Lore and Hors D'Oeuvre** I A Jones, D Ferguson
1992 June	**The Bed of Nails** I A Jones, R Wightman

A local activist was once kept out of his home by a wife who had nailed the front door shut – he was however 'Drunk as a Skunk' and very late back from the pub.

1992 July 31	**The Green Beam** P A Targett, C Davies
1992 July	**Ring Ouzel 2** G Smith, M Thomas
1992 Aug 1	**The Play-away Flake** I Lloyd-Jones, solo
1992 Aug 5	**Melondrama** N Dixon, T Dixon, C Dixon

The ascent was a family affair.

1992 Sept	**Autumn Acorns** P A Targett, unseconded
1993 March 13	**Partially Obscured by a Tall Sheep** J Green, I A Jones; **Ossum** I A Jones, J Green; **Annie Get Your Oakleys** J Green, I A Jones; **Alexandra Technique** I A Jones, J Green; **Matt's Pad** J Green (solo); **Herbie The Cat** I A Jones, J Green; **Llados** I A Jones (solo); **Bistromaths** J Green (solo); **The Rabbit Stu** J Green (solo)
1993 June 3	**Beginner's Mind** N Dixon, D Crilley
1993 June 6	**Catflea Massacre** S Wood, I A Jones
1993 June 23	**Fermat's Last Theorem** I A Jones, D Ferguson; **Belbin's Bull** D Ferguson, I A Jones; **Shed's Arête** D Ferguson, I A Jones; **Ejectamenta** I A Jones, D Ferguson (both solo)
1993 July 14	**God Told Me To Do It** G Farquhar, S Cameron
1993 July 27	**Ring My Bell** A Popp, N Dixon
1993 July 28	**6B Melonoma** N Dixon
1993 August 28	**Cut Back Crack, Going Over The Falls, Totally Tubular** I A Jones, P Croxford, G Sutherland, N Horwood, T Poltronetti, S Egerton, A J Stephenson, K Looker (Various combinations)
1993 August 28	**Salem's Slab** I A Jones, G Sutherland
1993 Sept 4	**Bryn Rhedyn** N Dixon, A Popp

Index

Mountain Rescue

In the event of a serious accident where assistance is required, a message giving all the factual information about the person(s) location (crag, climb, pitch etc.) should be passed on to the North Wales Police by dialling 999.

The Police will contact the respective Rescue Team/Post, and as coordinators will obtain further assistance (e.g. helicopter) as directed by those effecting the rescue.

The Police and/or the Rescue Team involved will require the names and addresses of the persons climbing with the injured party.

Avoid making rash or unconsidered statements to the press; refer any journalists to the mountaineer who has overall charge of the rescue.

Helicopter Notes

In the event of a helicopter evacuation ALL climbers ON or OFF the cliff should take heed. A helicopter flying close to the cliff will make verbal communications between climbers difficult, and small stones etc. will be dislodged by the rotor downdraft. All loose equipment must be secured and climbers in precarious positions should try to make themselves safe. A smoke grenade may be dropped from the helicopter to give wind direction.

The persons with the injured party should try to identify their location. NO attempt should be made to throw a rope at the helicopter, but assistance should be given to the helicopter crew/personnel if requested.

A helicopter will always be flown into the wind to effect a rescue and on landing there are three danger points: the main rotor and the tail rotor and the engine exhaust. The helicopter should not be approached until directed to do so by the aircrew.

Appendix:
Clogwyn Gafr

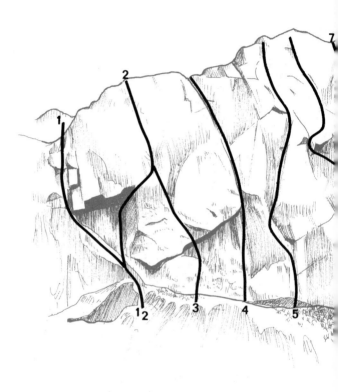

1. The Gangway   VD
2. Diapason   E1
3. Outspan   E5
4. Hanging Flake Route   VS
5. Satsumo Wrestler   E6
6. The Nectarine Run   E5

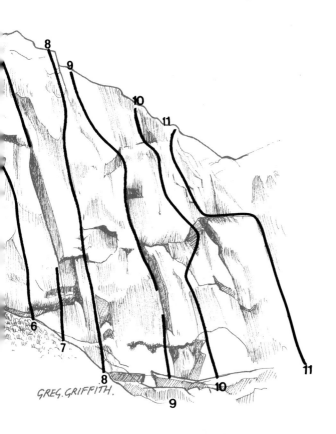

GREG.GRIFFITH.

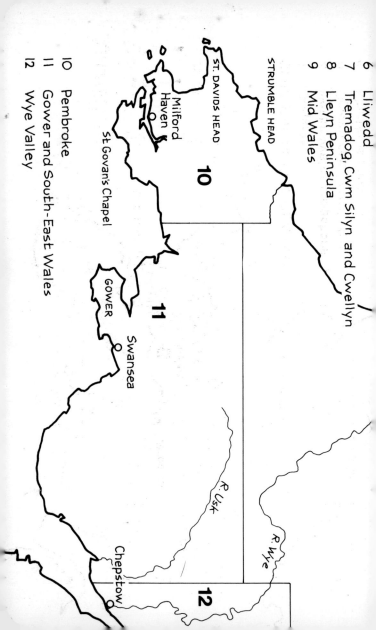

6 Lliwedd
7 Tremadog, Cwm Silyn and Cwellyn
8 Lleyn Peninsula
9 Mid Wales

10 Pembroke
11 Gower and South-East Wales
12 Wye Valley

STRUMBLE HEAD

ST. DAVIDS HEAD

St Govan's Chapel

Milford Haven

10

GOWER

11

Swansea

R. Usk

R. Wye

12

Chepstow